Learning to Program
in Structured COBOL
Parts 1 and 2

Edward Yourdon
Chris Gane
Trish Sarson
Timothy R. Lister

Prentice-Hall, Inc., Englewood Cliffs, New Jersey   07632

Library of Congress Cataloging in Publication Data

Main entry under title:
Learning to program in structured COBOL.

    (Prentice-Hall software series)
    Includes indexes.
    1.–COBOL (Computer program language)
2.–Structured programming. I.–Yourdon, Edward.
II.–Title. III.–Series.
QA76.73.C25L4   001.6'424   79-12427
ISBN 0-13-527713-2

PRENTICE-HALL SOFTWARE SERIES
Brian Kernighan, advisor

Production Supervision by Lynn Frankel
Cover Design by Suzanne Behnke
Manufacturing Buyer: Gordon Osbourne

Printed in the United States of America

10 9 8 7 6 5

PRENTICE-HALL INTERNATIONAL, INC., *London*
PRENTICE-HALL OF AUSTRALIA PTY. LIMITED, *Sydney*
PRENTICE-HALL OF CANADA, LTD., *Toronto*
PRENTICE-HALL OF INDIA PRIVATE LIMITED, *New Delhi*
PRENTICE-HALL OF JAPAN, INC., *Tokyo*
PRENTICE-HALL OF SOUTHEAST ASIA PTE. LTD., *Singapore*
WHITEHALL BOOKS LIMITED, *Wellington, New Zealand*

CONTENTS

Part 1

Part 2

ACKNOWLEDGMENT

The following paragraphs are reprinted from *American National Standard Programming Language COBOL,* published in 1974 by the American National Standards Institute, New York:

> COBOL is an industry language and is not the property of any company or group of companies, or of any organization or group of organizations.
>
> No warranty, expressed or implied, is made by any contributor or by the CODASYL Programming Language Committee as to the accuracy and functioning of the programming system and language. Moreover, no responsibility is assumed by any contributor, or by the committee, in connection therewith.
>
> The authors and copyright holders of the copyrighted material used herein
>
>> FLOW-MATIC (trademark of Sperry Rand Corporation), Programming for the UNIVAC® I and II, Data Automation Systems copyrighted 1958, 1959, by Sperry Rand Corporation; IBM Commercial Translator Form No. F 28-8013, copyrighted 1959 by IBM; FACT, DSI 27A5260-2760, copyrighted 1960 by Minneapolis-Honeywell
>
> have specifically authorized the use of this material in whole or in part, in the COBOL specifications. Such authorization extends to the reproduction and use of COBOL specifications in programming manuals or similar publications.

FOREWORD

Learning to Program in Structured COBOL is intended for people with no previous knowledge of computers, who want to learn to program in COBOL, the most widely used computer language. Parts 1 and 2 of the *Learning to Program* series incorporate the methods and styles of "structured" programming, which have been shown to be more productive than traditional programming techniques.

Learning to Program in Structured COBOL, Part 1 can be used as a stand-alone introduction to structured programming or it can be used in conjunction with the more advanced concepts and features that are presented in Part 2. Both are complete texts and can be used effectively with other structured programming texts; however, Parts 1 and 2 were designed to be used together as a teaching unit and are complementary in content and approach as well as style and format.

The books can be used either for self-study or as the texts for an industrial or college course. If you are an instructor, please read the following Notes for Instructors, which discuss possible uses of this book and its companion volume as basic texts. If you plan to use either or both of the books to study COBOL on your own, you will find the frequent questions and exercises helpful, especially if you work them *before* checking the answers provided.

We have tried to make your learning easy, thorough, and fun. If you actually can run some of the exercise programs on a computer, you will enhance your learning, and find it fascinating to build a realistic commercial data processing system.

New York   E.Y., C.G., T.S.

NOTES FOR INSTRUCTORS

One of the objectives of each book in this series is to serve as the text for a three-week full-time training course or a one-semester college course for people with little or no prior exposure to data processing.

Apart from teaching COBOL entirely in the context of structured programming, the course design incorporates several well-established educational techniques that have not, so far as we know, been applied in this area before. They are

- the concept of COBOL as a foreign language

- the concept of the spiral curriculum

- the concept of the "theory/practice sandwich"

COBOL as a foreign language

Teaching a foreign language using a grammar is not as effective as teaching via a set of syntactic structures. That is, it is better to learn a language by learning basic conversational exchanges, such as "Have you got an X? Yes, I have an X," rather than to learn "I have, you have, he has, she has. . . ." If we view COBOL in this light, we see that the standards manual and manufacturers' reference manuals are *grammars* of COBOL; they set forth the rules of the language in a formal way, exploring all the options of each statement, however obscure and rarely used. Many texts and courses explain the reference manual, but essentially follow the same pattern. In this text and in courses based on it, we use the four structures — process, decision, loop, and CASE — as the building blocks and teach the language with a structural rather than a grammatical orientation.

Regarding COBOL as a foreign language also suggests that we minimize the history and geography of the "country" concerned. While we do not question that a well-rounded professional should know the history of data processing from Hollerith to HISAM, we believe that history is irrelevant and confusing to the beginner, because it is of no help in performing his central task of solving problems with code. Likewise, while a professional COBOL programmer should know enough about the architecture of the hardware to appreciate the implications of alternative coding techniques, the beginner needs only a very simple model of main storage and common peripherals. We have taken pains to concentrate initially on the production of readable, changeable code, rather than on any considerations of run-time efficiency; for example, binary representation is not discussed until Chapter 10, in Part 2.

The spiral curriculum

Usually, topics in a subject can be arranged in a linear order, one after another. However, this is difficult to do in teaching programming, because of the amount of interdependence between topics; the instructor is in the chicken-egg situation of not being able to teach topic A properly before the students know about topic B, and not being able to teach B before they know about A. The solution is to design a *spiral* curriculum in which all topics are treated several times at progressively increasing levels of detail. As you will see, Parts 1 and 2 develop five levels of the spiral:

Chapter 1:	brief explanation of the whole program development process, and a walkthrough of a simple COBOL program
Chapters 2,3,4,5,6:	establishment of the basic structures and language subset, with a thorough discussion of COBOL logic
Chapters 7,8,9,10:	use of auxiliary storage, a larger subset of the language, and internal data representation
Chapters 11,12:	use of tables and advanced input-output techniques, including buffering and blocking, and indexed and relative input-output

Chapters 13,14,15:   use of sorting and merging techniques, testing and debugging
strategies, efficiency as well as optimization

The theory/practice sandwich

It is often a temptation for someone who is expert in a subject to teach theory at a more profound level than is desirable.
This is partly because the more deeply one understands the
theory behind a subject, the simpler it appears. So, the instructor may feel that the subject can be made simple to the learner
by teaching the underlying theory at the same depth as the instructor understands it. This is a fallacy; the learner needs to
start with familiar, concrete ideas and simple skills, and *then*
learn abstract concepts. After a while, he can treat these abstract
concepts as concrete things and then learn deeper-level concepts,
and so on.

Introducing the subject of computer programming by teaching binary arithmetic is a case in point; it is true that, at a deep
level, the computer is merely performing operations on binary
strings, but that is no help to the beginner. The temptation to
teach too much theory too early can be resisted by asking "What
is the simplest act of mastery the learner can do next? What is
the minimum theory he must know in order to do that act of
mastery?" The idea behind the "theory/practice sandwich,"
then, is a curriculum that, within each spiral, has the structure

minimum theory

simple act of mastery

next item of minimum theory

next act of mastery

and so on.

The sequence of acts of mastery around which the book builds is

read a simple program

make a small modification to a program

write a card-to-print program

enhance the program to do some arithmetic

enhance the program to do complex logic

enhance the program to write a tape file

maintain the tape file

use the tape file to create an indexed disk file

use the indexed disk file in a simple accounting system

and so on.

Throughout the texts, specific program exercises, as well as the overall concepts, build on each other in such a way as to combine the maximum of learning with the minimum of coding and keypunching.

In addition, instructors may find it useful to refer to the suggested lesson plans and lecture notes for the first thirty sessions of a course (three hours per session), provided in Appendix B of Part 1.

Learning to Program in Structured COBOL
Part 1

Ed Yourdon
Chris Gane
Trish Sarson

1 Making the Computer Do What You Want

1.1 Clerks, computers, compilers, and COBOL

You probably have heard a lot about computers before picking up this book. Some of it may be alarming — for example, how computers are invading and taking over our lives. Some of it may be optimistic, as in the predictions of computers doing all of the boring work, leaving people a life of ease and leisure. Neither of these statements is true, of course, and by the end of the book we hope you will be in a position to make up your own mind about the meaning of computers (from a position of strength), because *you* will be giving the orders.

That is what being a programmer is all about: giving the orders to computers. Think of the computer as a clerk without any common sense, and think of yourself as the clerk's boss. Whatever you tell the clerk to do, he will do *exactly* that, incredibly fast, all the time drawing on a vast memory of what you and others have told him in the past. But, if you tell the computer to send out a check for $100,000 when you mean only $100, the computer will blindly obey and pay the $100,000.

The key requirement of your job as a programmer is to understand in practical terms what work people need done by the computer, and then to translate exactly those needs into code the computer can read and obey. Computers work by streams of coded electronic pulses, which we shall discuss in detail later in the book. Since these pulses, of course, are meaningless to humans, a variety of computer *language translators* have been developed, to transform commands in an English-like language form into coded electronic instructions that direct the computer. The most common of these languages is COBOL, which is an acronym of *COmmon Business Oriented Language*. The vast majority of computers have a translator (or *compiler*), which accepts COBOL commands and produces coded instructions (called *machine language*), which drive that particular computer.

To see how this programming process works in practice, let's examine a simple computer job. Don't worry at this point if you don't understand all of the details of how the job is done; we will discuss the details in later chapters. The most important thing for you to understand now is how the parts of the process fit together; then the details will make sense when you are ready to learn them.

The problem is as follows: Suppose the firm for which you work has decided to start selling by mail order. They have advertised in the national magazines and newspapers and received a veritable blizzard of cut-out coupons — 30,000 in all — asking for catalogs. Have you ever seen 30,000 coupons? Going through them by hand is a chore. Our job is to send out the catalogs, and for that we need labels. We also want to enter these names and addresses into the computer, so we can send out additional mailings. Looking through the coupons, we notice that while most people have filled in their name, address, and phone number correctly, some have given only their name and phone number. Our first task is to write a program that will produce a list of all people who have sent in coupons, and mark prominently those whose addresses are missing, so that someone can call them, and complete the entry.

The list shown on the following page represents only the first twenty coupons of the total. The entries are typed in three columns, and in some cases, the address lines are missing. If these addresses were typed like this list with thirty on a page, how many pages would be needed for all 30,000? How thick a stack of paper would this be? If a typist types one label per minute, how long would it take to type the labels for a mailing to all 30,000 people?

Victor S Grasper
990 Gauntlet Ave
Burlingame CA 94010
(415) 243-7022

Dr P. Quackenbush

(602) 852-4822

Frances Paisano
2521 Edge Street
Fort Lee NJ 07024
(201) 614-7525

Ian S Inkerman
59 Pecan Valley Rd
Montvale NJ 07645
(201) 103-6061

Barbara diGiacomo

(918) 726-4401

C. Enchaine
212 Sleepy Hollow Dr
Greenwich CT 06830
(203) 886-7431

Saralee James
Parthenon Court
Athens MO 64065
(816) 542-0535

Scarlett O'Hara
Suite 414 Nat Bank
New Orleans LA 70012
(504) 815-1147

Lucy Lakeshore
7328 Main Street
Chicago IL 60619
(312) 838-9903

Susan Krupman
131 W 32nd Street
New York NY 10001
(212) 465-0330

I. Morris Good
1313 Porpoise
Dallas TX 75219
(214) 225-7013

Mel Harrison
4 Newton Plaza
Syracuse NY 13210
(315) 747-2121

Digital Datagrab
Apt 4R, 400 John St
Chicago IL 60611
(312) 494-1014

B. Hugh Thompson
1111 Sutter
San Francisco, CA 94103
(415) 263-4857

C.P. Foster Inc
8th & Chestnut
Philadelphia PA 77055
(215) 229-5575

Starlet Q. Freebody
12277 Sunset Blvd
Los Angeles CA 90024
(213) 574-2179

B Buchwald

(202) 936-1212

Francis T. Nord
1905 N. County Road
Minneapolis MN 55436
(612) 501-0631

John Woodside
12074 Milam
Houston TX 77023
(713) 292-8996

Z. Robertski
12 Jefferson Road
Newton MA 02160
(617) 569-8505

etc.

What we want to do is print all 30,000 names and addresses on computer stationery, or printout paper, which you've undoubtedly seen. It is continuous, has folds between pages, and holds sixty lines per page. It often has holes down both sides to allow toothed wheels in the computer printer to move the paper.

Whenever the coupon had no address, as in the cases of Dr. Quackenbush, Barbara diGiacomo, and B. Buchwald, we want the computer to print an obvious message (*flagging* is the computer jargon). Figure 1.1 shows how the printout will look.

VICTOR S GRASPER	990 GAUNTLET AVENUE	BURLINGAME	CA94010	415 243-7022
DR P.QUACKENBUSH				602 852-4022	**** ADDRESS MISSING ****
FRANCES PAISANO	2521 EDGE STREET	FORT LEE	NJ07024	201 614-7525
IAN S INKERMAN	59 PECAN VALLEY RD	MUNTVALE	NJ07645	201 101-6061
BARBARA DIGIACOMO				918 726-4401	· **** ADDRESS MISSING ****
C. ENCHAINE	312 SLEEPY HOLLOW DR	GREENWICH	CT06830	203 886-7431
SARALEE JANES	PARTHENON COURT	ATHENS	MO64065	816 542-0535
SCARLETT O'HARA	STE 414 NAT BANK	NEW ORLEANS	LA70012	504 815-1147
LUCY LAKESHORE	7328 MAIN STREET	CHICAGO	IL60619	312 838-9903
SUSAN KRUPMAN	131 W 32ND STREET	NEW YORK	NY10001	212 465-0330
I. MORRIS GOOD	1313 PORPOISE	DALLAS	TX75219	214 225-7013
MEL HARRISON	4 NEWTOWN PLAZA	SYRACUSE	NY13210	315 747-2121
DIGITAL DATAGRAB	APT 4R, 400 JOHN ST	CHICAGO	IL60611	312 494-1014
B. HUGH THOMPSON	1111 SUTTER	SAN FRANCISCO	CA94103	413 263-4857
C. P. FOSTER INC	8TH E CHESTNUT	PHILADELPHIA	PA77055	215 229-5575
STARLET Q. FREEBODY	12277 SUNSET BLVD	LOS ANGELES	CA90024	213 574-2179
B BUCHWALD				202 936-1212	**** ADDRESS MISSING ****
FRANCIS T. NORD	1905 N. COUNTY ROAD	MINNEAPOLIS	MN55434	612 501-0631
JOHN WOODSIDE	12074 MILAM	HOUSTON	TX77023	713 292-8996
Z. ROBERTSKI	12 JEFFERSON ROAD	NEWTOWN	MA02160	617 569-8505

**Figure 1.1. A computer printout of names, addresses,
and phone numbers, with missing addresses flagged.**

As you can see, in Fig. 1.1, we have made the computer list the names, addresses, and phone numbers, one to a line, and flag the missing addresses with a warning message.

1.2 Coding the data for the computer

Obviously, before the computer can print, it somehow must read in the data. There are several ways of changing data from the form humans read and use, such as handwriting, into a form that the machine can convert into coded pulses (called *machine-readable form*). The most common way is to punch holes in cards using a machine called a keypunch, which has a typewriter-like keyboard. A picture of a card with Victor Grasper's data is shown on the next page; study it carefully and try to figure out which combinations of hole-positions correspond to each letter and number on the top row.

Each group of columns is called a *field.* The whole card is said to contain a *record,* and a set of such cards makes up a *file.* Of course, there can be any number of records in the file, and up to eighty fields in each record. If you had punched a card for every coupon, you would have 30,000 cards; since a tray of 2,000 cards is about two feet long, you would have a file of cards thirty feet long! In addition to having a *card file* of this type, the computer treats the printout as a file, and each line on the printout as a record.

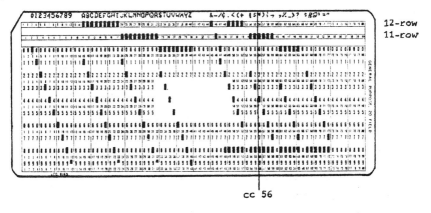

The specimen card below shows that each of the eighty columns can carry a digit (0 through 9), or a letter (A through Z), or a special character (+, −, *, and so on), or be blank and represent a space.

cc 56

Every column in a row is printed with the row number, except for the top two rows, which for historical reasons are called the 11-row and the 12-row as shown above.

A digit is coded as a single punch in the appropriate row; a letter is coded as two punches; for example, A is a 12-punch plus a 1-punch. Special characters have varying numbers of punches; for instance, the asterisk (*) is 11-4-8. This is shown above in card column 56 (abbreviated "cc 56").

Punched cards with characters printed along the top are said to be *interpreted*. Although you sometimes may need to read uninterpreted cards, don't bother to memorize the codes; just use this specimen for reference.

If you have access to a keypunch, get someone to show you how to use it; punch a set of twenty cards with the twenty names, addresses, and phone numbers listed previously. Be sure to use the same columns for the same type of data, uniform with Victor Grasper's card; that is, always start the name in cc 1, the address in cc 21, the city in cc 41, the state in cc 54, the ZIP code in cc 56, and the phone number in cc 61.

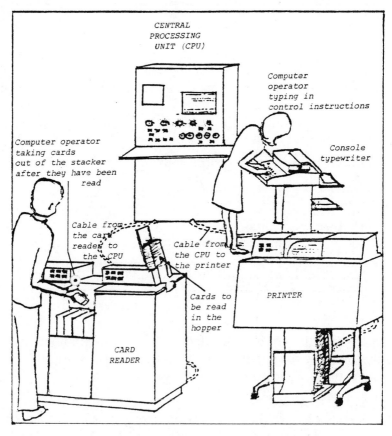

Figure 1.2. Components of a computer system.

In order to enter data into the computer, cards must be stacked and fed into a card reader, which senses where the holes have been punched in each card, with either fine metal brushes or light rays. The hole-positions are converted into coded electronic pulses that are fed along a cable into the Central Processing Unit (CPU), the brain of the computer. Figure 1.2 on the previous page shows an IBM System/370 Model 135 with a 2540 Card Reader/Punch and a 1403 Printer, which receives pulses along another cable from the CPU and produces the printout.

1.3 Getting the data printed out

Look at the layout of the printer listing on the next page (Fig. 1.3). This shows a *printer spacing chart,* which is the form that the programmer uses to plan the printout. Compare the position of the fields on the printer listing with the fields on the input card. You will see that the lengths are still the same, but they are spaced across the whole 132 columns of the printer. (Some printers have 120 columns, some 144, but 132 is most common.) Also, check the actual printout shown in Fig. 1.1 to see how the printer spacing chart corresponds to it.

Now, determine what you as the programmer must do in order for the computer to read your punched cards, and to list them on the printer in this format, detecting cards with no address and writing out the message

**** ADDRESS MISSING ****

The answer is to write the necessary instructions (which make up the *program*), punch them on cards, and feed them into the computer before entering your job. SAMPLE-1 (page 9) shows how you would write the instructions for this particular task. Don't worry if you can't follow every instruction; simply read the program and the annotations, and we will discuss details later.

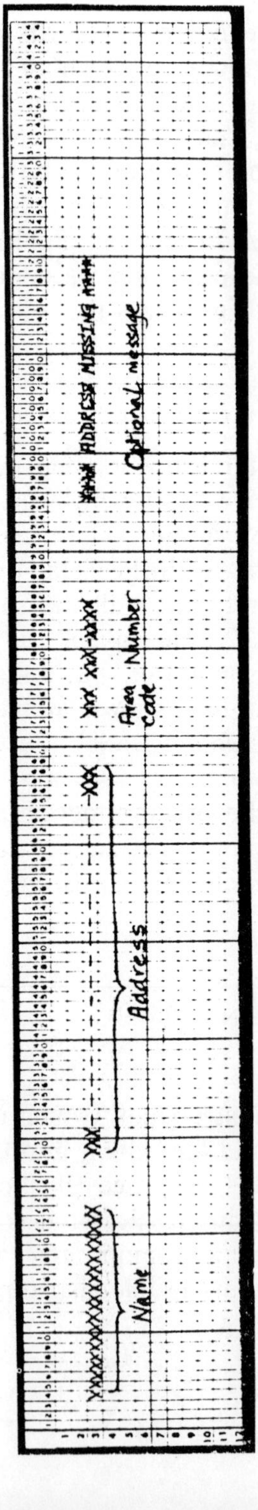

Figure 1.3. A printer spacing chart, used to plan the name and address listing.

COBOL Coding Form

SYSTEM		
PROGRAM	SAMPLE-1	
PROGRAMMER		Date

8   Every COBOL program is divided into four DIVISIONS.

```
IDENTIFICATION DIVISION.
PROGRAM-ID. SAMPLE-1.
```
The Identification Division tells what the program is called, and may give other details about who wrote it and when.

```
ENVIRONMENT DIVISION.
INPUT-OUTPUT SECTION.
FILE-CONTROL.
```
The Environment Division tells what files the program is to use. As well as the file of cards, called CARD-FILE in this case, the computer treats the printer as being a file (in this case called PRINT-FILE) with every line on the printer being a record.

```
    SELECT CARD-FILE ASSIGN TO SYS031-UR-2540R-S.
    SELECT PRINT-FILE ASSIGN TO SYS033-UR-1403-S.
```
These are the "system-names" of the files. They are usually different on each computer installation.

```
DATA DIVISION.
```
The Data Division tells how the files and records are structured and the names and sizes of fields they contain.

```
FILE SECTION.
FD CARD-FILE
   LABEL RECORDS ARE OMITTED.
01 CARD.
```
This part describes the layout of the card to the computer, and gives names to each field and subfield. Compare this description with the actual cards and check that the fields correspond exactly.

```
   05  NAME          PICTURE X(20).
   05  ADDR          PICTURE X(40).
   05  PHONE
       10  AREA-CODE PICTURE 9(3).
       10  NUMBER    PICTURE X(5).
   05  FILLER        PICTURE X(9).
```
Note that zero is written Ø to avoid confusing it with O.

This means a field 20 positions long holding numbers, letters or special characters (X).

This means a field 3 positions long holding only numbers (9).

```
FD PRINT-FILE
   LABEL RECORDS ARE OMITTED.
01 PRINT-RECORD.
   05  FILLER        PICTURE X(3).
   05 'NAME          PICTURE X(20).
   05  FILLER        PICTURE X(5).
   05  ADDR          PICTURE X(40).
   05  FILLER        PICTURE X(5).
   05  PHONE
       10  AREA-CODE PICTURE 9(3).
       10  FILLER    PICTURE X.
       10  NUMBER    PICTURE X(8).
   05  FILLER        PICTURE X(14).
   05  MESSAGE-AREA  PICTURE X(25).
   05  FILLER        PICTURE X(12).
```
This part describes the layout of the printer listing. Compare it with the printer layout chart and check that the lengths and types of each field, and the positions of the blanks (FILLER) are exactly right.

This sets up an area 25 characters long with the warning message ready to be printed out if the computer finds a missing address.

```
WORKING-STORAGE SECTION.
01  WARNING PICTURE X(25) VALUE '**** ADDRESS MISSING ****'.
01  CARDS-LEFT PICTURE X(3).
```

```
PROCEDURE DIVISION.
```
The Procedure Division tells the computer what to do with the data.

```
    OPEN INPUT  CARD-FILE
         OUTPUT PRINT-FILE.
```
"Get the files ready for processing"

```
    MOVE 'YES' TO CARDS-LEFT.
    READ CARD-FILE
       AT END MOVE 'NO ' TO CARDS-LEFT.
    PERFORM PROCESS-CARDS
       UNTIL CARDS-LEFT IS EQUAL TO 'NO '.
    CLOSE CARD-FILE PRINT-FILE.
    STOP RUN.
```
"Carry out the following group of instructions for each card"

```
PROCESS-CARDS.
    MOVE SPACES TO PRINT-RECORD.
    MOVE NAME IN CARD TO NAME IN PRINT-RECORD.
```
"Put the name on the card in its proper place in PRINT-RECORD".

```
    IF ADDR IN CARD IS EQUAL TO SPACES
        MOVE WARNING TO MESSAGE-AREA
    ELSE
        MOVE ADDR IN CARD TO ADDR IN PRINT-RECORD.
```
"If there was no address on the card, move the warning to its proper place in PRINT-RECORD. If there was an address, put it in its proper place".

```
    MOVE AREA-CODE IN CARD TO AREA-CODE IN PRINT-RECORD.
    MOVE NUMBER IN CARD TO NUMBER IN PRINT-RECORD.
    WRITE PRINT-RECORD.
```
"Print the contents of PRINT-RECORD"

```
    READ CARD-FILE
       AT END MOVE 'NO ' TO CARDS-LEFT.
```

Figure 1.4. SAMPLE-1.

And that's all there is to it!

After you punch each line of the COBOL program onto a card, you feed the cards in while running your computer's COBOL compiler program (which is already stored there ready for use). The compiler will check that everything has been punched correctly, as far as it can, and print out a listing of the cards with messages about anything the compiler can find wrong (*diagnostics*). In the case of errors, you will have to repunch some cards and rerun the compiler. When you have a *clean compilation* — no serious diagnostics — the computer will store the electronic instructions representing SAMPLE-1.

Following this procedure, you instruct the computer to prepare SAMPLE-1 for a *run* and feed in the data cards with name, address, and phone numbers, to get the printout.

Before reading further, we strongly recommend that you punch up SAMPLE-1 exactly as shown, have someone show you how to use your computer's COBOL compiler, and run your twenty data cards. Be sure you punch exactly what is written; every space and every period means something to the computer, as you will see later on. It's quite a thrill to get your first compilation and printout; and once you've seen the various stages in the cycle, everything else discussed hereafter will make much more sense. The listing on the next page shows how the program should look when printed out from your cards.

```
00001          IDENTIFICATION DIVISION.
00002          PROGRAM-ID. SAMPLE-1.
00003          ENVIRONMENT DIVISION.
00004          INPUT-OUTPUT SECTION.
00005          FILE-CONTROL.
00006              SELECT CARD-FILE      ASSIGN TO SYS031-UR-2540R-S.
00007              SELECT PRINT-FILE     ASSIGN TO SYS033-UR-1403-S.
00008          DATA DIVISION.
00009          FILE SECTION.
00010          FD  CARD-FILE
00011              LABEL RECORDS ARE OMITTED.
00012          01  CARD.
00013              05  NAME                 PICTURE     X(20).
00014              05  ADDR                 PICTURE     X(40).
00015              05  PHONE.
00016                  10  AREA-CODE        PICTURE     9(3).
00017                  10  NUMBR            PICTURE     X(8).
00018              05  FILLER               PICTURE     X(9).
00019          FD  PRINT-FILE
00020              LABEL RECORDS ARE OMITTED.
00021          01  PRINT-RECORD.
00022              05  FILLER               PICTURE     X(3).
00023              05  NAME                 PICTURE     X(20).
00024              05  FILLER               PICTURE     X(5).
00025              05  ADDR                 PICTURE     X(40).
00026              05  FILLER               PICTURE     X(5).
00027              05  PHONE.
00028                  10  AREA-CODE        PICTURE     9(3).
00029                  10  FILLER           PICTURE     X.
00030                  10  NUMBR            PICTURE     X(8).
00031              05  FILLER               PICTURE     X(10).
00032              05  MESSAGE-AREA         PICTURE     X(25).
00033              05  FILLER               PICTURE     X(12).
00034          WORKING-STORAGE SECTION.
00035          01  WARNING PICTURE X(25)    VALUE '**** ADDRESS MISSING ****'.
00036          01  CARDS-LEFT PICTURE X(3).
00037          PROCEDURE DIVISION.
00038              OPEN  INPUT    CARD-FILE
00039                    OUTPUT   PRINT-FILE.
00040              MOVE 'YES' TO CARDS-LEFT.
00041              READ CARD-FILE
00042                 AT END MOVE 'NO ' TO CARDS-LEFT.
00043              PERFORM PROCESS-CARDS
00044                 UNTIL CARDS-LEFT IS EQUAL TO 'NO '.
00045              CLOSE CARD-FILE PRINT-FILE.
00046              STOP RUN.
00047          PROCESS-CARDS.
00048              MOVE SPACES TO PRINT-RECORD.
00049              MOVE NAME IN CARD TO NAME IN PRINT-RECORD.
00050              IF ADDR IN CARD IS EQUAL TO SPACES
00051                  MOVE WARNING TO MESSAGE-AREA
00052              ELSE
00053                  MOVE ADDR IN CARD TO ADDR IN PRINT-RECORD.
00054              MOVE AREA-CODE IN CARD TO AREA-CODE IN PRINT-RECORD.
00055              MOVE NUMBR IN CARD TO NUMBR IN PRINT-RECORD.
00056              WRITE PRINT-RECORD.
00057              READ CARD-FILE
```

SAMPLE-1 listing

2 Processes, Decisions, and Loops

Now that you have seen what is involved in writing and running a COBOL program, let's look more closely at some of the instructions that we used.

2.1 Moving data from field to field

The MOVE statement is probably the statement you will use most as a COBOL programmer. Looking at the MOVE statements in SAMPLE-1, note that they all are of the general form

MOVE first-field TO second-field

where first-field and second-field vary depending on what you want to do. If first-field is WARNING and second-field is MESSAGE-AREA, the general form becomes

MOVE WARNING TO MESSAGE-AREA.

Picture the inside of the computer as consisting of thousands of storage positions, each normally capable of holding one character. When you write the Data Division (a portion of your COBOL program defined in Chapter 3), reserve some of these storage positions for your program. For example, WARNING is a field 25 positions long, with those positions filled like this:

WARNING: ****** ADDRESS MISSING ******

You set it up this way in the Working-Storage Section of the Data Division in SAMPLE-1.

MESSAGE-AREA is a field 25 positions long, defined as part of PRINT-RECORD, and full of blanks (spaces). When the computer obeys your MOVE instruction, it copies data position by position from WARNING to MESSAGE-AREA, working from the left, like this:

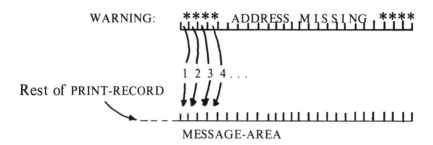

This whole MOVE operation may take only one ten-thousandth of a second!

The important thing to remember is that since the MOVE sequence is from left to right, and if MESSAGE-AREA is shorter than WARNING, the computer will stop copying characters when it comes to the end of MESSAGE-AREA.

Q.　What would be put in MESSAGE-AREA if it were only ten positions long?

A.　**** ADDRE

Since the MOVE is a copy operation, the contents of the field being copied (WARNING) are unchanged. If anything were in MESSAGE-AREA before the MOVE, however, it would be overwritten and consequently lost. If WARNING were *shorter* than MESSAGE-AREA, and if WARNING were moved, the rest of MESSAGE-AREA would be filled with blanks.

To illustrate the possibilities, cover the right-hand column in the table on the next page and work out, for each case, what will be in FIELD-A and FIELD-B after the computer executes the instruction

MOVE FIELD-A TO FIELD-B.

Assume in each case that FIELD-A and FIELD-B have been defined appropriately in the Data Division.

	BEFORE MOVE		AFTER MOVE	
	FIELD-A	FIELD-B	FIELD-A	FIELD-B
Case 1:	NAME	GONE	NAME	NAME
			(Fields are the same length so NAME over-writes GONE)	
Case 2:	NAME	GONETO	NAME	NAMEbb
			(FIELD-B is longer, so it is filled up with blanks)	
Case 3:	NAME	GO	NAME	NA
			(Moving stops when FIELD-B is full)	

Q. What would happen to FIELD-A if, after the MOVE shown in Case 2 above, you commanded

MOVE FIELD-B TO FIELD-A.

A. FIELD-A still would contain NAME.

Q. If MOVEing a field destroys the receiving field, how could you swap the contents of two locations in main storage?

A. You would need to set up a third location, say, one called FIELD-C, and store one field there temporarily, as shown on the next page:

FIELD-A   FIELD-B   FIELD-C

N A M E   G O N E   ⌀ ⌀ ⌀ ⌀

1.   **MOVE FIELD-B TO FIELD-C.**
     N A M E   G O N E   G O N E

2.   **MOVE FIELD-A TO FIELD-B.**

     N A M E   N A M E   G O N E

3.   **MOVE FIELD-C TO FIELD-A.**

     G O N E   N A M E   G O N E

Thus, you have swapped FIELD-A for FIELD-B.

When programming, always consider the contents of the computer storage at every step. If it helps, draw little diagrams like the ones above. Remember to distinguish the *name* of a field (the *data-name*), which stays the same throughout a given program, from the *contents* or *value* of that field at a particular time; the contents will change every time you do something in the program to modify the field.

Q.   In the swapping example above, which are data-names and which are field contents?

A.   FIELD-A, FIELD-B, FIELD-C are data-names; NAME, GONE are field contents or values.

2.2 Initializing fields

Computer main storage generally stays the way you set it until you reset it with another MOVE or similar instruction. However, often the section of main storage that your program uses has been used earlier by someone else's program, and so many of your fields may be filled with someone else's garbage. For this reason, the first step is to *initialize* the fields to be used (indeed, if you don't, your program has a high likelihood of mis-behaving — either printing garbage or not executing at all). One way of doing this is to MOVE SPACES to them. SPACES is a special reserved name supplied by COBOL, to provide all of the spaces (blanks) needed for any field.

To illustrate, consider statement 48 in SAMPLE-1, which says

MOVE SPACES TO PRINT-RECORD.

PRINT-RECORD is a field 132 positions long, which is used to build each line of printout. Fields from each card are moved into it, but nothing is moved into the FILLER fields between columns. So, we MOVE SPACES to clear out anybody else's gar-bage lurking there.

Take the card holding statement 48 out of SAMPLE-1, and re-compile and rerun the program. Examining the printout, you will see that SPACES fills the field in question without your having to specify the number of spaces needed.

2.3 Qualified data-names

In SAMPLE-1, we wrote

MOVE NAME IN CARD TO NAME IN PRINT-RECORD.

In the Data Division, there are, in fact, two fields that are both called NAME. Obviously, simply writing MOVE NAME TO NAME would not be sufficient for the computer to know which you meant; and a rude message, when you compiled the program, would tell you so.

Data-names, such as field names, must be written to be unique within a program. You can do so either by giving each field a different, though meaningful, name, or by providing addi-tional information, as above. For example, you could have called the fields in the card NAME-IN, ADDR-IN, and PHONE-IN, and the fields in the print-line NAME-OUT, and so on. By writing MOVE NAME-IN TO NAME-OUT, the computer would know exactly which fields you meant.

Or, as in SAMPLE-1, you may *qualify* a data-name by adding the name of the item of which it is a part, by writing NAME IN CARD or NAME OF CARD. The computer knows what you mean by reading the Data Division.

2.4 Literals

Suppose you want to set a field to a specific value — say, to put CALIF in a five-position field called STATE. COBOL allows you to do this directly by writing

MOVE 'CALIF' TO STATE.

You put single quotation marks (not the usual double quotes) around the specific value (called a *literal*) so that the computer knows you don't mean some field called CALIF, defined in the Data Division.

Q.   How would you put the value 243-7022 in an eight-position field called NUMB?

A.   **MOVE '243-7022' TO NUMB.**

You don't need to include a pure number in quotes, because it cannot be a data-name. For example,

MOVE 212 TO AREA-CODE.

would be acceptable. Note that in the Data Division of SAMPLE-1, AREA-CODE was defined by a PICTURE 9(3), meaning a field three positions long, containing only pure numbers (digits 0 through 9, with perhaps a + or − sign, and/or a decimal point).

Q.   How would you put the value 1492 into a field called YEAR, defined by a PICTURE 9(4)?

A.   **MOVE 1492 TO YEAR.**

Q.   Why can't you write

MOVE 243-7022 TO NUMB.

A.   243-7022 is a nonnumeric literal (not a pure number) because it contains a hyphen; it must be enclosed in quotes.

If the field is to contain a decimal point, the PICTURE must show its position with a V. Thus,

RATE   PICTURE 99V99

is a field that could be 19.95, or 14.0̸0̸, or 0̸1.25, or any such number. No space is left for an actual decimal point in the field; instead, its position is understood from the PICTURE.

Q.   How would you define a numeric field called PI, whose value is approximately 3.14159?

A.   **PI   PICTURE 9V9(5) or 9V99999.***

2.5 MOVEing numbers

When the computer receives an instruction to move one numeric field to another numeric field, instead of working from left to right, it *aligns the decimal point* in the sending field with the decimal point in the receiving field.

PIC is a standard abbreviation for PICTURE, which we shall use in the future. If FIELD-1 is defined as PIC 999V99 and contains

$$3 \quad 2 \quad 1.4 \quad 6$$

and is MOVEd to FIELD-2, defined as PIC 999V9, FIELD-2 then will contain

$$3 \quad 2 \quad 1.4$$

Note: You must be extremely careful when MOVEing numeric fields or you will lose digits. Note that we wrote the decimal point in its understood position between the digits, not in a space all of its own. If in doubt, draw diagrams to verify what will hap-

---

*Note that we use this bold typeface to signify extracts from programs.

pen. Two rules summarize our previous discussion:

1. When the compiler detects empty positions in the receiving fields, it fills them with zeros.

2. When no decimal point is specified in the sending field, the compiler assumes it is in the right-most position.

Bearing these rules in mind and remembering that the computer works outward from the decimal point, consider what will be the contents of FIELD-2 in the cases below after executing

MOVE FIELD-1 TO FIELD-2.

BEFORE MOVE		AFTER MOVE
FIELD-1	FIELD-2	FIELD-2
Case 1: PIC 99V99 |1|2.7|1|	PIC 99V99 |8|7.2|1|	|1|2.7|1|
Case 2: PIC 9(3) |3|1|4|	PIC 99V99 |8|7.2|1|	|1|4.Ø|Ø| (3 is lost; two decimal places filled with zeros)
Case 3: PIC 9V999 |3.1|4|2|	PIC 99V99 |8|7.2|1|	|Ø|3.1|4| (2 is lost; leading zero is supplied)
Case 4: PIC 9(4)V9(4) |1|2|3|4.5|6|7|8|	PIC 99V99 |8|7.2|1|	|3|4.5|6|

Just as you could set an alphanumeric field like PRINT-RECORD to blanks by moving spaces, so you can set a numeric field to zero by writing, for example,

MOVE ZEROS TO FIELD-1.

This is useful for initializing numeric fields.

In SAMPLE-1, the phone number punched in each card is defined as being composed of two fields: AREA-CODE PIC 9(3) and NUMBR PIC X(8). Defined this way, NUMBR is not a pure numeric field because it has a hyphen between the first three digits representing the telephone exchange and the last four digits representing the telephone number.

Q. How could you redefine these 11 characters or card columns so that all three fields of the number are numeric and can be manipulated separately?

A.
AREA-CODE	**PIC 9(3).**
EXCHANGE	**PIC 9(3).**
HYPHEN	**PIC X.** ◄——— a hyphen is not
TEL-NUMBR	**PIC 9(4).** a pure number.

Q. How would you set all of the positions of a field called PHONE to zero?

A. **MOVE ZEROS TO PHONE.**

Q. How would you set up (212) 936-4096 in the fields defined above, field by field?

A.
MOVE 212 TO AREA-CODE.
MOVE 936 TO EXCHANGE.
MOVE '-' TO HYPHEN. ◄——— must have quote
MOVE 4096 TO TEL-NUMBR.   marks because it is
    a nonnumeric literal.

A number of other more complex possibilities in defining and moving fields will be examined in detail in Part 2, Chapter 9.

2.6 Program logic: the IF statement

Apart from reading in cards and writing their contents on the printer, the most important operation of SAMPLE-1 is to test whether each card has an address, and to act based on that information. This is done with the IF statement (lines 50 through 53 in the program), for example,

IF ADDR IN CARD IS EQUAL TO SPACES
            MOVE WARNING TO MESSAGE-AREA
ELSE
            MOVE ADDR IN CARD TO ADDR IN PRINT-RECORD.

(Note that there is only one period, and it comes at the end of the whole statement.)

The general form of the IF statement is

IF condition is true
            Carry out specified operation
ELSE
            Carry out different operation.

The IF statement, properly programmed, enables the computer to make decisions and to appear to "think." Of course, the programmer, who works out the IF statements for the machine to follow mechanically, actually is doing the thinking.

The conditions tested by the IF can be extremely complex, as we shall see in Chapter 6. For the moment, let us concentrate on testing whether one field is equal to another, or equal to a literal.

Q.   Suppose you wanted to move FIELD-A to FIELD-B if AREA-CODE was 2Ø2; if AREA-CODE was anything else, you would want to move FIELD-A to FIELD-C. How would you code the test?

A.   **IF AREA-CODE IS EQUAL TO 202**
            MOVE FIELD-A TO FIELD-B
    ELSE
            MOVE FIELD-A TO FIELD-C.

Though COBOL does not require it, we recommend that you code the ELSE statement on a line by itself, aligned with its corresponding IF, and that you indent the imperative statements. This makes the structure of the text clear, which, as you will see later, is important when the IFs are complex. Most important of all is to be *consistent,* so that you learn to identify standard constructs using this format.

Q. Code a sentence that tests whether PHONE is punched in a card read by the program; if present, move PHONE to PRINT-LINE; if not, move WARNING-3 to MESSAGE-AREA.

A. IF PHONE IN CARD IS EQUAL TO SPACES
    MOVE WARNING-3 TO MESSAGE-AREA
ELSE
    MOVE PHONE IN CARD TO PHONE IN PRINT-LINE.

The ELSE clause can contain more than one imperative statement. For instance, you could write

IF PHONE IN CARD IS EQUAL TO SPACES
    MOVE WARNING-3 TO MESSAGE-AREA
ELSE
    MOVE AREA-CODE IN CARD TO AREA-CODE IN PRINT-LINE
    MOVE NUMBR IN CARD TO NUMBR IN PRINT-LINE.

Again, note that there is only one period, right at the end of the sentence. This type of decision can be shown graphically, which sometimes helps to display the control structure.

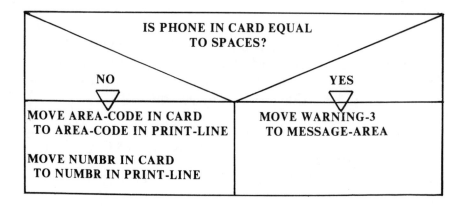

If the answer to the question in the central triangle is yes, then the right-hand rectangle is processed. If the answer is no, the statements in the left-hand rectangle are obeyed.

If the false alternative requires no action, but the true does, you may leave out the ELSE part. For instance,

IF AREA-CODE IS EQUAL TO 312
   MOVE 'CHICAGO NUMBER' TO MESSAGE-AREA.
MOVE PHONE IN CARD TO PHONE IN PRINT-LINE.

Q. What does this code do?

A. Tests if the area code is 312; and, if yes, moves a message to that effect, ready to be printed. No matter what the area code, the whole number is moved in preparation for printing.

Graphically, this looks like the following:

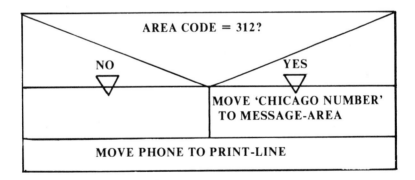

For obvious reasons, a rectangle containing an IF-ELSE structure is known as a "decision box"; a rectangle containing a MOVE or series of MOVEs is a "process box." The boxes can be put together in any order and are read from top to bottom.

Q. Write the code (program instructions) that will express process-decision-process.

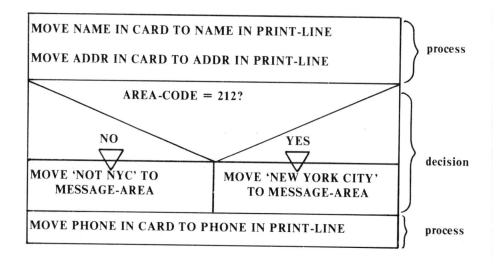

A. MOVE NAME IN CARD TO NAME IN PRINT-LINE.
    MOVE ADDR IN CARD TO ADDR IN PRINT-LINE.
    IF AREA-CODE IS EQUAL TO 212
        MOVE 'NEW YORK CITY' TO MESSAGE-AREA
    ELSE
        MOVE 'NOT NYC' TO MESSAGE-AREA.
    MOVE PHONE IN CARD TO PHONE IN PRINT-LINE.

2.7 Repeating blocks of code with loop structures

Very often in a program, we want to execute a group of instructions, either once or many times. In order to do this, we have to label these instructions as a group, called a *procedure.* For example, in SAMPLE-1, PROCESS-CARDS is written starting in column 8 to show that it is the name of a procedure, and all of the statements that follow PROCESS-CARDS (beginning four columns to the right) make up that procedure.

If we were to write

PERFORM PROCESS-CARDS.

we would mean "carry out all of the statements following the name PROCESS-CARDS, then come back, and carry on with the program." We can diagram the flow of control (the sequence in which instructions are executed) as shown on the following page:

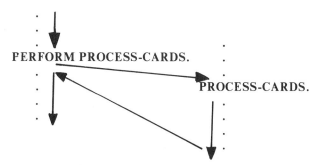

The computer knows where PROCESS-CARDS ends because it either runs out of instructions to execute (as in the case of SAM-
PLE-1) or it finds another package of code labeled with a
procedure-name. (We will define procedure-name in more detail
in Chapter 3.)

More commonly, we will want to perform a block of statements many times. For example, the block of statements called
PROCESS-CARDS in SAMPLE-1 (statements 47 through 58) is executed once for every card read in. If 30,000 cards are to be processed, this block of code will be executed 30,000 times. The
great strength of computer programming lies in our ability to
specify only once instructions that eventually are executed possibly millions of times.

We can arrange for this repeated processing by tagging an

" . . . UNTIL some condition is true"

onto the PERFORM. Thus,

PERFORM-PROCESS-CARDS
UNTIL CARDS-LEFT IS EQUAL TO 'NO '.

means "test to see if the field named CARDS-LEFT has the literal
'NO ' in it. If not, execute the block of code named PROCESS-
CARDS. When you have finished, go back to the PERFORM statement and do the test again. If the condition is still not true, execute the block again. Repeat until the condition *is* true, then go
on to the next statement after the PERFORM."

This "PERFORM procedure UNTIL condition is true" enables
us to set up *loops,* whereby the computer tirelessly repeats some
operation over and over, until it has completed what we want.

Q. Write a statement that will carry out repeatedly a procedure called READ-A-CARD, reading our name-and-address cards and stopping when one is found with a missing address.

A. **PERFORM READ-A-CARD**
UNTIL ADDRESS IN CARD IS EQUAL TO SPACES.

The PERFORM loop is shown graphically below.

PERFORM UNTIL CARDS-LEFT = 'NO '	
P R O C E S S – C A R D S	MOVE . . . .

If the condition tested is *not* true, the procedure in the inner box is carried out, and the condition is tested again. Only when the condition is made true does control go down the left-hand side into the box below.

Q. What happens if the procedure *never* makes the condition true?

A. The computer will perform the procedure over and over forever, unless something happens to stop it, such as the computer operator or operating system eventually halting your program.

Q. Use the process, decision, and loop boxes to show the structure of SAMPLE-1.

A.

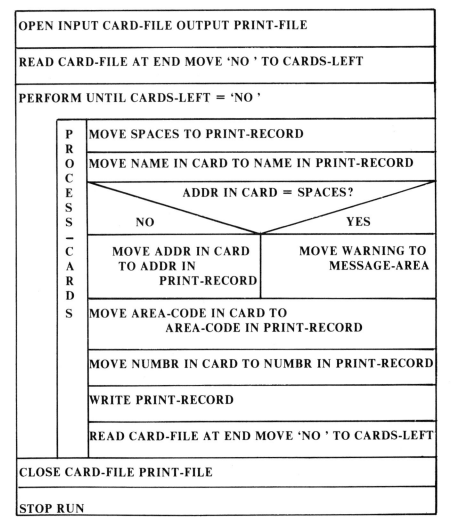

If not identical, your answer should be very similar to this. A diagram like the above is a *structured flowchart,* and it shows the flow of control in a program. As you can see, it is normal to have decisions within loops, process boxes within decisions, and every combination of structure *nested* within other structures.

2.8 Structuring a sample program

As coupons asking for catalogs continue to come in, we notice that some people are including their addresses, but omitting their phone numbers. Others are giving their addresses and phone numbers, but leaving off their names! Here are some examples of the cards you must process:

You are asked to write a slightly more complex program than the previous program, to be named SAMPLE-2, which will deal with the following possibilities:

1) Name only missing:
   Print **** NAME MISSING ****

2) Address only missing:
   Print **** ADDRESS MISSING ****

3) Whole phone number missing:
   Print **** PHONE MISSING ****

No other combination of mistakes occurs.

Q. Given that three warning messages are set up in Working-Storage (WARNING-1, WARNING-2, WARNING-3), redraw the structured flowchart for SAMPLE-1 to show the logic.

A.

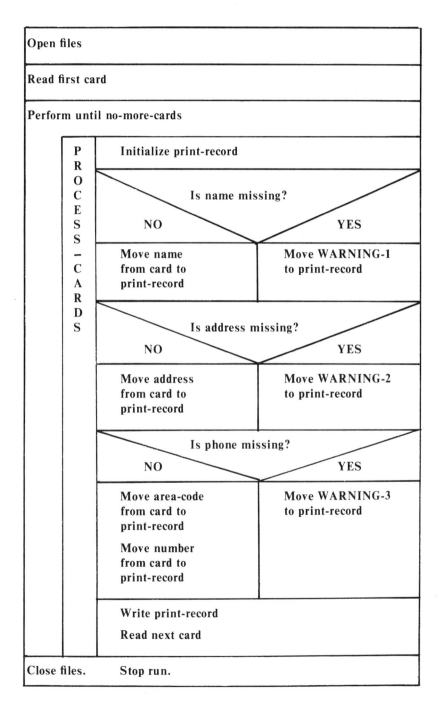

Note that we have used a precise shorthand description for some of the boxes, especially those that we already know how to code from SAMPLE-1.

2.9 Coding a sample program (SAMPLE-2)

Review the layout of the handwritten version of SAMPLE-1. You will notice that it is written on special COBOL coding sheets; use a pad of such sheets to write out your version of SAMPLE-2 from the structured flowchart just developed. Be sure to follow the format and punctuation used in the handwritten SAMPLE-1; note that most statements begin in column 12, except for certain names and headings, which begin in column 8. Most coding sheets have the statements already numbered for you; all you do is add the page number in column 3. Since the compiler will give numbers to your statements on the listing, the main reason for numbering the cards is in case you drop the deck. Columns 73-80 on the coding pad are reserved for the program name. Don't bother about that at this stage.

Find out your installation's requirements regarding transition SELECT statements, in the Environment Division.

When you have finished, compare your solution with the model solution on the next page. Have someone review your code before keypunching and compiling it; other people are better at finding errors in what you have written than you are, just as *you* are better at finding errors in what *they* have written. It always is worthwhile to take the time to have a walkthrough of your code with someone else.

You will find a compiled listing and a sample report on the following pages.

IBM   COBOL Coding Form

PROGRAM   SAMPLE-2

```
1 01   IDENTIFICATION DIVISION.
1 02   PROGRAM-ID. SAMPLE-2.
1 03   ENVIRONMENT DIVISION.
1 04   INPUT-OUTPUT SECTION.
1 05   FILE-CONTROL.
1 06        SELECT CARD-FILE  ASSIGN TO SYS031-UR-2540R-S.
1 07        SELECT PRINT-FILE ASSIGN TO SYS033-UR-1403-S.
1 08   DATA DIVISION.
1 09   FILE SECTION.
1 10   FD  CARD-FILE
1 11        LABEL RECORDS ARE OMITTED.
1 12   01   CARD.
1 13        05  NAME           PICTURE    X(20).
1 14        05  ADDR           PICTURE    X(40).
1 15        05  PHONE.
1 16            10  AREA-CODE   PICTURE    9(3).
1 17            10  NUMBR       PICTURE    X(8).
1 18        05  FILLER         PICTURE    X(9).
1 19   FD  PRINT-FILE
1 20        LABEL RECORDS ARE OMITTED.
1 21   01   PRINT-RECORD.
1 22        05  FILLER         PICTURE    X(3).
1 23        05  NAME           PICTURE    X(20).
1 24        05  FILLER         PICTURE    X(5).

2 01        05  ADDR           PICTURE    X(40).
2 02        05  FILLER         PICTURE    X(5).
2 03        05  PHONE.
2 04            10  AREA-CODE   PICTURE    9(3).
2 05            10  FILLER      PICTURE    X.
2 06            10  NUMBR       PICTURE    X(8).
2 07        05  FILLER         PICTURE    X(10).
2 08        05  MESSAGE-AREA   PICTURE    X(25).
2 09        05  FILLER         PICTURE    X(12).
2 10   WORKING-STORAGE SECTION.
2 11   01   WARNING-1 PICTURE X(25) VALUE '**** NAME MISSING ****'.
2 12   01   WARNING-2 PICTURE X(25) VALUE '**** ADDRESS MISSING ****'.
2 13   01   WARNING-3 PICTURE X(25) VALUE '**** PHONE MISSING ****'.
2 14   01   CARDS-LEFT PICTURE X(3).
2 15   PROCEDURE DIVISION.
2 16        OPEN INPUT  CARD-FILE
2 17             OUTPUT PRINT-FILE.
2 18        MOVE 'YES' TO CARDS-LEFT
2 19        READ CARD-FILE
2 20             AT END MOVE 'NO ' TO CARDS-LEFT.
2 21        PERFORM PROCESS-CARDS
2 22             UNTIL CARDS-LEFT IS EQUAL TO 'NO '.
2 23        CLOSE CARD-FILE PRINT-FILE.
2 24        STOP RUN.

3 01   PROCESS-CARDS.
3 02        MOVE SPACES TO PRINT-RECORD.
3 03        IF NAME IN CARD IS EQUAL TO SPACES
3 04             MOVE WARNING-1 TO MESSAGE-AREA
3 05        ELSE
3 06             MOVE NAME IN CARD TO NAME IN PRINT-RECORD.
3 07        IF ADDR IN CARD IS EQUAL TO SPACES
3 08             MOVE WARNING-2 TO MESSAGE-AREA
3 09        ELSE
3 10             MOVE ADDR IN CARD TO ADDR IN PRINT-RECORD.
3 11        IF PHONE IN CARD IS EQUAL TO SPACES
3 12             MOVE WARNING-3 TO MESSAGE-AREA
3 13        ELSE
3 14             MOVE AREA-CODE IN CARD TO AREA-CODE IN PRINT-RECORD
3 15             MOVE NUMBR IN CARD TO NUMBR IN PRINT-RECORD.
3 16        WRITE PRINT-RECORD.
3 17        READ CARD-FILE
3 18             AT END MOVE 'NO ' TO CARDS-LEFT.
```

Figure 2.1. COBOL coding sheet.

```
00001      IDENTIFICATION DIVISION.
00002      PROGRAM-ID. SAMPLE-2.
00003      ENVIRONMENT DIVISION.
00004      INPUT-OUTPUT SECTION.
00005      FILE-CONTROL.
00006          SELECT CARD-FILE   ASSIGN TO SYS031-UR-2540R-S.
00007          SELECT PRINT-FILE  ASSIGN TO SYS033-UR-1403-S.
00008      DATA DIVISION.
00009      FILE SECTION.
00010      FD  CARD-FILE
00011          LABEL RECORDS ARE OMITTED.
00012      01  CARD.
00013          05  NAME                    PICTURE     X(20).
00014          05  ADDR                    PICTURE     X(40).
00015          05  PHONE.
00016              10  AREA-CODE           PICTURE     9(3).
00017              10  NUMBR               PICTURE     X(8).
00018          05  FILLER                  PICTURE     X(9).
00019      FD  PRINT-FILE
00020          LABEL RECORDS ARE OMITTED.
00021      01  PRINT-RECORD.
00022          05  FILLER                  PICTURE     X(3).
00023          05  NAME                    PICTURE     X(20).
00024          05  FILLER                  PICTURE     X(5).
00025          05  ADDR                    PICTURE     X(40).
00026          05  FILLER                  PICTURE     X(5).
00027          05  PHONE.
00028              10  AREA-CODE           PICTURE     9(3).
00029              10  FILLER              PICTURE     X.
00030              10  NUMBR               PICTURE     X(8).
00031          05  FILLER                  PICTURE     X(10).
00032          05  MESSAGE-AREA            PICTURE     X(25).
00033          05  FILLER                  PICTURE     X(12).
00034      WORKING-STORAGE SECTION.
00035      01  WARNING-1 PICTURE X(25) VALUE   '**** NAME MISSING ****'.
00036      01  WARNING-2 PICTURE X(25) VALUE   '**** ADDRESS MISSING ****'.
00037      01  WARNING-3 PICTURE X(25) VALUE   '**** PHONE MISSING ****'.
00038      01  CARDS-LEFT PICTURE X(3).
00039      PROCEDURE DIVISION.
00040          OPEN  INPUT    CARD FILE
00041                OUTPUT   PRINT-FILE.
00042          MOVE 'YES' TO CARDS-LEFT.
00043          READ CARD-FILE
00044            AT END MOVE 'NO ' TO CARDS-LEFT.
00045          PERFORM PROCESS-CARDS
00046            UNTIL CARDS-LEFT IS EQUAL TO 'NO '.
00047          CLOSE   CARD-FILE
00048                  PRINT-FILE.
00049          STOP RUN.
```

```
00050    PROCESS-CARDS.
00051        MOVE SPACES TO PRINT-RECORD.
00052        IF NAME IN CARD IS EQUAL TO SPACES
00053            MOVE WARNING-1 TO MESSAGE-AREA
00054        ELSE
00055            MOVE NAME IN CARD TO NAME IN PRINT-RECORD.
00056        IF ADDR IN CARD IS EQUAL TO SPACES
00057            MOVE WARNING-2 TO MESSAGE-AREA
00058        ELSE
00059            MOVE ADDR IN CARD TO ADDR IN PRINT-RECORD.
00060        IF PHONE IN CARD IS EQUAL TO SPACES
00061            MOVE WARNING-3 TO MESSAGE-AREA
00062        ELSE
00063            MOVE AREA-CODE IN CARD TO AREA-CODE IN PRINT-RECORD
00064            MOVE NUMBR IN CARD TO NUMBR IN PRINT-RECORD.
00065        WRITE PRINT-RECORD.
00066        READ CARD-FILE
00067            AT END MOVE 'NO ' TO CARDS-LEFT.
```

Figure 2.2. Specimen printout from SAMPLE-2.

3 Defining Data for the Computer

Having seen how to make the computer manipulate data in the way you want, let's take a first look at how you define this data for the computer.

3.1 The COBOL character set

COBOL uses 51 characters:

the letters A through Z and ƀ	27	(ƀ stands for blank or space)
the digits 0 through 9	10	
the special characters + −* / = $, ; . ' ( ) > <	14	
	51	

Note that, except in nonnumeric literals, and unless you are working with a computer that permits it, you can't use characters like @ or !. As you know,

- the letters A−Z and ƀ are *alphabetic* characters (A)

- the digits 0 − 9 are *numeric* characters (9)

- a field that contains only digits, with perhaps a decimal point embedded in the field or maybe a plus or minus sign, is *numeric*

- a field that is not purely alphabetic or purely numeric, i.e., contains a mixture, maybe with some special characters, is *alphanumeric* (X)

34

Thus, to take some examples:

ACCT NUM is an A-type field (alphabetic), even though it contains a blank.

3.14159 is a 9-type field, even though it contains a decimal point.

$132435 is an X-type field because it contains a dollar sign.

-27.49 is a 9-type field, even though it contains a hyphen (-) used as a minus sign.

27-49 is an X-type field because the hyphen appears as a special character, not as a minus sign.

3.2 Group items and elementary items

With this in mind, let's take another look at our card layout. What is the most detailed way in which we could describe the fields that make up the names, addresses, and phone numbers? The table below shows that all of the cards have the following format:

Card Columns	Data	Length of Field	Type of Field	
cc 1 - 20	Name	20	A	
cc 21 - 40	Street Address	20	X	These fields make up "Address"
cc 41 - 53	City	13	A	
cc 54 - 55	State	2	A	
cc 56 - 60	ZIP Code	5	9	
cc 61 - 63	Area Code	3	9	These fields make up "Phone"
cc 64 - 66	Exchange	3	9	
cc 67	Hyphen	1	X	
cc 68 - 71	Local Number	4	9	
cc 72 - 80	Blank	9	A	

Make sure you agree with this table and that you understand why each field is given its particular field type.

As you will recall from Chapter 1, these fields together compose a record; within most records, several fields are collected into one or more *group items.* Each field that cannot be broken down further is called an *elementary item.*

> Q. Suppose we defined a field called "name-and-address." Would that be a group item?
>
> A. Yes. It would be composed of the elementary item "Name" and the group item "Address."

3.3 File Definition

Whenever a file is going to be used in a COBOL program, it must have a File Definition (FD) in the Data Division. Here is the layout of a detailed FD for CARD-FILE:

```
FD  CARD-FILE.
    01  CARD.
        05  NAME-AND-ADDRESS.
            10  NAME
            10  ADDR.
                15  STREET-ADDRESS
                15  CITY
                15  STATE-AND-ZIP.
                    20  STATE
                    20  ZIP
        05  PHONE.
            10  AREA-CODE
            10  NUMBR.
                15  EXCHANGE
                15  FILLER
                15  LOCAL-NUMBER
        05  FILLER
```

Within the outline are the *level-numbers.* Starting with Ø1 for the name of the whole record, they increase for each level of subdivision of a group item, up to a maximum level of 49. They don't necessarily have to go Ø1, Ø5, 1Ø, 15, as shown above; you could have Ø1, Ø2, Ø3, or, in fact, any ascending order. However, it's advisable to leave some gaps in case you want to interpose some levels later on; for this reason, we recommend the scheme shown above.

Recalling our detailed card layout in the previous section, we now can formulate a rule: *Only elementary items in a field have a PIC clause.*

Q. Bearing in mind that in a PIC

A means only alphabetic
9 means only numeric
X means alphanumeric

work out the PICs for the card as defined above.

A. **FD CARD-FILE.**

 01 CARD. ◄──────────────────────────────┐

  05 NAME-AND-ADDRESS. ◄────────────────┤

   10 NAME   PIC A (2Ø).

   10 ADDR. ◄─────────────────────────────┤

    15 STREET-ADDRESS   PIC X (20).

    15 CITY   PIC A (13).

    15 STATE-AND-ZIP. ◄─────────────┤

     20 STATE   PIC A (2).

     20 ZIP   PIC 9 (5).

  05 PHONE. ◄───────────────────────────┤

   10 AREA-CODE   PIC 9 (3).

   10 NUMBR. ◄────────────────────────────┤

    15 EXCHANGE   PIC 9 (3).

    15 FILLER   PIC X.

    15 LOCAL-NUMBER   PIC 9 (4).

  05 FILLER   PIC A (9).

These do not have PICs because they are group items and are further divided.

Q. Why would you want to have this degree of grouping and subdivision?

A. So that you could refer to any part or reasonable combination of parts of the record as a unit in the Procedure Division.

For example, if you had a 60-position field called NAMADD in the print-line, you could write

MOVE NAME-AND-ADDRESS TO NAMADD.

and the whole 60 characters would be moved. At the same time, you could test the state by writing,

IF STATE = 'NY'
        MOVE 'NEW YORK STATE' TO MESSAGE-AREA
ELSE
        MOVE 'OUT OF STATE' TO MESSAGE-AREA.

Q. Suppose you wanted to test the ZIP code, digit by digit, to check that the ZIP code and state matched (all ZIP codes beginning with 15 are in Pennsylvania, for example). Code the part of the FD that would enable you to do this; make ZIP a group item.

A.

```
            .
            .
            .
     20    ZIP.
           25  FIRST-DIGIT       PIC 9.
           25  SECOND-DIGIT      PIC 9.
           25  THIRD-DIGIT       PIC 9.
           25  FOURTH-DIGIT      PIC 9.
           25  FIFTH-DIGIT       PIC 9.
     05  PHONE.
            .
            .
            .
```

or similar structure.

3.4 Names

We have used many names for data fields and procedures, such as AREA-CODE and PROCESS-CARDS; strict rules must be followed in coding different sorts of names, or else the compiler will reject them.

The four divisions of COBOL all have names that must be coded exactly as we already have seen them. Each division consists of one or more sections. Section-names also must be coded exactly as we have seen them, for example, INPUT-OUTPUT SECTION or WORKING-STORAGE SECTION. Note that section-names are hyphenated, and that in code the word SECTION is followed by a period.

Each section consists of one or more paragraphs; paragraphs, in turn, consist of sentences, each followed by a period. Each sentence consists of one or more statements, which contain verbs and data-names. Each paragraph in the Procedure Division is a procedure, and its name is a procedure-name. You can see how this works by looking at the skeleton of SAMPLE-1, shown in Fig. 3.1.

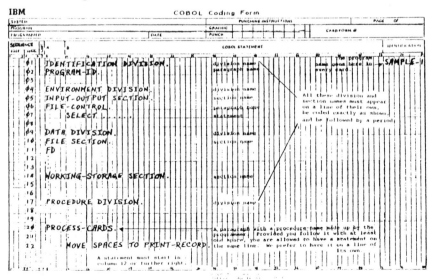

Figure 3.1. Skeleton of a COBOL program.

All of these are programmer-defined names, which

- can be up to 30 characters long
- can be any combination of A—Z, Ø—9, and hyphens, but may not begin or end with a hyphen
- must have at least one alphabetic character if they are to be data-names
- should always have a mnemonic meaning

Listed below are some data-names for you to decide if they are OK, and if not, why not.

Data-name

MESSAGE-AREA-FOR-WARNING-MESSAGES	Wrong; 3 characters too long
MSGØ6Ø	OK
NUMBERS-OF-$	Wrong; $ is a special character and therefore not allowed
64083	Wrong; data-names must have one alpha character, or the computer will think it is a numeric literal
MFACNO	OK; but cryptic
MAST-FILE-AC-NO-	Meaningful, but ends with a hyphen

Do the same for the following procedure-names:

Procedure-name

123456789Ø123456789Ø	This is legal; procedure-names may be all digits; quite meaningless
UPDATE-MASTER-FILE	OK

Programmer-defined names must not be the same as any of the standard words reserved for special use in COBOL, such as ADDRESS, NUMBER, SPACES, FILE-CONTROL, MOVE, DATA, among others. (This is why we have used ADDR instead of ADDRESS and NUMBR instead of NUMBER.) A list of these *reserved words* is given in Appendix A. Don't bother to memorize them all at this stage; just note the ones that have hyphens in them, and steer clear of them. Then, if you are in doubt, make up a name with a hyphen in it (which will help to make it more readable and meaningful anyway), and you should have no problem.

Of course, once you have chosen a name and defined it in the Data Division, it is essential to spell it *exactly* the same throughout the program. To the computer, MAST-FILE-AC-NO and MAS-FILE-AC-NO are *totally* different data-names; if you write one when you mean another, you most assuredly will receive a rude message from the computer. Generally, in defining names, make them as meaningful as possible, without making them so long that you get writer's cramp when coding.

3.4.1 Naming the same data in different places

In SAMPLE-1, we have the fields NAME and ADDR in two places: CARD and PRINT-RECORD. As you saw previously, we can distinguish between the fields by writing NAME IN CARD, for example. However, this method of using *qualified data-names* to get unique definitions is clumsy when the names are long and often referenced.

A good practice, instead, is to put a *suffix* on the data-name: -IN for an input field, and -OUT for an output field. Thus, if we defined the card fields as NAME-IN, ADDRESS-IN, and PHONE-IN, we could define the printer fields as NAME-OUT, ADDRESS-OUT, and so on.

You can see at a glance that NAME-IN and NAME-OUT contain the same data, and you can write

MOVE NAME-IN TO NAME-OUT

instead of

MOVE NAME IN CARD TO NAME IN PRINT-RECORD

We will use this technique in the sample programs throughout the rest of this book.

3.5 Punctuation, layout, and comments

The period (.) tells the compiler where a sentence ends; and since we normally write one statement per sentence, we will have a period at the end of every complete statement. The period also must be used

- at the end of the definition of each FD statement or group item statement or elementary item definition in the Data Division

- after every division, section-, or paragraph-name.

Each period must be followed by one or more spaces; while it is legal to have several statements on one line, we recommend that you always start a new line after each period. This makes your program much more readable.

Q. Put a period wherever needed in the code below:

```
DATA DIVISION
FILE SECTION
FD RECORD-IN
    LABEL RECORDS ARE OMITTED
01  REC
    02  PERSONNEL-NO                 PIC 9(6)
    02  JOB-DESCRIP
        03  DEPT
            04  FACTORY              PIC X(3)
            04  SHOP-NO              PIC 9(3)
PROCEDURE DIVISION
    MOVE PERSONNEL-NO TO WAGE-ACCT
    IF FACTORY IS EQUAL TO CODE-FOR-PODUNK
        MOVE SHOP-NO TO SHOP-NO-WS
    ELSE
        PERFORM OTHER-GROUP-ROUTINE
```

```
A.      DATA DIVISION.
        FILE SECTION.
        FD RECORD-IN
           LABEL RECORDS ARE OMITTED.
        01 REC.
           02 PERSONNEL-NO                    PIC 9(6).
           02 JOB-DESCRIP.
              03 DEPT.
                 04 FACTORY                   PIC X(3).
                 04 SHOP-NO                   PIC 9(3).
        PROCEDURE DIVISION.
           MOVE PERSONNEL-NO TO WAGE-ACCT.
           IF FACTORY IS EQUAL TO CODE-FOR-PODUNK
              MOVE SHOP-NO TO SHOP-NO-WS
           ELSE
              PERFORM OTHER-GROUP-ROUTINE.
```

Notice that the FD does not have a period until it is completed by the LABEL RECORDS clause, and there is only one period in the whole IF statement, right at the end.

3.5.1 Avoiding confusion with handwriting

As you have seen, we are using the convention of writing number zero as Ø to avoid confusion with the letter O. You may find the convention reversed in some installations.

The other pairs of characters that are sometimes confused are I and 1, S and 5, Z and 2, U and V. So, stick to these conventions:

Zero	Ø
Letter O for orange	O
Letter I for India	I
Number 1	I
Letter S for sugar	S
Number 5	5
Letter Z for zebra	Z
Number 2	2
Letter U for uncle	U
Letter V for Victor	Y

3.5.2 Comments and continuation

After writing a program more than a few statements long, and then reviewing it after a few months have elapsed, you may find that you have forgotten what the various statements do. If you have to check or change the program for any reason, you probably will have to work through the logic of the program and figure out afresh what each statement does.

You frequently may be asked to modify programs written by other people, either because the situation for which they were written has changed, or they didn't accomplish what they were supposed to do in the first place.

For these reasons, you must aim to write code that is easy to read and understand by anyone who knows COBOL. If you think any statement or group of statements is going to be hard to understand, and you can see no way to simplify them, write an explanatory *comment*. You do this by putting an asterisk (*) in column 7 of the line of code, as shown below; everything else on this line will be part of the program, but will not be executed by the computer.

SEQUENCE		CONT	A	B						
(PAGE)	(SERIAL)									
	01		PROCEDURE DIVISION.							
	02			MOVE PERSONNEL-NO TO WAGE-ACCT.						
	03			IF FACTORY IS EQUAL TO PODUNK-CODE						
	04			MOVE SHOP-NO TO SHOP-NO-WS						
	05			ELSE						
	06			PERFORM OTHER-GROUP-ROUTINE.						
	07	*	THIS PROGRAM ONLY DEALS WITH STAFF AT							
	08	*	THE PODUNK FACTORY							
	09			IF SHOP-NO-WS IS.......						
	10									

As we saw with the IF statement in SAMPLE-2, you can write a statement over several lines, with the separate parts (clauses) of the statement starting in column 14 or 16 of each line (or further to the right if you need to indent for clarity). You should always break the sentence at a *key word* such as UNTIL or TO. For example, do not write

PERFORM COMPUTE-PROCEDURE UNTIL CARDS-LEFT IS EQUAL TO 'NO '.

While this will work, your program will be much more readable if you always break the statement in a standard place, as follows:

**PERFORM COMPUTE-PROCEDURE
UNTIL CARDS-LEFT IS EQUAL TO 'NO '.**

By putting a *hyphen* in column 7, you can *split words* between lines; while this is legal, it is a poor practice except in the case of long nonnumeric literals. A nonnumeric literal can be up to 120 characters long (for example, in a report heading), so it would have to be split into at least two lines.

Q. Define in Working-Storage a field called ASTERISK-DELIMITER, which is 120 characters long and consists of alternating asterisks and hyphens, thus * - * - * - * - * etc.

A.

Note that in this case the continuation cards also must begin with a single quote to identify what follows as a nonnumeric literal.

3.6 FILE SECTION and WORKING-STORAGE SECTION

As we saw in SAMPLE-1 and SAMPLE-2, you must have an FD for each *external file* (e.g., cards, printer) that will provide data to the program (input) or accept data from the program (output). The FD does two things:

- ● tells the computer what the layout of the data record will be, and what data-names will be used for the various parts

- tells the compiler to reserve an area of storage that will hold each data record while the program deals with it

We can draw a diagram of computer storage like this:

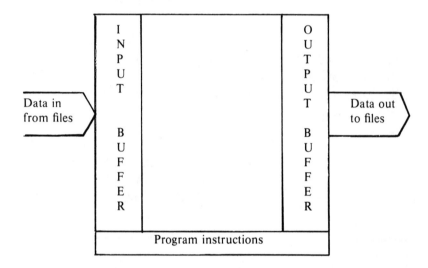

These reserved input-output work areas, called *buffers,* hold the data for each record. The input buffer holds the data from the most recently read card. When we issue an instruction like

MOVE NAME IN CARD TO NAME IN PRINT-RECORD.

the computer moves data from the input buffer to the output buffer, as specified by the appropriate FDs. Then, the instruction

WRITE PRINT-RECORD.

transfers data from the output buffer to the printer.

In addition to defining files and reserving space for buffers, we need to reserve other positions in storage for work areas in the program, for setting up messages and constants as is done in WARNING-1 and WARNING-2, and for all other storage of intermediate data between input and output. Storage is set up for these purposes in the Working-Storage Section, which, as you have seen, follows the File Section.

A common use for Working-Storage is to set up *flags*. A flag is a field that can be set to 'YES' or 'NO ', as a signal that something has or has not happened. For instance, in a more complex version of SAMPLE-1, we might want to defer processing of a card with a missing name until later in the program. In this case, we would write

> **IF NAME IN CARD IS EQUAL TO SPACES**
> ** MOVE 'YES' TO MISSING-NAME-FLAG**
> **ELSE**
>   . . .

and later in the program

> **IF MISSING-NAME-FLAG IS EQUAL TO 'YES'**
> ** MOVE WARNING-1 TO MESSAGE-AREA**
> **ELSE**
>   . . .

Setting MISSING-NAME-FLAG to 'YES' allows us to delay handling the situation. We set a flag in one part of the program, and test for it in another.

Q.   Code a Working-Storage Section entry to set up MISSING-NAME-FLAG.

A.   **01 MISSING-NAME-FLAG   PIC X(3).**

Q.   With MISSING-NAME-FLAG having PIC X(3), what is its contents if

MOVE 'NO' TO MISSING-NAME-FLAG
is executed.

A.   NOƄ; since the literal 'NO' is too short, the remaining position is filled with a blank. While this is adequate, we prefer to be doubly sure by moving 'NOƄ' to flags.

3.7 Initializing Working-Storage

As we said in Chapter 2, it is important that you know the contents of all work areas before you use them and, hence, you must initialize them to some known value.

3.7.1 Initializing constants with VALUE

Suppose you wanted to print a heading in the middle of a 132-position print-line, saying

SALES REPORT

Since the words consist of 12 characters, you will want 60 blanks on either side. You would use the VALUE clause to set up this print-line in Working-Storage by coding

```
WORKING-STORAGE SECTION.
01   HEADING-1.
     05   FILLER        PIC X(60) VALUE SPACES.
     05   FILLER        PIC X(12) VALUE 'SALES REPORT'.
     05   FILLER        PIC X(60) VALUE SPACES.
```

As you have seen, we use FILLER to name a field that will not be called, although it may be filled with blanks. Later, in the Procedure Division, you would write

```
     .
     .
     MOVE HEADING-1 TO PRINT-LINE.
     WRITE PRINT-LINE.

or
     WRITE PRINT-LINE FROM HEADING-1.
```
Note that these two are equivalent.

Use VALUE to set up any field that is a *constant,* or is not changed throughout the execution of the program. The general format of the VALUE clause has three options:

$$\text{VALUE} \begin{Bmatrix} \text{numeric literal} \\ \text{'nonnumeric literal'} \\ \text{figurative constant} \end{Bmatrix}$$

The braces show that these three are alternatives.

You might want to use ZERO or ZEROS to initialize a long numeric field, in much the same way as you use the figurative constant SPACES to initialize an alphabetic field.

3.7.2 Initializing flags, counters, and other fields

When a field is used as a flag, as in the case of MISSING-NAME-FLAG in the previous section, its contents will vary from time to time as the program is executed. Similarly, if a field is used to count the number of cards processed, its value also would change. Working-Storage fields like these must be initialized to a starting value before being used for the first time. While this *could* be done with the VALUE clause, it is better practice to reserve VALUE for constants, and to initialize flags and counters with a MOVE statement.

As you saw in SAMPLE-1 and SAMPLE-2, immediately before READing the card file, we wrote

MOVE 'YES' TO CARDS-LEFT.

CARDS-LEFT is a flag, whose value will be changed to 'NO ', when the program finds there are no more cards to be read.

So, to complete the previous picture of the storage inside the computer, visualize it as consisting of four areas:

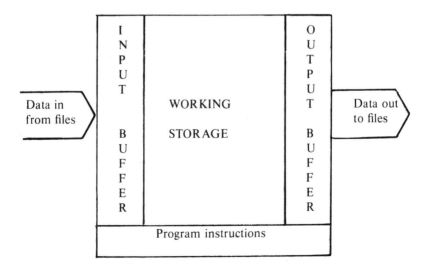

Data are read into the input buffer, moved to Working-Storage for processing, then moved to the output buffer for printing. The size and format of each buffer is specified automatically by

the size and format of the corresponding FD; Working-Storage must be defined separately according to your needs.

3.8 Condition-names

Suppose one column on a card were used to indicate a person's marital status: S for single, M for married, D for divorced, and W for widowed. We might describe the field as

```
01  CARD.
       .
       .

    05  MARITAL-STATUS        PIC X.
```

Since we often want to perform different operations depending on the contents of that column, we would have to write

```
IF MARITAL-STATUS = 'S' PERFORM SINGLE-ROUTINE.
IF MARITAL-STATUS = 'M' PERFORM MARRIED-ROUTINE.
IF MARITAL-STATUS = 'D' PERFORM DIVORCED-ROUTINE.
IF MARITAL-STATUS = 'W' PERFORM WIDOWED-ROUTINE.
```

To simplify this coding, we can set up condition-names for each of the possible card entries. This involves using the special level-number 88, as illustrated below:

```
01  CARD.
       .
       .

    05  MARITAL-STATUS                 PIC X.
        88  SINGLE        VALUE 'S'.
        88  MARRIED       VALUE 'M'.
        88  DIVORCED      VALUE 'D'.
        88  WIDOWED       VALUE 'W'.
```

Then we would code

```
IF SINGLE PERFORM SINGLE-ROUTINE.
IF MARRIED PERFORM MARRIED-ROUTINE.
```

and so on. The condition-name, e.g., DIVORCED, takes the place of the condition MARITAL STATUS = 'D'.

Q. A one-column field in CARD, called SEX, contains M for males and F for females. Set up condition-names.

A. 01 CARD.
.
.
.
```
05 SEX                        PIC X.
   88 MALE          VALUE 'M'.
   88 FEMALE        VALUE 'F'.
```

At this point, let's test ourselves. Turn to the Review Quiz on the following page.

REVIEW QUIZ*

1. Which of the characters shown in the specimen card on page 5 are *not* in the COBOL character set?

2. What is wrong with this FD?

```
FD  OUT-PRINT
01  LINE                    PIC X(132)
    05 FILLER               PIC X(60).
    05 FILLER               PIC X(12)  VALUE REPORT
    05 FILLER               PIC X(60).        HEADING.
```

3. What is wrong with this FD?

```
FD  CARD-FILE
01  CARD
    02 NAME.                PIC A (20).
    02 ADDRESS
        03 STREET.          PIC X (20).
        03 CITY.            PIC A (20).
        03 STATE-ZIP.       PIC X (20).
```

4. Here are some programmer-defined names. Decide if they are OK as data-names, or as procedure-names, and if not, why not.

MASTER-FILE-INVENTORY-CODE	LINE-COUNTER
M9999	ZIP CODE
HEADING-	ZIP.CODE
-TITLE-	POSITION
111X	666

5. What is wrong with this Working-Storage Section?

```
01  CARDS-LEFT-FLAG        PIC 999.
01  PRINT-LINE-WS          VALUE SPACES.
    05 FILLER.
    05 FILLER              PIC X(24)
                           VALUE 'MONTHLY PRODUCTION REPORT'.
    05 FILLER.
```

6. Write the FD entries to set up meaningful condition-names for a one-column card code called JOB-CODE with the following meanings:

T	Trainee	P Programmer
J	Junior Programmer	A Systems Analyst

7. ·Rewrite the Working-Storage Section specified in Question 5, using correct COBOL, and changing the print-line to read REPORT OF MONTH-LY SALES, PRODUCTION AND PROFITABILITY, centered in a 132-position print-line.

*Answers are in Appendix C.

3.9 Designing, structuring, and coding a sample program

The mail-order firm for which you work sent catalogs to the names and addresses that were processed in SAMPLE-1 and SAMPLE-2, and has received a number of orders together with applications to open credit accounts. Applicants for credit accounts must fill in a form giving family income, years employed at the current job, sex, marital status, number of dependents, status as home-owner or renter, amount of rent or mortgage paid monthly, and other payments made regularly.

For instance, Victor Grasper's form shows that he is a single male earning $15,700 per annum in a job held for four years. He has no dependents and owns an apartment for which he pays $250 per month. His other debt payments are $40 per month.

This information is entered into the computer on a second card for each person, who is assigned a six-digit number. That number is punched in cc 75-80 of the first name/address/phone card. Victor Grasper's and Ian Inkerman's name-and-address and credit information cards are shown below.

The layout of the second card is

cc	Data	Field Length	Field Type	Remarks
1	A letter 'C' for continuation	1	X	
2-7	6-digit account number	6	9	
8	blank	1	X	
9	Sex	1	X	M for male, F for female
1Ø	blank	1	X	
11	Marital status	1	X	S for single, etc.
12	blank	1	X	
13	Number of dependents	1	9	Number of people supported from Ø-9. More than 9 coded as 9.
14	blank	1	X	
15-17	Income in hundreds of dollars	3	9	e.g., 157 means $15,7ØØ
18	blank	1	X	
19-2Ø	Years employed in this job	2	99	e.g., Ø1 means 1 year. Less than 1 year coded as ØØ.
21	blank	1	X	
22	Own-or-rent	1	X	O for own; R for rent
23	blank	1	X	
24-26	Monthly payments on mortgage or rent	3	999	
27	blank	1	X	
28-3Ø	Monthly payments on other debts	3	999	

We want to read in the name-and-address and credit infor-mation cards in pairs, for one applicant at a time, and produce a report listing the details of the application (the application profile) in an easy-to-read form. To simplify the problem, we will assume that all of the fields are present and correctly punched; obviously, you would have to check for this in any pro-gram you write for your organization.

Figure 3.2 shows what the profile is to look like for the first six applicants. Study the details of the layout and compare the data printed with the data on the cards. You will notice that the printout is a bit clumsy where, for example, it says 1 DEPEN-DENTS and 04 YEARS. We did this purposely to simplify your programming work, and we'll clean up these finer points in a later chapter.

```
VICTOR S GRASPER      PHONE (415) 243-7022   MALE        INCOME       $15700 PER YEAR: IN THIS EMPLOY 04 YEARS
990 GAUNTLET AVE                             SINGLE      MORTGAGE:      $250 PER MTH
BURLINGAME    CA 94010  A/C: 010101          0 DEPENDENTS OTHER PAYMENTS $040 PER MTH

IAN S INKERMAN        PHONE (201) 103-6061   MALE        INCOME       $17500 PER YEAR: IN THIS EMPLOY LESS THAN 1 YEAR
59 PECAN VALLEY RD                            DIVORCED    RENTAL:       $325 PER MTH
MONTVALE      NJ 07645  A/C: 620202          1 DEPENDENTS OTHER PAYMENTS $110 PER MTH

SARALEE JAMES         PHONE (816) 542-0535   FEMALE      INCOME       $71000 PER YEAR: IN THIS EMPLOY 03 YEARS
PARTHENON COURT                              DIVORCED    MORTGAGE:     $775 PER MTH
ATHENS        MO 64065  A/C: 050505          1 DEPENDENTS OTHER PAYMENTS $ 75 PER MTH

SCARLETT O'HARA       PHONE (504) 815-1147   FEMALE      INCOME       $09500 PER YEAR: IN THIS EMPLOY 26 YEARS
SUITE 414 NAT BANK                           WIDOWED     RENTAL:       $110 PER MTH
NEW ORLEANS   LA 70012  A/C: 060606          2 DEPENDENTS OTHER PAYMENTS $ 20 PER MTH

SUSAN KRUPMAN         PHONE (212) 354-0330   FEMALE      INCOME       $12900 PER YEAR: IN THIS EMPLOY 01 YEARS
131 WEST 32ND ST                             SINGLE      RENTAL:       $150 PER MTH
NEW YORK      NY 10001  A/C: 040404          0 DEPENDENTS OTHER PAYMENTS $ 30 PER MTH

I. MORRIS GOOD        PHONE (214) 225-7013   MALE        INCOME       $27300 PER YEAR: IN THIS EMPLOY 11 YEARS
1313 PORPOISE                                MARRIED     MORTGAGE:     $400 PER MTH
DALLAS        TX 75219  A/C: 030303          4 DEPENDENTS OTHER PAYMENTS $150 PER MTH
```

Figure 3.2. Specimen printout of profiles for credit applicants.

As a first step, produce a printer spacing chart to correspond with the report layout; check carefully that the spac-ing between fields is correct. Now, how are we to proceed from the card data to the report giving a profile of each person? We obviously have to read in a pair of cards, somehow transform the data on them into correctly formatted print-lines, write the print-lines, move the paper up four lines, and repeat the process until we run out of cards.

Graphically, we can show the general process like this:

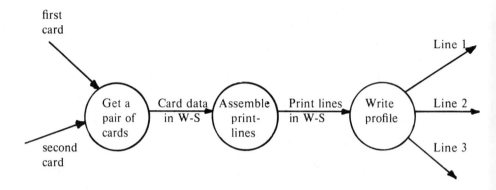

This is called a *program graph;* the circles show the basic data manipulations, and the lines connecting them represent the form that the data takes as it goes from input to output. Drawing a program graph is the first step in designing a program.

We can see from the program graph above that there are three basic procedures to be controlled in some way; we now draw a *structure chart* (not a flowchart), which shows the break down of the overall program's function (to print profiles).

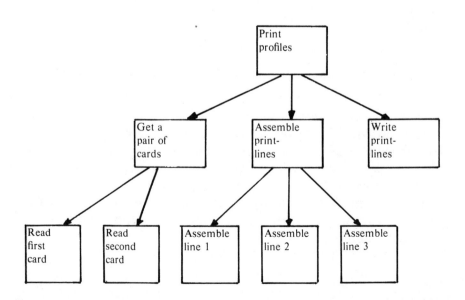

The structure chart shows that the overall function is composed of three subfunctions, one being "Get a pair of cards into Working-Storage" (which in turn breaks down to "Read first card" and "Read second card"). The structure of this program is fairly simple; the structure chart becomes very important when the program gets complex, as we shall see later.

Since we want to continue printing profiles until we run out of cards, the heart of the program is in the following shorthand form:

> Initialize (open files, read first card)
> PERFORM PRINT-PROFILES
>   UNTIL no-more-cards.
> Terminate (close files, stop-run)

PRINT-PROFILES will contain
>   PERFORM GET-A-PAIR-OF-CARDS-INTO-WS.
>   PERFORM ASSEMBLE-PRINT-LINES.
>   PERFORM WRITE-PRINT-LINES.

GET-A-PAIR-OF-CARDS must read in two cards, and move their contents to appropriate Working-Storage areas.

Q.   Since COBOL normally provides only one input buffer for each FD, what would happen if the first card were not moved to Working-Storage before reading the second card?

A.   The data in the second card would over-write the data from the first card in the buffer, and the data from the first card would be lost.

ASSEMBLE-PRINT-LINES must move data from the card-holding areas in Working-Storage to print-line holding areas, also in Working-Storage, ready for printing.

The Data Division must consist of

●   an FD for the card file to read in cards with two formats

- an FD for the printer file

- a holding area for the card data

- three holding areas for the formatted information in each print-line

Before going further, write the Data Division for this program, to be called SAMPLE-3. Remember to use 88 levels for condition-names. To deal with several types of records in one file (two types of cards in this case), give each 01 entry a different name and write in the FD

DATA RECORDS ARE name-1 name-2, etc.

In this case, if the first card were described with an Ø1 called NAME-ADDRESS-AND-PHONE-IN, and the second card of each pair were described with an Ø1 called CREDIT-INFORMATION, the FD might read

    FD APPLICATION-CARDS
          LABEL RECORDS ARE OMITTED
          DATA RECORDS ARE NAME-ADDRESS-AND-PHONE-IN
                  CREDIT-INFORMATION.

After you have coded the Data Division, compare it with the sample that follows. If your answer differs in any significant way, be sure that you understand why.

```
00001          IDENTIFICATION DIVISION.
00002          PROGRAM-ID.  SAMPLE-3.
00003
00004          ENVIRONMENT DIVISION.
00005          INPUT-OUTPUT SECTION.
00006          FILE-CONTROL.
00007               SELECT APPLICATION-CARDS-FILE    ASSIGN TO SYS031-UR-2540R-S.
00008               SELECT PROFILE-LISTING           ASSIGN TO SYS033-UR-1403-S.
00009
00010          DATA DIVISION.
00011          FILE SECTION.
00012
00013          FD   APPLICATION-CARDS-FILE
00014               LABEL RECORDS ARE OMITTED
00015               DATA RECORDS ARE NAME-ADDRESS-AND-PHONE-IN
00016                              CREDIT-INFORMATION-IN.
00017          01   NAME-ADDRESS-AND-PHONE-IN.
00018               05   NAME-IN                    PIC X(20).
00019               05   ADDRESS-IN                 PIC X(40).
00020               05   PHONE-IN                   PIC X(11).
00021               05   FILLER                     PIC X(3).
00022               05   ACCT-NUM-IN1               PIC 9(6).
00023          01   CREDIT-INFORMATION-IN.
00024               05   CARD-TYPE-IN               PIC X.
00025               05   ACCT-NUM-IN2               PIC 9(6).
00026               05   FILLER                     PIC X.
00027               05   CREDIT-INFO-IN             PIC X(22).
00028               05   FILLER                     PIC X(50).
00029
00030          FD   PROFILE-LISTING
00031               LABEL RECORDS ARE OMITTED.
00032          01   PRINT-LINE-OUT                  PIC X(132).
00033
00034          WORKING-STORAGE SECTION.
00035          01   CARDS-LEFT                      PIC X(3).
00036
00037          01   APPLICATION-DATA.
00038               05   NAME-AND-ADDRESS-WS.
00039                    10   NAME-WS               PIC X(20).
00040                    10   ADDRESS-WS.
00041                         15   STREET-WS        PIC X(20).
00042                         15   CITY-WS          PIC X(13).
00043                         15   STATE-WS         PIC XX.
00044                         15   ZIP-WS           PIC X(5).
00045               05   PHONE-WS.
00046                    10   AREA-CODE-WS          PIC 9(3).
00047                    10   NUMBR-WS              PIC X(8).
00048               05   FILLER                     PIC X(3).
00049               05   ACCT-NUM-WS                PIC 9(6).
00050               05   CREDIT-INFO-WS.
00051                    10   SEX-WS                PIC X.
00052                         88   MALE     VALUE 'M'.
00053                         88   FEMALE   VALUE 'F'.
00054                    10   FILLER                PIC X.
00055                    10   MARITAL-STATUS-WS     PIC X.
00056                         88   SINGLE    VALUE 'S'.
00057                         88   MARRIED   VALUE 'M'.
00058                         88   DIVORCED  VALUE 'D'.
00059                         88   WIDOWED   VALUE 'W'.
00060                    10   FILLER                PIC X.
```

```
00061                 10   NUMBER-DEPENS-WS              PIC 9.
00062                 10   FILLER                        PIC X.
00063                 10   INCOME-HUNDREDS-WS            PIC 9(3).
00064                 10   FILLER                        PIC X.
00065                 10   YEARS-EMPLOYED-WS             PIC 99.
00066                 10   FILLER                        PIC X.
00067                 10   OWN-OR-RENT-WS                PIC X.
00068                     88   OWNED        VALUE 'O'.
00069                     88   RENTED       VALUE 'R'.
00070                 10   FILLER                        PIC X.
00071                 10   MORTGAGE-OR-RENTAL-WS         PIC 9(3).
00072                 10   FILLER                        PIC X.
00073                 10   OTHER-PAYMENTS-WS             PIC 9(3).
00074
00075       01   LINE-1-WS.
00076            05   FILLER                          PIC X(5)     VALUE SPACES.
00077            05   NAME-L1                         PIC X(20).
00078            05   FILLER                          PIC X(11).
00079                                 VALUE          PHONE ('.
00080            05   AREA-CODE-L1                    PIC 9(3).
00081            05   FILLER                          PIC XX       VALUE ') '.
00082            05   NUMBR-L1                        PIC X(8).
00083            05   FILLER                          PIC X(3)     VALUE SPACES.
00084            05   SEX-L1                          PIC X(6).
00085            05   FILLER                          PIC X(9)     VALUE SPACES.
00086            05   FILLER                          PIC X(14)
00087                                 VALUE 'INCOME      $'.
00088            05   INCOME-HUNDREDS-L1              PIC 9(3).
00089            05   FILLER                          PIC X(28)
00090                             VALUE '00 PER YEAR; IN THIS EMPLOY '.
00091            05   YEARS-EMPLOYED-L1.
00092                 10   YEARS-L1                   PIC XX.
00093                 10   DESCN-L1                   PIC X(16).
00094
00095       01   LINE-2-WS.
00096            05   FILLER                          PIC X(5)     VALUE SPACES.
00097            05   STREET-L2                       PIC X(20).
00098            05   FILLER                          PIC X(27)    VALUE SPACES.
00099            05   MARITAL-STATUS-L2               PIC X(8).
00100            05   FILLER                          PIC X(7)     VALUE SPACES.
00101            05   OUTGO-DESCN                     PIC X(16).
00102            05   MORTGAGE-OR-RENTAL-L2           PIC 9(3).
00103            05   MESSAGE-L2                      PIC X(46)    VALUE ' PER MTH
00104
00105       01   LINE-3-WS.
00106            05   FILLER                          PIC X(5)     VALUE SPACES.
00107            05   CITY-L3                         PIC X(13).
00108            05   FILLER                          PIC X        VALUE SPACE.
00109            05   STATE-L3                        PIC XX.
00110            05   FILLER                          PIC X        VALUE SPACE.
00111            05   ZIP-L3                          PIC X(5).
00112            05   FILLER                          PIC X(7)     VALUE ' A/C: '.
00113            05   ACCT-NUM-L3                     PIC 9(6).
00114            05   FILLER                          PIC X(12)    VALUE SPACES.
00115            05   NUMBER-DEPENS-L3                PIC 9.
00116            05   FILLER                          PIC X(14)
00117                                 VALUE ' DEPENDENTS  '
00118            05   FILLER                          PIC X(16)
00119                                 VALUE 'OTHER PAYMENTS $'.
00120            05   OTHER-PAYMENTS-L3               PIC 9(3).
00121            05   MESSAGE-L3                      PIC X(46)    VALUE ' PER MTH
```

Now that we have the Data Division specified, we can work out the Procedure Division in detail. We can imagine that each box on the structure chart is a *mini-program* or *module* with its own input and output. For example, the input to ASSEMBLE-PRINT-LINES is the data from the two cards stored in APPLICATION-DATA; the output is the three lines formatted for printing. This data flow is shown on the structure chart by an arrow with a circle on its tail, thus:

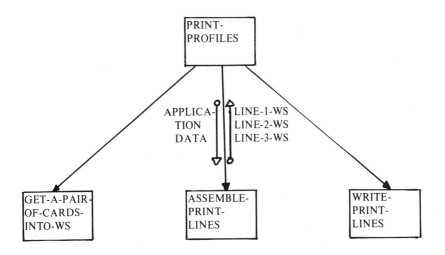

APPLICATION-DATA is, of course, the output of GET-A-PAIR-OF-CARDS. GET-A-PAIR-OF-CARDS also returns a *control variable*, CARDS-LEFT, with a value of Ø at the end of the card file. Control variables are shown by an arrow terminating in a dark, or filled, circle.

Q.   What is the input to WRITE-PRINT-LINES?

A.   The three formatted lines LINE-1-WS, LINE-2-WS, and LINE-3-WS.

Since we also have to include the initialization and termination functions, the full structure chart looks as follows:

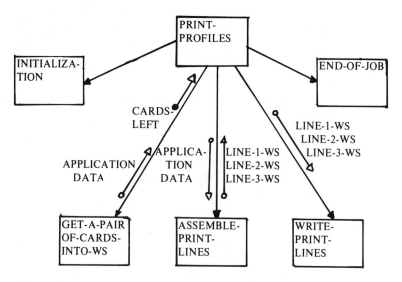

The structure chart doesn't show any of the detailed logic, nor does it show that we want a loop to print profiles until we run out of cards; but it *does* show major modules of the program, their relationship to one another, and the main data flows. To see the loop logic and the order in which the modules are executed, we need to draw a structured flowchart, like this:

INITIALIZATION	
PERFORM UNTIL CARDS-LEFT = 'NO '	
P R I N T - P R O F I L E S	GET-A-PAIR-OF-CARDS-INTO-WS
	ASSEMBLE-PRINT-LINES
	WRITE-PRINT-LINES
TERMINATION	

In this SAMPLE-3, the initialization is more complicated than in SAMPLE-1 or in SAMPLE-2. Before we can read cards or write reports, we have to instruct the computer to prepare the card file and printer file by coding an OPEN statement. In this case, the card file (APPLICATION-CARDS-FILE) will provide the input, and the printer file (PROFILE-LISTING) will receive the output; so we will code

OPEN INPUT APPLICATION-CARDS-FILE
OUTPUT PROFILE-LISTING.

Note that there is only one period, right at the end of the statement, and that we line up the file names to make them easier to read. Every file that is OPENed must be included in a CLOSE statement, which will be part of program termination. You do not need to specify whether files are input or output in a CLOSE statement, but you do need to name the files.

In addition to OPENing the files in INITIALIZATION, we need to read the first card of the card file into the input buffer. (You will see the reason why as soon as we design the logic of GET-A-PAIR-OF-CARDS.) We thus will make INITIALIZATION into a separate paragraph.

When control goes to GET-A-PAIR-OF-CARDS-INTO-WS for the first time, the first card is already in the buffer. For this reason, you have to move the card fields NAME-IN, and so on, to Working-Storage, NAME-WS, read in the second card, move *its* fields to Working-Storage, and then read in the first card of the *next* pair of cards, so that a card is in the buffer next time the program is ready to perform GET-A-PAIR-OF-CARDS-INTO-WS. We can summarize the paragraph in shorthand, thus:

```
GET-A-PAIR-OF-CARDS-INTO-WS.
        Move fields from first card into fields in APPLICATION-DATA
        Read the second card of the pair
        Move fields from second card into fields in APPLICATION-DATA
        Read the first card of the next pair.
```

This sort of shorthand summary is called *pseudocode;* it is not quite COBOL, but easily can be translated into COBOL statements. If we put the pseudocode for INITIALIZATION and GET-A-PAIR-OF-CARDS into the flowchart, we will have

```
┌─────────────────────────────────────────────────────────────┐
│  INITIALIZATION.                                             │
│        Open files                                           │
│        Initialize CARDS-LEFT                                │
│        Read the first card                                  │
├─────────────────────────────────────────────────────────────┤
│  PERFORM UNTIL CARDS-LEFT = 'NO '                           │
│   ┌───┬─────────────────────────────────────────────────┐   │
│   │ P │  GET-A-PAIR-OF-CARDS-INTO-WS                     │   │
│   │ R │     Move fields from first card into fields in   │   │
│   │ I │        APPLICATION-DATA                           │   │
│   │ N │     Read the second card of the pair             │   │
│   │ T │     Move fields from second card into fields in  │   │
│   │ - │        APPLICATION-DATA                           │   │
│   │ P │     Read the first card of the next pair          │   │
│   │ R ├─────────────────────────────────────────────────┤   │
│   │ O │                                                 │   │
│   │ F │  ASSEMBLE-PRINT-LINES                            │   │
│   │ I │                                                 │   │
│   │ L ├─────────────────────────────────────────────────┤   │
│   │ E │                                                 │   │
│   │ S │  WRITE-PRINT-LINES                               │   │
│   └───┴─────────────────────────────────────────────────┘   │
│  TERMINATION.                                               │
└─────────────────────────────────────────────────────────────┘
```

ASSEMBLE-PRINT-LINES has to transfer the fields from APPLICATION-DATA to the appropriate places in the print-lines. So the pseudocode might begin:

> Move name to line 1.
> Move street to line 2.
> Move city, state, ZIP to line 3.
> Move area-code, number to line 1.
> Move account-number to line 3.
> IF male, set up MALE in line 1 sex field.
> IF female, set up FEMALE in line 1 sex field.

Q. Complete the pseudocode for ASSEMBLE-PRINT-LINES.

A.

> IF single, set up SINGLE in line 2 marital status.
>   (similarly for married, divorced, widowed)
> Move number of dependents to line 3.
> Move income to line 1 and format with last two zeros.
> IF years employed is Ø
>   Set up IN THIS EMPLOY LESS THAN 1 YEAR
>   on line 1
> ELSE
>   Move years employed to line 1.
> IF owned, set up MORTGAGE on line 2.
> IF rented, set up RENTAL on line 2.
> Move mortgage/rental to line 2.
> Move other payments to line 3.

or similar answer.

Note how we have capitalized the IFs and the ELSE, and lined them up appropriately.

When we are ready to write the print-lines, we want to move the paper up four lines before printing the first time, then move the paper up one time each for the second and third lines.

Termination simply involves closing the files with the STOP RUN instruction, which ends the execution of your program.

Q. Complete the structured flowchart, showing pseudocode for all of the boxes.

A.

INITIALIZATION.
    Open files.
    Initialize CARDS-LEFT.
    Read the first card.		

PERFORM UNTIL CARDS-LEFT = 'NO '

<table>
<tr>
<td rowspan="4">P
R
I
N
T
—
P
R
O
F
I
L
E
S</td>
<td>GET-A-PAIR-OF-CARDS-INTO-WS
    Move fields from first card into fields in
        APPLICATION-DATA.
    Read the second card of the pair.
    Move fields from second card into fields in
        APPLICATION-DATA.
    Read the first card of the next pair.</td>
</tr>
<tr>
<td>ASSEMBLE-PRINT-LINES
    Move name to line 1.
    Move street to line 2.
    Move city, state, ZIP to line 3.
    Move area-code, number to line 1.
    Move account-number to line 3.
    IF male, set up MALE in line 1 sex field.
    IF female, set up FEMALE in line 1 sex field.
    IF single, set up SINGLE in line 2 marital status
        (similarly for married, divorced, widowed).
    Move number of dependents to line 3.
    Move income to line 1 and format with last two zeros.
    IF years employed is $\emptyset$
        set up IN THIS EMPLOY LESS THAN 1 YEAR
                on line 1
    ELSE
        move years employed to line 1.
    IF owned, set up MORTGAGE on line 2.
    IF rented, set up RENTAL on line 2.
    Move mortgage/rental to line 2.</td>
</tr>
<tr>
<td>WRITE-PRINT-LINES
    Move paper up four lines; write line 1.
    Move paper up one line; write line 2.
    Move paper up one line; write line 3.</td>
</tr>
<tr>
<td colspan="1" style="border:none"></td>
</tr>
</table>

TERMINATION
    Close files.
    Stop run.

or equivalent answer.

It is good practice to have the STOP RUN statement in the highest level module on the structure chart, so that the Procedure Division will begin

```
PROCEDURE DIVISION.
    PERFORM INITIALIZATION.
    PERFORM PRINT-PROFILES
        UNTIL CARDS-LEFT = 'NO '.
    PERFORM END-OF-JOB.
    STOP RUN.
```

Even though END-OF-JOB merely closes the files in this program, we will make it a separate module.

In INITIALIZATION, we want to open the card file and the printer file, initialize CARDS-LEFT, and read the first card into the buffer.

Q.   Code the INITIALIZATION paragraph.

A.
```
INITIALIZATION.
    OPEN INPUT APPLICATION-CARDS-FILE
         OUTPUT PROFILE-LISTING.
    MOVE 'YES' TO CARDS-LEFT.
    READ APPLICATION-CARD
        AT END MOVE 'NO ' TO CARDS-LEFT.
*   THE FIRST CARD OF A PAIR IS NOW IN THE BUFFER
```

Note the comment to remind later readers of the program.

Q.   Code the PRINT-PROFILES paragraph and the END-OF-JOB paragraph.

A.
```
PRINT-PROFILES.
    PERFORM GET-A-PAIR-OF-CARDS-INTO-WS.
    PERFORM ASSEMBLE-PRINT-LINES.
    PERFORM WRITE-PRINT-LINES.

END-OF-JOB.
    CLOSE APPLICATION-CARDS-FILE
          PROFILE-LISTING.
```

In WRITE-PRINT-LINES, you should clear the print-line by moving in spaces before each WRITE statement. As we indicated in pseudocode, you want to separate each profile by spacing four lines between the last line of one and the first line of the next. This is done by adding AFTER ADVANCING to the WRITE statement, like this:

WRITE PRINT-LINE-OUT FROM LINE-1-WS
AFTER ADVANCING 4 LINES.

will move the paper up four lines before writing. The only drawback is that, in some current versions of COBOL, use of AFTER ADVANCING on one WRITE statement requires use on all the others. This means that if you want to space one line, which is normally done automatically by a simple WRITE statement, you have to write AFTER ADVANCING 1 LINES. This annoying lack of grammar will be removed in new versions of COBOL, but you may be stuck with it in your installation.

You now have all the information you need to code the Procedure Division for SAMPLE-3; when you have done so, compare it with the solution on the following pages.

```
00122
00123          PROCEDURE DIVISION.
00124             PERFORM INITIALIZATION.
00125             PERFORM PRINT-PROFILES
00126                UNTIL CARDS-LEFT IS EQUAL TO 'NO '.
00127             PERFORM END-OF-JOB.
00128             STOP RUN.
00129
00130          INITIALIZATION.
00131             OPEN INPUT      APPLICATION-CARDS-FILE
00132                   OUTPUT    PROFILE-LISTING.
00133             MOVE 'YES' TO CARDS-LEFT.
00134             READ APPLICATION-CARDS-FILE
00135                AT END MOVE 'NO ' TO CARDS-LEFT.
00136          * THE FIRST CARD OF A PAIR IS NOW IN THE BUFFER
00137
00138          PRINT-PROFILES.
00139             PERFORM GET-A-PAIR-OF-CARDS-INTO-WS.
00140             PERFORM ASSEMBLE-PRINT-LINES.
00141             PERFORM WRITE-PROFILE.
00142
00143          END-OF-JOB.
00144             CLOSE   APPLICATION-CARDS-FILE
00145                     PROFILE-LISTING.
00146
00147          GET-A-PAIR-OF-CARDS-INTO-WS.
00148             MOVE NAME-IN TO NAME-WS.
00149             MOVE ADDRESS-IN TO ADDRESS-WS.
00150             MOVE PHONE-IN TO PHONE-WS.
00151             MOVE ACCT-NUM-IN1 TO ACCT-NUM-WS.
00152             READ APPLICATION-CARDS-FILE
00153                AT END MOVE 'NO ' TO CARDS-LEFT.
00154          * THE SECOND CARD OF THE PAIR IS NOW IN THE BUFFER
00155             MOVE CREDIT-INFO-IN TO CREDIT-INFO-WS.
00156             READ APPLICATION-CARDS-FILE
00157                AT END MOVE 'NO ' TO CARDS-LEFT.
00158          * THE FIRST CARD OF THE NEXT PAIR IS NOW IN THE BUFFER
00159
```

```
00160    ASSEMBLE-PRINT-LINES.
00161        MOVE NAME-WS TO NAME-L1.
00162        MOVE STREET-WS TO STREET-L2.
00163        MOVE CITY-WS TO CITY-L3.
00164        MOVE STATE-WS TO STATE-L3.
00165        MOVE ZIP-WS TO ZIP-L3.
00166        MOVE AREA-CODE-WS TO AREA-CODE-L1.
00167        MOVE NUMBR-WS TO NUMBR-L1.
00168        MOVE ACCT-NUM-WS TO ACCT-NUM-L3.
00169        IF MALE    MOVE 'MALE     ' TO SEX-L1.
00170        IF FEMALE  MOVE 'FEMALE ' TO SEX-L1.
00171        IF SINGLE     MOVE 'SINGLE     ' TO MARITAL-STATUS-L2.
00172        IF MARRIED  MOVE 'MARRIED ' TO MARITAL-STATUS-L2.
00173        IF DIVORCED MOVE 'DIVORCED' TO MARITAL-STATUS-L2.
00174        IF WIDOWED  MOVE 'WIDOWED ' TO MARITAL-STATUS-L2.
00175        MOVE NUMBER-DEPENS-WS TO NUMBER-DEPENS-L3.
00176        MOVE INCOME-HUNDREDS-WS TO INCOME-HUNDREDS-L1.
00177        IF YEARS-EMPLOYED-WS IS EQUAL TO 0
00178            MOVE 'LESS THAN 1 YEAR' TO YEARS-EMPLOYED-L1
00179        ELSE
00180            MOVE YEARS-EMPLOYED-WS TO YEARS-L1
00181            MOVE ' YEARS           ' TO DESCN-L1.
00182        IF OWNED MOVE 'MORTGAGE:      $' TO OUTGO-DESCN.
00183        IF RENTED MOVE 'RENTAL:        $' TO OUTGO-DESCN.
00184        MOVE MORTGAGE-OR-RENTAL-WS TO MORTGAGE-OR-RENTAL-L2.
00185        MOVE OTHER-PAYMENTS-WS TO OTHER-PAYMENTS-L3.
00186
00187    WRITE-PROFILE.
00188        MOVE SPACES TO PRINT-LINE-OUT.
00189        WRITE PRINT-LINE-OUT FROM LINE-1-WS
00190                        AFTER ADVANCING 4 LINES.
00191        MOVE SPACES TO PRINT-LINE-OUT.
00192        WRITE PRINT-LINE-OUT FROM LINE-2-WS
00193                        AFTER ADVANCING 1 LINES.
00194        MOVE SPACES TO PRINT-LINE-OUT.
00195        WRITE PRINT-LINE-OUT FROM LINE-3-WS
00196                        AFTER ADVANCING 1 LINES.
00197
```

3.10 Getting the program to run

Now that you have coded a substantial program, punch it onto cards; it is preferable for you to do this yourself to practice using the keypunch. If you cannot do it, make sure that your writing on the coding sheet is completely accurate and clear before you submit the program to the keypunch department, and check every character on every card returned to you.

The *deck* of cards containing your program statements is called the *source deck,* as it is the source from which the compiler will prepare the machine language or *object* program. When you are satisfied that you have an accurately punched source deck, arrange to get the program compiled. Depending on the installation you are using, you will have to put two or three Job Control cards before and after your program deck for compilation. This is because different installations use different *operating systems,* that is, special sets of programs supplied by the computer manufacturer, which partly automate the job of the computer operations staff.

The Job Control cards give operating system's programs the information needed to process your job. We will deal with Job Control later in detail, so don't bother about what needs to go on the Job Control cards now; just get someone who knows the installation to specify them for you.

Before compiling, check the cards again, making sure that all names are spelled correctly, that statements do not begin to the left of column 12, and, most importantly, that there is a period everywhere there should be, and nowhere else (such as, in the middle of an IF statement). Try to get into the habit of scanning through the deck for periods, which should be the last character on each card, except where the statement is split over two cards. So if you do find a period, ask yourself, "Should it be there?" and if you *don't* find a period as the last character on a card, ask yourself, "Why isn't there a period here?" Misplaced periods are one of the most common coding errors.

Now submit your job for compilation; you may be required to operate the computer yourself in a small installation, and that is outside the scope of this book. More likely, you will take your deck of cards to someone responsible for Computer Operations, complete a form telling the computer operator what should be done with your job, and come back when the job has been run. The Operations staff may hold your job until a number of similar jobs are ready for processing, to make the best use of the computer facility.

3.10.1 Compiler diagnostics

When you receive your program from compilation, you will see that, after the listing of the cards, there is a section headed CARD and ERROR MESSAGE. These messages are called *diagnostics*. Figure 3.4 on the next page shows a listing of SAMPLE-1 with some deliberate (but common) errors, and the resulting diagnostics. The codes under ERROR MESSAGE are those for an IBM compiler, but all compilers produce similar messages. You will notice that the code is suffixed by -W, -C, or -E; you occasionally may see a -D.

The -W means a *warning* diagnostic on this compiler. It flags conditions that you should check, but does not necessarily mean that anything is wrong. For example, every time you write a paragraph to be PERFORMed, you will get the warning

ILA4072I-W EXIT FROM PERFORMED PROCEDURE ASSUMED
BEFORE PROCEDURE-NAME.

This means that the compiler correctly assumes that you intend the procedure to terminate at the next procedure-name (or at the end of the program, in this case). But

ILA1043I-W END OF SENTENCE SHOULD PRECEDE 05. ASSUMED PRESENT.

arises because the period has been left out after Ø1 PRINT-RECORD; while the compiler in this case assumes that you meant to put a period, it should be corrected.

-C means a *conditional* diagnostic, meaning that you should correct the problem because it probably will affect the object program that results from the compilation.

```
00001          IDENTIFICATION DIVISION.
00002          PROGRAM-ID. SAMPLE-1.
00003          * THIS VERSION OF SAMPLE-1 HAS 3 DELIBERATE ERRORS
00004          ENVIRONMENT DIVISION.
00005          INPUT-OUTPUT SECTION.
00006          FILE-CONTROL.
00007              SELECT CARD-FILE  ASSIGN TO SYS031-UR-2540R-S.
00008              SELECT PRINT-FILE ASSIGN TO SYS033-UR-1403-S.
00009          DATA DIVISION.
00010          FILE SECTION.
00011          FD   CARD-FILE
00012              LABEL RECORDS ARE OMITTED.
00013          01   CARD.
00014              05  NAME                       PICTURE      X(20).
00015              05  ADDR                       PICTURE      X(40).
00016              05  PHONE.
00017                  10   AREA-CODE             PICTURE      9(3).
00018                  10   NUMBR                 PICTURE      X(8).
00019              05  FILLER                     PICTURE      X(9).
00020          FD   PRINT-FILE
00021              LABEL RECORDS ARE OMITTED.
00022          01   PRINT-RECORD
00023              05  FILLER                     PICTURE      X(3).
00024              05  NAME                       PICTURE      X(20).
00025              05  FILLER                     PICTURE      X(5).
00026              05  ADDR                       PICTURE      X(40).
00027              05  FILLER                     PICTURE      X(5).
00028              05  PHONE.
00029                  10   AREA-CODE             PICTURE      9(3).
00030                  10   FILLER                PICTURE      X.
00031                  10   NUMBR                 PICTURE      X(8).
00032              05  FILLER                     PICTURE      X(10).
00033              05  MESSAGE-AREA               PICTURE      X(25).
00034              05  FILLER                     PICTURE      X(12).
00035          WORKING-STORAGE SECTION.
00036          01   WARNING PICTURE X(25) VALUE '**** ADDRESS MISSING ****'.
00037          01   CARDS-LEFT PICTURE 9(3).
00038          PROCEDURE DIVISION.
00039              OPEN INPUT   CARD-FILE
00040                   OUTPUT  PRINT-FILE.
00041              MOVE 'YES' TO CARDS-LEFT.
00042              READ CARD-FILE
00043                      AT END MOVE 'NO ' TO CARDS-LEFT.
00044              PERFORM PROCESS-CARDS
00045                  UNTIL CARDS-LEFT IS EQUAL TO 'NO '.
00046              CLOSE  CARD-FILE
00047                     PRINT-FILE.
00048              STOP RUN.
00049          PROCESS-CARDS.
00050              MOVE SPACES TO PRINT-RECORD.
00051              MOVE NAME IN CARD TO NAME IN PRINT-RECORD.
00052              IF ADDR IN CARD IS EQUAL TO SPACES
00053                  MOVE WARNING TO MESSAGE AREA
00054              ELSE
00055                  MOVE ADDR IN CARD TO ADDR IN PRINT-RECORD.
00056              MOVE AREA-CODE IN CARD TO AREA-CODE IN PRINT-RECORD.
00057              MOVE NUMBR IN CARD TO NUMBR IN PRINT-RECORD.
00058              WRITE PRINT-RECORD.
00059              READ CARD-FILE
00060                  AT END MOVE 'NO ' TO CARDS-LEFT.
```

CARD	ERROR MESSAGE	
23	ILA1043I-W	END OF SENTENCE SHOULD PRECEDE 05. ASSUMED PRESENT.
41	ILA4044I-C	ALPHANUMERIC LITERAL (AN) SHOULD NOT BE MOVED TO NUMERIC FIELD. SUBSTITUTING ZERO .
43	ILA4044I-C	ALPHANUMERIC LITERAL (AN) SHOULD NOT BE MOVED TO NUMERIC FIELD. SUBSTITUTING ZERO .
53	ILA3001I-E	MESSAGE NOT DEFINED. DISCARDED.
53	ILA4052I-E	AREA MAY NOT BE TARGET FIELD FOR ONM-1-490 (AN) IN MOVE STATEMENT. AND IS DISCARDED.
60	ILA4044I-C	ALPHANUMERIC LITERAL (AN) SHOULD NOT BE MOVED TO NUMERIC FIELD. SUBSTITUTING ZERO .
60	ILA4072I-W	EXIT FROM PERFORMED PROCEDURE ASSUMED BEFORE PROCEDURE-NAME.
60	ILA5029I-W	STOP RUN GENERATED AFTER LAST STATEMENT.

Figure 3.4. Version of SAMPLE-1 showing three deliberate errors.

-E means an *error* diagnostic; the program will not run until the error has been corrected. As you can see, leaving out the hyphen from MESSAGE-AREA in statement 53 has caused the compiler to look for a field called MESSAGE for which it can find no Data Division entry, so it tells you

ILA3001I-E   MESSAGE NOT DEFINED. DISCARDED.

Then, of course, the compiler is really in trouble because it finds the word AREA and has no instruction as to what to do with it.

-D means a *disaster* diagnostic, which usually indicates an error within the compiler itself. If you ever come across this, ask for help.

3.10.2 Diagnosing diagnostics

Given the way in which we are writing COBOL, you always will get one or more

EXIT FROM PERFORMED PROCEDURE ASSUMED BEFORE PROCEDURE-NAME.

and one

STOP RUN GENERATED AFTER LAST STATEMENT.

If these are the only diagnostics you have, your program is ready for a test run. If you have any others, work through the program, diagnostic by diagnostic, checking each statement indicated to locate the error.

Always bear in mind:

● A single mistake may give rise to more than one diagnostic. For example, if you fail to define a field, you will get a diagnostic for every statement in which that field is used. In Fig. 3.4, the C-level diagnostics for statements 41, 43, and 60 all are caused by giving CARDS-LEFT a PIC of 9(3) in statement 37.

- If you leave out a period, you may see some very strange messages, because the compiler tries to process everything up to the next period as though it were part of the original statement.

- O looks very much iike 0 on a source listing and on a card. If you define OWNER and punch 0WNER by mistake, you will get a lovely crop of diagnostics and may be unable to understand the reason. Be suspicious and check back to the punching of the original card.

When you have located as many errors as you can, and you still have some diagnostics that you cannot understand, ask someone's advice, or recompile the program. There are hundreds of possible diagnostic messages; sometimes, an obscure diagnostic will go away when a few simple things have been fixed in the program.

Bear in mind also that a compilation for a program of the size with which we are working costs between $5 and $10; depending upon how you value your time, it may be better to check out your corrections with a compile rather than scratch your head for an hour. By the same token, though, don't burn up $10 worth of machine time to find out something that five minutes' quiet thought would have enabled you to see.

3.10.3 Executing the program

When you have a compile with no serious errors (a *clean* compile), test the program by running it with the cards needed to produce the six profiles in Fig. 3.2 as input. Be sure to punch the codes in the second card of each pair in exactly the right columns. If the cards are punched correctly, and your program is equivalent to the model solution, you should get the report printed out. As we said, you will need the Job Control cards that your installation requires in order to execute the program with the test data. If the report is printed out incorrectly, or if your program fails to run for any reason, carefully check the punching of the test data cards. If you still can't find anything wrong, seek advice and help; we deal with testing in Chapter 5.

4 Doing Arithmetic

So far, we have written useful programs without doing any arithmetic on our data; but for most kinds of problems we need to be able to add, subtract, multiply, and divide. In this chapter, we will deal with the basic arithmetic statements.

4.1 Arithmetic statements

4.1.1 ADD and SUBTRACT

There are two forms of the ADD instruction, one being

Form 1:   ADD FIELD-1 TO FIELD-2.

In this case, the total of the contents of the two fields is stored in FIELD-2. For example,

Before addition		After addition	
FIELD-1	FIELD-2	FIELD-1	FIELD-2
1 2 3 4	5 4 3 2	1 2 3 4	6 6 6 6

The value that was in FIELD-2 is lost.

The second form of the ADD instruction is

Form 2:   ADD FIELD-1 FIELD-2 GIVING FIELD-3.

As expected, the total is stored in FIELD-3. For example,

FIELD-1	FIELD-2	FIELD-3	FIELD-1	FIELD-2	FIELD-3
1 2 3 4	5 4 3 2	1 1 1 1	1 2 3 4	5 4 3 2	6 6 6 6

Q.   Write a statement that will add MORTGAGE-OR-RENTAL and OTHER-PAYMENTS to produce a figure for TOTAL-OUTGO.

A.   **ADD MORTGAGE-OR-RENTAL OTHER-PAYMENTS GIVING TOTAL-OUTGO.**

Note that ADD FIELD-1 TO FIELD-2 GIVING FIELD-3 is *wrong;* you are not allowed to have TO and GIVING in the same statement.

There also are two forms of the SUBTRACT instruction:

Form 1:   SUBTRACT FIELD-1 FROM FIELD-2.

In this case, the difference will appear in FIELD-2 after subtraction. The other form of the instruction is

Form 2:   SUBTRACT FIELD-1 FROM FIELD-2 GIVING FIELD-3.

In this case FIELD-1 and FIELD-2 are undisturbed; the answer is in FIELD-3.

Q.   Code a statement that will reduce the value in COUNTER by 1.

A.   **SUBTRACT 1 FROM COUNTER.**

Q.   Code a statement taking TAXES away from GROSS-INCOME with NET-INCOME as the result.

A.   **SUBTRACT TAXES FROM GROSS-INCOME GIVING NET-INCOME.**

4.1.2 *MULTIPLY and DIVIDE*

The instructions MULTIPLY and DIVIDE similarly have two forms:

Form 1:   MULTIPLY FIELD-1 BY FIELD-2.   Result is in
           DIVIDE FIELD-1 INTO FIELD-2.   FIELD-2

Form 2:

MULTIPLY FIELD-1 BY FIELD-2 GIVING FIELD-3.   Result is in
DIVIDE FIELD-1 INTO FIELD-2 GIVING FIELD-3.   FIELD-3

Q.   Code a statement to calculate GROSS-PAY by multiplying PAY-RATE by HOURS-WORKED.

A.   **MULTIPLY PAY-RATE BY HOURS-WORKED GIVING GROSS-PAY.**

Q.   Code a statement to calculate MONTHLY-SALARY from ANNUAL-SALARY.

A.   **DIVIDE MONTHS-IN-YEAR INTO ANNUAL-SALARY GIVING MONTHLY-SALARY.**

Note that it is good practice never to code a numeric literal into a statement, with the possible exception of Ø and 1. Even with a value that is very unlikely to change, such as 12 months in the year, you may forget what the 12 stands for. With the data-name, MONTHS-IN-YEAR, initialized to 12 in Working-Storage, it always will be perfectly clear.

In SAMPLE-3, we read in annual income: INCOME-HUNDREDS and two lots of monthly-outgoings: MORTGAGE-OR-RENTAL and OTHER-PAYMENTS.

Company policy is to base credit on discretionary income, the amount of income left each month after deducting all outgoing amounts. While everybody's tax bracket varies, it is your company's practice to deduct a flat 25 percent of income to estimate income-after-taxes.

Q.   Write the code to calculate discretionary income in SAMPLE-3 and check through it with Victor Grasper's data (assume that all of the fields you use are defined in the Data Division).

A.   **MULTIPLY INCOME-HUNDREDS BY 100 GIVING INCOME.**
MULTIPLY INCOME BY TAX-RATE GIVING ESTIMATED-TAX.
SUBTRACT ESTIMATED-TAX FROM INCOME GIVING NET-INCOME.
DIVIDE MONTHS-IN-YEAR INTO NET-INCOME
GIVING MONTHLY-NET.
SUBTRACT MORTGAGE-OR-RENTAL-WS OTHER-PAYMENTS-WS
FROM MONTHLY-NET
GIVING DISCRETIONARY-INCOME.

or equivalent answer.

Data for Victor Grasper:

INCOME	15,700.00
ESTIMATED TAX	3,925.00
NET INCOME	11,775.00
MONTHLY-NET	981.25
MORTGAGE-OR-RENTAL	250.00
OTHER-PAYMENTS	40.00
DISCRETIONARY-INCOME	691.25

Note that we have defined TAX-RATE in Working-Storage, rather than using a numeric literal in the program. If the tax rate is changed, we will have to make only one change to the program. If we had coded the literal 0.25 in several places in the program, by contrast, we would have had to hunt through it to make sure they all were changed. However, since INCOME-HUNDREDS, by definition, needs to be multiplied by 100 to give income, it is acceptable to code 100 as a literal at this point.

4.1.3 Rounding

When we discussed MOVEing numeric items in Chapter 2, we said that numeric items are lined up by their decimal points. The same is true with arithmetic operations; so if MONTHLY-NET had been defined with PIC 999 (with an assumed decimal point at the right), the .25 of $981.25 would be lost, giving $981. In this case, the loss may not matter so much; but what if the value had been $981.95? You would have lost 95 cents.

You can avoid this problem by using the key word ROUND-ED. If ROUNDED is added at the end of an arithmetic statement, then the computer will add 1 to the right-most position retained if the next digit to its right would have been 5 or more.

For example, if we want to know what 563 divided by 5 to the nearest whole number equals, we would carry out the division, as follows:

112.6 —————— *but the next digit is*
/ *more than 5, so we add*
this is the right-most *1 to the right-most*
position of the whole number *position, getting 113.*

If RESULT is defined as PIC 99,

DIVIDE 12 INTO 141 GIVING RESULT   gives 11 (losing .75)

DIVIDE 12 INTO 141 GIVING RESULT ROUNDED gives 12

Note that, for the sake of clarity, we are breaking our own rules about using literals.

> Q.   ANSWER is defined as PIC 99V99. What appears in ANSWER with and without ROUNDED when DIVIDE DEN INTO NUM GIVING ANSWER is executed with
>
> NUM : 23.986 and DEN : 3

> A. $\dfrac{23.986}{3}$ = 7.995333
>
> Without ROUNDED, ANSWER is 07.99 losing 5333.
> With ROUNDED, ANSWER is 08.00.

> Q.   What about $\dfrac{23.984}{3}$?

> A. $\dfrac{23.984}{3}$ = 7.994666
>
> Without ROUNDED, ANSWER is 07.99.
> With ROUNDED, ANSWER is 07.99.
> Since 4666 is less than 5000, the result is rounded down.

4.1.4 COMPUTE

When a formula must be worked out over several statements as with the DISCRETIONARY-INCOME calculation, it is often more convenient and easier to grasp if the whole calculation is condensed into one statement. This can be done with the COMPUTE statement. Use the symbols shown on the following page:

=
+
−
/ for divide
* for multiply

to make an algebraic expression. For example:

COMPUTE ESTIMATED-TAX = INCOME-HUNDREDS * 100 * TAX-RATE.

Note that a space
must be left on each side.

When + or − are combined with * or / in an arithmetic expression, parentheses should be used to make the meaning clear. For example, does

A + B * C   mean

(A + B) * C or A + (B * C)   ?

There's a lot of difference, as you'll see if you substitute values in each case.

If you leave the parentheses out for any reason, the computer will do multiplication and division before addition and subtraction. In fact, it would interpret A + B * C as A + (B * C). As a general rule, don't leave the parentheses out; even if *you* and the computer understand it, someone else who someday reads your program may not.

Q. Code the computation of DISCRETIONARY-INCOME as five COMPUTE statements.

A. **COMPUTE ANNUAL-INCOME = INCOME-HUNDREDS * 100.**
   COMPUTE ANNUAL-TAX = ANNUAL-INCOME * TAX-RATE.
   COMPUTE MONTHLY-NET =
   (ANNUAL-INCOME − ANNUAL-TAX) / MONTHS-IN-YEAR.
   COMPUTE MONTHLY-PAYMENTS = MORTGAGE-OR-RENTAL
   + OTHER-PAYMENTS.
   COMPUTE DISCRETIONARY-INCOME =
   MONTHLY-NET − MONTHLY-PAYMENTS.

   or similar answer.

4.1.5 Dealing with result fields that are too small

Suppose AA, BB, and CC all were defined PIC 9(3). You could code COMPUTE CC = AA + BB. But what would happen if both AA and BB were more than 500? The result would not fit into AA. In this case, the computer would not know what to do. It probably would halt your program, and print a message telling you that a field had overflowed.

Unless you are sure you have a result field big enough for any conceivable combination of input data, you should use the ON SIZE ERROR clause. For example,

COMPUTE ANSWER = BIG-FIELD + LARGE-FIELD
ON SIZE ERROR PERFORM OVERFLOW-ROUTINE.

You should code OVERFLOW-ROUTINE to deal with the condition, possibly by rejecting the current transaction and printing an error message. In any case, code the routine to keep the program running if at all possible.

Q. Suppose MONTHLY-NET and MONTHLY-PAY-MENTS both are defined as 9(4) and DISCRETIONARY-INCOME is defined as 9(3).

Code a COMPUTE statement that will calculate DISCRETIONARY-INCOME, and set its value at $999 if the computed value is greater than that.

A. **COMPUTE DISCRETIONARY-INCOME =**
MONTHLY-NET — MONTHLY-PAYMENTS
ON SIZE ERROR MOVE 999 TO DISCRETIONARY-INCOME.

4.1.6 Defining signed variables

Q. Using the formula coded previously, what is the discretionary income of a person making $16,000 a year, who is spending $750 per month for rent and has other debt payments of $300 per month?

A. -$50 per month; an outflow of $50. Either this person is understating his income, or he's in real trouble.

DISCRETIONARY-INCOME is an example of a field that could have a negative value, and the definition of its PICTURE should reflect the fact by including an S for sign: PIC S9 (3). The S ensures that the computer will keep track of whether the value is positive or negative. It also allows us to test for the sign of the value, and to program accordingly, by coding IF DISCRETIONARY-INCOME NEGATIVE. . . .

A signed picture should be used whenever a numeric field might be negative. If you do not include a sign, the computer will assume that all numbers are positive. As in the case above, the program will proceed happily, showing the person has an *inflow* of $50 per month, instead of the true situation.

Q. Write the Data Division entries and the Procedure Division code needed to take the quantity of an item ordered away from the number in stock, and perform the out-of-stock routine if the order cannot be fully met.

A.

DATA DIVISION.

    .
    .

ORDER-QUANTITY	**PIC 9(3).**
STOCK-ON-HAND	**PIC S9(4).**

    .
    .

PROCEDURE DIVISION.

    .
    .

SUBTRACT ORDER-QUANTITY FROM STOCK-ON-HAND.

IF STOCK-ON-HAND IS NEGATIVE.
    PERFORM OUT-OF-STOCK-ROUTINE.

or similar answer.

REVIEW QUIZ*

1. Write the code to increase the value of VERMOUTH by the amount stored in GIN, and store the new value in MARTINI.

2. Write the code to increase the value of LOOP-COUNT by 1.

3. If field TOTAL contains 480 and field NUMBR contains 24, what is in each field after executing

   DIVIDE NUMBR INTO TOTAL.

4. If RESULT is defined as PIC 9V99, what is in RESULT after execution of

   DIVIDE 8 INTO 9 GIVING RESULT ROUNDED.

5. If ABSOLUTE-VALUE is defined as PIC 9(3), what is in ABSOLUTE-VALUE after execution of

   SUBTRACT 1000 FROM 2 GIVING ABSOLUTE-VALUE.

6. Use the COMPUTE statement to write the code calculating the interest due on an amount up to $100,000 at a rate of interest that may be set to the nearest one-quarter percent up to twenty percent, over a period to the nearest year, expressing the result to the nearest cent. Include the Data Division entries for your data-names.

---

*Answers are in Appendix C.

5 Developing Programs

5.1 Using the Source Statement Library

Before we apply the last chapter's arithmetic statements to a program, let us deal with an important feature that makes the programming job easier.

Very often, a program that you need to write has much in common with programs you have written before; you may use the same FDs time and time again, or you may use a procedure like ASSEMBLE-PRINT-LINES in several programs.

To save having to code and keypunch the same statements, it is possible to *catalog* groups of statements in a special computer file known as the *Source Statement Library* (SSL). For the moment, all you need to know is how to use it.

5.1.1 The COPY statement

Suppose the following statements have been cataloged and given the name FDCARDS:

```
            LABEL RECORDS ARE OMITTED
            DATA RECORDS ARE NAME-ADDRESS-AND-PHONE-IN
                        CREDIT-INFORMATION.
   01    NAME-ADDRESS-AND-PHONE-IN.
            05  NAME-IN                    PIC X(20).
            05  ADDRESS-IN                 PIC X(40).
            05  PHONE-IN                   PIC X(11).
            05  FILLER                     PIC X(3).
            05  ACCT-NUM-IN1               PIC 9(6).
   01    CREDIT-INFORMATION-IN.
            05  CARD-TYPE-IN               PIC X.
            05  ACCT-NUM-IN2               PIC 9(6).
            05  FILLER                     PIC X.
            05  CREDIT-INFO-IN             PIC X(22).
            05  FILLER                     PIC X(50).
```

You will recognize these as the statements making up the FD for APPLICATION-CARDS. Suppose you wanted to use this FD in a program. You simply would write the following:

FD APPLICATION-CARDS-FILE COPY FDCARDS.

When the program is compiled, the compiler will fetch all of the statements cataloged under the name FDCARDS and *copy them into the program* so that the listing will look like this:

```
     FD  APPLICATION-CARDS-FILE COPY FDCARDS.
C            LABEL RECORDS ARE OMITTED
C            DATA RECORDS ARE NAME-ADDRESS-AND-PHONE-IN
C                             CREDIT-INFORMATION-IN.
C    01  NAME-ADDRESS-AND-PHONE-IN.
C        05  NAME-IN                          PIC X(20).
C        05  ADDRESS-IN                       PIC X(40).
C        05  PHONE-IN                         PIC X(11).
C        05  FILLER                           PIC X(3).
C        05  ACCT-NUM-IN1                     PIC 9(6).
C    01  CREDIT-INFORMATION-IN.
C        05  CARD-TYPE-IN                     PIC X.
```

and so on.

On IBM systems, copied statements are identified by a C to the left of each listed statement. If the group of statements being cataloged is an 01 level with the statements following it, then the 01 statement itself must be cataloged. For example, if APPLICATION-DATA were cataloged with the name of CARDSWS, the library entry would have to begin

```
01  APPLICATION-DATA.
    05  NAME-WS                           PIC X(20).
    05  ADDRESS-WS                        PIC X(40).
```

and so on.

In your program you would write, for example,

01 CARD-DATA-IN-WS COPY CARDSWS.

The compiler copies the library entry, changing APPLICATION-DATA to the name that you supplied, so that the listing now becomes the following:

```
   01   CARD-DATA-IN-WS COPY CARDSWS.
C  01   CARD-DATA-IN-WS.
C       05   NAME-WS                                    PIC X(20).
C       05   ADDRESS-WS                                 PIC X(40).
```

and so on.

In the Procedure Division, the body of a paragraph is cataloged. Under the name WRITPRFL, you might have

MOVE SPACES TO PRINT-LINE-OUT.
WRITE PRINT-LINE-OUT FROM LINE-1-WS
AFTER ADVANCING 4 LINES.

You would write in your program

PRINT-APPLICATION-PROFILE. COPY WRITPRFL.

Note that there is a period after the procedure-name; this is only used in Procedure Division COPY statements.

5.1.2 COPY REPLACING

Sometimes, what is cataloged in the library may not be exactly what you want; you would like to make use of a library in your program, but need to make some changes in it. For example, you might want to copy WRITPRFL but you need to call the three print-lines, FIRST-LINE, SECOND-LINE, and THIRD-LINE. You can do this with the REPLACING option of the COPY statement, thus,

PRINT-APPLICATION-PROFILE. COPY WRITPRFL
REPLACING LINE-1-WS BY FIRST-LINE
LINE-2-WS BY SECOND-LINE
LINE-3-WS BY THIRD-LINE.

Notice that REPLACING appears only once; also note the placing of the periods.

> Q.   Given that WRITPRFL is the name in the library of the statements in the paragraph called WRITE-PROFILE in SAMPLE-3, what listing will result from the above COPY statement?

A.
```
C        MOVE SPACES TO PRINT-LINE-OUT.
C        WRITE PRINT-LINE-OUT FROM FIRST-LINE
C            AFTER ADVANCING 4 LINES.
C        MOVE SPACES TO PRINT-LINE-OUT.
C        WRITE PRINT-LINE-OUT FROM SECOND-LINE
C            AFTER ADVANCING 1 LINES.
C        MOVE SPACES TO PRINT-LINE-OUT.
C        WRITE PRINT-LINE-OUT FROM THIRD-LINE
C            AFTER ADVANCING 1 LINES.
```

In most COBOL compilers, it is possible to REPLACE only one data-name with another data-name or with a literal. New compilers will enable you to REPLACE any group of characters by any other group, for example, to change -IN to -OUT on every data-name in a paragraph.

You have to specify to the compiler that you are using the SSL facility. This is done in various ways depending upon the operating system you are using; the programs in this section were compiled under IBM's Disk Operating System (DOS), for which you have to punch a card with CBL LIB, beginning in cc 2, and insert it immediately before the IDENTIFICATION DIVISION.

5.2 Steps to follow in developing a program

In a business situation, the development of a program normally begins with a *user request,* as when a manager says, "I want a program (or a system) to do such and such." Often a *systems analyst* then will study the request and work with the user to understand exactly what he needs, what purpose it is to serve, and precisely what information the user will supply to the computer department.

From this *systems study,* the systems analyst produces a *functional specification,* which sets out the form of the report(s) to be produced, describes the rules and policies to be used in producing them, and explains the nature of the input data. This is the point at which you, the programmer, should get involved. You should understand the functional specification, and from it be able to produce the *program graph,* showing the data flow through the program.

From the program graph, you should produce a *structure chart,* which breaks down the whole function of the program into *functional modules* as we have seen, and specifies the input and output of each module.

After developing the structure chart, you should be able to write the pseudocode for each module; review it to make sure that the logic you have written will do what you want. It is very helpful to get together with a group of your colleagues and guide or walk them through the structure chart and the pseudocode, explaining your code, its intended function, and your reasons for doing it this way. Many errors (bugs) are discovered in a *structured walkthrough* of this type.

After you have written the COBOL code and gotten a clean compile, you may find it useful to walkthrough the code again, to uncover any bugs that may have crept in during coding.

You now are ready to begin testing the program with some representative test data, such as the cards we specified for SAMPLE-3. Almost certainly, the testing will reveal that your program is not perfect! You may find that the program either does not run at all, or runs but gives the wrong output. *Debugging* is the process of finding the cause of these faults and correcting them. You may need to go through several cycles of test, debug, test, debug. Obviously, the more carefully you design and code your program, and the more carefully you review the structure chart, the pseudocode, and the COBOL, the less time you will need to spend in testing. This is important, because debugging is extremely difficult. Your time is *much* better spent avoiding bugs than finding them.

Only when the program delivers good output on all tests can you hand it over to the user for *user acceptance.* The user will need your help to train his staff in the use of the program, the correct preparation of the input data, and the resolution of any problems. You also will need to produce operational instructions, which tell the computer operator the following:

- how to set up the computer for this job
- how to respond to messages on the console typewriter
- how to recognize successful completion of the job
- what to do in case of error

Before going on to the next programming problem, let us look at the testing and debugging phase in more detail.

5.2.1 Specifying test data

If the program is at all complex, test it first with data that you know to be reasonable and correctly punched. When the program correctly processes good data, you should start to feed in data in which

- the values of the fields are at the extreme ends of the possible range, e.g., income of $99,900 per annum and income of $0 per annum
- all reasonable combinations of inputs are dealt with, e.g., we include applications that are from both males *and* females, owners *and* renters, and so forth
- the values of fields are just out of range, or way out of range
- data fields have been mispunched or are missing

Every commercial system should *edit* the incoming data thoroughly, checking as much as possible that fields are present and of reasonable value; in SAMPLE-2, we edited the cards for the presence of name, address, and phone number.

As you can imagine, comprehensive editing can require a lot of programming, so we shall not discuss it in detail until later chapters. The creation of thorough test data also is important and will be dealt with in Part 2, Chapter 14.

5.2.2 Program checks

When you run a program with test data, it may fail the test for one of two reasons:

- The program runs OK, and ends normally, but the output is incorrect; e.g., you get garbage in the print-lines because you did not initialize them correctly

- The program *bombs,* that is, comes to an *abnormal end* (abend); you see a message on the output saying, for example,

    0S03I PROGRAM CHECK INTERRUPTION . . . . . DATA EXCEPTION

    There will be some more detail in the middle of the message, but it doesn't concern us at present.

If you get a program check, it means that the operating system has cancelled (terminated) your program because it tried to do something invalid. There are several types of program checks, only three of which you will commonly meet:

1) DATA EXCEPTION — occurs when you have tried to do arithmetic on nonnumeric data, perhaps because letters are punched in a card where there should be numbers, or more commonly because you have not initialized a Working-Storage field. For example, if you define in Working-Storage

    TOTAL-DISCR-INCOME   PIC 9(7)

    and later in the program write

    ADD DISCRETIONARY-INCOME TO TOTAL-DISCR-INCOME.

    your program almost certainly will bomb with a Data Exception when it tries to add the numeric DISCRETIONARY-INCOME to the uninitialized garbage in TOTAL-DISCR-INCOME.

Q.   How do you avoid this?

A.   By being sure to initialize every field that may have arithmetic done on it. In this case, you should add MOVE ZEROS TO TOTAL-DISCR-INCOME, before using TOTAL-DISCR-INCOME the first time.

2)   OVERFLOW EXCEPTION — occurs when a result field is too large for its receiving field, and you have not specified ON SIZE ERROR.

3)   DIVIDE EXCEPTION — occurs when you try to divide a field by another field that is zero.

Other types of EXCEPTIONs may occur if something goes wrong inside the computer. This is rare; seek advice if it happens.

5.2.3 Simple debugging

If your program abends, check to see its probable cause. If you cannot locate it by examining the date and the program, you must look more closely at what is happening during execution. There are several ways of doing this; the simplest way, which also enables you to locate the most errors, is to use the TRACE and EXHIBIT statements.

Put a card bearing the command READY TRACE (starting in column 12) after the card with PROCEDURE DIVISION on it. This will invoke a facility that prints out all statement numbers of paragraph-names of paragraphs that actually are executed. Run the program again. The last number appearing on the printout will be the paragraph causing the program check.

If you still cannot see what is wrong with this paragraph (Are all the data-names initialized? What should their values be during execution?), after each statement of the paragraph, insert a card with EXHIBIT NAMED (starting in column 12) and a list of the data-names of which you would like to know the contents.

For example, suppose the last paragraph to be executed is

00113 CALCULATE-GROSS.
   ADD OVERTIME REGULAR GIVING TOTAL-HOURS.
   MULTIPLY TOTAL-HOURS BY RATE GIVING GROSS-PAY.
statement number

You insert three EXHIBIT statements, thus:

CALCULATE-GROSS   *Exhibit all*
1) _____ **EXHIBIT NAMED OVERTIME REGULAR TOTAL-HOURS** — *data-names used*
   ADD OVERTIME REGULAR GIVING TOTAL-HOURS.   *in the paragraph*
2) _____ **EXHIBIT NAMED TOTAL-HOURS RATE GROSS-PAY**
   MULTIPLY TOTAL-HOURS BY RATE GIVING GROSS-PAY.
3) _____ **EXHIBIT NAMED GROSS-PAY**

In each case, include in the EXHIBIT statement the data-names that should have been changed by the previous program statement, plus the ones that will be used by the next program statement. (Note there is no period after the READY TRACE statement or the EXHIBIT statements.)

Run the program again. You may get a printout like this:

```
113
OVERTIME = 07     REGULAR = 38   TOTAL HOURS = 000
TOTAL-HOURS = 45 RATE = &AC:     GROSS-PAY = 000.00
0S03I  PROGRAM CHECK INTERRUPTION. . . . . DATA EXCEPTION
```
These are the first two EXHIBIT statements.
This is the statement number of the paragraph-name.

The EXHIBIT NAMED statement has printed out the contents of the data-names that you specified, with their names in each case.

Q. What can we conclude from this printout?

A. We know that abend was caused by the MULTIPLY statement because only the first two EXHIBIT statements were executed before the error message. We can see that RATE contains garbage instead of some reasonable figure like 11.25. Clearly, this is the cause of the data exception. Where was this value &AC: loaded into RATE? Maybe you left out the statement in which you were going to set up the value of RATE.

Of course, when you have fixed the bug, you will want to take out the READY TRACE and EXHIBIT statements and recompile the program. It's a good idea to put them on two cards that are different in color from the rest of the cards in the program, making them easy to locate.

5.2.4 User acceptance

Now you have a program that delivers valid output. Compare the output carefully with the data cards used as input. Is the output *exactly* what you intended? If, for example, you have a logic error that is causing the program to compute one person's payroll check based on the salary of the previous person in the file, the output is going to *look* right, but some people will be justifiably unhappy if you allow this program to be put into production. When you can produce good output from good input and can reject bad transactions, in a well-chosen variety of cases, you can take the program to the user who requested it, and have him test it with his own data.

The normal method of user acceptance test is to use the program with real data from the user's operation and compare the program output with the product of the current, probably clerical, operation. When this *parallel* run has functioned satisfactorily, the program can be *cut over,* or used on a routine basis by the user department.

Most programs need work on them after they have been cut over for a variety of reasons, including

- the programmer did not test with a wide enough range of test data, and actual data cause an unsuspected abend or incorrect output

- the user's business needs a change or he wants *enhancements* to what the program does for him

Whatever the reason, this sort of work is called program *maintenance,* and can be very time-consuming. For this reason, you always should write your programs to be easy to maintain; that is, with clear layout, meaningful data-names, and comments about anything that is not evident from reading the listings.

If in doubt, imagine that you are someone else writing the program, and that in two weeks' time the real you will be responsible for maintaining it. Imagine that you get a phone call at 1 a.m. from the night-shift computer operator telling you that the program has bombed with a data exception, and asking you to come in to fix it, because the report must be ready for the Board of Directors at 9 a.m. Write programs that you would be prepared to maintain in the middle of the night.

5.3 Enhancing SAMPLE-3

To give you a taste of maintenance now that SAMPLE-3 is working, the Marketing Manager wants you to modify it. Each applicant's discretionary income should be calculated as in Chapter 4, based on the previously stated assumption that everyone pays 25 percent tax. This profile should print, on the second line, underneath

IN THIS EMPLOY
DISCRETIONARY INCOME $nnn PER MTH

(nnn standing for whatever the value is). If any applicant's discretionary income works out to $1,000 or more, set it to $999. The resulting report should resemble Fig. 5.1.

```
VICTOR S GRASPER        PHONE (415) 243-7022    MALE        INCOME      $15700 PER YEAR: IN THIS EMPLOY 04 YEARS
990 GAUNTLET AVE                                SINGLE      MORTGAGE:     $250 PER MTH   DISCRETIONARY INCOME $691 PER MTH
BURLINGAME     CA 94010  A/C: 010101            0 DEPENDENTS OTHER PAYMENTS $040 PER MTH


IAN S INKERMAN          PHONE (201) 103-6061    MALE        INCOME      $17500 PER YEAR: IN THIS EMPLOY LESS THAN 1 YEAR
55 PECAN VALLEY RD                              DIVORCED    RENTAL:       $325 PER MTH   DISCRETIONARY INCOME $650 PER MTH
MONTVALE       NJ 07645  A/C: 020202            1 DEPENDENTS OTHER PAYMENTS $110 PER MTH


SARALEE JAMES           PHONE (816) 542-0535    FEMALE      INCOME      $21000 PER YEAR: IN THIS EMPLOY 03 YEARS
PARTHENON COURT                                 DIVORCED    MORTGAGE:     $275 PER MTH   DISCRETIONARY INCOME $963 PER MTH
ATHENS         MO 64065  A/C: 050505            1 DEPENDENTS OTHER PAYMENTS $ 75 PER MTH


SCARLETT O'HARA         PHONE (504) 815-1147    FEMALE      INCOME      $09500 PER YEAR: IN THIS EMPLOY 26 YEARS
SUITE 414 NAT BANK                              WIDOWED     RENTAL:       $110 PER MTH   DISCRETIONARY INCOME $464 PER MTH
NEW ORLEANS    LA 70012  A/C: 060606            2 DEPENDENTS OTHER PAYMENTS $ 20 PER MTH


SUSAN KRUPMAN           PHONE (212) 354-0330    FEMALE      INCOME      $12900 PER YEAR: IN THIS EMPLOY 01 YEARS
131 WEST 32ND ST                                SINGLE      RENTAL:       $150 PER MTH   DISCRETIONARY INCOME $626 PER MTH
NEW YORK       NY 10001  A/C: 040404            0 DEPENDENTS OTHER PAYMENTS $ 30 PER MTH


I. MORRIS GOOD          PHONE (214) 225-7013    MALE        INCOME      $27300 PER YEAR: IN THIS EMPLOY 11 YEARS
1313 PORPOISE                                   MARRIED     MORTGAGE:     $400 PER MTH   DISCRETIONARY INCOME $999 PER MTH
DALLAS         TX 75219  A/C: 030303            4 DEPENDENTS OTHER PAYMENTS $150 PER MTH
```

Figure 5.1. Output of SAMPLE-4.

From this functional specification, we can develop the structure chart for SAMPLE-4, as we will call the enhanced program. For ease of reference in the body of the program, we will prefix each module name with a letter and a number, thus:

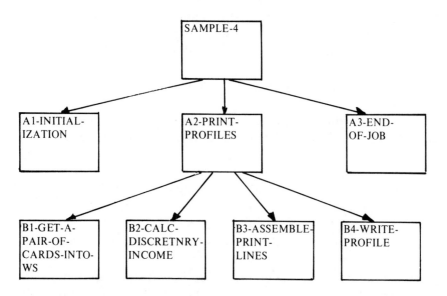

To make the problem simpler, you can assume that the paragraphs and data definitions shown on the next two pages have been cataloged in the Source Statement Library for your use. Furthermore, the senior programmer in your group wishes you to use COMPUTE statements for your calculation.

From this information, code SAMPLE-4, using COPY statements as much as possible. You can assume that the cards you use for input are all correctly punched, and so you need not worry about any further editing (although this would, of course, be very important in the real world).

When you have completed your coding, compare it with the model solution on the following pages. The code as you would write it is given first, followed by the output from the compilation with the COPY statements expanded.

Contents of Source Statement Library

Library Name

```
              FILE-CONTROL.
FILECONT          SELECT APPLICATION-CARDS-FILE    ASSIGN TO SYS031-UR-2540R-S.
                  SELECT PROFILE-LISTING           ASSIGN TO SYS033-UR-1403-S.

              DATA DIVISION.
              FILE SECTION.

              FD  APPLICATION-CARDS-FILE
                      LABEL RECORDS ARE OMITTED
                      DATA RECORDS ARE NAME-ADDRESS-AND-PHONE-IN
                                      CREDIT-INFORMATION-IN.
              01  NAME-ADDRESS-AND-PHONE-IN.
                  05   NAME-IN                      PIC X(20).
                  05   ADDRESS-IN                   PIC X(40).
FDCARDS           05   PHONE-IN                     PIC X(11).
                  05   FILLER                       PIC X(3).
                  05   ACCT-NUM-IN1                 PIC 9(6).
              01  CREDIT-INFORMATION-IN.
                  05   CARD-TYPE-IN                 PIC X.
                  05   ACCT-NUM-IN2                 PIC 9(6).
                  05   FILLER                       PIC X.
                  05   CREDIT-INFO-IN               PIC X(22).
                  05   FILLER                       PIC X(50).

              FD  PROFILE-LISTING
                      LABEL RECORDS ARE OMITTED.
              01  PRINT-LINE-OUT                    PIC X(132).

              WORKING-STORAGE SECTION.
              01  CARDS-LEFT                        PIC X(3).
              01  APPLICATION-DATA.
                  05   NAME-AND-ADDRESS-WS.
                       10   NAME-WS                 PIC X(20).
                       10   ADDRESS-WS.
                            15   STREET-WS          PIC X(20).
                            15   CITY-WS            PIC X(13).
                            15   STATE-WS           PIC XX.
                            15   ZIP-WS             PIC X(5).
                  05   PHONE-WS.
                       10   AREA-CODE-WS            PIC 9(3).
                       10   NUMBR-WS                PIC X(8).
                  05   FILLER                       PIC X(3).
                  05   ACCT-NUM-WS                  PIC 9(6).
                  05   CREDIT-INFO-WS.
                       10   SEX-WS                  PIC X.
                            88   MALE     VALUE 'M'.
CARDSWS                     88   FEMALE   VALUE 'F'.
                       10   FILLER                  PIC X.
                       10   MARITAL-STATUS-WS       PIC X.
                            88   SINGLE    VALUE 'S'.
                            88   MARRIED   VALUE 'M'.
                            88   DIVORCED  VALUE 'D'.
                            88   WIDOWED   VALUE 'W'.
                       10   FILLER                  PIC X.
                       10   NUMBER-DEPENS-WS        PIC 9.
                       10   FILLER                  PIC X.
                       10   INCOME-HUNDREDS-WS      PIC 9(3).
                       10   FILLER                  PIC X.
                       10   YEARS-EMPLOYED-WS       PIC 99.
                       10   FILLER                  PIC X.
                       10   OWN-OR-RENT-WS          PIC X.
                            88   OWNED    VALUE 'O'.
                            88   RENTED   VALUE 'R'.
                       10   FILLER                  PIC X.
                       10   MORTGAGE-OR-RENTAL-WS   PIC 9(3).
                       10   FILLER                  PIC X.
                       10   OTHER-PAYMENTS-WS       PIC 9(3).
```

```
        01  LINE-1-WS.
            05  FILLER                        PIC X(5)    VALUE SPACES.
            05  NAME-L1                       PIC X(20).
            05  FILLER                        PIC X(11)
                                          VALUE '        PHONE ('.
            05  AREA-CODE-L1                  PIC 9(3).
            05  FILLER                        PIC XX      VALUE ') '.
            05  NUMBR-L1                      PIC X(8).
            05  FILLER                        PIC X(3)    VALUE SPACES.
            05  SEX-L1                        PIC X(6).
            05  FILLER                        PIC X(9)    VALUE SPACES.
            05  FILLER                        PIC X(14)
                                          VALUE 'INCOME        $'.
            05  INCOME-HUNDREDS-L1            PIC 9(3).
            05  FILLER                        PIC X(28)
                                          VALUE '00 PER YEAR; IN THIS EMPLOY '.
            05  YEARS-EMPLOYED-L1.
                10  YEARS-L1                  PIC XX.
                10  DESCN-L1                  PIC X(16).
        01  LINE-2-WS.
            05  FILLER                        PIC X(5)    VALUE SPACES.
            05  STREET-L2                     PIC X(20).
            05  FILLER                        PIC X(27)   VALUE SPACES.
            05  MARITAL-STATUS-L2             PIC X(8).
            05  FILLER                        PIC X(7)    VALUE SPACES.
            05  OUTGO-DESCN                   PIC X(16).
            05  MORTGAGE-OR-RENTAL-L2         PIC 9(3).
            05  MESSAGE-L2                    PIC X(46)   VALUE ' PER MTH'.
        01  LINE-3-WS.
            05  FILLER                        PIC X(5)    VALUE SPACES.
            05  CITY-L3                       PIC X(13).
            05  FILLER                        PIC X       VALUE SPACE.
            05  STATE-L3                      PIC XX.
            05  FILLER                        PIC X       VALUE SPACE.
            05  ZIP-L3                        PIC X(5).
            05  FILLER                        PIC X(7)    VALUE ' A/C: '.
            05  ACCT-NUM-L3                   PIC 9(6).
            05  FILLER                        PIC X(12)   VALUE SPACES.
            05  NUMBER-DEPENS-L3              PIC 9.
            05  FILLER                        PIC X(14)
                                          VALUE ' DEPENDENTS '.
            05  FILLER                        PIC X(16)
                                          VALUE 'OTHER PAYMENTS $'.
            05  OTHER-PAYMENTS-L3             PIC 9(3).
            05  MESSAGE-L3                    PIC X(46)   VALUE ' PER MTH'.

        GET-A-PAIR-OF-CARDS-INTO-WS.
            MOVE NAME-IN TO NAME-WS.
            MOVE ADDRESS-IN TO ADDRESS-WS.
            MOVE PHONE-IN TO PHONE-WS.
            MOVE ACCT-NUM-IN1 TO ACCT-NUM-WS.
            READ APPLICATION-CARDS-FILE
                AT END MOVE 'NO ' TO CARDS-LEFT.
        * THE SECOND CARD OF THE PAIR IS NOW IN THE BUFFER
            MOVE CREDIT-INFO-IN TO CREDIT-INFO-WS.
            READ APPLICATION-CARDS-FILE
                AT END MOVE 'NO ' TO CARDS-LEFT.
        * THE FIRST CARD OF THE NEXT PAIR IS NOW IN THE BUFFER
```

Labels in left margin: LINE1WS, LINE2WS, LINE3WS, GETPAIR

ASSEMBLE-PRINT-LINES.

ASSMBLPR

```
    MOVE NAME-WS TO NAME-L1.
    MOVE STREET-WS TO STREET-L2.
    MOVE CITY-WS TO CITY-L3.
    MOVE STATE-WS TO STATE-L3.
    MOVE ZIP-WS TO ZIP-L3.
    MOVE AREA-CODE-WS TO AREA-CODE-L1.
    MOVE NUMBR-WS TO NUMBR-L1.
    MOVE ACCT-NUM-WS TO ACCT-NUM-L3.
    IF MALE     MOVE 'MALE    ' TO SEX-L1.
    IF FEMALE MOVE 'FEMALE' TO SEX-L1.
    IF SINGLE     MOVE 'SINGLE     ' TO MARITAL-STATUS-L2.
    IF MARRIED   MOVE 'MARRIED   ' TO MARITAL-STATUS-L2.
    IF DIVORCED MOVE 'DIVORCED ' TO MARITAL-STATUS-L2.
    IF WIDOWED   MOVE 'WIDOWED  ' TO MARITAL-STATUS-L2.
    MOVE NUMBER-DEPENS-WS TO NUMBER-DEPENS-L3.
    MOVE INCOME-HUNDREDS-WS TO INCOME-HUNDREDS-L1.
    IF YEARS-EMPLOYED-WS IS EQUAL TO 0
        MOVE 'LESS THAN 1 YEAR' TO YEARS-EMPLOYED-L1
    ELSE
        MOVE YEARS-EMPLOYED-WS TO YEARS-L1
        MOVE ' YEARS        ' TO DESCN-L1.
    IF OWNED MOVE 'MORTGAGE:        $' TO OUTGO-DESCN.
    IF RENTED MOVE 'RENTAL:          $' TO OUTGO-DESCN.
    MOVE MORTGAGE-OR-RENTAL-WS TO MORTGAGE-OR-RENTAL-L2.
    MOVE OTHER-PAYMENTS-WS TO OTHER-PAYMENTS-L3.
```

WRITE-PROFILE.

WRITPRFL

```
    MOVE SPACES TO PRINT-LINE-OUT.
    WRITE PRINT-LINE-OUT FROM LINE-1-WS
                    AFTER ADVANCING 4 LINES.
    MOVE SPACES TO PRINT-LINE-OUT.
    WRITE PRINT-LINE-OUT FROM LINE-2-WS
                    AFTER ADVANCING 1 LINES.
    MOVE SPACES TO PRINT-LINE-OUT.
    WRITE PRINT-LINE-OUT FROM LINE-3-WS
                    AFTER ADVANCING 1 LINES.
```

CBL LIB
    IDENTIFICATION DIVISION.
    PROGRAM-ID. SAMPLE-4.

    ENVIRONMENT DIVISION.
    INPUT-OUTPUT SECTION.
    FILE-CONTROL. COPY FILECONT.

    DATA DIVISION.
    FILE SECTION.

    FD APPLICATION-CARDS-FILE COPY FDCARDS.

    FD PROFILE-LISTING
         LABEL RECORDS ARE OMITTED.
    01 PRINT-LINE-OUT   PIC X(132).

    WORKING-STORAGE SECTION.
    01 COMMON-WS.
        05 CARDS-LEFT   PIC X(3).
    01 APPLICATION-DATA-WSB1 COPY CARDSWS.
    01 DISCR-INCOME-CALC-FIELDS-WSB2.
        05 ANNUAL-INCOME-WS   PIC 9(5).
        05 ANNUAL-TAX-WS   PIC 9(5).
        05 TAX-RATE-WS   PIC 9V99   VALUE 0.25.
        05 MONTHS-IN-YEAR   PIC 99   VALUE 12.
        05 MONTHLY-NET-INCOME-WS   PIC 9(4).
        05 MONTHLY-PAYMENTS-WS   PIC 9(4).
        05 DISCR-INCOME-WS   PIC S9(3).
    01 LINE-1-WSB3 COPY LINE1WS.
    01 LINE-2-WSB3 COPY LINE2WS.
        05 FILLER   PIC X(11)
        05 FILLER   PIC X(22)
                       VALUE 'DISCRETIONARY INCOME $'.
        05 DISCR-INCOME-L2   PIC 9(3).
        05 FILLER   PIC X(9)
                       VALUE ' PER MTH '.
    01 LINE-3-WSB3 COPY LINE3WS.

```
PROCEDURE DIVISION.
        PERFORM A1-INITIALIZATION.
        PERFORM A2-PRINT-PROFILES
          UNTIL CARDS-LEFT = 'NO '.
        PERFORM A3-END-OF-JOB.
        STOP RUN.

A1-INITIALIZATION.
        OPEN  INPUT APPLICATION-CARDS-FILE
              OUTPUT PROFILE-LISTING.
        MOVE ZEROS TO ANNUAL-INCOME-WS.
        MOVE ZEROS TO ANNUAL-TAX-WS.
        MOVE ZEROS TO MONTHLY-NET-INCOME-WS.
        MOVE ZEROS TO MONTHLY-PAYMENTS-WS.
        MOVE ZEROS TO DISCR-INCOME-WS.
        MOVE 'YES' TO CARDS-LEFT.
        READ APPLICATION-CARDS-FILE
          AT END MOVE 'NO ' TO CARDS-LEFT.
* THE FIRST CARD OF A PAIR IS NOW IN THE BUFFER

A2-PRINT-PROFILES.
        PERFORM B1-GET-A-PAIR-OF-CARDS-INTO-WS.
        PERFORM B2-CALC-DISCRETNRY-INCOME.
        PERFORM B3-ASSEMBLE-PRINT-LINES.
        PERFORM B4-WRITE-PROFILE.

A3-END-OF-JOB.
        CLOSE   APPLICATION-CARDS-FILE
                PROFILE-LISTING.

B1-GET-A-PAIR-OF-CARDS-INTO-WS.  COPY GETPAIR.

B2-CALC-DISCRETNRY-INCOME.
        COMPUTE ANNUAL-INCOME-WS = INCOME-HUNDREDS-WS * 100.
        COMPUTE ANNUAL-TAX-WS        = ANNUAL-INCOME-WS * TAX-RATE-WS.
        COMPUTE MONTHLY-NET-INCOME-WS ROUNDED
           = (ANNUAL-INCOME-WS − ANNUAL-TAX-WS) / MONTHS-IN-YEAR.
        COMPUTE MONTHLY-PAYMENTS-WS = MORTGAGE-OR-RENTAL-WS
                                    + OTHER-PAYMENTS-WS.
        COMPUTE DISCR-INCOME-WS = MONTHLY-NET-INCOME-WS
                                − MONTHLY-PAYMENTS-WS
           ON SIZE ERROR MOVE 999 TO DISCR-INCOME-WS.
* DISCRETIONARY INCOMES OVER $999 PER MONTH ARE SET AT $999

B3-ASSEMBLE-PRINT-LINES.  COPY ASSMBLPR.
        MOVE DISCR-INCOME-WS TO DISCR-INCOME-L2.

B4-WRITE-PROFILE.  COPY WRITPRFL
             REPLACING LINE-1-WS BY LINE-1-WSB3
                       LINE-2-WS BY LINE-2-WSB3
                       LINE-3-WS BY LINE-3-WSB3.
```

```
CBL LIB
00001          IDENTIFICATION DIVISION.
00002          PROGRAM-ID. SAMPLE-4.
00003
00004          ENVIRONMENT DIVISION.
00005          INPUT-OUTPUT SECTION.
00006          FILE-CONTROL. COPY FILECONT.
00007 C           SELECT APPLICATION-CARDS-FILE     ASSIGN TO SYS031-UR-2540R-S.
00008 C           SELECT PROFILE-LISTING            ASSIGN TO SYS033-UR-1403-S.
00009
00010          DATA DIVISION.
00011          FILE SECTION.
00012
00013          FD   APPLICATION-CARDS-FILE  COPY FDCARDS.
00014 C              LABEL RECORDS ARE OMITTED
00015 C              DATA RECORDS ARE     NAME-ADDRESS-AND-PHONE-IN
00016 C                                   CREDIT-INFORMATION-IN.
00017 C        01   NAME-ADDRESS-AND-PHONE-IN.
00018 C             05    NAME-IN                    PIC X(20).
00019 C             05    ADDRESS-IN                 PIC X(40).
00020 C             05    PHONE-IN                   PIC X(11).
00021 C             05    FILLER                     PIC X(3).
00022 C             05    ACCT-NUM-IN1               PIC 9(6).
00023 C        01   CREDIT-INFORMATION-IN.
00024 C             05    CARD-TYPE-IN               PIC X.
00025 C             05    ACCT-NUM-IN2               PIC 9(6).
00026 C             05    FILLER                     PIC X.
00027 C             05    CREDIT-INFO-IN             PIC X(22).
00028 C             05    FILLER                     PIC X(50).
00029
00030          FD   PROFILE-LISTING
00031               LABEL RECORDS ARE OMITTED.
00032          01   PRINT-LINE-OUT                   PIC X(132).
00033
```

```
00034          WORKING-STORAGE SECTION.
00035          01    COMMON-WS.
00036                05    CARDS-LEFT                      PIC X(3).
00037          01    APPLICATION-DATA-WSB1 COPY CARDSWS.
00038 C        01    APPLICATION-DATA-WSB1.
00039 C              05    NAME-AND-ADDRESS-WS.
00040 C                    10    NAME-WS                   PIC X(20).
00041 C                    10    ADDRESS-WS.
00042 C                          15    STREET-WS           PIC X(20).
00043 C                          15    CITY-WS             PIC X(13).
00044 C                          15    STATE-WS            PIC XX.
00045 C                          15    ZIP-WS              PIC X(5).
00046 C              05    PHONE-WS.
00047 C                    10    AREA-CODE-WS              PIC 9(3).
00048 C                    10    NUMBR-WS                  PIC X(8).
00049 C              05    FILLER                          PIC X(3).
00050 C              05    ACCT-NUM-WS                     PIC 9(6).
00051 C              05    CREDIT-INFO-WS.
00052 C                    10    SEX-WS                    PIC X.
00053 C                          88    MALE        VALUE 'M'.
00054 C                          88    FEMALE      VALUE 'F'.
00055 C                    10    FILLER                    PIC X.
00056 C                    10    MARITAL-STATUS-WS         PIC X.
00057 C                          88    SINGLE      VALUE 'S'.
00058 C                          88    MARRIED     VALUE 'M'.
00059 C                          88    DIVORCED    VALUE 'D'.
00060 C                          88    WIDOWED     VALUE 'W'.
00061 C                    10    FILLER                    PIC X.
00062 C                    10    NUMBER-DEPENS-WS          PIC 9.
00063 C                    10    FILLER                    PIC X.
00064 C                    10    INCOME-HUNDREDS-WS        PIC 9(3).
00065 C                    10    FILLER                    PIC X.
00066 C                    10    YEARS-EMPLOYED-WS         PIC 99.
00067 C                    10    FILLER                    PIC X.
00068 C                    10    OWN-OR-RENT-WS            PIC X.
00069 C                          88    OWNED       VALUE 'O'.
00070 C                          88    RENTED      VALUE 'R'.
00071 C                    10    FILLER                    PIC X.
00072 C                    10    MORTGAGE-OR-RENTAL-WS     PIC 9(3).
00073 C                    10    FILLER                    PIC X.
00074 C                    10    OTHER-PAYMENTS-WS         PIC 9(3).
00075          01    DISCR-INCOME-CALC-FIELDS-WSB2.
00076                05    ANNUAL-INCOME-WS                PIC 9(5).
00077                05    ANNUAL-TAX-WS                   PIC 9(5).
00078                05    TAX-RATE-WS                     PIC 9V99      VALUE 0.25.
00079                05    MONTHS-IN-YEAR                  PIC 99        VALUE 12.
00080                05    MONTHLY-NET-INCOME-WS           PIC 9(4).
00081                05    MONTHLY-PAYMENTS-WS             PIC 9(4).
00082                05    DISCR-INCOME-WS                 PIC S9(3).
```

```
00083        01    LINE-1-WSB3 COPY LINE1WS.
00084 C      01    LINE-1-WSB3.
00085 C            05   FILLER                        PIC X(5)      VALUE SPACES.
00086 C            05   NAME-L1                       PIC X(20).
00087 C            05   FILLER                        PIC X(11).
00088 C                                       VALUE '   PHONE ('.
00089 C            05   AREA-CODE-L1                  PIC 9(3).
00090 C            05   FILLER                        PIC XX        VALUE ') '.
00091 C            05   NUMBR-L1                      PIC X(8).
00092 C            05   FILLER                        PIC X(3)      VALUE SPACES.
00093 C            05   SEX-L1                        PIC X(6).
00094 C            05   FILLER                        PIC X(9)      VALUE SPACES.
00095 C            05   FILLER                        PIC X(14)
00096 C                                       VALUE 'INCOME      $'.
00097 C            05   INCOME-HUNDREDS-L1            PIC 9(3).
00098 C            05   FILLER                        PIC X(28)
00099 C                                       VALUE '00 PER YEAR;  IN THIS EMPLOY '.
00100 C            05   YEARS-EMPLOYED-L1.
00101 C                 10   YEARS-L1                 PIC XX.
00102 C                 10   DESCN-L1                 PIC X(16).
00103        C1    LINE-2-WSB3 COPY LINE2WS.
00104 C      01    LINE-2-WSB3.
00105 C            05   FILLER                        PIC X(5)      VALUE SPACES.
00106 C            05   STREET-L2                     PIC X(20).
00107 C            05   FILLER                        PIC X(27)     VALUE SPACES.
00108 C            05   MARITAL-STATUS-L2             PIC X(8).
00109 C            05   FILLER                        PIC X(7)      VALUE SPACES.
00110 C            05   OUTGO-DESCN                   PIC X(16).
00111 C            05   MORTGAGE-OR-RENTAL-L2         PIC 9(3).
00112              05   FILLER                        PIC X(11)
00113                                        VALUE ' PER MTH   '.
00114              05   FILLER                        PIC X(22)
00115                                        VALUE 'DISCRETIONARY INCOME $'.
00116              05   DISCR-INCOME-L2               PIC 9(3).
00117              05   FILLER                        PIC X(9)
00118                                        VALUE ' PER MTH '.
00119        01    LINE-3-WSB3 COPY LINE3WS.
00120 C      01    LINE-3-WSB3.
00121 C            05   FILLER                        PIC X(5)      VALUE SPACES.
00122 C            05   CITY-L3                       PIC X(13).
00123 C            05   FILLER                        PIC X         VALUE SPACE.
00124 C            05   STATE-L3                      PIC XX.
00125 C            05   FILLER                        PIC X         VALUE SPACE.
00126 C            05   ZIP-L3                        PIC X(5).
00127 C            05   FILLER                        PIC X(7)      VALUE ' A/C: '.
00128 C            05   ACCT-NUM-L3                   PIC 9(6).
00129 C            05   FILLER                        PIC X(12)     VALUE SPACES.
00130 C            05   NUMBER-DEPENS-L3              PIC 9.
00131 C            05   FILLER                        PIC X(14)
00132 C                                       VALUE ' DEPENDENTS  '.
00133 C            05   FILLER                        PIC X(16)
00134 C                                       VALUE 'OTHER PAYMENTS $'.
00135 C            05   OTHER-PAYMENTS-L3             PIC 9(3).
00136
```

```
00137            PROCEDURE DIVISION.
00138                PERFORM A1-INITIALIZATION.
00139                PERFORM A2-PRINT-PROFILES
00140                   UNTIL CARDS-LEFT = 'NO '.
00141                PERFORM A3-END-OF-JOB.
00142                STOP RUN.
00143
00144            A1-INITIALIZATION.
00145                OPEN   INPUT APPLICATION-CARDS-FILE
00146                       OUTPUT PROFILE-LISTING.
00147                MOVE ZEROS TO ANNUAL-INCOME-WS.
00148                MOVE ZEROS TO ANNUAL-TAX-WS.
00149                MOVE ZEROS TO MONTHLY-NET-INCOME-WS.
00150                MOVE ZEROS TO MONTHLY-PAYMENTS-WS.
00151                MOVE ZEROS TO DISCR-INCOME-WS.
00152                MOVE 'YES' TO CARDS-LEFT.
00153                READ APPLICATION-CARDS-FILE
00154                   AT END MOVE 'NO ' TO CARDS-LEFT.
00155          * THE FIRST CARD OF A PAIR IS NOW IN THE BUFFER
00156
00157            A2-PRINT-PROFILES.
00158                PERFORM B1-GET-A-PAIR-OF-CARDS-INTO-WS.
00159                PERFORM B2-CALC-DISCRETNRY-INCOME.
00160                PERFORM B3-ASSEMBLE-PRINT-LINES.
00161                PERFORM B4-WRITE-PROFILE.
00162
00163            A3-END-OF-JOB.
00164                CLOSE APPLICATION-CARDS-FILE
00165                      PROFILE-LISTING.
00166
00167            B1-GET-A-PAIR-OF-CARDS-INTO-WS.  COPY GETPAIR.
00168 C              MOVE NAME-IN TO NAME-WS.
00169 C              MOVE ADDRESS-IN TO ADDRESS-WS.
00170 C              MOVE PHONE-IN TO PHONE-WS.
00171 C              MOVE ACCT-NUM-IN1 TO ACCT-NUM-WS.
00172 C              READ APPLICATION-CARDS-FILE
00173 C                 AT END MOVE 'NO ' TO CARDS-LEFT.
00174 C        * THE SECOND CARD OF THE PAIR IS NOW IN THE BUFFER
00175 C              MOVE CREDIT-INFO-IN TO CREDIT-INFO-WS.
00176 C              READ APPLICATION-CARDS-FILE
00177 C                 AT END MOVE 'NO ' TO CARDS-LEFT.
00178 C        * THE FIRST CARD OF THE NEXT PAIR IS NOW IN THE BUFFER
```

```
00179
00180          B2-CALC-DISCRETNRY-INCOME.
00181              COMPUTE ANNUAL-INCOME-WS = INCOME-HUNDREDS-WS * 100.
00182              COMPUTE ANNUAL-TAX-WS      = ANNUAL-INCOME-WS * TAX-RATE-WS.
00183              COMPUTE MONTHLY-NET-INCOME-WS ROUNDED
00184                  = (ANNUAL-INCOME-WS — ANNUAL-TAX-WS) / MONTHS-IN-YEAR.
00185              COMPUTE MONTHLY-PAYMENTS-WS = MORTGAGE-OR-RENTAL-WS
00186                            + OTHER-PAYMENTS-WS.
00187              COMPUTE DISCR-INCOME-WS = MONTHLY-NET-INCOME-WS
00188                          — MONTHLY-PAYMENTS-WS
00189              ON SIZE ERROR MOVE 999 TO DISCR-INCOME-WS.
00190          * DISCRETIONARY INCOMES OVER $999 PER MONTH ARE SET AT $999
00191
00192          B3-ASSEMBLE-PRINT-LINES.  COPY ASSMBLPR.
00193 C          MOVE NAME-WS TO NAME-L1.
00194 C          MOVE STREET-WS TO STREET-L2.
00195 C          MOVE CITY-WS TO CITY-L3.
00196 C          MOVE STATE-WS TO STATE-L3.
00197 C          MOVE ZIP-WS TO ZIP-L3.
00198 C          MOVE AREA-CODE-WS TO AREA-CODE-L1.
00199 C          MOVE NUMBR-WS TO NUMBR-L1.
00200 C          MOVE ACCT-NUM-WS TO ACCT-NUM-L3.
00201 C          IF MALE    MOVE 'MALE    ' TO SEX-L1.
00202 C          IF FEMALE MOVE 'FEMALE' TO SEX-L1.
00203 C          IF SINGLE     MOVE 'SINGLE     ' TO MARITAL-STATUS-L2.
00204 C          IF MARRIED   MOVE 'MARRIED  ' TO MARITAL-STATUS-L2.
00205 C          IF DIVORCED MOVE 'DIVORCED ' TO MARITAL-STATUS-L2.
00206 C          IF WIDOWED  MOVE 'WIDOWED  ' TO MARITAL-STATUS-L2.
00207 C          MOVE NUMBER-DEPENS-WS TO NUMBER-DEPENS-L3.
00208 C          MOVE INCOME-HUNDREDS-WS TO INCOME-HUNDREDS-L1.
00209 C          IF YEARS-EMPLOYED-WS IS EQUAL TO 0
00210 C              MOVE 'LESS THAN 1 YEAR' TO YEARS-EMPLOYED-L1
00211 C          ELSE
00212 C              MOVE YEARS-EMPLOYED-WS TO YEARS-L1
00213 C              MOVE ' YEARS        ' TO DESCN-L1.
00214 C          IF OWNED MOVE 'MORTGAGE:       $' TO OUTGO-DESCN.
00215 C          IF RENTED MOVE 'RENTAL:         $' TO OUTGO-DESCN.
00216 C          MOVE MORTGAGE-OR-RENTAL-WS TO MORTGAGE-OR-RENTAL-L2.
00217 C          MOVE OTHER-PAYMENTS-WS TO OTHER-PAYMENTS-L3.
00218          MOVE DISCR-INCOME-WS TO DISCR-INCOME-L2.
00219
00220          B4-WRITE-PROFILE.    COPY WRITPRFL
00221              REPLACING    LINE-1-WS BY LINE-1-WSB3
00222                           LINE-2-WS BY LINE-2-WSB3
00223                           LINE-3-WS BY LINE-3-WSB3.
00224 C          MOVE SPACES TO PRINT-LINE-OUT.
00225 C          WRITE PRINT-LINE-OUT FROM LINE-1-WSB3
00226 C                              AFTER ADVANCING 4 LINES.
00227 C          MOVE SPACES TO PRINT-LINE-OUT.
00228 C          WRITE PRINT-LINE-OUT FROM LINE-2-WSB3
00229 C                              AFTER ADVANCING 1 LINES.
00230 C          MOVE SPACES TO PRINT-LINE-OUT.
00231 C          WRITE PRINT-LINE-OUT FROM LINE3-WSB3
00232 C                              AFTER ADVANCING 1 LINES.
```

6 Program Logic

6.1 Testing for conditions

There are a variety of useful tests that we can make in addition to the simple tests that we already have done, for example, IF NAME IS EQUAL TO SPACES. These tests are of five types:

Relational: Is field-1 GREATER THAN, LESS THAN, OR EQUAL TO field-2?

Class: Is field-1 NUMERIC or ALPHABETIC?

Condition-name: IF MARRIED . . . (where MARRIED has previously been defined in an 88 level).

Sign: Is field-1 POSITIVE, NEGATIVE, or ZERO?

Complex: Is (condition-1 true) $\begin{Bmatrix} \text{AND} \\ \text{OR} \end{Bmatrix}$ (condition-2 true)?

Let us look at each type of test in turn.

6.1.1 Relational tests

The general form is:

IF   field-1 $\begin{Bmatrix} \text{IS GREATER THAN} \\ \text{IS LESS THAN} \\ \text{IS EQUAL TO} \end{Bmatrix}$ field-2

statement-1

ELSE

statement-2.

Q. Code a test to perform OK-ROUTINE if TOTAL-OUTGO is less than NET-INCOME, and perform BANKRUPT-ROUTINE if TOTAL-OUTGO is more than or equal to NET-INCOME.

A. **IF TOTAL-OUTGO IS LESS THAN NET-INCOME**
       PERFORM OK-ROUTINE
    ELSE
       PERFORM BANKRUPT-ROUTINE.

Q. In the preceding question, what is wrong with

  IF TOTAL-OUTGO IS GREATER THAN NET-INCOME
     PERFORM BANKRUPT-ROUTINE
  ELSE
     PERFORM OK-ROUTINE.

A. This test gives the wrong result when TOTAL-OUTGO and NET-INCOME are exactly equal.

Most computers will allow you to use the characters

  > for IS GREATER THAN
  < for IS LESS THAN
  = for IS EQUAL TO

We prefer to stay away from > and < because some people find them confusing, and the printers of some computers can't handle them. We prefer to use = only in a COMPUTE statement or when followed by a literal, e.g., IF CARDS-LEFT = 'NO '.

6.1.2 Class tests

A field is NUMERIC when it contains only Ø — 9 and decimal points, with a ± sign; and ALPHABETIC when it contains only A — Z and/or spaces.

Q. FIELD-A contains 243-7022. Which routine will be performed when the statement on the next page is executed:

> **IF FIELD-A IS NUMERIC**
> **PERFORM NUMBER-ROUTINE**
> **ELSE**
> **PERFORM GARBAGE-ROUTINE.**

A.   GARBAGE-ROUTINE will be performed; FIELD-A fails the test of being numeric because it contains a hyphen. Thus, control goes to the ELSE clause, where the imperative statement is obeyed.

Q.   Given the format of PHONE-IN as we have used it, how could you use class tests to make sure that the digits have been punched correctly?

A.   Define the card with three fields, say, EX-CHANGE, HYPHEN, and NUMBER, and test EX-CHANGE and NUMBER to make sure they are numeric. This will not guarantee that the digits punched are the ones that *should* be there, but at least you will catch any spaces (which will fail the test), and any letters or other characters which were punched by accident.

Q.   If NAME-IN is blank, will it pass an ALPHABETIC test?

A.   Yes. Since blanks are alpha characters, you would need to test specifically for SPACES to detect a missing field.

As you can see, class tests can be useful in editing: If you know a field contains a dollar amount, then test it for NUMERIC. If the test fails, something is wrong, and the transactions should not be processed until the error is corrected.

6.1.3 Condition-name tests

We used condition-names extensively in SAMPLE-3 and SAMPLE-4. Provided MARRIED, SINGLE, OWNED, and RENTED, and so on, have been defined in 88 levels, you test as follows:

```
IF OWNED
    . . .
ELSE . . .
```

When a condition-name can have one of two values, it is good practice to test for both. For example,

```
IF OWNED
    perform owned-routine
ELSE IF RENTED
    perform rented-routine
ELSE
    perform error-routine.
```

Note that we have combined the two separate IF statements used in SAMPLE-3 and SAMPLE-4, into the form IF . . . ELSE IF . . . . One advantage of this form is that it provides for the situation in which OWNED is not true and RENTED is not true. This is a problem, which you must deal with in "error-routine"; maybe something other than O or R is punched in the card. Anyway, don't assume that because OWNED is not true, RENTED is automatically true: *Always test.*

This is an example of *defensive* programming: trying to anticipate anything that might go wrong and dealing with it.

Q. Code a defensive routine to add 1 to MEN if MALE, and add 1 to WOMEN if FEMALE.

A. **IF MALE**
    ADD 1 TO MEN
    ELSE IF FEMALE
    ADD 1 TO WOMEN
    ELSE
    PERFORM SEX-ERROR-ROUTINE.

Note that where we have ELSE IF we prefer to continue on the same line, rather than our normal practice of leaving the ELSE on a line of its own.

6.1.4 Sign tests

These allow you to test whether a field defined as numeric is positive, negative, or zero, as follows:

IF DISCRETIONARY-INCOME IS NEGATIVE
    PERFORM BANKRUPT-ROUTINE
ELSE
    PERFORM OK-ROUTINE.

Q.   IF DISCRETIONARY-INCOME is defined as PIC 9(3), will BANKRUPT-ROUTINE ever be performed?

A.   No, the field always will appear positive. Only signed fields, e.g., PIC S9(3), should be tested with a sign test.

6.1.5 Complex tests

You can combine various conditions in one test, using the logical operators AND, OR, and NOT. For example, you may want to write

IF MALE AND MARRIED
    ADD 1 TO MARRIED-MEN
ELSE
    ADD 1 TO OTHER-PEOPLE.

Or, you might have occasion to write

IF SINGLE OR DIVORCED OR WIDOWED
    ADD 1 TO UNMARRIED-PERSONS.

First, let's see what the operators (AND, OR, NOT) really mean. The AND operator, for example, forms expressions whose values are true if and only if *both* of the conditions ANDed together are individually true.

MALE AND INCOME-HUNDREDS IS GREATER THAN 150 is true only for people who *both* are men and also earn more than $15,000 per annum. If the condition on either side of the AND is false, the whole expression is false.

We can demonstrate this formally with a *truth table,* which shows the various combinations of truth and falsity:

X	Y	X AND Y
True	True	True
True	False	False
False	True	False
False	False	False

On the other hand, the operator OR creates expressions that are true if either one or both of the conditions on either side of the OR is true.

Thus "FEMALE OR MARRIED" is true for men if they are married, and also true for all women whether married or not, and certainly true for married women.

Q. Draw up a truth table for the expression X OR Y.

A.

X	Y	X OR Y
T	T	T
T	F	T
F	T	T
F	F	F

The NOT operator allows us to form the logical negation, or reversal of truth value, of a condition. Thus, if condition X is true, NOT-X is false; conversely, if X is false, NOT-X is true.

Q. Is NOT GREATER THAN 100 true or false for the number 101?

A. False. GREATER THAN 100 is true for 101, so the negation must be false.

The human mind has a lot of difficulty with expressions involving NOT; experiments suggest that they are about twice as hard to follow as positive expressions. The real trouble comes, though, when we start to combine AND, OR, and NOT. For example, is NOT MARRIED OR AGE NOT GREATER THAN 21 true of a married person aged 20? It is difficult to evaluate this without working through the truth table. The answer is

NOT MARRIED is false

AGE NOT GREATER THAN 21 is true

and the truth table shows that if condition X is false and condition Y is true, X or Y is true.

You would expect that NOT NOT MARRIED would be the same as MARRIED, but COBOL does not allow you to have two NOTs together. You must enclose the inner NOT condition in parentheses. Thus, you can write

IF A NOT (NOT NUMERIC)
    PERFORM NUMBER-ROUTINE
ELSE
    PERFORM ALPHA-ROUTINE.

While you would rarely want to do this, the *use of parentheses is vital whenever two or more different operators are used.* To see why this is so, try answering the following:

Q.   IS MARRIED AND FEMALE OR AGE GREATER THAN 21 true for a single man of 30?

A.   Your answer will depend on how you interpret the expression. If you read it as

(MARRIED AND FEMALE) OR (AGE GREATER THAN 21)

you have   False   OR   True

which is True.

If you read it as

(MARRIED) AND (FEMALE OR AGE GREATER THAN 21), you have

    False AND   True

which is False.

The placing of the parentheses alters the meaning of the whole expression. To put it another way, if A is false and C is true, then

(A AND B) OR C is always true, no matter what the value of B, and

A AND (B OR C) is always false.

Watch out for this problem of *precedence of operators* in program specifications; if, for example, you read "If the person is married and lives in the state or is a veteran, apply a discount of five percent," you should be aware that this is an ambiguous sentence programmable in two ways. Make sure the one you choose also is the one that the user intends.

Complicating the issue is the fact that COBOL has its built-in rules for inserting parentheses if you leave them out; if you code A AND B OR NOT C, the compiler will treat it as though you had written (A AND B) OR (NOT C). So, always include parentheses when you have two or more operands. The only exception to this rule is when you have a string of expressions all connected by the same operand. Thus, it's OK to write

    IF MALE AND MARRIED AND OWNER AND INCOME GREATER THAN 10000

or

    AGE IS LESS THAN 21   OR INCOME IS LESS THAN 15000
                           OR RENTER
                           OR OUT-OF-STATE

Once we have made proper use of parentheses to clearly specify the intended precedence of logical operations, we still are left with one problem: When more than three operators are involved, Boolean algebra (the rules for combining operators) is not trivial. That is, when we write the COBOL statement

    IF A OR (NOT (B OR (NOT (C AND D))))
        MOVE P TO Q
    ELSE
        MOVE X TO Y.

even a competent mathematician probably would scratch his head for a while to determine the conditions under which P is moved to Q. We're tempted at this point to make the flat statement, "You should never write statements as complex as that," which is true 95 percent of the time. If the situation is genuinely complex, you will need to draw up a type of truth table known as a decision table, discussed in Section 6.3.

6.2 Nested IF statements

Suppose we had occasion to count the number of people with blue eyes, count separately the number of people with a height of over six feet, and count separately the number of people from California, we would code (assuming appropriate definition of data-names)

```
IF COLOR-OF-EYES = 'BLUE' ADD 1 TO BLUE-EYES.
IF HEIGHT IS GREATER THAN HEIGHT-LIMIT
       ADD 1 TO SIX-FOOTERS.
IF HOME-STATE = 'CA' ADD 1 TO CALIFORNIANS.
```

If the program is processing data for a very tall, blue-eyed person from San Francisco, all three of the counter fields will be incremented; for a short, brown-eyed New Yorker, none would be incremented. You can imagine all combinations of counters being incremented, because the conditions tested are *independent* of one another; home state has nothing to do with having blue eyes or with height.

However, suppose we counted the number of married men, counted separately the number of married women, and similarly counted the number of single men and single women; suppose further that we have defined the condition-names so that divorced and widowed people are considered single. What sort of COBOL statements could we write to accomplish this?

One sequence of statements comes to mind immediately:

```
IF MALE AND MARRIED ADD 1 TO MARRIED-MEN.
IF FEMALE AND MARRIED ADD 1 TO MARRIED-WOMEN.
IF MALE AND SINGLE ADD 1 TO SINGLE-MEN.
IF FEMALE AND SINGLE ADD 1 TO SINGLE-WOMEN.
```

There is no question that this code is simple and straightforward; it can be understood by anyone who reads it. On the other hand, this code is misleading: The separate IF statements imply the testing of independent conditions.

We know that the four combinations of conditions are very far from being independent. For instance, if we discover that a person is male and married, we know that he cannot be simultaneously female and married, so there is no point even asking the question. In other words, although only *one* of the IF statements in the example above can have a value of true, all four IF statements will be tested.

Worse than this, though, is the clumsiness of the form when more than two conditions are involved. For instance, suppose we wanted to take property ownership into account. We would have to write

IF MALE AND MARRIED AND OWNER ADD 1 TO MARRIED-MALE-OWNERS.
IF MALE AND MARRIED AND RENTER ADD 1 TO MARRIED-MALE-RENTERS.
.
. etc.

> Q. How many statements would be required to cover all possible cases?
>
> A. Eight: Each of the three conditions can have one of two values, and $2^3 = 8$.

This provides the motivation for another approach: the *nested IF*. Consider, for example, our original problem of counting separate categories of single men, married men, single women, and married women. We could accomplish this with the following COBOL statement:

```
IF MALE
    IF MARRIED
        ADD 1 TO MARRIED-MEN
    ELSE
        ADD 1 TO SINGLE-MEN
ELSE
    IF MARRIED
        ADD 1 TO MARRIED-WOMEN
    ELSE
        ADD 1 TO SINGLE-WOMEN.
```

This kind of statement does what we want, and also avoids most of the problems that arose in the previous scheme with combinations of dependent conditions. On the other hand, it requires clear thinking to use correctly, and, if carelessly used, can create unbelievable trouble. Consequently, we must look closely at the nested IF to see how it works, and to see how to avoid the problems associated with it.

First of all, let's look more closely at how the nested IF works. The outer *layer* of logic expressed in our statement above could be written informally as

```
IF MALE
     male-logic
ELSE
     female-logic.
```

From this point of view, it is clear that we have a very simple "either-or" binary situation; either MALE is true or it is not. What we must emphasize, though, is that if MALE *is* true, then we want to carry out "male-logic," whatever that is, *and then proceed to the next COBOL sentence.* That is, we want to skip over the ELSE clause, since it is obviously irrelevant to us. Let's keep that in mind as we investigate what male-logic entails. From the original statement of the problem, we see that it can be expressed as

IF MARRIED
    ADD 1 TO MARRIED-MEN
ELSE
    ADD 1 TO SINGLE-MEN.

Thus, if it turns out that we are dealing with a married man, we will execute the statement that adds one to the MARRIED-MEN counter. What next? Well, we certainly don't want to execute the ELSE clause; that is, we don't want to add one to SINGLE-MEN, having just decided that we had a married man. In fact, we want to skip over the ELSE clause . . . and we recognize at this point that we are through with male-logic.

What do we do next? We had decided before we got involved in the details of male-logic that, once it was accomplished, we wanted to proceed to the next COBOL statement. Thus, when we look at the fully nested IF statement,

IF MALE
    IF MARRIED
        ADD 1 TO MARRIED-MEN
    ELSE
        ADD 1 TO SINGLE-MEN
    ELSE
        IF MARRIED
            ADD 1 TO MARRIED-WOMEN
        ELSE
            ADD 1 TO SINGLE-WOMEN.

it becomes clear that if MALE is true, we then will execute the first IF MARRIED . . . clause. And, if the object of our investigation is not only male but also married, we will execute the statement ADD 1 TO MARRIED-MEN *and then skip over the ELSE that matches the IF-MARRIED* (since we have dispensed with male-logic). *Furthermore, we will skip over the ELSE that matches the IF MALE* (since we obviously have no interest in executing any statements associated with female-logic).

We can generalize all of this by saying that an IF statement is of the form

> IF logical-condition-1
>   statement-1
> ELSE
>   statement-2.

where statement-1 and statement-2 can be any of the simple COBOL statements with which you are familiar, or a linear sequence of such statements, *or another IF statement.* Thus, it is possible for statement-1 to be a simple MOVE statement, and statement-2 to be of the form

> IF logical-condition-2
>   statement-3
> ELSE
>   statement-4.

Sooner or later, the "statement-i's" will have been fully expanded into simple statements, or linear sequences of such statements. Keep in mind that, no matter how deeply nested, the IF statement is just one COBOL sentence with only one period at the very end.

By a *linear sequence* of simple statements, we mean that it is permissible to write such statements as shown at the top of the next page:

```
IF logical-condition-1
        MOVE A TO B
        MOVE C TO D
        MOVE E TO F
ELSE
        IF logical-condition-2
                MOVE P1 TO Q1
                MOVE P2 TO Q2
        ELSE
                MOVE X1 TO Y1
                MOVE X2 TO Y2.
```

Once again, note that there is only one period in this structure!

Q. What happens when the nested IF statement shown above is executed, assuming that "logical-condition-1" is false, and "logical-condition-2" is true?

A. P1 will be moved to Q1 and P2 will be moved to Q2. Nothing else will be moved and execution will continue at the statement following the IF.

Q. Write out the nested IF that is equivalent to the eight sequential IFs started on page 116.

A.
```
IF MALE
    IF MARRIED
        IF OWNER
            ADD 1 TO MARRIED-MALE-OWNERS
        ELSE
            ADD 1 TO MARRIED-MALE RENTERS
    ELSE
        IF OWNER
            ADD 1 TO SINGLE-MALE-OWNERS
        ELSE
            ADD 1 TO SINGLE-MALE-RENTERS
ELSE
    IF MARRIED
        IF OWNER
            ADD 1 TO MARRIED-FEMALE-OWNERS
        ELSE
            ADD 1 TO MARRIED-FEMALE-RENTERS
    ELSE
        IF OWNER
            ADD 1 TO SINGLE-FEMALE-OWNERS
        ELSE
            ADD 1 TO SINGLE-FEMALE-RENTERS.
```

6.2.1 Block structures

Let's be sure that we understand the consequences of having multiple MOVE statements in linear sequences in nested IFs. We observed that the outer layer of the IF statement was of the following form:

```
IF logical-condition-1
    statement-1
ELSE
    statement-2.
```

Suppose, as in the earlier example, that statement-1 consists of three MOVE statements. How does COBOL know when we've finished doing everything we wanted to do in statement-1? The answer is that *statement-1 is terminated by the ELSE clause that matches the IF clause within which statement-1 is embedded.* In more formal terms, statement-1 is known as a *block*. In some programming languages, blocks are delimited with the explicit words BEGIN and END; but in COBOL, blocks are delimited by the presence of an ELSE (in the case of statement-1), or by the period that ends the sentence (as with statement-2).

In case you think we're making a lot of noise about something relatively insignificant, we hasten to point out that it's a *very* significant issue — and failure to understand it has caused enormous problems for a lot of COBOL programmers. To illustrate the potential problems, let's consider a slight variation to the original problem of counting categories of married men, and single men. Suppose we were required to make a cumulative count of all males and all females, as well as individual counts of married males, married females, single males, and single females. We might be tempted to write the following IF statement:

```
IF MALE                            *
    IF MARRIED                     *
        ADD 1 TO MARRIED-MEN       *    THIS IS AN
    ELSE                           *
        ADD 1 TO SINGLE-MEN        *    EXAMPLE
    ADD 1 TO MALE-COUNTER          *
ELSE                               *    OF
    IF MARRIED                     *
        ADD 1 TO MARRIED-WOMEN     *    INCORRECT
    ELSE                           *
        ADD 1 TO SINGLE-WOMEN      *    CODE
    ADD 1 TO FEMALE-COUNTER.       *
```

The intention of this code is fairly clear: Once we have determined that a person is male, we check further to see if he is married in order to increment MARRIED-MEN or SINGLE-MEN — but in either case, the intention is to increment MALE-COUNTER. Obviously, the code is trying to do the same thing with females.

> Q.   Does the code shown above achieve this? If not, why not?

> A.   No, because according to the formal definition of COBOL, the statement ADD 1 TO MALE-COUNTER is included as part of a linear block of statements imbedded within the ELSE clause corresponding to unmarried males. Thus, if we discover that a person is *male* and is *married,* we will increment MARRIED-MEN, then skip around the next ELSE clause (since we aren't concerned with unmarried males), and skip around the outer-level ELSE clause (since we aren't concerned with females of any variety). In other words, MALE-COUNTER is incremented *only* when we are dealing with unmarried males, which is not what we intended; similarly, FEMALE-COUNTER is incremented only when we are dealing with unmarried females.

How do we cope with the problem? The simplest way in this case is to increment MALE-COUNTER *before* determining whether the male is married; obviously, the same applies to females. Thus, we might write

```
IF MALE
    ADD 1 TO MALE-COUNTER
    IF MARRIED
        ADD 1 TO MARRIED-MEN
    ELSE
        ADD 1 TO SINGLE-MEN
ELSE
    ADD 1 TO FEMALE-COUNTER
    IF MARRIED
        ADD 1 TO MARRIED-WOMEN
    ELSE
        ADD 1 TO SINGLE-WOMEN.
```

Q. Is there any other easy way to do the increment-
ing of MALE-COUNTER and FEMALE-COUNTER?

A. One way that comes to mind is to compute
MALE-COUNTER and FEMALE-COUNTER separately, *after* the nested IF has been executed. Thus,
we would have

```
IF MALE
    IF MARRIED
        ADD 1 TO MARRIED-MEN
    ELSE
        ADD 1 TO SINGLE-MEN
ELSE
    IF MARRIED
        ADD 1 TO MARRIED-WOMEN
    ELSE
        ADD 1 TO SINGLE-WOMEN.
ADD MARRIED-MEN SINGLE-MEN
    GIVING MALE-COUNTER.
ADD MARRIED-WOMEN SINGLE-WOMEN
    GIVING FEMALE-COUNTER.
```

While we're on the subject of minor issues that can become
major problems, we should point out that it's not always practical
to solve the block-structure problem by moving a statement before the IF statement (as we did with the ADD 1 TO MALE-
COUNTER in the example above). For example, suppose we decided that MALE-COUNTER should be computed each time by adding MARRIED-MEN to SINGLE-MEN to produce the result. Our
initial attempt might be as follows:

```
IF MALE                                   *
    IF MARRIED                            *
        ADD 1 TO MARRIED-MEN              *       THIS IS AN
    ELSE                                  *
        ADD 1 TO SINGLE-MEN               *       EXAMPLE
    ADD MARRIED-MEN SINGLE-MEN            *
        GIVING MALE-COUNTER               *       OF
ELSE                                      *
    IF MARRIED                            *       INCORRECT
        ADD 1 TO MARRIED-WOMEN            *
    ELSE                                  *       CODE
        ADD 1 TO SINGLE-WOMEN             *
    ADD MARRIED-WOMEN SINGLE-WOMEN        *
        GIVING FEMALE-COUNTER.            *
```

However, as we already have discovered, this code will compute MALE-COUNTER only for unmarried males, and FEMALE-COUNTER only for unmarried females. So, we could attempt to solve the problem as we did before, by moving the computational statement before the appropriate IF MARRIED clause. This would give us

```
IF MALE                                       *
    ADD MARRIED-MEN SINGLE-MEN                *
        GIVING MALE-COUNTER                   *    THIS IS AN
    IF MARRIED                                *
        ADD 1 TO MARRIED-MEN                  *    EXAMPLE
    ELSE                                      *
        ADD 1 TO SINGLE-MEN                   *    OF
ELSE                                          *
    ADD MARRIED-WOMEN SINGLE-WOMEN            *    INCORRECT
        GIVING FEMALE-COUNTER                 *
    IF MARRIED                                *    CODE
        ADD 1 TO MARRIED-WOMEN                *
    ELSE                                      *
        ADD 1 TO SINGLE-WOMEN.                *
```

Unfortunately, this doesn't do what we want either. The way we've coded things now, MALE-COUNTER is computed *before* we have incremented MARRIED-MEN (or SINGLE-MEN, as the case may be), which means that MALE-COUNTER is off by one. In the event that this IF statement occurs in the middle of a loop being executed once for each person in a large file, the result will be that the program concludes with MARRIED-MEN, SINGLE-MEN, MARRIED-WOMEN, and SINGLE-WOMEN computed correctly, but MALE-COUNTER and FEMALE-COUNTER computed incorrectly.

There is one remaining aspect of nested IFs that you must learn about: the *null* ELSE. It can be illustrated by suggesting still another variation on our original problem. Suppose we have decided to count only the married men and the married women; unmarried men and unmarried women are of no interest to us, and should not be counted. Our first attempt might result in the following code:

```
IF MALE                               *    THIS IS AN
    IF MARRIED                        *
        ADD 1 TO MARRiED-MEN          *    EXAMPLE OF
ELSE                                  *
    IF MARRIED                        *    INCORRECT
        ADD 1 TO MARRIED-WOMEN.       *
                                      *    CODE
```

Sad to say, the code shown on the previous page doesn't do what we want it to do. A general rule of COBOL is that ELSE clauses are matched with IF clauses much the way right parentheses are paired with left parentheses in an arithmetic expression; specifically, an ELSE is matched up with the last preceding unmatched IF clause in the statement.

> Q. Reformat the statement on the preceding page to show this matching rule.

> A.
> ```
> IF MALE
>     IF MARRIED
>         ADD 1 TO MARRIED-MEN
>     ELSE
>         IF MARRIED
>             ADD 1 TO MARRIED-WOMEN.
> ```

This reformatted code says that if the subject is female, *no* counter is incremented; however, if the subject is male, then another test is made to see if he is married — in which case MARRIED-MEN is incremented. If the subject is male but unmarried, the logic falls into the ELSE clause, in which another useless test is made to see if he is married!

So, how do we get the COBOL statements to do what we originally wanted to do — count married men and married women, but ignore unmarried men and unmarried women? It turns out that the ELSE NEXT SENTENCE clause is particularly appropriate for saying "otherwise, do nothing." Our code now reads

```
IF MALE
    IF MARRIED
        ADD 1 TO MARRIED-MEN
    ELSE
        NEXT SENTENCE
ELSE
    IF MARRIED
        ADD 1 TO MARRIED-WOMEN
    ELSE
        NEXT SENTENCE.
```

The first NEXT SENTENCE clause does just what we want: It says, "There really isn't anything more to do — processing should continue at the next COBOL sentence." Its effect, then, is to allow us to skip around all of the logic pertaining to females. The second NEXT SENTENCE clause has the same effect, but it turns out to be redundant; there is nothing left to skip around, since it occurred at the very end of the nested IF statement. Then, we would accomplish the same thing by writing the code as

```
IF MALE
    IF MARRIED
        ADD 1 TO MARRIED-MEN
    ELSE
        NEXT SENTENCE
ELSE
    IF MARRIED
        ADD 1 TO MARRIED-WOMEN.
```

We highly recommend that you use ELSE NEXT SENTENCE (where appropriate) to ensure that you have an ELSE to match each IF. Once you have gone through this exercise, you can eliminate the redundant ELSE NEXT SENTENCEs at the end of the nested IF.

6.2.2 The CASE structure

Suppose that we had defined condition-names to allow us to distinguish separately the categories of single men, married men, single women, and married women. In that case, the nested IF statement that we have been studying throughout this section could be rewritten in the following form:

```
IF SINGLE-MALE
    ADD 1 TO SINGLE-MALE-COUNTER
ELSE
    IF MARRIED-MALE
        ADD 1 TO MARRIED-MALE-COUNTER
    ELSE
        IF SINGLE-FEMALE
            ADD 1 TO SINGLE-FEMALE-COUNTER
        ELSE
            IF MARRIED-FEMALE
                ADD 1 TO MARRIED-FEMALE-COUNTER
            ELSE
                ADD 1 TO UNUSUAL-PERSON-COUNTER.
```

We can understand why such a logic structure has been termed a *CASE;* it simply asks, "Which case are we dealing with: single male, married male, single female, married female, or some other kind of person?" Only one of these cases is presumed to be true, and the nested IF statement simply is trying to find out which one.

You can see that such a structure can be extended indefinitely without becoming too hard to read; that is, you should be able to write a CASE structure with 198 different cases, and someone else should be able to read it easily. However, if we continue to indent each CASE by four spaces on our coding sheet, we obviously shall run out of room after eight or ten levels. Moreover, since the logic is not of the "level-within-level-within-level" type but rather of the "which-one-of-the-following-N-cases" type, there is no need to indent each successive statement on the coding sheet. The previous statement is just as readable if written:

```
IF      SINGLE-MALE
        ADD 1 TO SINGLE-MALE-COUNTER
ELSE IF MARRIED-MALE
        ADD 1 TO MARRIED-MALE-COUNTER
ELSE IF SINGLE-FEMALE
        ADD 1 TO SINGLE-FEMALE-COUNTER
ELSE IF MARRIED-FEMALE
        ADD 1 TO MARRIED-FEMALE-COUNTER
ELSE
        ADD 1 TO UNUSUAL-PERSON-COUNTER.
```

This CASE structure is shown in a structured flowchart like this:

SINGLE-MALE	MARRIED-MALE	SINGLE-FEMALE	MARRIED-FEMALE	DEFAULT
ADD 1 TO SINGLE-MALE-COUNTER	ADD 1 TO MARRIED-MALE-COUNTER	ADD 1 TO SINGLE-FEMALE-COUNTER	ADD 1 TO MARRIED-FEMALE-COUNTER	ADD 1 TO UNUSUAL-PERSON-COUNTER

The default case is handled by the trailing ELSE; it is obeyed if all the earlier tests fail.

> Q. Write a case structure that tests a two-digit card code and writes the corresponding part-name as a literal in a field called PART-NAME, PIC X(15) according to the following table:

Code	Part-Name
06	12 IN. RULER
07	24 IN. RULER
19	PENCILS, GROSS
21	PENS, BALL-POINT
27	TEMPLATE

> A.
> ```
> IF        CODE = 06
>     MOVE '12 IN. RULER' TO PART-NAME
> ELSE IF  CODE = 07
>     MOVE '24 IN. RULER' TO PART-NAME
> ELSE IF  CODE = 19
>     MOVE 'PENCILS, GROSS' TO PART-NAME
> etc.
> ```

6.2.3 Simplifying nested IFs

The complexity of nested IFs increases mainly when the problem demands levels of IFs within IFs; that is, by COBOL statements of the form

> IF a
>   IF b
>   IF c
> and so forth.

The reason why this is complicated is that the person who reads your program has to keep several things in his head simultaneously; in the example above, he has to think about all possible combinations of a, b, and c at the same time. Naturally, *you* also have to worry about all combinations of a, b, and c when you write the code, which is equally difficult.

How can you circumvent this complexity? The first answer, of course, is not to work on such complex problems! Another, more serious, solution is to express some or all of such logic with the complex tests discussed in Section 6.1.5. That is, instead of writing three levels of nested IFs as we did above, we may well be able to write

IF a AND b AND c

A dead giveaway in situations of this sort is the sequence of code

```
IF X
    IF Y
        IF Z
            MOVE A TO B
        ELSE NEXT SENTENCE
    ELSE NEXT SENTENCE
ELSE NEXT SENTENCE.
```

This should certainly be rewritten in the form

```
IF X AND Y AND Z
    MOVE A TO B.
```

Still another way of simplifying deeply nested IF structures is to break the job into smaller pieces, each one of which can be written and comprehended separately. Earlier in this section, we paraphrased our nested IF example by writing

```
IF MALE
        male-logic
ELSE
        female-logic
```

There is a formal way of doing this in COBOL; utilizing the PERFORM statement, we would write

```
IF MALE
        PERFORM MALE-LOGIC
ELSE
        PERFORM FEMALE-LOGIC.
```

In some other part of our program, we would have the paragraph of logic named MALE-LOGIC that would carry out the familiar processing shown at the top of the next page:

```
MALE-LOGIC.
        IF MARRIED
                ADD 1 TO MARRIED-MEN
        ELSE
                ADD 1 TO SINGLE-MEN.
```

This makes use of the concept of *subroutines* in which a large complex structure can be tackled by breaking it into smaller bite-sized chunks.

As we mentioned in the section on complex logic tests, as soon as a nested IF becomes too complicated to handle comfortably, you should analyze the problem with a decision table, as described in the next section.

6.3 Decision tables

A decision table is an extension of the truth table we saw earlier, and is valuable for analyzing problems. Suppose you must write a program to deal with the following problem:

> If a customer has placed an order that exceeds his credit limit, the order should be sent to the credit department. However, the order always should be accepted if it comes from one of our special customers, i.e., one who does business with us regularly and whose credit has been assured. Also, if the order is less than the minimum shipping quantity, the order should be rejected and sent to the shipping manager. However, the computer system should be capable of receiving "exceptions" to these rules, as there will be cases when a customer will insist that his order be shipped, even though it is too small.

There are four *conditions,* or *variables,* in this problem:

- the dollar order amount exceeds the credit limit

- the customer has special approval from the credit department

- the size of the order is less than the minimum allowed for shipping

- the shipping department has given special approval for shipment.

There are three possible *actions* that the program might be required to take:

- the order can be rejected and sent to the credit department

- the order can be rejected and sent to the shipping department

- the order can be processed normally.

We want to show the somewhat complicated relationship between conditions and actions as clearly as possible, and the best way of doing it is with a decision table, as shown on the next page.

The conditions, or variables, forming the top rows of the decision table often are referred to as *condition stubs;* we shall call them simply conditions. In our example are four conditions.

Similarly, our example contains three actions, often called *action stubs.* Note that the action stubs form the lower rows of the decision table, and that they represent computations to be performed, or in a general sense, procedures to be executed.

The most important part of the decision table is the *rule,* which is a specification that certain combinations of conditions should cause certain actions to be performed. Indeed, this is just what the narrative description of our order-entry problem contains; but the rules in the narrative description are generally less precisely stated, more error-prone, and more subject to misinterpretation. The rules form the columns of the diagram; note that they are numbered at the top simply as a convenient way of referring to them. The rules can be in a variety of orders, depending upon the alternation of sequence of true and false for the conditions.

This rule shows what to do with one particular combination of conditions: If it is *true* that the dollar amount of the order exceeds the credit limit
and the customer *does not* have special approval,
and the size of the order is *not* less than minimum,
and the customer *does not* have special approval from the shipping department,
then reject the order and send it to the credit department.

	Conditions and actions	1	2	3	4	5	6	7	8	9	10	11	12	13	14	15	16
four condi-tions	Dollar amount of order exceeds credit limit	F	F	F	F	F	F	F	F	T	T	T	T	T	T	T	T
	Cust. has sp. approval from credit dept.	F	F	F	F	T	T	T	T	F	F	F	F	T	T	T	T
	Size of order is less than minimum	F	F	T	T	F	F	T	T	F	F	T	T	F	F	T	T
	Cust. has sp. approval from shipping dept.	F	T	F	T	F	T	F	T	F	T	F	T	F	T	F	T
three actions	REJECT ORDER, SEND TO CREDIT DEPT.									X	X	X	X				
	REJECT ORDER, SEND TO SHIPPING DEPT.			X				X				X				X	
	PROCESS ORDER AND SHIP IT NORMALLY	X	X		X	X	X		X					X	X		X

Note that this rule calls for two rejections: we will assume that only action 1 is necessary.

As you will see from the example, the way to be sure you have covered all possible combinations of conditions is

- start with the last condition (in this case, "Customer has special approval from the Shipping Department"), and alternate F T F T (or T F T F)

- for the next-to-last condition, alternate F F T T (or T T F F)

- as you work up, alternate F and T in groups that, in each case, are twice as large as for the condition immediately below them.

Q. How do you know how many combinations of conditions (rules) for which to allow?

A. In this type of decision table (called *exhaustive* because it exhaustively covers all possible combinations), there will be 2^C rules, where C is the number of conditions.

Q. Redraw the decision table, with the conditions and actions in the same order, but alternating T F instead of F T.

A. Your decision table should look like this:

Conditions and actions	16	15	14	13	12	11	10	9	8	7	6	5	4	3	2	1
Dollar amount of order exceeds credit limit	T	T	T	T	T	T	T	T	F	F	F	F	F	F	F	F
Cust. has sp. approval from credit dept.	T	T	T	T	F	F	F	F	T	T	T	T	F	F	F	F
Size of order is less than minimum	T	T	F	F	T	T	F	F	T	T	F	F	T	T	F	F
Cust. has sp. approval from shipping dept.	T	F	T	F	T	F	T	F								
REJECT ORDER, SEND TO CREDIT DEPT.					X	X	X	X								
REJECT ORDER, SEND TO SHIPPING DEPT.		X								X				X		
PROCESS ORDER AND SHIP IT NORMALLY	X		X	X					X		X	X	X		X	X

(Rules)

Note that we have kept the original numbering of the rules.

This decision table deals with conditions that are either true or false; it is called a *limited-entry* decision table. You sometimes may meet *extended-entry* decision tables, in which the conditions can have three, four, or more values and are, consequently, more awkward to use.

We already have said that ours is an *exhaustive* decision table; a *selective* decision table contains only those rules that you can find in the original specification of the problem. Imagine a programmer trying to develop a decision table from the simple order-entry problem described earlier. He might notice that there are only three unique situations mentioned in the narrative specification; if the customer has exceeded his limit and is *not* a special customer, then his order should be rejected; if the customer has placed an order too small for shipment and does not have special approval from the shipping department, then his order should be rejected; otherwise, his order should be filled. This situation may be represented by the selective decision table below, which has only three rules:

Dollar amount of order exceeds credit limit	T	–	
Cust. has special **approval** from credit dept.	F	–	E
Size of order is less than minimum	–	T	L S
Cust. has special approval from shipping dept.	–	F	E
REJECT ORDER, SEND TO CREDIT DEPT.	X		
REJECT ORDER, SEND TO SHIPPING DEPT.		X	
PROCESS ORDER AND SHIP NORMALLY			X

Note that there are two items in this new decision table that did not appear in the original exhaustive table: the "-" entry for some of the rules and the "else" rule.

The "dash" (-) entry represents a "don't care" situation; that is, we don't care if the specified condition is true or false because the action is the same in either case.

The "else" rule has an effect similar to the ELSE in COBOL. In the case of the decision table above, we see that if rule 1 is satisfied, we will perform action 1; if rule 2 is satisfied, we will perform action 2; *otherwise, the "else" rule will take effect, and we will perform action 3*. Note that, in this case, using the "else" saves us several rules.

Q. How many rules in the exhaustive decision table are replaced by the else rule in the selective table?

A. Nine: rules 1, 2, 4, 5, 6, 8, 13, 14, and 16.

The primary difference between the exhaustive decision table and the selective decision table is one of emphasis and orientation. In the case of the exhaustive table, we *first* write down all 2^C combinations of conditions, and *then* go back to the narrative specification of the problem to determine which action should accompany each combination of conditions (note that we did not use the word rule in this sentence; we don't have a rule until *after* we have associated an action with a set of conditions). In the case of the selective table, we *first* look at the narrative description of the problem, and *then* try to write down rules that are, in effect, a more precise restatement of the problem.

This difference of orientation often is overlooked because of more practical aspects of the selective or exhaustive approach. If we have only a small number of conditions — perhaps 2, 3, or 4 — then it is quite easy to write down all 2^C possible combinations, using the easy *binary counting sequence* of T F T F. In any case, by forcing ourselves to write down *all* possible rules, we know that we haven't overlooked any, and this can be a major consideration.

On the other hand, the exhaustive approach also can be exhaust*ing!* For example, it is quite common to find an order-entry policy with ten conditions. Much as we might like to, it clearly would be impractical to write down all 2^{10} (1,024) possible combinations. Hence, we may be forced to choose the selective approach in this case.

6.3.1 Applying decision tables and nested IFs to a problem

The Marketing Manager and Comptroller of the company you work for have decided that they will open credit accounts for the people who have applied, with a credit limit based on the following policy:

A person's credit ceiling is set at a certain multiple of his or her monthly discretionary income, computed as follows:

For married home-owners who have been two years or more at present job	5 times
For married persons who either are home-owners or who have been two years or more at present job	4 times
For unmarried home-owners who have been two years or more at present job	3 times
For married persons who rent homes and for unmarried home-owners with less than two years at present job	2 times
For single, widowed, or divorced persons who rent	amount equal to their discretionary income.

Notwithstanding the above, no one will receive a credit limit of more than $2,500.

You are required to produce a program called CREDCALC, which is an upgrade of SAMPLE-4. As well as calculating monthly discretionary income, CREDCALC will calculate the credit limit for each person according to the above policy, and print out the credit limit on the third line of each profile. As a first step to this, let us produce a decision table covering the credit limit policy outlined above.

Q. How many conditions are there? How many actions are there?

A. Three conditions: Married — yes or no;
Owner — yes or no;
Two or more years
in present job — yes or no.

Five actions: These correspond to multiples of discretionary income from 1 to 5.

Note that the upper limit of $2,500 should not be considered as part of the decision table, but should be applied once the credit limit is calculated as a multiple of income.

Since there are three conditions, there will be eight rules for an exhaustive table. With this information, we develop an exhaustive limited-entry decision table to represent the credit policy:

		1	2	3	4	5	6	7	8
Married?		Y	Y	Y	Y	N	N	N	N
Home-owner?		Y	Y	N	N	Y	Y	N	N
2 or more years in job?		Y	N	Y	N	Y	N	Y	N
Credit limit is this multiple of discr. income	1 times							X	X
	2 times				X		X		
	3 times					X			
	4 times		X	X					
	5 times	X							

Can we simplify this decision table? Yes, a little. Consider rules 7 and 8: They both lead to the same action and have the same combination of Y and N except for one condition. This means that we can put in a - (meaning don't care) for this condition, and reduce the two rules to one rule:

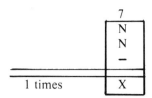

This is in accordance with the original policy; if the person is *not* married, and *not* an owner, he/she gets a credit limit of one multiple, no matter how long he/she has been at a job.

> Q. Using the 88 levels MARRIED, OWNED, and STABLE-JOB as the conditions, and MOVE 1 TO CREDIT-FACTOR, and so on, as the actions, code the decision table as a nested IF.

> A.
> ```
> IF MARRIED
>     IF OWNED
>         IF STABLE-JOB
>             MOVE 5 TO CREDIT-FACTOR
>         ELSE
>             MOVE 4 TO CREDIT-FACTOR
>     ELSE
>         IF STABLE-JOB
>             MOVE 4 TO CREDIT-FACTOR
>         ELSE
>             MOVE 2 TO CREDIT-FACTOR
> ELSE
>     IF OWNED
>         IF STABLE-JOB
>             MOVE 3 TO CREDIT-FACTOR
>         ELSE
>             MOVE 2 TO CREDIT-FACTOR
>     ELSE
>         MOVE 1 TO CREDIT-FACTOR.
> ```

Whenever you code a nested IF as complex as the above, it is good practice to include the decision table as a series of comment lines.

Now that we have the decision table and the essential logic, we can proceed to implement CREDCALC. Here is the full functional specification:

Main function. CREDCALC is to read in the same pairs of cards as SAMPLE-4 and to print a similar report, with the exception that under DISCRETIONARY IN-COME will be printed CREDIT LIMIT IS $nnnn, where nnnn is the amount determined by company policy as already stated.

Heading. The first page of this report is to be headed

APPLICANT CREDIT LIMIT REPORT

Editing. CREDCALC should check the input cards for missing name, missing address, missing phone, and unmatched account numbers. CREDCALC also must check to be sure that the second card of each pair has a 'C' in cc 1. If any of these errors is found, both cards should be rejected and their contents written out, one card to a line, with a suitable error message. Similarly, if a pair of cards passes these editing tests, but the discretionary income turns out to be negative, both cards should be rejected.

Summary report. After all the cards have been read, you should calculate the average credit limit granted to each accepted applicant, and print out a one-line summary, with a border of asterisks, stating total credit granted, average credit granted per accepted applicant, number of applications accepted, and number of applications rejected.

Figure 6.1 on the next page shows a sample of the report required; four pairs of cards, each containing some error, follow seven valid applications.

From this functional specification, draw a program graph, showing the main flow of data and the main transformations. Don't show errors on the program graph. Then develop a struc-ture chart, breaking down the major functions into single in-dependent ones, and indicating which modules will need to per-form error-handling modules. Compare your charts with the samples in Fig. 6.2.

From the structure chart, you can see that the key module is A2-PRINT-CREDIT-PROFILES. The highest-level *executive* module will PERFORM this until all the cards have been read, when it will go on to PERFORM A3-PRINT-SUMMARY.

```
                                      APPLICANT CREDIT LIMIT REPORT

VICTOR S GRASPER      PHONE (415) 243-7022  MALE          INCOME         $15700 PER YEAR: IN THIS EMPLOY 04 YEARS
990 GAUNTLET AVE                            SINGLE        MORTGAGE:        $250 PER MTH   DISCRETIONARY INCOME $691 PER MTH
BURLINGAME   CA 94010 A/C: 010101           0 DEPENDENTS  OTHER PAYMENTS $040 PER MTH   CREDIT LIMIT IS $2073

IAN S INKERMAN        PHONE (201) 103-6061  MALE          INCOME         $17500 PER YEAR: IN THIS EMPLOY LESS THAN 1 YEAR
59 PECAN VALLEY RD                          DIVORCED      RENTAL:          $325 PER MTH   DISCRETIONARY INCOME $659 PER MTH
MONTVALE     NJ 07645 A/C: 020202           1 DEPENDENTS  OTHER PAYMENTS $110 PER MTH   CREDIT LIMIT IS $0659

SARALEE JAMES         PHONE (816) 542-0535  FEMALE        INCOME         $21000 PER YEAR: IN THIS EMPLOY 03 YEARS
PARTHENON COURT                             DIVORCED      MORTGAGE:        $275 PER MTH   DISCRETIONARY INCOME $963 PER MTH
ATHENS       MO 64065 A/C: 050505           1 DEPENDENTS  OTHER PAYMENTS $ 75 PER MTH   CREDIT LIMIT IS $2500

SCARLETT O'HARA       PHONE (504) 815-1147  FEMALE        INCOME         $09500 PER YEAR: IN THIS EMPLOY 26 YEARS
SUITE 414 NAT BANK                          WIDOWED       RENTAL:          $110 PER MTH   DISCRETIONARY INCOME $464 PER MTH
NEW ORLEANS  LA 70012 A/C: 060606           2 DEPENDENTS  OTHER PAYMENTS $ 20 PER MTH   CREDIT LIMIT IS $0464

SUSAN KRUPMAN         PHONE (212) 354-0330  FEMALE        INCOME         $12900 PER YEAR: IN THIS EMPLOY 01 YEARS
131 WEST 32ND ST                            SINGLE        RENTAL:          $150 PER MTH   DISCRETIONARY INCOME $626 PER MTH
NEW YORK     NY 10001 A/C: 040404           0 DEPENDENTS  OTHER PAYMENTS $ 30 PER MTH   CREDIT LIMIT IS $0626

I. MORRIS GOOD        PHONE (214) 225-7013  MALE          INCOME         $27300 PER YEAR: IN THIS EMPLOY 11 YEARS
1313 PORPOISE                               MARRIED       MORTGAGE:        $400 PER MTH   DISCRETIONARY INCOME $999 PER MTH
DALLAS       TX 75219 A/C: 030303           4 DEPENDENTS  OTHER PAYMENTS $150 PER MTH   CREDIT LIMIT IS $2500

FRANCES PAISANO       PHONE (201) 614-7525  FEMALE        INCOME         $96000 PER YEAR: IN THIS EMPLOY LESS THAN 1 YEAR
2521 EDGE STREET                            SINGLE        MORTGAGE:        $100 PER MTH   DISCRETIONARY INCOME $999 PER MTH
FORT LEE     NJ 07024 A/C: 070707           0 DEPENDENTS  OTHER PAYMENTS $050 PER MTH   CREDIT LIMIT IS $1999

FIRST CARD  GOOD  STARLET Q. FREEBODY 12277 SUNSET BLVD   LOS ANGELES  CA90024213574-2179   080808
SECOND CARD GOOD  C080807 F S 0 060 00 R 350 100                                                  ACCOUNT NUMBERS DO NOT MATCH

FIRST CARD  BAD   DR P.QUACKENBUSH    **** ADDRESS MISSING ****                 602852-4822   090909
SECOND CARD GOOD  C090909 M M 8 120 10 0 320 135

FIRST CARD  GOOD  C. ENCHAINE          212 SLEEPY HOLLOW DRGREENWICH   CT06830203886-7431   101010
SECONC CARD BAD   X101010 F S 1 130 08 R 240 050

FIRST CARD        B. HUGH THOMPSON    1111 SUTTER          SAN FRANCISCOCA94103413263-4857   111111
SECOND CARD       M S 0 065 00 R 360 110                                                          OUTGO EXCEEDS INCOME: REJECT


**************************************************************************************************************
*                                                                                                            *
*  TOTAL CREDIT GIVEN: $0010920   AVERAGE CREDIT GIVEN: $001546 ON 0007 ACCEPTED APPLICATIONS.   NUMBER REJECTED 004 *
*                                                                                                            *
**************************************************************************************************************
```

Figure 6.1. Applicant credit limit report.

The pseudocode for A2-PRINT-CREDIT-PROFILES is

```
Get a pair of cards.
IF pair of cards passes the edit tests
      calculate discretionary income
      IF discretionary income is positive
            calculate credit limit
            assemble print lines
            write normal credit profile
      ELSE
            write the cards as an error profile with
                  message OUTGO EXCEEDS INCOME
ELSE
      write the cards as an error profile with
                  message indicating error.
```

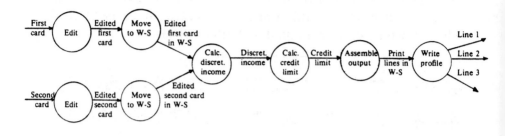

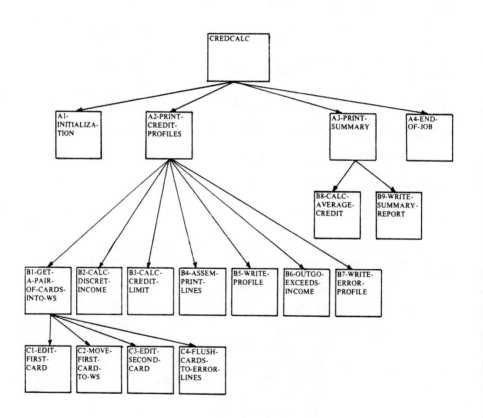

Figure 6.2. Sample program graph and structure chart.

Once again, assume you have available to you in the SSL all of the data structures and procedures used in SAMPLE-4, with the addition of

DISCR-INCOME-CALC-FIELDS   (called DISIFLDS) and

CALC-DISCRETNRY-INCOME   (called DISCINCM)

You will need to set up Data Division entries for the fields used in calculating credit limit. It is good practice to set up data-names FACTOR1, FACTOR2, and so forth, for the various values of CREDIT-FACTOR, and for UPPER-LIMIT ($2,500), and to set these fields to the specified amounts with VALUE clauses.

Q.   What is the value of using data-names in this way? Why not code literals in the program?

A.   It is a safeguard in case of change; if the policy were to change, say, to allow an upper limit of $3,000, you would only have to change the value once in Working-Storage, and you would be sure the correct value would be used wherever you had referred to it.

You also will need to set up formats for the initial heading, for the error-lines, and for the summary report lines.

After you have done this, you will be ready to write the pseudocode for the whole of CREDCALC from the structure chart and from the suggestions already given. Get a colleague to walk through your pseudocode with you, to see if he can spot any errors in logic, before you code the Data Division and the Procedure Division.

The model solution to CREDCALC given on the following pages is a listing of the cards as you would punch them (called an "80:80" listing because the 80 columns on the card are shown in the first 80 print positions).

Following that is a complete listing of the program with the COPY statements expanded by the compiler.

```
IDENTIFICATION DIVISION.
PROGRAM-ID.  CREDCALC.

ENVIRONMENT DIVISION.
INPUT-OUTPUT SECTION.
FILE-CONTROL.  COPY FILECONT.

DATA DIVISION.
FILE SECTION.

FD    APPLICATION-CARDS-FILE   COPY FDCARDS.

FD    PROFILE-LISTING
          LABEL RECORDS ARE OMITTED.
01    PRINT-LINE-OUT                      PIC X(132).
WORKING-STORAGE SECTION.

01    COMMON-WS.
      05  CARDS-LEFT                      PIC X(3).
      05  FIRST-CARD                      PIC X(4).
      05  SECOND-CARD                     PIC X(4).
      05  ACCT-NUM-MATCH                  PIC X(4).
      05  PAIR-VALIDITY                   PIC X(4).
      05  APPLICATIONS-ACCEPTED-ACCUM     PIC 9(4).
      05  APPLICATIONS-REJECTED-ACCUM     PIC 9(4).

01    HEADER-WS1.
      05  FILLER                          PIC X(52)    VALUE SPACES.
      05  TITLE                           PIC X(29)
                          VALUE 'APPLICANT CREDIT LIMIT REPORT'.
      05  FILLER                          PIC X(52)    VALUE SPACES.

01    APPLICATION-DATA-WSB1 COPY CARDSWS.

01    DISCR-INCOME-CALC-FIELDS-WSB2  COPY DISIFLDS.

01    CRED-LIMIT-CALC-FIELDS-WSB3.
      05  CREDIT-FACTOR                   PIC 9.
      05  FACTOR1                         PIC 9        VALUE 1.
      05  FACTOR2                         PIC 9        VALUE 2.
      05  FACTOR3                         PIC 9        VALUE 3.
      05  FACTOR4                         PIC 9        VALUE 4.
      05  FACTOR5                         PIC 9        VALUE 5.
      05  CREDIT-LIMIT-WS                 PIC 9(4).
      05  UPPER-LIMIT-WS                  PIC 9(4)     VALUE 2500.
      05  TOTAL-CREDIT-GIVEN-WS           PIC 9(7).

01    LINE-1-WSB4 COPY LINE1WS.

01    LINE-2-WSB4 COPY LINE2WS.
      05  FILLER                          PIC X(11)
                          VALUE ' PER MTH   '.
      05  FILLER                          PIC X(22)
                          VALUE 'DISCRETIONARY INCOME  $'.
      05  DISCR-INCOME-L2                 PIC 9(3).
      05  FILLER                          PIC X(9)
                          VALUE '  PER MTH  '.
```

```
01  LINE-3-WSB4 COPY LINE3WS.
    05  FILLER                          PIC X(8)     VALUE ' PER MTH'.
    05  FILLER                          PIC X(20)
        VALUE ' CREDIT LIMIT IS $'.
    05  CREDIT-LIMIT-L3                 PIC 9(4).

01  LINE-OF-ASTERISKS-WSB9.
    05  FILLER                          PIC X(6)     VALUE '     *'.
    05  FILLER                          PIC X(120)
        VALUE '***********************************************************
    ***********************************************************************
    **********'.
    05  FILLER                          PIC X(6)     VALUE '*     '.

01  SIDE-DELIMITER-WSB9.
    05  FILLER                          PIC X(6)     VALUE '     *'.
    05  FILLER                          PIC X(120)   VALUE SPACES.
    05  FILLER                          PIC X(6)     VALUE '*     '.

01  SUMMARY-LINE-WSB9.
    05  FILLER                          PIC X(6)     VALUE '     *'.
    05  FILLER                          PIC X(24)
        VALUE ' TOTAL CREDIT GIVEN: $'.
    05  TOTAL-CREDIT-GIVEN              PIC 9(7).
    05  FILLER                          PIC X(27)
        VALUE '  AVERAGE CREDIT GIVEN: $'.
    05  AVERAGE CREDIT                  PIC 9(6).
    05  FILLER                          PIC X(4)     VALUE ' ON '.
    05  APPLICATIONS-ACCEPTED           PIC 9(4).
    05  FILLER                          PIC X(24)
        VALUE ' ACCEPTED APPLICATIONS. '.
    05  FILLER                          PIC X(20)
        VALUE '   NUMBER REJECTED '.
    05  APPLICATIONS-REJECTED           PIC 9(3).
    05  FILLER                          PIC X(10)
        VALUE ' *       '.

01  CARD-ERROR-LINE1-WSC4.
    05  FILLER                          PIC X(5)     VALUE SPACES.
    05  FILLER                          PIC X(12)
        VALUE 'FIRST CARD  '.
    05  FIRST-CARD-ERR1                 PIC X(4).
    05  FILLER                          PIC XX       VALUE SPACES.
    05  NAME-ERR1                       PIC X(20).
    05  ADDRESS-ERR1                    PIC X(40).
    05  PHONE-ERR1                      PIC X(11).
    05  FILLER                          PIC X(3)     VALUE SPACES.
    05  ACCT-NUM-ERR1                   PIC 9(6).

01  CARD-ERROR-LINE2-WSC4.
    05  FILLER                          PIC X(5)     VALUE SPACES.
    05  FILLER                          PIC X(12)
        VALUE 'SECOND CARD '.
    05  SECOND-CARD-ERR2                PIC X(4).
    05  FILLER                          PIC X(2)     VALUE SPACES.
    05  CREDIT-INFO-ERR2                PIC X(80).
    05  MESSAGE-ERR-LINE-2              PIC X(29)    VALUE SPACES.
```

```
PROCEDURE DIVISION.
    PERFORM A1-INITIALIZATION.
    PERFORM A2-PRINT-CREDIT-PROFILES
        UNTIL CARDS-LEFT = 'NO '.
    PERFORM A3-PRINT-SUMMARY.
    PERFORM A4-END-OF-JOB.
    STOP RUN.
A1-INITIALIZATION.
    OPEN   INPUT APPLICATION-CARDS-FILE
           OUTPUT PROFILE-LISTING.
    WRITE PRINT-LINE-OUT FROM HEADER-WS1
                    AFTER ADVANCING 2 LINES.
    MOVE ZEROS TO APPLICATIONS-ACCEPTED-ACCUM.
    MOVE ZEROS TO APPLICATIONS-REJECTED-ACCUM.
    MOVE ZEROS TO ANNUAL-INCOME-WS.
    MOVE ZEROS TO ANNUAL-TAX-WS.
    MOVE ZEROS TO MONTHLY-NET-INCOME-WS.
    MOVE ZEROS TO MONTHLY-PAYMENTS-WS.
    MOVE ZEROS TO DISCR-INCOME-WS.
    MOVE ZEROS TO CREDIT-FACTOR.
    MOVE ZEROS TO CREDIT-LIMIT-WS.
    MOVE ZEROS TO TOTAL-CREDIT-GIVEN-WS.
    MOVE ZEROS TO TOTAL-CREDIT-GIVEN.
    MOVE ZEROS TO AVERAGE-CREDIT.
    MOVE ZEROS TO APPLICATIONS-ACCEPTED.
    MOVE ZEROS TO APPLICATIONS-REJECTED.
    MOVE SPACES TO FIRST-CARD.
    MOVE SPACES TO SECOND-CARD.
    MOVE SPACES TO ACCT-NUM-MATCH.
    MOVE SPACES TO PAIR-VALIDITY.
    MOVE 'YES' TO CARDS-LEFT.
    READ APPLICATION-CARDS-FILE
        AT END MOVE 'NO ' TO CARDS-LEFT.
* FIRST CARD IS NOW IN BUFFER

A2-PRINT-CREDIT-PROFILES.
    PERFORM B1-GET-A-PAIR-OF-CARDS.
    IF PAIR-VALIDITY = 'GOOD'
            PERFORM B2-CALC-DISCRETNRY-INCOME
            IF DISCR-INCOME-WS IS POSITIVE
                PERFORM B3-CALC-CREDIT-LIMIT
                PERFORM B4-ASSEMBLE-PRINT-LINES
                PERFORM B5-WRITE-PROFILE
            ELSE
                PERFORM B6-OUTGO-EXCEEDS-INCOME
    ELSE
            PERFORM B7-WRITE-ERROR-PROFILE.

A3-PRINT-SUMMARY.
    PERFORM B8-CALC-AVERAGE-CREDIT.
    PERFORM B9-WRITE-SUMMARY-REPORT.

A4-END-OF-JOB.
    CLOSE APPLICATION-CARDS-FILE
            PROFILE-LISTING.
```

```
  B1-GET-A-PAIR-OF-CARDS.
      PERFORM C1-EDIT-FIRST-CARD.
      PERFORM C2-MOVE-FIRST-CARD-TO-WS.
      READ APPLICATION-CARDS-FILE
          AT END MOVE 'NO ' TO CARDS-LEFT.
* SECOND CARD OF PAIR IS NOW IN BUFFER
      PERFORM C3-EDIT-SECOND-CARD.
      IF        (FIRST-CARD = 'GOOD')
          AND   (SECOND-CARD = 'GOOD')
          AND   (ACCT-NUM-MATCH = 'GOOD')
                MOVE 'GOOD' TO PAIR-VALIDITY
                MOVE CREDIT-INFO-IN TO CREDIT-INFO-WS
      ELSE
              MOVE 'BAD ' TO PAIR-VALIDITY
              PERFORM C4-FLUSH-CARDS-TO-ERROR-LINES.
      READ APPLICATION-CARDS-FILE
          AT END MOVE 'NO ' TO CARDS-LEFT.
* FIRST CARD OF NEXT PAIR IS NOW IN BUFFER

  B2-CALC-DISCRETNRY-INCOME.  COPY DISCINCM.

  B3-CALC-CREDIT-LIMIT.
*     MARRIED?              Y Y Y Y N N N N    THIS DECISION TABLE      *
*     OWNED?                Y Y N N Y Y N N    SETS OUT COMPANY POLICY *
*     2 OR MORE YEARS?      Y N Y N Y N Y N    FOR DETERMINING CREDIT  *
*     ---------------------------------------  LIMIT FROM DISCRETIONARY*
*     CREDIT FACTOR 1                   X X    INCOME. FACTOR1 ETC ARE *
*     LIMIT IS      2           X   X          SET UP IN WSB3.         *
*     MULTIPLE      3             X             *
*     OF DISCR      4       X X                 *
*     INCOME.       5     X                     *
      IF MARRIED
          IF OWNED
              IF YEARS-EMPLOYED-WS NOT LESS THAN 02
                  MOVE FACTOR5 TO CREDIT-FACTOR
              ELSE
                  MOVE FACTOR4 TO CREDIT-FACTOR
          ELSE
              IF YEARS-EMPLOYED-WS NOT LESS THAN 02
                  MOVE FACTOR4 TO CREDIT-FACTOR
              ELSE
                  MOVE FACTOR2 TO CREDIT-FACTOR
      ELSE
          IF OWNED
              IF YEARS-EMPLOYED-WS NOT LESS THAN 02
                  MOVE FACTOR3 TO CREDIT-FACTOR
              ELSE
                  MOVE FACTOR2 TO CREDIT-FACTOR
          ELSE
              MOVE FACTOR1 TO CREDIT-FACTOR.
      COMPUTE CREDIT-LIMIT-WS = DISCR-INCOME-WS * CREDIT-FACTOR.
      IF CREDIT-LIMIT-WS IS GREATER THAN UPPER-LIMIT-WS
          MOVE UPPER-LIMIT-WS TO CREDIT-LIMIT-WS.
      ADD CREDIT-LIMIT-WS TO TOTAL-CREDIT-GIVEN-WS.
```

```
B4-ASSEMBLE-PRINT-LINES.
    MOVE NAME-WS TO NAME-L1.
    MOVE STREET-WS TO STREET-L2.
    MOVE CITY-WS TO CITY-L3.
    MOVE STATE-WS TO STATE-L3.
    MOVE ZIP-WS TO ZIP-L3.
    MOVE AREA-CODE-WS TO AREA-CODE-L1.
    MOVE NUMBR-WS TO NUMBR-L1.
    MOVE ACCT-NUM-WS TO ACCT-NUM-L3.
    IF        MALE      MOVE 'MALE     ' TO SEX-L1
    ELSE IF   FEMALE    MOVE 'FEMALE' TO SEX-L1
    ELSE                MOVE '* * * * * *' TO SEX-L1.
    IF        SINGLE    MOVE 'SINGLE     ' TO MARITAL-STATUS-L2
    ELSE IF   MARRIED   MOVE 'MARRIED ' TO MARITAL-STATUS-L2
    ELSE IF   DIVORCED  MOVE 'DIVORCED' TO MARITAL-STATUS-L2
    ELSE IF   WIDOWED   MOVE 'WIDOWED ' TO MARITAL-STATUS-L2
    ELSE                MOVE ' * * * * * * *' TO MARITAL-STATUS-L2.
    MOVE NUMBER-DEPENS-WS TO NUMBER-DEPENS-L3.
    MOVE INCOME-HUNDREDS-WS TO INCOME-HUNDREDS-L1.
    IF YEARS-EMPLOYED-WS IS EQUAL TO 0
        MOVE 'LESS THAN 1 YEAR' TO YEARS-EMPLOYED-L1
    ELSE
        MOVE YEARS-EMPLOYED-WS TO YEARS-L1
        MOVE ' YEARS     ' TO DESCN-L1.
    IF        OWNED     MOVE 'MORTGAGE:     $' TO OUTGO-DESCN
    ELSE IF   RENTED    MOVE 'RENTAL:       $' TO OUTGO-DESCN
    ELSE                MOVE '*****************  ' TO OUTGO-DESCN.
    MOVE MORTGAGE-OR-RENTAL-WS TO MORTGAGE-OR-RENTAL-L2.
    MOVE OTHER-PAYMENTS-WS TO OTHER-PAYMENTS-L3.
    MOVE DISCR-INCOME-WS TO DISCR-INCOME-L2.
    MOVE CREDIT-LIMIT-WS TO CREDIT-LIMIT-L3.

B5-WRITE-PROFILE.  COPY WRITPRFL
        REPLACING LINE-1-WS BY LINE-1-WSB4
                  LINE-2-WS BY LINE-2-WSB4
                  LINE-3-WS BY LINE-3-WSB4. .
    ADD 1 TO APPLICATIONS-ACCEPTED-ACCUM.

B6-OUTGO-EXCEEDS-INCOME.
    MOVE SPACES TO FIRST-CARD-ERR1.
    MOVE NAME-WS TO NAME-ERR1.
    MOVE ADDRESS-WS TO ADDRESS-ERR1.
    MOVE PHONE-WS TO PHONE-ERR1.
    MOVE ACCT-NUM-WS TO ACCT-NUM-ERR1.
    MOVE SPACES TO SECOND-CARD-ERR2.
    MOVE CREDIT-INFO-WS TO CREDIT-INFO-ERR2.
    MOVE 'OUTGO EXCEEDS INCOME: REJECT' TO MESSAGE-ERR-LINE-2.
    PERFORM B7-WRITE-ERROR-PROFILE.

B7-WRITE-ERROR-PROFILE.
    MOVE SPACES TO PRINT-LINE-OUT.
    WRITE PRINT-LINE-OUT FROM CARD-ERROR-LINE1-WSC4
                    AFTER ADVANCING 4 LINES.
    WRITE PRINT-LINE-OUT FROM CARD-ERROR-LINE2-WSC4
                    AFTER ADVANCING 1 LINES.
    ADD 1 TO APPLICATIONS-REJECTED-ACCUM.
```

B8-CALC-AVERAGE-CREDIT.
    MOVE TOTAL-CREDIT-GIVEN-WS TO TOTAL-CREDIT-GIVEN.
    IF TOTAL-CREDIT-GIVEN = 0
        MOVE ZEROS TO AVERAGE-CREDIT
    ELSE
        DIVIDE APPLICATIONS-ACCEPTED-ACCUM
            INTO TOTAL-CREDIT-GIVEN
            GIVING AVERAGE-CREDIT ROUNDED.
B9-WRITE-SUMMARY-REPORT.
    MOVE APPLICATIONS-ACCEPTED-ACCUM TO APPLICATIONS-ACCEPTED.
    MOVE APPLICATIONS-REJECTED-ACCUM TO APPLICATIONS-REJECTED.
    WRITE PRINT-LINE-OUT FROM LINE-OF-ASTERISKS-WSB9
                      AFTER ADVANCING 6 LINES.
    WRITE PRINT-LINE-OUT FROM SIDE-DELIMITER-WSB9
                      AFTER ADVANCING 1 LINES.
    WRITE PRINT-LINE-OUT FROM SUMMARY-LINE-WSB9
                      AFTER ADVANCING 1 LINES.
    WRITE PRINT-LINE-OUT FROM SIDE-DELIMITER-WSB9
                      AFTER ADVANCING 1 LINES.
    WRITE PRINT-LINE-OUT FROM LINE-OF-ASTERISKS-WSB9
                      AFTER ADVANCING 1 LINES.
C1-EDIT-FIRST-CARD.
    MOVE 'GOOD' TO FIRST-CARD.
    IF NAME-IN IS EQUAL TO SPACES
        MOVE '*** NAME MISSING ***' TO NAME-IN
        MOVE 'BAD ' TO FIRST-CARD.
    IF ADDRESS-IN IS EQUAL TO SPACES
        MOVE '**** ADDRESS MISSING ****' TO ADDRESS-IN
        MOVE 'BAD ' TO FIRST-CARD.
    IF PHONE-IN IS EQUAL TO SPACES
        MOVE 'NO PHONE **' TO PHONE-IN
        MOVE 'BAD ' TO FIRST-CARD.
C2-MOVE-FIRST-CARD-TO-WS.
    MOVE NAME-IN TO NAME-WS.
    MOVE ADDRESS-IN TO ADDRESS-WS.
    MOVE PHONE-IN TO PHONE-WS.
    MOVE ACCT-NUM-IN1 TO ACCT-NUM-WS.
C3-EDIT-SECOND-CARD.
    MOVE 'GOOD' TO SECOND-CARD.
    MOVE 'GOOD' TO ACCT-NUM-MATCH.
    IF CARD-TYPE-IN IS NOT EQUAL TO 'C'
        MOVE 'BAD ' TO SECOND-CARD.
    IF ACCT-NUM-IN2 IS NOT EQUAL TO ACCT-NUM-WS
        MOVE 'BAD' TO ACCT-NUM-MATCH.
C4-FLUSH-CARDS-TO-ERROR-LINES.
    MOVE FIRST-CARD TO FIRST-CARD-ERR1.
    MOVE NAME-WS TO NAME-ERR1.
    MOVE ADDRESS-WS TO ADDRESS-ERR1.
    MOVE PHONE-WS TO PHONE-ERR1.
    MOVE ACCT-NUM-WS TO ACCT-NUM-ERR1.
    MOVE SECOND-CARD TO SECOND-CARD-ERR2.
    MOVE CREDIT-INFO-WS TO CREDIT-INFO-ERR2.
    IF ACCT-NUM-MATCH = 'BAD '
        MOVE 'ACCOUNT NUMBERS DO NOT MATCH'
                      TO MESSAGE-ERR-LINE-2
    ELSE
        MOVE SPACES TO MESSAGE-ERR-LINE-2.

```
CBL LIB
00001           IDENTIFICATION DIVISION.
00002           PROGRAM-ID. CREDCALC.
00003
00004           ENVIRONMENT DIVISION.
00005           INPUT-OUTPUT SECTION.
00006           FILE-CONTROL. COPY FILECONT.
00007 C             SELECT APPLICATION-CARDS-FILE ASSIGN TO SYS031-UR-2540R-S.
00008 C             SELECT PROFILE-LISTING          ASSIGN TO SYS033-UR-1403-S.
00009
00010           DATA DIVISION.
00011           FILE SECTION.
00012
00013           FD   APPLICATION-CARDS-FILE    COPY FDCARDS.
00014 C               LABEL RECORDS ARE OMITTED
00015 C               DATA RECORDS ARE NAME-ADDRESS-AND-PHONE-IN
00016 C                           CREDIT-INFORMATION-IN.
00017 C         01   NAME-ADDRESS-AND-PHONE-IN.
00018 C              05   NAME-IN                   PIC X(20).
00019 C              05   ADDRESS-IN                PIC X(40).
00020 C              05   PHONE-IN                  PIC X(11).
00021 C              05   FILLER                    PIC X(3).
00022 C              05   ACCT-NUM-IN1              PIC 9(6).
00023 C         01   CREDIT-INFORMATION-IN.
00024 C              05   CARD-TYPE-IN              PIC X.
00025 C              05   ACCT-NUM-IN2              PIC 9(6).
00026 C              05   FILLER                    PIC X.
00027 C              05   CREDIT-INFO-IN            PIC X(22).
00028 C              05   FILLER                    PIC X(50).
00029
00030           FD   PROFILE-LISTING
00031                    LABEL RECORDS ARE OMITTED.
00032           01   PRINT-LINE-OUT                 PIC X(132).
00033           WORKING-STORAGE SECTION.
00034
00035           01   COMMON-WS.
00036                05   CARDS-LEFT                PIC X(3).
00037                05   FIRST-CARD                PIC X(4).
00038                05   SECOND-CARD               PIC X(4).
00039                05   ACCT-NUM-MATCH            PIC X(4).
00040                05   PAIR-VALIDITY             PIC X(4).
00041                05   APPLICATIONS-ACCEPTED-ACCUM  PIC 9(4).
00042                05   APPLICATIONS-REJECTED-ACCUM  PIC 9(4).
00043
00044           01   HEADER-WS1.
00045                05   FILLER                    PIC X(52)  VALUE SPACES.
00046                05   TITLE                     PIC X(29)
00047                                     VALUE 'APPLICANT CREDIT LIMIT REPORT'.
00048                05   FILLER                    PIC X(52)  VALUE SPACES.
00049
```

```
00050          01    APPLICATION-DATA-WSB1 COPY CARDSWS.
00051 C        01    APPLICATION-DATA-WSB1.
00052 C               05    NAME-AND-ADDRESS-WS.
00053 C                     10    NAME-WS                        PIC X(20).
00054 C                     10    ADDRESS-WS.
00055 C                           15    STREET-WS                PIC X(20).
00056 C                           15    CITY-WS                  PIC X(13).
00057 C                           15    STATE-WS                 PIC XX.
00058 C                           15    ZIP-WS                   PIC X(5).
00059 C               05    PHONE-WS.
00060 C                     10    AREA-CODE-WS                   PIC 9(3).
00061 C                     10    NUMBR-WS                       PIC X(8).
00062 C               05    FILLER                               PIC X(3).
00063 C               05    ACCT-NUM-WS                          PIC 9(6).
00064 C               05    CREDIT-INFO-WS.
00065 C                     10    SEX-WS                         PIC X.
00066 C                           88    MALE        VALUE 'M'.
00067 C                           88    FEMALE      VALUE 'F'.
00068 C                     10    FILLER                         PIC X.
00069 C                     10    MARITAL-STATUS-WS              PIC X.
00070 C                           88    SINGLE      VALUE 'S'.
00071 C                           88    MARRIED     VALUE 'M'.
00072 C                           88    DIVORCED    VALUE 'D'.
00073 C                           88    WIDOWED     VALUE 'W'.
00074 C                     10    FILLER                         PIC X.
00075 C                     10    NUMBER-DEPENS-WS               PIC 9.
00076 C                     10    FILLER                         PIC X.
00077 C                     10    INCOME-HUNDREDS-WS             PIC 9(3).
00078 C                     10    FILLER                         PIC X.
00079 C                     10    YEARS-EMPLOYED-WS              PIC 99.
00080 C                     10    FILLER                         PIC X.
00081 C                     10    OWN-OR-RENT-WS                 PIC X.
00082 C                           88    OWNED       VALUE 'O'.
00083 C                           88    RENTED      VALUE 'R'.
00084 C                     10    FILLER                         PIC X.
00085 C                     10    MORTGAGE-OR-RENTAL-WS          PIC 9(3).
00086 C                     10    FILLER                         PIC X.
00087 C                     10    OTHER-PAYMENTS-WS              PIC 9(3).
00088
00089          01    DISCR-INCOME-CALC-FIELDS-WSB2    COPY DISIFLDS.
00090 C        01    DISCR-INCOME-CALC-FIELDS-WSB2.
00091 C               05    ANNUAL-INCOME-WS               PIC 9(5).
00092 C               05    ANNUAL-TAX-WS                  PIC 9(5).
00093 C               05    TAX-RATE-WS                    PIC 9V99 VALUE 0.25.
00094 C               05    MONTHS-IN-YEAR                 PIC 99     VALUE 12.
00095 C               05    MONTHLY-NET-INCOME-WS          PIC 9(4).
00096 C               05    MONTHLY-PAYMENTS-WS            PIC 9(4).
00097 C               05    DISCR-INCOME-WS                PIC S9(3).
00098
00099          01    CRED-LIMIT-CALC-FIELDS-WSB3.
00100                 05    CREDIT-FACTOR                  PIC 9.
00101                 05    FACTOR1                        PIC 9      VALUE 1.
00102                 05    FACTOR2                        PIC 9      VALUE 2.
00103                 05    FACTOR3                        PIC 9      VALUE 3.
00104                 05    FACTOR4                        PIC 9      VALUE 4.
00105                 05    FACTOR5                        PIC 9      VALUE 5.
00106                 05    CREDIT-LIMIT-WS                PIC 9(4).
00107                 05    UPPER-LIMIT-WS                 PIC 9(4)   VALUE 2500.
00108                 05    TOTAL-CREDIT-GIVEN-WS          PIC 9(7).
```

```
00109
00110        01    LINE-1-WSB4 COPY LINE1WS.
00111 C      01    LINE-1-WSB4.
00112 C            05    FILLER                         PIC X(5)      VALUE SPACES.
00113 C            05    NAME-L1                        PIC X(20).
00114 C            05    FILLER                         PIC X(11)
00115 C                                         VALUE '    PHONE ('.
00116 C            05    AREA-CODE-L1                   PIC 9(3).
00117 C            05    FILLER                         PIC XX        VALUE ') '.
00118 C            05    NUMBR-L1                       PIC X(8).
00119 C            05    FILLER                         PIC X(3)      VALUE SPACES.
00120 C            05    SEX-L1                         PIC X(6).
00121 C            05    FILLER                         PIC X(9)      VALUE SPACES.
00122 C            05    FILLER                         PIC X(14)
00123 C                                         VALUE 'INCOME       $'.
00124 C            05    INCOME-HUNDREDS-L1             PIC 9(3).
00125 C            05    FILLER                         PIC X(28)
00126 C                                  VALUE '00 PER YEAR;  IN THIS EMPLOY '.
00127 C            05    YEARS-EMPLOYED-L1.
00128 C            10    YEARS-L1                       PIC XX.
00129 C            10    DESCN-L1                       PIC X(16).
00130
00131        01    LINE-2-WSB4 COPY LINE2WS.
00132 C      01    LINE-2-WSB4.
00133 C            05    FILLER                         PIC X(5)      VALUE SPACES.
00134 C            05    STREET-L2                      PIC X(20).
00135 C            05    FILLER                         PIC X(27)     VALUE SPACES.
00136 C            05    MARITAL-STATUS-L2              PIC X(8).
00137 C            05    FILLER                         PIC X(7)      VALUE SPACES.
00138 C            05    OUTGO-DESCN                    PIC X(16).
00139 C            05    MORTGAGE-OR-RENTAL-L2          PIC 9(3).
00140              05    FILLER                         PIC X(11)
00141                                          VALUE ' PER MTH '.
00142              05    FILLER                         PIC X(22)
00143                                          VALUE 'DISCRETIONARY INCOME $'.
00144              05    DISCR-INCOME-L2                PIC 9(3).
00145              05    FILLER                         PIC X(9)
00146                                          VALUE ' PER MTH '.
00147
00148        01    LINE-3-WSB4 COPY LINE3WS.
00149 C      01    LINE-3-WSB4.
00150 C            05    FILLER                         PIC X(5)      VALUE SPACES.
00151 C            05    CITY-L3                        PIC X(13).
00152 C            05    FILLER                         PIC X         VALUE SPACE.
00153 C            05    STATE-L3                       PIC XX.
00154 C            05    FILLER                         PIC X         VALUE SPACE.
00155 C            05    ZIP-L3                         PIC X(5).
00156 C            05    FILLER                         PIC X(7)      VALUE ' A/C: '.
00157 C            05    ACCT-NUM-L3                    PIC 9(6).
00158 C            05    FILLER                         PIC X(12)     VALUE SPACES.
00159 C            05    NUMBER-DEPENS-L3               PIC 9.
00160 C            05    FILLER                         PIC X(14)
00161 C                                         VALUE ' DEPENDENTS '.
00162 C            05    FILLER                         PIC X(16)
00163 C                                         VALUE 'OTHER PAYMENTS $'.
00164 C            05    OTHER-PAYMENTS-L3              PIC 9(3).
00165              05    FILLER                         PIC X(8)      VALUE ' PER MT
00166              05    FILLER                         PIC X(20)
00167                                          VALUE '  CREDIT LIMIT IS $'.
00168              05    CREDIT-LIMIT-L3                PIC 9(4).
00169
```

```
00170          01  LINE-OF-ASTERISKS-WSB9.
00171              05    FILLER                           PIC X(6)      VALUE '   *'.
00172              05    FILLER                           PIC X(120)
00173                    VALUE '*******************************************************
00174        -    ********************************************************************
00175        -    '****************'.
00176              05    FILLER                           PIC X(6)      VALUE '*    '.
00177
00178          01  SIDE-DELIMITER-WSB9.
00179              05    FILLER                           PIC X(6)      VALUE '   *'.
00180              05    FILLER                           PIC X(120)    VALUE SPACES.
00181              05    FILLER                           PIC X(6)      VALUE '*    '.
00182
00183          01  SUMMARY-LINE-WSB9.
00184              05    FILLER                           PIC X(6)      VALUE '   *'.
00185              05    FILLER                           PIC X(24)
00186                         VALUE ' TOTAL CREDIT GIVEN: $'.
00187              05    TOTAL-CREDIT-GIVEN               PIC 9(7).
00188              05    FILLER                           PIC X(27)
00189                         VALUE '  AVERAGE CREDIT GIVEN: $'.
00190              05    AVERAGE-CREDIT                   PIC 9(6).
00191              05    FILLER                           PIC X(4)      VALUE '  ON '.
00192              05    APPLICATIONS-ACCEPTED            PIC 9(4).
00193              05    FILLER                           PIC X(24)
00194                         VALUE ' ACCEPTED APPLICATIONS. '.
00195              05    FILLER                           PIC X(20)
00196                         VALUE ' NUMBER REJECTED '.
00197              05    APPLICATIONS-REJECTED            PIC 9(3).
00198              05    FILLER                           PIC X(10)
00199                         VALUE '  *    '.
00200
00201          01  CARD-ERROR-LINE1-WSC4.
00202              05    FILLER                           PIC X(5)      VALUE SPACES.
00203              05    FILLER                           PIC X(12)
00204                         VALUE 'FIRST CARD '.
00205              05    FIRST-CARD-ERR1                  PIC X(4).
00206              05    FILLER                           PIC XX        VALUE SPACES.
00207              05    NAME-ERR1                        PIC X(20).
00208              05    ADDRESS-ERR1                     PIC X(40).
00209              05    PHONE-ERR1                       PIC X(11).
00210              05    FILLER                           PIC X(3)      VALUE SPACES.
00211              05    ACCT-NUM-ERR1                    PIC 9(6).
00212
00213          01  CARD-ERROR-LINE2-WSC4.
00214              05    FILLER                           PIC X(5)      VALUE SPACES.
00215              05    FILLER                           PIC X(12)
00216                         VALUE 'SECOND CARD '.
00217              05    SECOND-CARD-ERR2                 PIC X(4).
00218              05    FILLER                           PIC X(2)      VALUE SPACES.
00219              05    CREDIT-INFO-ERR2                 PIC X(80).
00220              05    MESSAGE-ERR-LINE-2               PIC X(29)     VALUE SPACES.
```

```
00222          PROCEDURE DIVISION.
00223             PERFORM A1-INITIALIZATION.
00224             PERFORM A2-PRINT-CREDIT-PROFILES
00225                UNTIL CARDS-LEFT = 'NO '.
00226             PERFORM A3-PRINT-SUMMARY.
00227             PERFORM A4-END-OF-JOB.
00228             STOP RUN.
00229          A1-INITIALIZATION.
00230             OPEN   INPUT APPLICATION-CARDS-FILE
00231                       OUTPUT PROFILE-LISTING.
00232             WRITE PRINT-LINE-OUT FROM HEADER-WS1
00233                                AFTER ADVANCING 2 LINES.
00234             MOVE ZEROS TO APPLICATIONS-ACCEPTED-ACCUM.
00235             MOVE ZEROS TO APPLICATIONS-REJECTED-ACCUM.
00236             MOVE ZEROS TO ANNUAL-INCOME-WS.
00237             MOVE ZEROS TO ANNUAL-TAX-WS.
00238             MOVE ZEROS TO MONTHLY-NET-INCOME-WS.
00239             MOVE ZEROS TO MONTHLY-PAYMENTS-WS.
00240             MOVE ZEROS TO DISCR-INCOME-WS.
00241             MOVE ZEROS TO CREDIT-FACTOR.
00242             MOVE ZEROS TO CREDIT-LIMIT-WS.
00243             MOVE ZEROS TO TOTAL-CREDIT-GIVEN-WS.
00244             MOVE ZEROS TO TOTAL-CREDIT-GIVEN.
00245             MOVE ZEROS TO AVERAGE-CREDIT.
00246             MOVE ZEROS TO APPLICATIONS-ACCEPTED.
00247             MOVE ZEROS TO APPLICATIONS-REJECTED.
00248             MOVE SPACES TO FIRST-CARD.
00249             MOVE SPACES TO SECOND-CARD.
00250             MOVE SPACES TO ACCT-NUM-MATCH.
00251             MOVE SPACES TO PAIR-VALIDITY.
00252             MOVE 'YES' TO CARDS-LEFT.
00253             READ APPLICATION-CARDS-FILE
00254                AT END MOVE 'NO ' TO CARDS-LEFT.
00255      * FIRST CARD IS NOW IN BUFFER
00256
00257
00258          A2-PRINT-CREDIT-PROFILES.
00259             PERFORM B1-GET-A-PAIR-OF-CARDS.
00260             IF PAIR-VALIDITY = 'GOOD'
00261                PERFORM B2-CALC-DISCRETNRY-INCOME
00262                IF DISCR-INCOME-WS IS POSITIVE
00263                   PERFORM B3-CALC-CREDIT-LIMIT
00264                   PERFORM B4-ASSEMBLE-PRINT-LINES
00265                   PERFORM B5-WRITE-PROFILE
00266                ELSE
00267                   PERFORM B6-OUTGO-EXCEEDS-INCOME
00268                ELSE
00269                   PERFORM B7-WRITE-ERROR-PROFILE.
00270
00271          A3-PRINT-SUMMARY.
00272             PERFORM B8-CALC-AVERAGE-CREDIT.
00273             PERFORM B9-WRITE-SUMMARY-REPORT.
00274
00275          A4-END-OF-JOB.
00276             CLOSE APPLICATION-CARDS-FILE
00277                       PROFILE-LISTING.
00278
```

```
00279          B1-GET-A-PAIR-OF-CARDS.
00280              PERFORM C1-EDIT-FIRST-CARD.
00281              PERFORM C2-MOVE-FIRST-CARD-TO-WS.
00282              READ APPLICATION-CARDS-FILE
00283                  AT END MOVE 'NO ' TO CARDS-LEFT.
00284      * SECOND CARD OF PAIR IS NOW IN BUFFER
00285              PERFORM C3-EDIT-SECOND-CARD.
00286              IF        (FIRST-CARD = 'GOOD')
00287                  AND (SECOND-CARD = 'GOOD')
00288                  AND (ACCT-NUM-MATCH = 'GOOD')
00289                      MOVE 'GOOD' TO PAIR-VALIDITY
00290                      MOVE CREDIT-INFO-IN TO CREDIT-INFO-WS
00291              ELSE
00292                  MOVE 'BAD ' TO PAIR-VALIDITY
00293                  PERFORM C4-FLUSH-CARDS-TO-ERROR-LINES.
00294              READ APPLICATION-CARDS-FILE
00295                  AT END MOVE 'NO ' TO CARDS-LEFT.
00296      * FIRST CARD OF NEXT PAIR IS NOW IN BUFFER
00297
00298          B2-CALC-DISCRETNRY-INCOME. COPY DISCINCM.
00299 C            COMPUTE ANNUAL-INCOME-WS = INCOME-HUNDREDS-WS * 100
00300 C            COMPUTE ANNUAL-TAX-WS       = ANNUAL-INCOME-WS * TAX-RATE-WS.
00301 C            COMPUTE MONTHLY-NET-INCOME-WS ROUNDED
00302 C                = (ANNUAL-INCOME-WS − ANNUAL-TAX-WS) / MONTHS-IN-YEAR.
00303 C            COMPUTE MONTHLY-PAYMENTS-WS = MORTGAGE-OR-RENTAL-WS
00304 C                                              + OTHER-PAYMENTS-WS.
00305 C            COMPUTE DISCR-INCOME-WS     = MONTHLY-NET-INCOME-WS
00306 C                                          − MONTHLY-PAYMENTS-WS
00307 C                ON SIZE ERROR MOVE 999 TO DISCR-INCOME-WS.
00308 C      * DISCRETIONARY INCOMES OVER $999 PER MONTH ARE SET AT $999
00309
```

```
00310          B3-CALC-CREDIT-LIMIT.
00311      *    MARRIED?              Y Y Y Y N N N N    THIS DECISION TABLE
00312      *    OWNED?                Y Y N N Y Y N N    SETS OUT COMPANY POLICY
00313      *    2 OR MORE YEARS?      Y N Y N Y N Y N    FOR DETERMINING CREDIT
00314      *    --------------------------------------------------------    LIMIT FROM DISCRETIONARY
00315      *    CREDIT   FACTOR 1                 X X    INCOME.  FACTOR1 ETC ARE
00316      *    LIMIT IS        2         X   X         SET UP IN WSB3.
00317      *    MULTIPLE        3             X
00318      *    OF DISCR        4     X X
00319      *    INCOME.         5   X
00320
00321          IF MARRIED
00322             IF OWNED
00323                IF YEARS-EMPLOYED-WS NOT LESS THAN 02
00324                   MOVE FACTOR5 TO CREDIT-FACTOR
00325                ELSE
00326                   MOVE FACTOR4 TO CREDIT-FACTOR
00327             ELSE
00328                IF YEARS-EMPLOYED-WS NOT LESS THAN 02
00329                   MOVE FACTOR4 TO CREDIT-FACTOR
00330                ELSE
00331                   MOVE FACTOR2 TO CREDIT-FACTOR
00332          ELSE
00333             IF OWNED
00334                IF YEARS-EMPLOYED-WS NOT LESS THAN 02
00335                   MOVE FACTOR3 TO CREDIT-FACTOR
00336                ELSE
00337                   MOVE FACTOR2 TO CREDIT-FACTOR
00338             ELSE
00339                MOVE FACTOR1 TO CREDIT-FACTOR.
00340          COMPUTE CREDIT-LIMIT-WS = DISCR-INCOME-WS * CREDIT-FACTOR.
00341          IF CREDIT-LIMIT-WS IS GREATER THAN UPPER-LIMIT-WS.
00342             MOVE UPPER-LIMIT-WS TO CREDIT-LIMIT-WS.
00343          ADD CREDIT-LIMIT-WS TO TOTAL-CREDIT-GIVEN-WS.
00344
```

```
00345          B4-ASSEMBLE-PRINT-LINES.
00346              MOVE NAME-WS TO NAME-L1.
00347              MOVE STREET-WS TO STREET-L2.
00348              MOVE CITY-WS TO CITY-L3.
00349              MOVE STATE-WS TO STATE-L3.
00350              MOVE ZIP-WS TO ZIP-L3.
00351              MOVE AREA-CODE-WS TO AREA-CODE-L1.
00352              MOVE NUMBR-WS TO NUMBR-L1.
00353              MOVE ACCT-NUM-WS TO ACCT-NUM-L3.
00354              IF       MALE    MOVE 'MALE  ' TO SEX-L1
00355              ELSE IF  FEMALE  MOVE 'FEMALE' TO SEX-L1
00356              ELSE             MOVE '* * * * *' TO SEX-L1.
00357              IF       SINGLE     MOVE 'SINGLE   ' TO MARITAL-STATUS-L2
00358              ELSE IF  MARRIED    MOVE 'MARRIED ' TO MARITAL-STATUS-L2
00359              ELSE IF  DIVORCED   MOVE 'DIVORCED' TO MARITAL-STATUS-L2
00360              ELSE IF  WIDOWED    MOVE 'WIDOWED ' TO MARITAL-STATUS-L2
00361              ELSE                MOVE '************' TO MARITAL-STATUS-L2.
00362              MOVE NUMBER-DEPENS-WS TO NUMBER-DEPENS-L3.
00363              MOVE INCOME-HUNDREDS-WS TO INCOME-HUNDREDS-L1.
00364              IF YEARS-EMPLOYED-WS IS EQUAL TO 0
00365                  MOVE 'LESS THAN 1 YEAR' TO YEARS-EMPLOYED-L1
00366              ELSE
00367                  MOVE YEARS-EMPLOYED-WS TO YEARS-L1
00368                  MOVE ' YEARS     ' TO DESCN-L1.
00369              IF       OWNED  MOVE 'MORTGAGE:    $' TO OUTGO-DESCN
00370              ELSE IF  RENTED MOVE 'RENTAL:      $' TO OUTGO-DESCN
00371              ELSE            MOVE '***************** ' TO OUTGO-DESCN.
00372              MOVE MORTGAGE-OR-RENTAL-WS TO MORTGAGE-OR-RENTAL-L2.
00373              MOVE OTHER-PAYMENTS-WS TO OTHER-PAYMENTS-L3.
00374              MOVE DISCR-INCOME-WS TO DISCR-INCOME-L2.
00375              MOVE CREDIT-LIMIT-WS TO CREDIT-LIMIT-L3.
00376
00377          B5-WRITE-PROFILE.  COPY WRITPRFL
00378                  REPLACING   LINE-1-WS BY LINE-1-WSB4
00379                              LINE-2-WS BY LINE-2-WSB4
00380                              LINE-3-WS BY LINE-3-WSB4.
00381 C            MOVE SPACES TO PRINT-LINE-OUT.
00382 C            WRITE PRINT-LINE-OUT FROM LINE-1-WSB4
00383 C                                      AFTER ADVANCING 4 LINES.
00384 C            MOVE SPACES TO PRINT-LINE-OUT.
00385 C            WRITE PRINT-LINE-OUT FROM LINE-2-WSB4
00386 C                                      AFTER ADVANCING 1 LINES.
00387 C            MOVE SPACES TO PRINT-LINE-OUT.
00388 C            WRITE PRINT-LINE-OUT FROM LINE-3-WSB4
00389 C                                      AFTER ADVANCING 1 LINES.
00390              ADD 1 TO APPLICATIONS-ACCEPTED-ACCUM.
00391
00392          B6-OUTGO-EXCEEDS-INCOME.
00393              MOVE SPACES TO FIRST-CARD-ERR1.
00394              MOVE NAME-WS TO NAME-ERR1.
00395              MOVE ADDRESS-WS TO ADDRESS-ERR1.
00396              MOVE PHONE-WS TO PHONE-ERR1.
00397              MOVE ACCT-NUM-WS TO ACCT-NUM-ERR1.
00398              MOVE SPACES TO SECOND-CARD-ERR2.
00399              MOVE CREDIT-INFO-WS TO CREDIT-INFO-ERR2.
00400              MOVE 'OUTGO EXCEEDS INCOME: REJECT' TO MESSAGE-ERR-LINE-2.
00401              PERFORM B7-WRITE-ERROR-PROFILE.
00402
```

```
00403          B7-WRITE-ERROR-PROFILE.
00404              MOVE SPACES TO PRINT-LINE-OUT.
00405              WRITE PRINT-LINE-OUT FROM CARD-ERROR-LINE1-WSC4
00406                                  AFTER ADVANCING 4 LINES.
00407              WRITE PRINT-LINE-OUT FROM CARD-ERROR-LINE2-WSC4
00408                                  AFTER ADVANCING 1 LINES.
00409              ADD 1 TO APPLICATIONS-REJECTED-ACCUM.
00410
00411          B8-CALC-AVERAGE-CREDIT.
00412              MOVE TOTAL-CREDIT-GIVEN-WS TO TOTAL-CREDIT-GIVEN.
00413              IF TOTAL-CREDIT-GIVEN = 0
00414                  MOVE ZEROS TO AVERAGE-CREDIT
00415              ELSE
00416                  DIVIDE APPLICATIONS-ACCEPTED-ACCUM
00417                      INTO TOTAL-CREDIT-GIVEN
00418                      GIVING AVERAGE-CREDIT  ROUNDED.
00419
00420          B9-WRITE-SUMMARY-REPORT.
00421              MOVE APPLICATIONS-ACCEPTED-ACCUM TO APPLICATIONS-ACCEPTED.
00422              MOVE APPLICATIONS-REJECTED-ACCUM TO APPLICATIONS-REJECTED.
00423              WRITE PRINT-LINE-OUT FROM LINE-OF-ASTERISKS-WSB9
00424                                  AFTER ADVANCING 6 LINES.
00425              WRITE PRINT-LINE-OUT FROM SIDE-DELIMITER-WSB9
00426                                  AFTER ADVANCING 1 LINES.
00427              WRITE PRINT-LINE-OUT FROM SUMMARY-LINE-WSB9
00428                                  AFTER ADVANCING 1 LINES.
00429              WRITE PRINT-LINE-OUT FROM SIDE-DELIMITER-WSB9
00430                                  AFTER ADVANCING 1 LINES.
00431              WRITE PRINT-LINE-OUT FROM LINE-OF-ASTERISKS-WSB9
00432                                  AFTER ADVANCING 1 LINES.
00433
```

```
00434          C1-EDIT-FIRST-CARD.
00435              MOVE 'GOOD' TO FIRST-CARD.
00436              IF NAME-IN IS EQUAL TO SPACES
00437                  MOVE '*** NAME MISSING ***' TO NAME-IN
00438                  MOVE 'BAD ' TO FIRST-CARD.
00439              IF ADDRESS-IN IS EQUAL TO SPACES
00440                  MOVE '**** ADDRESS MISSING ****' TO ADDRESS-IN
00441                  MOVE 'BAD ' TO FIRST-CARD.
00442              IF PHONE-IN IS EQUAL TO SPACES
00443                  MOVE 'NO PHONE **' TO PHONE-IN
00444                  MOVE 'BAD ' TO FIRST-CARD.
00445
00446          C2-MOVE-FIRST-CARD-TO-WS.
00447              MOVE NAME-IN TO NAME-WS.
00448              MOVE ADDRESS-IN TO ADDRESS-WS.
00449              MOVE PHONE-IN TO PHONE-WS.
00450              MOVE ACCT-NUM-IN1 TO ACCT-NUM-WS.
00451
00452          C3-EDIT-SECOND-CARD.
00453              MOVE 'GOOD' TO SECOND-CARD.
00454              MOVE 'GOOD' TO ACCT-NUM-MATCH.
00455              IF CARD-TYPE-IN IS NOT EQUAL TO 'C'
00456                  MOVE 'BAD ' TO SECOND-CARD.
00457              IF ACCT-NUM-IN2 IS NOT EQUAL TO ACCT-NUM-WS
00458                  MOVE 'BAD' TO ACCT-NUM-MATCH.
00459
00460          C4-FLUSH-CARDS-TO-ERROR-LINES.
00461              MOVE FIRST-CARD-TO FIRST-CARD-ERR1.
00462              MOVE NAME-WS TO NAME-ERR1.
00463              MOVE ADDRESS-WS TO ADDRESS-ERR1.
00464              MOVE PHONE-WS TO PHONE-ERR1.
00465              MOVE ACCT-NUM-WS TO ACCT-NUM-ERR1.
00466              MOVE SECOND-CARD TO SECOND-CARD-ERR2.
00467              MOVE CREDIT-INFO-WS TO CREDIT-INFO-ERR2.
00468              IF ACCT-NUM-MATCH = 'BAD '
00469                  MOVE 'ACCOUNT NUMBERS DO NOT MATCH'
00470                                    TO MESSAGE-ERR-LINE-2
00471              ELSE
00472                  MOVE SPACES TO MESSAGE-ERR-LINE-2.
```

7 Getting Data into and out of the Computer

Up until now we have done some quite complex processing of data, all stored on punched cards. As you will realize, cards are very convenient for small volumes of data of the kind you have been using. However, once you start dealing with more than a few hundred records, the cards begin to get heavy, they wear and cause reading problems when used a lot, and they may get out of order. Have you ever dropped a card deck, and had to put it back in sequence? It happens.

7.1 Magnetic tape

For large volumes of data, *magnetic tape* often is used. This is a larger, more precision-engineered version of the tape used in a tape recorder, with the recording consisting of magnetized spots corresponding to the holes in a card. Figure 7.1 shows a modern tape drive, with a reel of computer tape mounted on it. The tape typically can hold 1,600 characters per inch, that is, *twenty punched cards can be recorded on one inch of magnetic tape.*

> Q. If a reel of tape is 2,400 feet long, how many punched cards in principle could be recorded on one reel?
>
> A. 2,400 feet × 12 inches × 20 cards per inch = 576,000 cards

Not only can magnetic tape store information much more compactly than can punched cards, but tape also can be read by the computer much more quickly. The schematic in Fig. 7.1 shows a magnified version of the contents of a short piece of tape. It is standard for the tape to have a gap of three-quarters of an inch between areas on which data are recorded; this is called the *inter-record gap* (IRG). You can see that if you record cards one by one on tape, and if each card takes up only one-twentieth of an inch, you would waste a lot of tape. For this reason, it is better to write five, ten, twenty, or more records on tape together as a *block,* as shown in the insert.

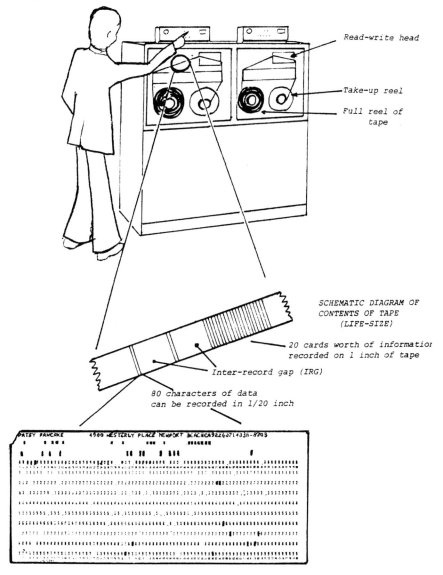

Read-write head

Take-up reel

Full reel of tape

SCHEMATIC DIAGRAM OF
CONTENTS OF TAPE
(LIFE-SIZE)

20 cards worth of information
recorded on 1 inch of tape

Inter-record gap (IRG)

80 characters of data
can be recorded in 1/20 inch

Figure 7.1. Schematic representation of a magnetic tape drive.

In addition to being blocked, a tape file has a coded label written by the computer as the first and last record on the tape. Although you can specify your own format for the label, it is more common to use the standard format provided by the operating system.

Here is a sample FD for a file to be written on tape:

```
FD   TAPE-FILE
     LABEL RECORDS ARE STANDARD
     BLOCK CONTAINS 10 RECORDS.
01   NAME-AND-ADDRESS                    PIC X(80).
```

Q.   How many characters will there be in each block on this tape?

A.   800: 80 per record, 10 records per block.

7.1.1 *FILE-CONTROL paragraph for tape files*

The SELECT statements for tape files are written in a way similar to the card and print files with which you already are familiar. The system-name can take a wide variety of forms depending upon the operating system. Find out which form is appropriate for your installation. For example, the SELECT statement for a tape file might read

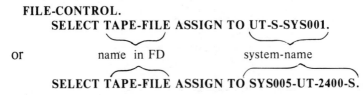

```
     FILE-CONTROL.
         SELECT TAPE-FILE ASSIGN TO UT-S-SYS001.
```
or   name in FD   system-name
```
         SELECT TAPE-FILE ASSIGN TO SYS005-UT-2400-S.
```

7.1.2 *OPEN and CLOSE for tape files*

When an OPEN is executed for a tape file, the computer system checks to see that the correct tape with a correct label is mounted on the correct tape drive ready for use, and positions the first block of records to be read. You don't have to worry about separating each block into its component records; the computer system will do that for you and will present you with a record in the input buffer, as specified in your FD, every time you issue a READ statement. You must open a tape file as either INPUT or OUTPUT depending on whether you want to read from it or write to it.

When you write CLOSE for a tape file, the system will write the correct label on the tape, if necessary, so that it can be used again; rewind the tape to the beginning, so that the computer operator can take the reel off the tape drive; and put it away until the next time it is needed.

7.1.3 READ and WRITE for tape files

You code the READ and WRITE statements much as you coded other statements for a card file. A tape file has a special end-of-file record, which is inserted automatically by the system. Reading this record results in the AT END condition, which can be used to set a flag, as we have done in previous chapters.

Once you have written the BLOCK CONTAINS clause in the FD, you do not have to worry about separating records from blocks on a READ or combining them into blocks on a WRITE; that is all handled by the computer system.

7.1.4 Creating a tape file

We want to store all the data about those mail-order customers, in the previous chapter's example, for whom we have approved a credit limit. To do this, we want to build a Customer Master File on tape, so that we do not have to keep on reading punched cards.

You now have to design and code a program, to be called CREATEMF, which will read pairs of cards as in CREDCALC, make the same checks on the cards, calculate discretionary income and credit limit, and write a record onto tape for each accepted applicant, printing out error messages for each rejected applicant, and rejecting their cards. When all the good applicants have been processed, we want to rewind the tape. Then, we check that we actually have written our master file on tape by reading the records on the tape and printing out the contents of the file, one record to a line.

This means that when all the cards have been processed, you will need to CLOSE the tape file, and OPEN it again as an IN-PUT file. Remember that the CLOSE statement automatically will rewind the tape.

The tape master file should have the record format as shown below.

Account number	6
Name	20
Street	20
City	13
State	2
ZIP code	5
Phone	10 - ten digits, no hyphen
Sex	1
Marital status	1
Number of dependents	2
Income in hundreds	3
Years in present job	2
Owner or renter	1
Mortgage or rental	3
Other monthly payments	3
Discretionary income	4
Credit limit	4
Current balance owing	8 - this field will be used later
Spare	20
	128

We have added twenty characters to set the size of the record at 128 characters, because we may want to add some additional fields later, and because many computers handle blocking more effectively when the lengths of the records are a power of two characters: 64, 128, 256, and so on. Though we do not have many records in our test data, we want to be able to open accounts for up to 100,000 applicants; so we will use a block size of ten records, to give a reasonably efficient use of the tape.

Given this information, draw a program graph and structure chart for CREATEMF, showing what functions you will need performed, and compare them with the models on the next page. Notice that in this case we are using a slightly different convention for naming modules, in which 21 performs 211, 212, . . . ;

22 would perform 221, 222, 223, . . . ; and 211 would perform 2111, 2112, and so on. While this method is somewhat more trouble to code than the letter-plus-digit system that we used in SAMPLE-4 and in CREDCALC, it is a helpful technique in large programs, because you can see at a glance that, say, 3242 is performed from 324 (though remember it may be performed from other places as well).

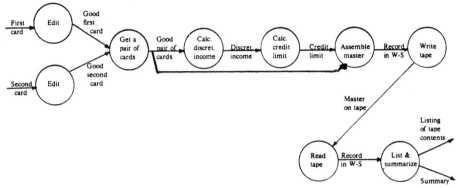

Figure 7.2. Program graph for tape master file creation.

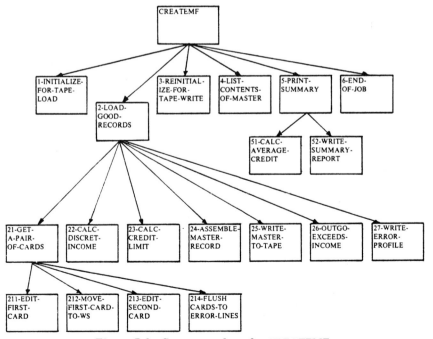

Figure 7.3. Structure chart for CREATEMF.

Assume that the data structures and all the procedures of
CREDCALC are cataloged for you in the Source Statement Library
with the library names as set out below.

	cataloged as
FD APPLICATION-CARDS	FDCARDS
HEADER-WS	HEADRWS
APPLICATION-DATA	CARDSWS
DISCR-INCOME-CALC-FIELDS	DISIFLDS
CRED-LIMIT-CALC-FIELDS	CREDFLDS
LINE-OF-ASTERISKS	LINASTSK
SIDE-DELIMITER	SIDELIMT
SUMMARY-LINE	SUMARYLN
CARD-ERROR-LINE1	ERRLINE1
CARD-ERROR-LINE2	ERRLINE2
GET-A-PAIR-OF-CARDS	GETPRCDS
CALC-DISCRETNRY-INCOME	DISCINCM
CALC-CREDIT-LIMIT	CALCREDT
OUTGO-EXCEEDS-INCOME	OUTEXCDI
WRITE-ERROR-PROFILE	WRTERRPR
CALC-AVERAGE-CREDIT	CALAVGEC
WRITE-SUMMARY-REPORT	WRITSMRY
EDIT-FIRST-CARD	EDT1STCD
MOVE-FIRST-CARD-TO-WS	MOV1STCD
EDIT-SECOND-CARD	EDT2NDCD
FLUSH-CARDS-TO-ERROR-LINES	FLUSHCDS

Use these library entries to code CREATEMF; the model
solution on the following pages gives the 80:80 listing before the
COPY statements are expanded, followed by the completely compiled listing.

CBL LIB
```
         IDENTIFICATION DIVISION.
         PROGRAM-ID.  CREATEMF.

         ENVIRONMENT DIVISION.
         INPUT-OUTPUT SECTION.
         FILE-CONTROL.  COPY FILECONT.
             SELECT CREDIT-MASTER-FILE     ASSIGN TO SYS005-UT-2400-S.

         DATA DIVISION.
         FILE SECTION.

         FD  APPLICATION-CARDS-FILE   COPY FDCARDS.

         FD  PROFILE-LISTING
                 LABEL RECORDS ARE OMITTED.
         01  PRINT-LINE-OUT                         PIC X(132).

         FD  CREDIT-MASTER-FILE
             LABEL RECORDS ARE STANDARD
             BLOCK CONTAINS 10 RECORDS.
         01  CREDIT-MASTER-RECORD.
             05   ACCT-NUM-MAS                      PIC 9(6).
             05   NAME-AND-ADDRESS-MAS.
                  10   NAME-MAS                     PIC X(20).
                  10   STREET-MAS                   PIC X(20).
                  10   CITY-MAS                     PIC X(13).
                  10   STATE-MAS                    PIC XX.
                  10   ZIP-MAS                      PIC 9(5).
             05   PHONE-MAS.
                  10   AREA-CODE-MAS                PIC 9(3).
                  10   NUMBR-MAS                    PIC 9(7).
             05   CREDIT-INFO-MAS.
                  10   SEX-MAS                      PIC X.
                  10   MARITAL-STATUS-MAS           PIC X.
                  10   NUMBER-DEPENS-MAS            PIC 99.
                  10   INCOME-HUNDREDS-MAS          PIC 9(3).
                  10   YEARS-EMPLOYED-MAS           PIC 99.
                  10   OWN-OR-RENT-MAS              PIC X.
                  10   MORTGAGE-OR-RENTAL-MAS       PIC 9(3).
                  10   OTHER-PAYMENTS-MAS           PIC 9(3).
             05   ACCOUNT-INFO-MAS.
                  10   DISCR-INCOME-MAS             PIC S9(3).
                  10   CREDIT-LIMIT-MAS             PIC 9(4).
                  10   CURRENT-BALANCE-OWING        PIC S9(6)V99.
             05   SPARE-CHARACTERS                  PIC X(20).
```

WORKING-STORAGE SECTION.

```
01      COMMON-WS
        05   CARDS-LEFT                      PIC X(3).
        05   MASTER-RECORDS-LEFT             PIC X(3).
        05   FIRST-CARD                      PIC X(4).
        05   SECOND-CARD                     PIC X(4).
        05   ACCT-NUM-MATCH                  PIC X(4).
        05   PAIR-VALIDITY                   PIC X(4).
        05   APPLICATIONS-ACCEPTED-ACCUM     PIC 9(4).
        05   APPLICATIONS-REJECTED-ACCUM     PIC 9(4).

01      HEADER-WS3.
        05   FILLER                          PIC X(51)     VALUE SPACES.
        05   TITLE                           PIC X(30)
                        VALUE 'CONTENTS OF CREDIT MASTER FILE'.
        05   FILLER                          PIC X(51)     VALUE SPACES.

01      APPLICATION-DATA-WS21 COPY CARDSWS.

01      DISCR-INCOME-CALC-FIELDS-WS22 COPY DISIFLDS.

01      CRED-LIMIT-CALC-FIELDS-WS23 COPY CREDFLDS.

01      ASSEMBLE-MASTER-WS24.
        05   TEL-NUMBR-WITH-HYPHEN-WS24.
             10   EXCHANGE-IN                PIC 9(3).
             10   FILLER                     PIC X.
             10   FOUR-DIGIT-NUMBR-IN        PIC 9(4).
        05   TEL-NUMBR-WITHOUT-HYPHEN-WS24.
             10   EXCHANGE                   PIC 9(3).
             10   FOUR-DIGIT-NUMBR           PIC 9(4).


01      LINE-OF-ASTERISKS-WS52 COPY LINASTSK.

01      SIDE-DELIMITER-WS52 COPY SIDELIMT.

01      SUMMARY-LINE-WS52 COPY SUMARYLN.

01      CARD-ERROR-LINE1-WS214 COPY ERRLINE1.

01      CARD-ERROR-LINE2-WS214 COPY ERRLINE2.
```

```
PROCEDURE DIVISION.
    PERFORM 1-INITIALIZE-FOR-TAPE-LOAD.
    PERFORM 2-LOAD-GOOD-RECORDS-TO-MASTER
        UNTIL CARDS-LEFT IS EQUAL TO 'NO '.
    PERFORM 3-REINITIALIZE-FOR-TAPE-WRITE.
    PERFORM 4-LIST-CONTENTS-OF-MASTER
        UNTIL MASTER-RECORDS-LEFT = 'NO '.
    PERFORM 5-PRINT-SUMMARY.
    PERFORM 6-END-OF-JOB.
    STOP RUN.


1-INITIALIZE-FOR-TAPE-LOAD.
    OPEN INPUT APPLICATION-CARDS-FILE
            OUTPUT PROFILE-LISTING
                    CREDIT-MASTER-FILE.
    MOVE SPACES TO FIRST-CARD.
    MOVE SPACES TO SECOND-CARD.
    MOVE SPACES TO PAIR-VALIDITY.
    MOVE ZEROS TO APPLICATIONS-ACCEPTED-ACCUM.
    MOVE ZEROS TO APPLICATIONS-REJECTED-ACCUM.
    MOVE ZEROS TO ANNUAL-INCOME-WS.
    MOVE ZEROS TO ANNUAL-TAX-WS.
    MOVE ZEROS TO MONTHLY-NET-INCOME-WS.
    MOVE ZEROS TO MONTHLY-PAYMENTS-WS.
    MOVE ZEROS TO DISCR-INCOME-WS.
    MOVE ZEROS TO CREDIT-FACTOR.
    MOVE ZEROS TO CREDIT-LIMIT-WS.
    MOVE ZEROS TO TOTAL-CREDIT-GIVEN-WS.
    MOVE ZEROS TO TOTAL-CREDIT-GIVEN.
    MOVE ZEROS TO AVERAGE-CREDIT.
    MOVE ZEROS TO APPLICATIONS-ACCEPTED.
    MOVE ZEROS TO APPLICATIONS-REJECTED.
    MOVE 'YES' TO CARDS-LEFT.
    READ APPLICATION-CARDS-FILE
        AT END MOVE 'NO ' TO CARDS-LEFT.
* FIRST CARD IS NOW IN BUFFER
```

```
2-LOAD-GOOD-RECORDS-TO-MASTER.
    PERFORM 21-GET-A-PAIR-OF-CARDS.
    IF PAIR-VALIDITY = 'GOOD'
        PERFORM 22-CALC-DISCRETNRY-INCOME
        IF DISCR-INCOME-WS IS POSITIVE
            PERFORM 23-CALC-CREDIT-LIMIT
            PERFORM 24-ASSEMBLE-MASTER-RECORD
            PERFORM 25-WRITE-MASTER-TO-TAPE
        ELSE
            PERFORM 26-OUTGO-EXCEEDS-INCOME
    ELSE
        PERFORM 27-WRITE-ERROR-PROFILE.

3-REINITIALIZE-FOR-TAPE-WRITE.
    CLOSE CREDIT-MASTER-FILE.
    OPEN INPUT CREDIT-MASTER-FILE.
    WRITE PRINT-LINE-OUT FROM HEADER-WS3
                        AFTER ADVANCING 10 LINES.
    MOVE 'YES' TO MASTER-RECORDS-LEFT.
    READ CREDIT-MASTER-FILE
        AT END MOVE 'NO ' TO MASTER-RECORDS-LEFT.

4-LIST-CONTENTS-OF-MASTER.
    MOVE SPACES TO PRINT-LINE-OUT.
    WRITE PRINT-LINE-OUT FROM CREDIT-MASTER-RECORD
                        AFTER ADVANCING 2 LINES.
    READ CREDIT-MASTER-FILE
        AT END MOVE 'NO ' TO MASTER-RECORDS-LEFT.

5-PRINT-SUMMARY.
    PERFORM 51-CALC-AVERAGE-CREDIT.
    PERFORM 52-WRITE-SUMMARY-REPORT.

6-END-OF-JOB.
    CLOSE   APPLICATION-CARDS-FILE
            PROFILE-LiSTING
            CREDIT-MASTER-FILE.
```

```
21-GET-A-PAIR-OF-CARDS.  COPY GETPRCDS REPLACING
            C1-EDIT-FIRST-CARD            BY  211-EDIT-FIRST-CARD
            C2-MOVE-FIRST-CARD-TO-WS      BY  212-MOVE-FIRST-CARD-TO-WS
            C3-EDIT-SECOND-CARD           BY  213-EDIT-SECOND-CARD
            C4-FLUSH-CARDS-TO-ERROR-LINES
                                          BY
            214-FLUSH-CARDS-TO-ERROR-LINES.

22-CALC-DISCRETNRY-INCOME.  COPY DISCINCM.

23-CALC-CREDIT-LIMIT.  COPY CALCREDT.

24-ASSEMBLE-MASTER-RECORD.
            MOVE ACCT-NUM-WS TO ACCT-NUM-MAS.
            MOVE NAME-AND-ADDRESS-WS TO NAME-AND-ADDRESS-MAS.
            MOVE AREA-CODE-WS TO AREA-CODE-MAS.
            PERFORM 241-REMOVE-HYPHEN-FROM-TEL-NUM.
            MOVE CREDIT-INFO-WS TO CREDIT-INFO-MAS.
            MOVE DISCR-INCOME-WS TO DISCR-INCOME-MAS.
            MOVE CREDIT-LIMIT-WS TO CREDIT-LIMIT-MAS.
            MOVE ZEROS TO CURRENT-BALANCE-OWING.
            MOVE SPACES TO SPARE-CHARACTERS.

25-WRITE-MASTER-TO-TAPE.
            WRITE CREDIT-MASTER-RECORD.
            ADD 1 TO APPLICATIONS-ACCEPTED-ACCUM.

26-OUTGO-EXCEEDS-INCOME.  COPY OUTEXCDI REPLACING
            B7-WRITE-ERROR-PROFILE        BY  27-WRITE-ERROR-PROFILE.

27-WRITE-ERROR-PROFILE.  COPY WRTERRPR REPLACING
            CARD-ERROR-LINE1-WSC4         BY  CARD-ERROR-LINE1-WS214
            CARD-ERROR-LINE2-WSC4         BY  CARD-ERROR-LINE2-WS214.

51-CALC-AVERAGE-CREDIT.  COPY CALAVGEC.

52-WRITE-SUMMARY-REPORT.  COPY WRITSMRY REPLACING
            LINE-OF-ASTERISKS-WSB9 BY LINE-OF-ASTERISKS-WS52
            SIDE-DELIMITER-WSB9 BY SIDE-DELIMITER-WS52
            SUMMARY-LINE-WSB9 BY SUMMARY-LINE-WS52.

211-EDIT-FIRST-CARD.  COPY EDT1STCD.

212-MOVE-FIRST-CARD-TO-WS.  COPY MOV1STCD.

213-EDIT-SECOND-CARD.  COPY EDT2NDCD.

214-FLUSH-CARDS-TO-ERROR-LINES.  COPY FLUSHCDS.

241-REMOVE-HYPHEN-FROM-TEL-NUM.
            MOVE NUMBR-WS TO TEL-NUMBR-WITH-HYPHEN-WS24.
            MOVE EXCHANGE-IN TO EXCHANGE.
            MOVE FOUR-DIGIT-NUMBR-IN TO FOUR-DIGIT-NUMBR.
            MOVE TEL-NUMBR-WITHOUT-HYPHEN-WS24 TO NUMBR-MAS.
```

```
CBL LIB
00001                 IDENTIFICATION DIVISION.
00002                 PROGRAM-ID.  CREATEMF.
00003
00004                 ENVIRONMENT DIVISION.
00005                 INPUT-OUTPUT SECTION.
00006                 FILE-CONTROL.  COPY FILECONT.
00007 C                   SELECT APPLICATION-CARDS-FILE   ASSIGN TO SYS031-UR-2540R-S.
00008 C                   SELECT PROFILE-LISTING          ASSIGN TO SYS033-UR-1403-S.
00009                     SELECT CREDIT-MASTER-FILE       ASSIGN TO SYS005-UT-2400-S
00010
00011                 DATA DIVISION.
00012                 FILE SECTION.
00013
00014                 FD   APPLICATION-CARDS-FILE   COPY FDCARDS.
00015 C                        LABEL RECORDS ARE OMITTED
00016 C                        DATA RECORDS ARE NAME-ADDRESS-AND-PHONE-IN
00017 C                                            CREDIT-INFORMATION-IN.
00018 C               01   NAME-ADDRESS-AND-PHONE-IN.
00019 C                    05   NAME-IN                   PIC X(20).
00020 C                    05   ADDRESS-IN                PIC X(40).
00021 C                    05   PHONE-IN                  PIC X(11).
00022 C                    05   FILLER                    PIC X(3).
00023 C                    05   ACCT-NUM-IN1              PIC 9(6).
00024 C               01   CREDIT-INFORMATION-IN.
00025 C                    05   CARD-TYPE-IN              PIC X.
00026 C                    05   ACCT-NUM-IN2              PIC 9(6).
00027 C                    05   FILLER                    PIC X.
00028 C                    05   CREDIT-INFO-IN            PIC X(22).
00029 C                    05   FILLER                    PIC X(50).
00030
00031                 FD   PROFILE-LISTING
00032                          LABEL RECORDS ARE OMITTED.
00033                 01   PRINT-LINE-OUT                 PIC X(132).
00034
```

```
00035       FD  CREDIT-MASTER-FILE
00036           LABEL RECORDS ARE STANDARD
00037           BLOCK CONTAINS 10 RECORDS.
00038       01  CREDIT-MASTER-RECORD.
00039           05  ACCT-NUM-MAS                    PIC 9(6).
00040           05  NAME-AND-ADDRESS-MAS.
00041               10  NAME-MAS                    PIC X(20).
00042               10  STREET-MAS                  PIC X(20).
00043               10  CITY-MAS                    PIC X(13).
00044               10  STATE-MAS                   PIC XX.
00045               10  ZIP-MAS                     PIC 9(5).
00046           05  PHONE-MAS.
00047               10  AREA-CODE-MAS               PIC 9(3).
00048               10  NUMBR-MAS                   PIC 9(7).
00049           05  CREDIT-INFO-MAS.
00050               10  SEX-MAS                     PIC X.
00051               10  MARITAL-STATUS-MAS          PIC X.
00052               10  NUMBER-DEPENS-MAS           PIC 99.
00053               10  INCOME-HUNDREDS-MAS         PIC 9(3).
00054               10  YEARS-EMPLOYED-MAS          PIC 99.
00055               10  OWN-OR-RENT-MAS             PIC X.
00056               10  MORTGAGE-OR-RENTAL-MAS      PIC 9(3).
00057               10  OTHER-PAYMENTS-MAS          PIC 9(3).
00058           05  ACCOUNT-INFO-MAS.
00059               10  DISCR-INCOME-MAS            PIC S9(3).
00060               10  CREDIT-LIMIT-MAS            PIC 9(4).
00061               10  CURRENT-BALANCE-OWING       PIC S9(6)V99.
00062           05  SPARE-CHARACTERS                PIC X(20).
```

```
00064          WORKING-STORAGE SECTION
00065
00066      01  COMMON-WS.
00067          05   CARDS-LEFT                      PIC X(3).
00068          05   MASTER-RECORDS-LEFT             PIC X(3).
00069          05   FIRST-CARD                      PIC X(4).
00070          05   SECOND-CARD                     PIC X(4).
00071          05   ACCT-NUM-MATCH                  PIC X(4).
00072          05   PAIR-VALIDITY                   PIC X(4).
00073          05   APPLICATIONS-ACCEPTED-ACCUM     PIC 9(4).
00074          05   APPLICATIONS-REJECTED-ACCUM     PIC 9(4).
00075
00076      01  HEADER-WS3.
00077          05   FILLER                          PIC X(51)     VALUE SPACES.
00078          05   TITLE                           PIC X(30)
00079                          VALUE 'CONTENTS OF CREDIT MASTER FILE'.
00080          05   FILLER                          PIC X(51)     VALUE SPACES.
00081
00082      01  CREDIT-MASTER-PRINT-LINE-WS4.
00083          05   FILLER                          PIC X(4)      VALUE SPACES.
00084          05   CREDIT-MASTER-OUT               PIC X(128).
00085
00086      01  APPLICATION-DATA-WS21 COPY CARDSWS.
00087 C    01  APPLICATION-DATA-WS21.
00088 C        05   NAME-AND-ADDRESS-WS.
00089 C            10   NAME-WS                     PIC X(20).
00090 C            10   ADDRESS-WS.
00091 C                15   STREET-WS               PIC X(20).
00092 C                15   CITY-WS                 PIC X(13).
00093 C                15   STATE-WS                PIC XX.
00094 C                15   ZIP-WS                  PIC X(5).
00095 C        05   PHONE-WS.
00096 C            10   AREA-CODE-WS                PIC 9(3).
00097 C            10   NUMBR-WS                    PIC X(8).
00098 C        05   FILLER                          PIC X(3).
00099 C        05   ACCT-NUM-WS                     PIC 9(6).
00100 C        05   CREDIT-INFO-WS.
00101 C            10   SEX-WS                      PIC X.
00102 C                88   MALE        VALUE 'M'.
00103 C                88   FEMALE      VALUE 'F'.
00104 C            10   FILLER                      PIC X.
00105 C            10   MARITAL-STATUS-WS           PIC X.
00106 C                88   SINGLE      VALUE 'S'.
00107 C                88   MARRIED     VALUE 'M'.
00108 C                88   DIVORCED    VALUE 'D'.
00109 C                88   WIDOWED     VALUE 'W'.
00110 C            10   FILLER                      PIC X.
00111 C            10   NUMBER-DEPENS-WS            PIC 9.
00112 C            10   FILLER                      PIC X.
00113 C            10   INCOME-HUNDREDS-WS          PIC 9(3).
00114 C            10   FILLER                      PIC X.
00115 C            10   YEARS-EMPLOYED-WS           PIC 99.
00116 C            10   FILLER                      PIC X.
00117 C            10   OWN-OR-RENT-WS              PIC X.
00118 C                88   OWNED       VALUE 'O'.
00119 C                88   RENTED      VALUE 'R'.
00120 C            10   FILLER                      PIC X.
00121 C            10   MORTGAGE-OR-RENTAL-WS       PIC 9(3).
00122 C            10   FILLER                      PIC X.
00123 C            10   OTHER-PAYMENTS-WS           PIC 9(3).
```

```
00124
00125        01  DISCR-INCOME-CALC-FIELDS-WS22 COPY DISIFLDS.
00126 C      01  DISCR-INCOME-CALC-FIELDS-WS22.
00127 C          05    ANNUAL-INCOME-WS              PIC 9(5)
00128 C          05    ANNUAL-TAX-WS                 PIC 9(5).
00129 C          05    TAX-RATE-WS                   PIC 9V99      VALUE 0.25.
00130 C          05    MONTHS-IN-YEAR                PIC 99        VALUE 12.
00131 C          05    MONTHLY-NET-INCOME-WS         PIC 9(4).
00132 C          05    MONTHLY-PAYMENTS-WS           PIC 9(4).
00133 C          05    DISCR-INCOME-WS               PIC S9(3).
00135        01  CRED-LIMIT-CALC-FIELDS-WS23 COPY CREDFLDS.
00136 C      01  CRED-LIMIT-CALC-FIELDS-WS23.
00137 C          05    CREDIT-FACTOR                 PIC 9.
00138 C          05    FACTOR1                       PIC 9         VALUE 1.
00139 C          05    FACTOR2                       PIC 9         VALUE 2.
00140 C          05    FACTOR3                       PIC 9         VALUE 3.
00141 C          05    FACTOR4                       PIC 9         VALUE 4.
00142 C          05    FACTOR5                       PIC 9         VALUE 5.
00143 C          05    CREDIT-LIMIT-WS               PIC 9(4).
00144 C          05    UPPER-LIMIT-WS                PIC 9(4)      VALUE 2500.
00145 C          05    TOTAL-CREDIT-GIVEN-WS         PIC 9(7).
00146
00147        01  ASSEMBLE-MASTER-WS24.
00148            05    TEL-NUMBR-WITH-HYPHEN-WS24.
00149                10    EXCHANGE-IN               PIC 9(3).
00150                10    FILLER                    PIC X.
00151                10    FOUR-DIGIT-NUMBR-IN       PIC 9(4).
00152            05    TEL-NUMBR-WITHOUT-HYPHEN-WS24.
00153                10    EXCHANGE                  PIC 9(3).
00154                10    FOUR-DIGIT-NUMBR          PIC 9(4).
00155
00156
00157        01  LINE-OF-ASTERISKS-WS52 COPY LINASTSK.
00158 C      01  LINE-OF-ASTERISKS-WS52.
00159 C          05    FILLER                        PIC X(6)      VALUE '    *
00160 C          05    FILLER                        PIC X(120)
00161 C                VALUE '*********************************************************
00162 C      -        '.*********************************************************
00163 C      -        '***************'
00164 C          05    'FILLER                       PIC X(6)      VALUE '*
00165
00166        01  SIDE-DELIMITER-WS52 COPY SIDELIMT.
00167 C      01  SIDE-DELIMITER-WS52.
00168 C          05    FILLER                        PIC X(6)      VALUE '    *
00169 C          05    FILLER                        PIC X(120)    VALUE SPACES.
00170 C          05    FILLER                        PIC X(6)      VALUE '*
00171
```

```
00172          01   SUMMARY-LINE-WS52 COPY SUMARYLN.
00173 C        01   SUMMARY-LINE-WS52.
00174 C             05   FILLER                         PIC X(6)       VALUE '   *'.
00175 C             05   FILLER                         PIC X(24)
00176 C                            VALUE '   TOTAL CREDIT GIVEN: $'.
00177 C             05   TOTAL-CREDIT-GIVEN             PIC 9(7).
00178 C             05   FILLER                         PIC X(27)
00179 C                            VALUE '   AVERAGE CREDIT GIVEN: $'.
00180 C             05   AVERAGE-CREDIT                 PIC 9(6).
00181 C             05   FILLER                         PIC X(4)       VALUE ' ON '.
00182 C             05   APPLICATIONS-ACCEPTED          PIC 9(4).
00183 C             05   FILLER                         PIC X(24)
00184 C                            VALUE ' ACCEPTED APPLICATIONS. '.
00185 C             05   FILLER                         PIC X(20)
00186 C                            VALUE ' NUMBER REJECTED '.
00187 C             05   APPLICATIONS-REJECTED          PIC 9(3).
00188 C             05   FILLER                         PIC X(10)
00189 C                            VALUE '*   '.
00190
00191          01   CARD-ERROR-LINE1-WS214 COPY ERRLINE1.
00192 C        01   CARD-ERROR-LINE1-WS214.
00193 C             05   FILLER                         PIC X(5)       VALUE SPACES.
00194 C             05   FILLER                         PIC X(12)
00195 C                            VALUE 'FIRST CARD '.
00196 C             05   FIRST-CARD-ERR1                PIC X(4).
00197 C             05   FILLER                         PIC XX         VALUE SPACES.
00198 C             05   NAME-ERR1                      PIC X(20).
00199 C             05   ADDRESS-ERR1                   PIC X(40).
00200 C             05       PHONE-ERR1                 PIC X(11).
00201 C             05   FILLER                         PIC X(3)       VALUE SPACES.
00202 C             05   ACCT-NUM-ERR1                  PIC 9(6).
00203
00204          01   CARD-ERROR-LINE2-WS214 COPY ERRLINE2.
00205 C        01   CARD-ERROR-LINE2-WS214.
00206 C             05   FILLER                         PIC X(5)       VALUE SPACES.
00207 C             05   FILLER                         PIC X(12)
00208 C                            VALUE 'SECOND CARD '.
00209 C             05   SECOND-CARD-ERR2               PIC X(4).
00210 C             05   FILLER                         PIC X(2)       VALUE SPACES.
00211 C             05   CREDIT-INFO-ERR2               PIC X(80).
00212 C             05   MESSAGE-ERR-LINE-2             PIC X(29)      VALUE SPACES.
00213
```

```
00214          PROCEDURE DIVISION.
00215              PERFORM 1-INITIALIZE-FOR-TAPE-LOAD.
00216              PERFORM 2-LOAD-GOOD-RECORDS-TO-MASTER
00217                  UNTIL CARDS-LEFT IS EQUAL TO 'NO '.
00218              PERFORM 3-REINITIALIZE-FOR-TAPE-WRITE.
00219              PERFORM 4-LIST-CONTENTS-OF-MASTER
00220                  UNTIL MASTER-RECORDS-LEFT = 'NO '.
00221              PERFORM 5-PRINT-SUMMARY.
00222              PERFORM 6-END-OF-JOB.
00223              STOP RUN.
00224
00225          1-INITIALIZE-FOR-TAPE-LOAD.
00226              OPEN INPUT  APPLICATION-CARDS-FILE
00227                  OUTPUT PROFILE-LISTING
00228                         CREDIT-MASTER-FILE.
00229              MOVE SPACES TO FIRST-CARD.
00230              MOVE SPACES TO SECOND-CARD.
00231              MOVE SPACES TO PAIR-VALIDITY.
00232              MOVE ZEROS TO APPLICATIONS-ACCEPTED-ACCUM.
00233              MOVE ZEROS TO APPLICATIONS-REJECTED-ACCUM.
00234              MOVE ZEROS TO ANNUAL-INCOME-WS.
00235              MOVE ZEROS TO ANNUAL-TAX-WS.
00236              MOVE ZEROS TO MONTHLY-NET-INCOME-WS.
00237              MOVE ZEROS TO MONTHLY-PAYMENTS-WS.
00238              MOVE ZEROS TO DISCR-INCOME-WS.
00239              MOVE ZEROS TO CREDIT-FACTOR.
00240              MOVE ZEROS TO CREDIT-LIMIT-WS.
00241              MOVE ZEROS TO TOTAL-CREDIT-GIVEN-WS.
00242              MOVE ZEROS TO TOTAL-CREDIT-GIVEN.
00243              MOVE ZEROS TO AVERAGE-CREDIT.
00244              MOVE ZEROS TO APPLICATIONS-ACCEPTED.
00245              MOVE ZEROS TO APPLICATIONS-REJECTED.
00246              MOVE 'YES' TO CARDS-LEFT.
00247              READ APPLICATION-CARDS-FILE
00248                  AT END MOVE 'NO ' TO CARDS-LEFT.
00249          * FIRST CARD IS NOW IN BUFFER
00250
00251          2-LOAD-GOOD-RECORDS-TO-MASTER.
00252              PERFORM 21-GET-A-PAIR-OF-CARDS.
00253              IF PAIR-VALIDITY = 'GOOD'
00254                  PERFORM 22-CALC-DISCRETNRY-INCOME
00255                  IF DISCR-INCOME-WS IS POSITIVE
00256                      PERFORM 23-CALC-CREDIT-LIMIT
00257                      PERFORM 24-ASSEMBLE-MASTER-RECORD
00258                      PERFORM 25-WRITE-MASTER-TO-TAPE
00259                  ELSE
00260                      PERFORM 26-OUTGO-EXCEEDS-INCOME
00261              ELSE
00262                  PERFORM 27-WRITE-ERROR-PROFILE.
00263
00264          3-REINITIALIZE-FOR-TAPE-WRITE.
00265              CLOSE CREDIT-MASTER-FILE.
00266              OPEN INPUT CREDIT-MASTER-FILE.
00267              WRITE PRINT-LINE-OUT FROM HEADER-WS3
00268                                      AFTER ADVANCING 10 LINES.
00269              MOVE 'YES' TO MASTER-RECORDS-LEFT.
00270              READ CREDIT-MASTER-FILE.
00271                  AT END MOVE 'NO ' TO MASTER-RECORDS-LEFT.
```

```
00272
00273              4-LIST-CONTENTS-OF-MASTER.
00274                 MOVE SPACES TO CREDIT-MASTER-PRINT-LINE-WS4.
00275                 MOVE CREDIT-MASTER-RECORD TO CREDIT-MASTER-OUT.
00276                 WRITE PRINT-LINE-OUT FROM CREDIT-MASTER-PRINT-LINE-WS4
00277                       AFTER ADVANCING 2 LINES.
00278                 READ CREDIT-MASTER-FILE
00279                   AT END MOVE 'NO ' TO MASTER-RECORDS-LEFT.
00280
00281            5-PRINT-SUMMARY.
00282               PERFORM 51-CALC-AVERAGE-CREDIT.
00283               PERFORM 52-WRITE-SUMMARY-REPORT.
00284
00285            6-END-OF-JOB.
00286              CLOSE APPLICATION-CARDS-FILE
00287                    PROFILE-LISTING
00288                    CREDIT-MASTER-FILE.

00290            21-GET-A-PAIR-OF-CARDS.  COPY GETPRCDS REPLACING
00291                    C1-EDIT-FIRST-CARD            BY   211-EDIT-FIRST-CARD
00292                    C2-MOVE-FIRST-CARD-TO-WS      BY   212-MOVE-FIRST-CARD-TO-WS
00293                    C3-EDIT-SECOND-CARD           BY   213-EDIT-SECOND-CARD
00294                    C4-FLUSH-CARDS-TO-ERROR-LINES
00295                                                  BY
00296                       214-FLUSH-CARDS-TO-ERROR-LINES.
00297 C          PERFORM 211-EDIT-FIRST-CARD.
00298 C          PERFORM 212-MOVE-FIRST-CARD-TO-WS.
00299 C          READ APPLICATION-CARDS-FILE
00300 C            AT END MOVE 'NO ' TO CARDS-LEFT.
00301 C  * SECOND CARD OF PAIR IS NOW IN BUFFER
00302 C          PERFORM 213-EDIT-SECOND-CARD.
00303 C          IF     (FIRST-CARD = 'GOOD')
00304 C              AND (SECOND-CARD = 'GOOD')
00305 C              AND (ACCT-NUM-MATCH = 'GOOD')
00306 C                  MOVE 'GOOD' TO PAIR-VALIDITY
00307 C                  MOVE CREDIT-INFO-IN TO CREDIT-INFO-WS
00308 C          ELSE
00309 C                  MOVE 'BAD ' TO PAIR-VALIDITY
00310 C                  PERFORM 214-FLUSH-CARDS-TO-ERROR-LINES.
00311 C          READ APPLICATION-CARDS-FILE
00312 C            AT END MOVE 'NO ' TO CARDS-LEFT.
00313 C  * FIRST CARD OF NEXT PAIR IS NOW IN BUFFER
00314
00315            22-CALC-DISCRETNRY-INCOME.  COPY DISCINCM.
00316 C          COMPUTE ANNUAL-INCOME-WS  = INCOME-HUNDREDS-WS * 100.
00317 C          COMPUTE ANNUAL-TAX-WS       = ANNUAL-INCOME-WS * TAX-RATE-WS
00318 C          COMPUTE MONTHLY-NET-INCOME-WS ROUNDED
00319 C             = (ANNUAL-INCOME-WS - ANNUAL-TAX-WS) / MONTHS-IN-YEAR.
00320 C          COMPUTE MONTHLY-PAYMENTS-WS  = MORTGAGE-OR-RENTAL-WS
00321 C                                       + OTHER-PAYMENTS-WS.
00322 C          COMPUTE DISCR-INCOME-WS     = MONTHLY-NET-INCOME-WS
00323 C                                       - MONTHLY-PAYMENTS-WS
00324 C             ON SIZE ERROR MOVE 999 TO DISCR-INCOME-WS.
00325 C  * DISCRETIONARY INCOMES OVER $999 PER MONTH ARE SET AT $999
```

```
00327              23-CALC-CREDIT-LIMIT.  COPY CALCREDT.
00328 C     *    MARRIED?              Y Y Y Y N N N N    THIS DECISION TABLE        *
00329 C     *    OWNED?                Y Y N N Y Y N N    SETS OUT COMPANY POLICY     *
00330 C     *    2 OR MORE YEARS?      Y N Y N Y N Y N    FOR DETERMINING CREDIT      *
00331 C     *    --------------------------------------   LIMIT FROM DISCRETIONARY    *
00332 C     *    CREDIT    FACTOR 1            X X        INCOME.  FACTOR1 ETC ARE     *
00333 C     *    LIMIT IS       2          X   X          SET UP IN WSB3.             *
00334 C     *    MULTIPLE       3            X                                        *
00335 C     *    OF DISCR       4       X X                                           *
00336 C     *    INCOME.        5     X                                              *
00337 C          IF MARRIED
00338 C             IF OWNED
00339 C                IF YEARS-EMPLOYED-WS NOT LESS THAN 02
00340 C                      MOVE FACTOR5 TO CREDIT-FACTOR
00341 C                ELSE
00342 C                      MOVE FACTOR4 TO CREDIT-FACTOR
00343 C             ELSE
00344 C                IF YEARS-EMPLOYED-WS NOT LESS THAN 02
00345 C                      MOVE FACTOR4 TO CREDIT-FACTOR
00346 C                ELSE
00347 C                      MOVE FACTOR2 TO CREDIT-FACTOR
00348 C          ELSE
00349 C             IF OWNED
00350 C                IF YEARS-EMPLOYED-WS NOT LESS THAN 02
00351 C                      MOVE FACTOR3 TO CREDIT-FACTOR
00352 C                ELSE
00353 C                      MOVE FACTOR2 TO CREDIT-FACTOR
00354 C             ELSE
00355 C                MOVE FACTOR1 TO CREDIT-FACTOR.
00356 C          COMPUTE CREDIT-LIMIT-WS = DISCR-INCOME-WS * CREDIT-FACTOR.
00357 C          IF CREDIT-LIMIT-WS IS GREATER THAN UPPER-LIMIT-WS
00358 C             MOVE UPPER-LIMIT-WS TO CREDIT-LIMIT-WS.
00359 C          ADD CREDIT-LIMIT-WS TO TOTAL-CREDIT-GIVEN-WS.

00361          24-ASSEMBLE-MASTER-RECORD.
00362             MOVE ACCT-NUM-WS TO ACCT-NUM-MAS.
00363             MOVE NAME-AND-ADDRESS-WS TO NAME-AND-ADDRESS-MAS.
00364             MOVE AREA-CODE-WS TO AREA-CODE-MAS.
00365             PERFORM 241-REMOVE-HYPHEN-FROM-TEL-NUM.
00366             MOVE SEX-WS                 TO SEX-MAS.
00367             MOVE MARITAL-STATUS-WS       TO MARITAL-STATUS-MAS.
00368             MOVE NUMBER-DEPENS-WS        TO NUMBER-DEPENS-MAS.
00369             MOVE INCOME-HUNDREDS-WS      TO INCOME-HUNDREDS-MAS.
00370             MOVE YEARS-EMPLOYED-WS       TO YEARS-EMPLOYED-MAS.
00371             MOVE OWN-OR-RENT-WS          TO OWN-OR-RENT-MAS.
00372             MOVE MORTGAGE-OR-RENTAL-WS   TO MORTGAGE-OR-RENTAL-MAS.
00373             MOVE OTHER-PAYMENTS-WS       TO OTHER-PAYMENTS-MAS.
00374             MOVE DISCR-INCOME-WS TO DISCR-INCOME-MAS.
00375             MOVE CREDIT-LIMIT-WS TO CREDIT-LIMIT-MAS.
00376             MOVE ZEROS TO CURRENT-BALANCE-OWING.
00377             MOVE SPACES TO SPARE-CHARACTERS.
00378
```

```
00379          25-WRITE-MASTER-TO-TAPE.
00380              WRITE CREDIT-MASTER-RECORD.
00381              ADD 1 TO APPLICATIONS-ACCEPTED-ACCUM.
00382
00383          26-OUTGO-EXCEEDS-INCOME.  COPY OUTEXCDI REPLACING
00384              B7-WRITE-ERROR-PROFILE  BY  27-WRITE-ERROR-PROFILE.
00385 C            MOVE SPACES TO FIRST-CARD-ERR1.
00386 C            MOVE NAME-WS TO NAME-ERR1.
00387 C            MOVE ADDRESS-WS TO ADDRESS-ERR1.
00388 C            MOVE PHONE-WS TO PHONE-ERR1.
00389 C            MOVE ACCT-NUM-WS TO ACCT-NUM-ERR1.
00390 C            MOVE SPACES TO SECOND-CARD-ERR2.
00391 C            MOVE CREDIT-INFO-WS TO CREDIT-INFO-ERR2.
00392 C            MOVE 'OUTGO EXCEEDS INCOME:  REJECT' TO MESSAGE-ERR-LINE-2.
00393 C            PERFORM 27-WRITE-ERROR-PROFILE.
00394
00395          27-WRITE-ERROR-PROFILE.  COPY WRTERRPR REPLACING
00396              CARD-ERROR-LINE1-WSC4   BY       CARD-ERROR-LINE1-WS214
00397              CARD-ERROR-LINE2-WSC4   BY       CARD-ERROR-LINE2-WS214.
00398 C            MOVE SPACES TO PRINT-LINE-OUT.
00399 C            WRITE PRINT-LINE-OUT FROM CARD-ERROR-LINE1-WS214
00400 C                                     AFTER ADVANCING 4 LINES.
00401 C            WRITE PRINT-LINE-OUT FROM CARD-ERROR-LINE2-WS214
00402 C                                     AFTER ADVANCING 1 LINES.
00403 C            ADD 1 TO APPLICATIONS-REJECTED-ACCUM.
00404
00405          51-CALC-AVERAGE-CREDIT.  COPY CALAVGEC.
00406 C            MOVE TOTAL-CREDIT-GIVEN-WS TO TOTAL-CREDIT-GIVEN.
00407 C            IF TOTAL-CREDIT-GIVEN = 0
00408 C                MOVE ZEROS TO AVERAGE-CREDIT
00409 C            ELSE
00410 C                DIVIDE APPLICATIONS-ACCEPTED-ACCUM
00411 C                    INTO TOTAL-CREDIT-GIVEN
00412 C                    GIVING AVERAGE-CREDIT  ROUNDED.
00413
00414          52-WRITE-SUMMARY-REPORT.  COPY WRITSMRY REPLACING
00415              LINE-OF-ASTERISKS-WSB9 BY LINE-OF-ASTERISKS-WS52
00416              SIDE-DELIMITER-WSB9 BY SIDE-DELIMITER-WS52
00417              SUMMARY-LINE-WSB9 BY SUMMARY-LINE-WS52.
00418 C            MOVE APPLICATIONS-ACCEPTED-ACCUM TO APPLICATIONS-ACCEPTED.
00419 C            MOVE APPLICATIONS-REJECTED-ACCUM TO APPLICATIONS-REJECTED.
00420 C            WRITE PRINT-LINE-OUT FROM LINE-OF-ASTERISKS-WS52
00421 C                                     AFTER ADVANCING 6 LINES.
00422 C            WRITE PRINT-LINE-OUT FROM SIDE-DELIMITER-WS52
00423 C                                     AFTER ADVANCING 1 LINES.
00424 C            WRITE PRINT-LINE-OUT FROM SUMMARY-LINE-WS52
00425 C                                     AFTER ADVANCING 1 LINES.
00426 C            WRITE PRINT-LINE-OUT FROM SIDE-DELIMITER-WS52
00427 C                                     AFTER ADVANCING 1 LINES.
00428 C            WRITE PRINT-LINE-OUT FROM LINE-OF-ASTERISKS-WS52
00429 C                                     AFTER ADVANCING 1 LINES.
00430
```

```
00431          211-EDIT-FIRST-CARD.  COPY EDT1STCD.
00432 C            MOVE 'GOOD' TO FIRST-CARD.
00433 C            IF NAME-IN IS EQUAL TO SPACES
00434 C                MOVE '*** NAME MISSING ***' TO NAME-IN
00435 C                MOVE 'BAD ' TO FIRST-CARD.
00436 C            IF ADDRESS-IN IS EQUAL TO SPACES
00437 C                MOVE '**** ADDRESS MISSING ****' TO ADDRESS-IN
00438 C                MOVE 'BAD ' TO FIRST-CARD.
00439 C            IF PHONE-IN IS EQUAL TO SPACES
00440 C                MOVE 'NO PHONE **' TO PHONE-IN
00441 C                MOVE 'BAD ' TO FIRST-CARD.

00443          212-MOVE-FIRST-CARD-TO-WS.  COPY MOV1STCD.
00444 C            MOVE NAME-IN TO NAME-WS.
00445 C            MOVE ADDRESS-IN TO ADDRESS-WS.
00446 C            MOVE PHONE-IN TO PHONE-WS.
00447 C            MOVE ACCT-NUM-IN1 TO ACCT-NUM-WS.
00448
00449          213-EDIT-SECOND-CARD.  COPY EDT2NDCD.
00450 C            MOVE 'GOOD' TO SECOND-CARD.
00451 C            MOVE 'GOOD' TO ACCT-NUM-MATCH.
00452 C            IF CARD-TYPE-IN IS NOT EQUAL TO '0'
00453 C                MOVE 'BAD ' TO SECOND-CARD.
00454 C            IF ACCT-NUM-IN2 IS NOT EQUAL TO ACCT-NUM-WS
00455 C                MOVE 'BAD' TO ACCT-NUM-MATCH.
00456
00457          214-FLUSH-CARDS-TO-ERROR-LINES.  COPY FLUSHCDS.
00458 C            MOVE FIRST-CARD TO FIRST-CARD-ERR1.
00459 C            MOVE NAME-WS TO NAME-ERR1.
00460 C            MOVE ADDRESS-WS TO ADDRESS-ERR1.
00461 C            MOVE PHONE-WS TO PHONE-ERR1.
00462 C            MOVE ACCT-NUM-WS TO ACCT-NUM-ERR1.
00463 C            MOVE SECOND-CARD TO SECOND-CARD-ERR2.
00464 C            MOVE CREDIT-INFO-WS TO CREDIT-INFO-ERR2.
00465 C            IF ACCT-NUM-MATCH = 'BAD '
00466 C                MOVE 'ACCOUNT NUMBERS DO NOT MATCH'
00467 C                                    TO MESSAGE-ERR-LINE-2
00468 C            ELSE
00469 C                MOVE SPACES TO MESSAGE-ERR-LINE-2.
00470
00471          241-REMOVE-HYPHEN-FROM-TEL-NUM.
00472              MOVE NUMBR-WS TO TEL-NUMBR-WITH-HYPHEN-WS24.
00473              MOVE EXCHANGE-IN TO EXCHANGE.
00474              MOVE FOUR-DIGIT-NUMBR-IN TO FOUR-DIGIT NUMBR.
00475              MOVE TEL-NUMBR-WITHOUT-HYPHEN-WS24 TO NUMBR-MAS.
```

7.2 Maintaining a sequential file on tape

Now that we have created a tape master file and rid our-selves of the large decks of cards and of the problems in han-dling them, we have to consider how to update the tape file. Remember, with the card decks, how easy it was to change a record merely by repunching the cards and replacing them in the original decks?

> Q.   What types of changes have you made to your card decks?
>
> A.   *Changes* or *updates* to fields on existing cards, *adding* new cards, and *removing* cards.

Maintaining tape files also requires changing fields and either ad-ding or deleting records as people relocate, open new accounts, or close accounts.

The tapes that we create normally are read and written in only one sequence — either forward or backward. It is usually impractical to skip forward from the beginning of the tape to the first record that we wish to deal with, and then backward toward the beginning of the tape to deal with the next record, and then forward again. Instead, we read each record one after the other and deal with any required changes as the records are read; in most cases, only a small fraction of the tape records will require any kind of processing.

> Q.   What would happen if we tried to add a new record in the middle of a tape file?
>
> A.   We would over-write the next record and there-fore lose one original record.

Each time we must update a tape file, we will need to create a copy of the tape file containing all of the new additions, changes, and deletions. These updates have to be made in such a way as to maintain the original sequence of the file.

Q. What would be the sequence of the new customer file if we add a new customer with an account number of 012345 to an existing tape file whose account number sequence was:

> 010101
> 020202
> 030303
>
> etc.

A. The new customer file would now look like this:

> 010101
> 012345
> 020202
> 030303
>
> etc.

Each time we update a tape file, we must remember to copy *all* existing records that have not been changed, together with all changes and additions. Since we are creating a new copy, we delete a record by *not* copying it. Let us look at how we would program all of the updates for a tape file, one at a time. In all tape-file changes, the file of the changes must be in the same sequence as is the tape file.

7.2.1 Changes to a record

Assuming that we have only changes to existing records, we would write

```
READ old-tape-record
READ change-record
While there are more old-tape-records or change-records
    IF the change applies to this old-tape-record
        While there are more old-tape-record fields
            IF field is to be changed
                MOVE update-field to new-tape-field
            ELSE
                MOVE old-tape-field to new-tape-field
        WRITE new-tape-record
        READ next-change-record
        READ next-old-tape-record
    ELSE
        WRITE new-tape-record from old-tape-record
        READ next-old-tape-record.
```

7.2.2 Additions

Assuming that we have only additions to the tape, we still must find the correct sequential position for the record addition in the new tape file. We will need to find the first old-tape record that will follow the new addition in order to be certain that the new record is added in the correct position, as follows:

```
READ old-tape-record
READ record-addition
While there are more tape-records or additions
    IF the old-tape-record-number is higher than the
                               record-addition-number
        WRITE new-tape-record from record-addition
        READ next-record-addition
    ELSE
        WRITE new-tape-record from old-tape-record
        READ next-old-tape-record.
```

7.2.3 Deletions

Assuming that we have only deletions to the file, we would follow the pseudocode:

```
READ delete-record
READ old-tape-record
While there are more old-tape-records or delete-records
    IF delete applies to this old-tape-record
        READ next-old-tape-record
        READ next-delete-record
    ELSE
        WRITE new-tape-record from old-tape-record
        READ next-old-tape-record.
```

In all of the above pseudocode examples of updating a tape file, we have assumed that only one type of update is expected. In most of the file maintenance work that you will do, you normally will be expected to make additions, changes, and deletions on the file with the same program.

Q. Assuming that you have read the first old-tape record and the first update record, what action would you take?

A.

a. If the update record did not apply to that tape record, then WRITE the new tape record from the old tape record.

b. If the update did apply to that tape record, the tape record would be updated depending upon the type of update: change or delete.

If the update were a delete, then no new tape record would be written.

If the update were a change to existing fields, the new fields would be updated and then the new tape record written from the updated record.

c. If the update were an addition to the file that had a record number less than the first old-tape record, then the first new-tape record would be written from the addition record, and the second new-tape record written from the old tape record.

Since the contents of the new tape file records must be determined each time we read a record from the update file and from the old tape file, we need a simple means of determining the possible types of updates. We use the record number sequence on both files to determine whether the update is a change or deletion, or an addition, or whether any update is required, as shown on the following page:

Old-tape-record-number is equal to update-record-number:	change or delete
Old-tape-record-number is less than update-record-number:	no change
Old-tape-record-number is greater than update-record-number:	add new record

In pseudocode, we can express the logic of all possible updates resulting from the first record on each file, as follows:

```
READ first-update-record
READ first-old-tape-record

IF old-tape-record-number less tnan update-record-number
    WRITE new-tape-record from old-tape-record

ELSE IF old-tape-record-number equal to update-record-number
    PERFORM CHANGE-OR-DELETE-ROUTINE

ELSE old-tape-record-number is greater than update-record-number
    WRITE new-tape-record from update-record.
```

The above pseudocode processes the first record from each of the files.

Q. Modify the pseudocode to process all records on both the update file and the old tape file. Whenever the old tape records are modified, or additions made, PERFORM a routine at the time of the change that will print out the update. For the sake of simplicity, assume that both the update file and the old tape file reach end-of-file (eof) at the same time; we will look at how to deal with other end-of-file situations once we have the basic logic correct.

A.
READ first-update-record
READ first-old-tape-record
PERFORM UPDATE-TAPE
    UNTIL eof on both files.

UPDATE-TAPE.

    IF old-tape-record-number less than update-record-number
        WRITE new-tape-record from old-tape-record
        READ next-old-tape-record

    ELSE IF old-tape-record-number is equal to update-record-number
        PERFORM CHANGE-OR-DELETE-ROUTINE
        READ next-update-record
        READ next-old-tape-record

    ELSE
        PERFORM ADD-NEW-RECORD
        READ next-update-record.

CHANGE-OR-DELETE-ROUTINE.

    IF change
        While there are more old-tape-fields
            IF field is to be changed
                MOVE update-field to new-tape-field
            ELSE
                MOVE old-tape-field to new-tape-field
        WRITE new-tape-record from merged field
        PERFORM PRINT-CHANGE
        READ next-update-record
        READ next-old-tape-record

    ELSE IF deletion
        Double-check that this is a deletion — it is much
        more difficult to recover from an accidentally
        deleted record than to double-check in the first place.

        PERFORM PRINT-CHANGE
        READ next-update-record
        READ next-old-tape-record

    ELSE
        PERFORM UPDATE-NOT-CHANGE-OR-DELETE.

ADD-NEW-RECORD.

    Check that all mandatory fields are present, and
    do any calculations that may be necessary.

    MOVE update-fields to new-tape-fields
    WRITE new-tape-record
    PERFORM PRINT-CHANGE
    READ next-update-record.

Now that we have the pseudocode for the basic logic, we must consider the case in which both files do not reach end-of-file at the same time; it would be very unusual if they did in a normal updating program.

Q.   What processing would be required if the update file reached end-of-file and the old tape file had not?

A.   We would want to copy the remaining old tape records onto the new tape file.

Q.   What processing would be required if the old tape file reached end-of-file but there were still more update records?

A.   All of the update records would be additions at the end of the master file, so we would want to add the update records to the new tape file.

This situation is best dealt with by performing normal processing until there are either no more old tape records or no more update records, then testing to see which condition has caused processing to halt, and reacting accordingly. The pseudocode of the highest-level module is this:

```
PERFORM UPDATE-MASTER
        UNTIL no-more-old-tape-records
           OR no-more-updates.

IF no-more-updates
        PERFORM copy-remaining-old-tape-records
            UNTIL no-more-old-tape-records

ELSE
        PERFORM add-remaining-updates
            UNTIL no-more-updates.
```

Now that we have the pseudocode for a tape maintenance program, we can prepare to write a program, MAINTMFS, which has the following specifications:

Customer master file to be updated is the same file that we created with the program CREATEMF.

Updates to the tape file will be submitted on pairs of cards as in SAMPLE-4. Any updates to the file should be printed so that we can check that the right updates were made.

Additions to the master file each will be contained on the pair of cards, which should be edited in the same manner as in CREDCALC.

Changes to existing customer records will be indicated by the letters "CH" in cc 73 and 74 of the first card. All changes will contain the name, address, and phone number in the first three fields on the first card. Any changes to the credit information on the second card must be punched together with the unchanged credit information. You can assume that all credit information on the second card will be correct, although you should check that the second card is with the correct first card, as in CREDCALC.

Deletions to the existing customer master file will be indicated by the letters "DE" in cc 73 and 74 of the first card. The name, address, and phone number will be on the first card to allow cross-checking of the information in case any records are deleted by mistake. For now, just check that they exist on the first card. There will be no credit information on the second card, just a "C" in cc 1 and the account number in cc 2 − 7. If there is any credit information on the second card, do not delete the original customer record.

As a check on the program's logic and as a sound business practice, we want to create a *log* of all changes made to the master file. Thus, after making an addition, print out the contents of the update cards and of the new tape record with a message saying that the record has been added. Likewise, when you delete a record, print out the card contents and the record that you deleted, with an appropriate message. If you change a record, print out the record *before* the change; print out the card contents, and the record *after* the change.

When all the updates have been processed, rewind the tape and list the contents of the new master file. This will serve as an additional check that the updates have been made correctly.

Before you design and code MAINTMFS, specify the test data that you are going to use as updates, and the contents of the master file as a result of these updates. A solution for MAINTMFS appears on the following pages.

```
CBL LIB
00001          IDENTIFICATION DIVISION.
00002          PROGRAM-ID.  MAINTMFS.
00003
00004          ENVIRONMENT DIVISION.
00005          INPUT-OUTPUT SECTION.
00006          FILE-CONTROL.
00007               SELECT APPLICATION-CARDS-FILE     ASSIGN TO SYS031-UR-2540R-S.
00008               SELECT UPDATE-LISTING             ASSIGN TO SYS033-UR-1403-S.
00009               SELECT CREDIT-MASTER-OLD-FILE     ASSIGN TO SYS005-UT-2400-S.
00010               SELECT CREDIT-MASTER-NEW-FILE     ASSIGN TO SYS005-UT-2400-S.
00011
00012          DATA DIVISION.
00013          FILE SECTION.
00014
00015          FD   APPLICATION-CARDS-FILE
00016               LABEL RECORDS ARE OMITTED
00017               DATA RECORDS ARE NAME-ADDRESS-AND-PHONE-IN
00018                              CREDIT-INFORMATION-IN.
00019          01   NAME-ADDRESS-AND-PHONE-IN.
00020               05   NAME-AND-ADDRESS-IN.
00021                    10   NAME-IN                 PIC X (20).
00022                    10   ADDRESS-IN.
00023                         15   STREET-IN          PIC X (20).
00024                         15   CITY-IN            PIC X (13).
00025                         15   STATE-IN           PIC XX.
00026                         15   ZIP-IN             PIC X (5).
00027               05   PHONE-IN                     PIC X (11).
00028               05   FILLER                       PIC X.
00029               05   CHANGE-CODE-IN               PIC XX.
00030               05   ACCT-NUM-IN1                 PIC 9 (6).
00031          01   CREDIT-INFORMATION-IN.
00032               05   CARD-TYPE-IN                 PIC X.
00033               05   ACCT-NUM-IN2                 PIC 9 (6).
00034               05   FILLER                       PIC X.
00035               05   CREDIT-INFO-IN               PIC X (22).
00036               05   FILLER                       PIC X (50).
00037
00038          FD   UPDATE-LISTING
00039               LABEL RECORDS ARE OMITTED.
00040          01   PRINT-LINE-OUT                    PIC X (132).
00041
```

```
00042        FD  CREDIT-MASTER-OLD-FILE
00043            LABEL RECORDS ARE STANDARD
00044            BLOCK CONTAINS 10 RECORDS.
00045        01  CREDIT-MASTER-OLD-RECORD.
00046            05  ACCT-NUM-MAS-OLD                        PIC 9(6).
00047            05  NAME-AND-ADDRESS-MAS-OLD.
00048                10  NAME-MAS-OLD                        PIC X(20).
00049                10  STREET-MAS-OLD                      PIC X(20).
00050                10  CITY-MAS-OLD                        PIC X(13).
00051                10  STATE-MAS-OLD                       PIC XX.
00052                10  ZIP-MAS-OLD                         PIC 9(5).
00053            05  PHONE-MAS-OLD.
00054                10  AREA-CODE-MAS-OLD                   PIC 9(3).
00055                10  NUMBR-MAS-OLD                       PIC 9(7).
00056            05  CREDIT-INFO-MAS-OLD.
00057                10  SEX-MAS-OLD                         PIC X.
00058                10  MARITAL-STATUS-MAS-OLD              PIC X.
00059                10  NUMBER-DEPENS-MAS-OLD               PIC 99.
00060                10  INCOME-HUNDREDS-MAS-OLD             PIC 9(3).
00061                10  YEARS-EMPLOYED-MAS-OLD              PIC 99.
00062                10  OWN-OR-RENT-MAS-OLD                 PIC X.
00063                10  MORTGAGE-OR-RENTAL-MAS-OLD          PIC 9(3).
00064                10  OTHER-PAYMENTS-MAS-OLD              PIC 9(3).
00065            05  ACCOUNT-INFO-MAS-OLD.
00066                10  DISCR-INCOME-MAS-OLD                PIC S9(3).
00067                10  CREDIT-LIMIT-MAS-OLD                PIC 9(4).
00068                10  CURRENT-BALANCE-OWING-OLD           PIC S9(6)V99.
00069            05  SPARE-CHARACTERS-OLD                    PIC X(20).
00070
00071        FD  CREDIT-MASTER-NEW-FILE
00072            LABEL RECORDS ARE STANDARD
00073            BLOCK CONTAINS 10 RECORDS.
00074        01  CREDIT-MASTER-NEW-RECORD.
00075            05  ACCT-NUM-MAS-NEW                        PIC 9(6).
00076            05  NAME-AND-ADDRESS-MAS-NEW.
00077                10  NAME-MAS-NEW                        PIC X(20).
00078                10  STREET-MAS-NEW                      PIC X(20).
00079                10  CITY-MAS-NEW                        PIC X(13).
00080                10  STATE-MAS-NEW                       PIC XX.
00081                10  ZIP-MAS-NEW                         PIC 9(5).
00082            05  PHONE-MAS-NEW.
00083                10  AREA-CODE-MAS-NEW                   PIC 9(3).
00084                10  NUMBR-MAS-NEW                       PIC 9(7).
00085            05  CREDIT-INFO-MAS-NEW.
00086                10  SEX-MAS-NEW                         PIC X.
00087                10  MARITAL-STATUS-MAS-NEW              PIC X.
00088                10  NUMBER-DEPENS-MAS-NEW               PIC 99.
00089                10  INCOME-HUNDREDS-MAS-NEW             PIC 9(3).
00090                10  YEARS-EMPLOYED-MAS-NEW              PIC 99.
00091                10  OWN-OR-RENT-MAS-NEW                 PIC X.
00092                10  MORTGAGE-OR-RENTAL-MAS-NEW          PIC 9(3).
00093                10  OTHER-PAYMENTS-MAS-NEW              PIC 9(3).
00094            05  ACCOUNT-INFO-MAS-NEW.
00095                10  DISCR-INCOME-MAS-NEW                PIC S9(3).
00096                10  CREDIT-LIMIT-MAS-NEW                PIC 9(4).
00097                10  CURRENT-BALANCE-OWING-NEW           PIC S9(6)V99.
00098            05  SPARE-CHARACTERS-NEW                    PIC X(20).
00099
00100
```

```
00101        WORKING-STORAGE SECTION.
00102
00103    01  COMMON-WS.
00104        05   CARDS-LEFT                         PIC X(3).
00105        05   OLD-MASTER-RECORDS-LEFT            PIC X(3).
00106        05   NEW-MASTER-RECORDS-LEFT            PIC X(3).
00107        05   FIRST-CARD                         PIC X(4).
00108        05   SECOND-CARD                        PIC X(4).
00109        05   ACCT-NUM-MATCH                     PIC X(4).
00110        05   PAIR-VALIDITY                      PIC X(4).
00111
00112    01  LOG-HEADER-WSA1.
00113        05   FILLER                             PIC X(47)   VALUE SPACES.
00114        05   FILLER                             PIC X(38)
00115                       VALUE 'LOG OF ADDITIONS DELETIONS AND CHANGES'.
00116        05   FILLER                             PIC X(47)   VALUE SPACES.

00118    01  HEADER-WSA5.
00119        05   FILLER                             PIC X(51)   VALUE SPACES.
00120        05   TITLE                              PIC X(30)
00121                       VALUE 'CONTENTS OF CREDIT MASTER FILE'.
00122        05   FILLER                             PIC X(51)   VALUE SPACES.

00124    01  APPLICATION-DATA-WSB2.
00125        05   NAME-AND-ADDRESS-WS.
00126             10   NAME-WS                       PIC X(20).
00127             10   ADDRESS-WS.
00128                  15   STREET-WS                PIC X(20).
00129                  15   CITY-WS                  PIC X(13).
00130                  15   STATE-WS                 PIC XX.
00131                  15   ZIP-WS                   PIC X(5).
00132        05   PHONE-WS.
00133             10   AREA-CODE-WS                  PIC 9(3).
00134             10   NUMBR-WS                      PIC X(8).
00135        05   FILLER                             PIC X       VALUE SPACE.
00136        05   CHANGE-CODE-WS                     PIC XX.
00137        05   ACCT-NUM-WS                        PIC 9(6).
00138        05   CREDIT-INFO-WS.
00139             10   SEX-WS                        PIC X.
00140                  88   MALE      VALUE 'M'.
00141                  88   FEMALE    VALUE 'F'.
00142             10   FILLER                        PIC X.
00143             10   MARITAL-STATUS-WS             PIC X.
00144                  88   SINGLE    VALUE 'S'.
00145                  88   MARRIED   VALUE 'M'.
00146                  88   DIVORCED  VALUE 'D'.
00147                  88   WIDOWED   VALUE 'W'.
00148             10   FILLER                        PIC X.
00149             10   NUMBER-DEPENS-WS              PIC 9.
00150             10   FILLER                        PIC X.
00151             10   INCOME-HUNDREDS-WS            PIC 9(3).
00152             10   FILLER                        PIC X.
00153             10   YEARS-EMPLOYED-WS             PIC 99.
00154             10   FILLER                        PIC X.
00155             10   OWN-OR-RENT-WS                PIC X.
00156                  88   OWNED     VALUE 'O'.
00157                  88   RENTED    VALUE 'R'.
00158             10   FILLER                        PIC X.
00159             10   MORTGAGE-OR-RENTAL-WS         PIC 9(3).
00160             10   FILLER                        PIC X.
00161             10   OTHER-PAYMENTS-WS             PIC 9(3).
```

```
00162
00163      01   UPDATE-MESSAGE-AREA-WSB2.
00164           05   UPDATE-MESSAGE-AREA          PIC X(15).
00165
00166      01   CREDIT-MASTER-PRINT-LINE.
00167           05   FILLER                       PIC X(4)      VALUE SPACES.
00168           05   CREDIT-MASTER-OUT            PIC X(128).
00169
00170      01   UPDATE-RECORD-PRINT-LINE.
00171           05   FILLER                       PIC X(4)      VALUE SPACES.
00172           05   APPLICATION-DATA-OUT         PIC X(102).
00173           05   FILLER                       PIC X(4)      VALUE SPACES.
00174           05   MESSAGE-AREA-OUT             PIC X(15).
00175
00176      01   DISCR-INCOME-CALC-FIELDS-WSC8  COPY DISIFLDS.
00177 C    01   DISCR-INCOME-CALC-FIELDS-WSC8.
00178 C         05   ANNUAL-INCOME-WS             PIC 9(5).
00179 C         05   ANNUAL-TAX-WS                PIC 9(5).
00180 C         05   TAX-RATE-WS                  PIC 9V99      VALUE 0.25.
00181 C         05   MONTHS-IN-YEAR               PIC 99        VALUE 12.
00182 C         05   MONTHLY-NET-INCOME-WS        PIC 9(4).
00183 C         05   MONTHLY-PAYMENTS-WS          PIC 9(4).
00184 C         05   DISCR-INCOME-WS              PIC S9(3).
00185
00186      01   CRED-LIMIT-CALC-FIELDS-WSC9  COPY CREDFLDS.
00187 C    01   CRED-LIMIT-CALC-FIELDS-WSC9.
00188 C         05   CREDIT-FACTOR                PIC 9.
00189 C         05   FACTOR1                      PIC 9         VALUE 1.
00190 C         05   FACTOR2                      PIC 9         VALUE 2.
00191 C         05   FACTOR3                      PIC 9         VALUE 3.
00192 C         05   FACTOR4                      PIC 9         VALUE 4.
00193 C         05   FACTOR5                      PIC 9         VALUE 5.
00194 C         05   CREDIT-LIMIT-WS              PIC 9(4).
00195 C         05   UPPER-LIMIT-WS               PIC 9(4)      VALUE 2500.
00196 C         05   TOTAL-CREDIT-GIVEN-WS        PIC 9(7).
```

```
00198     01    ASSEMBLE-TEL-NUM-WSD1.
00199           05    TEL-NUMBR-WITH-HYPHEN.
00200                 10    EXCHANGE-IN              PIC 9(3).
00201                 10    FILLER                   PIC X.
00202                 10    FOUR-DIGIT-NUMBR-IN      PIC 9(4).
00203           05    TEL-NUMBR-WITHOUT-HYPHEN.
00204                 10    EXCHANGE                 PIC 9(3).
00205                 10    FOUR-DIGIT-NUMBR         PIC 9(4).
00206
00207     01    CARD-ERROR-LINE1-WS    COPY ERRLINE1.
00208 C   01    CARD-ERROR-LINE1-WS.
00209 C         05    FILLER                   PIC X(5)     VALUE SPACES.
00210 C         05    FILLER                   PIC X(12)
00211 C                            VALUE 'FIRST CARD  '.
00212 C         05    FIRST-CARD-ERR1          PIC X(4).
00213 C         05    FILLER                   PIC XX       VALUE SPACES.
00214 C         05    NAME-ERR1                PIC X(20).
00215 C         05    ADDRESS-ERR1             PIC X(40).
00216 C         05    PHONE-ERR1               PIC X(11).
00217 C         05    FILLER                   PIC X(3)     VALUE SPACES.
00218 C         05    ACCT-NUM-ERR1            PIC 9(6).
00219
00220     01    CARD-ERROR-LINE2-WS   COPY ERRLINE2.
00221 C   01    CARD-ERROR-LINE2-WS.
00222 C         05    FILLER                   PIC X(5)     VALUE SPACES.
00223 C         05    FILLER                   PIC X(12)
00224 C                            VALUE 'SECOND CARD '.
00225 C         05    SECOND-CARD-ERR2         PIC X(4).
00226 C         05    FILLER                   PIC X(2)     VALUE SPACES.
00227 C         05    CREDIT-INFO-ERR2         PIC X(80).
00228 C         05    MESSAGE-ERR-LINE-2       PIC X(29)    VALUE SPACES.
00229
```

```
00231          PROCEDURE DIVISION.
00232
00233
00234              PERFORM A1-INITIALIZE.
00235              PERFORM A2-UPDATE-MASTER
00236                UNTIL OLD-MASTER-RECORDS-LEFT = 'NO '
00237                  OR CARDS-LEFT = 'NO '.
00238              IF CARDS-LEFT = 'NO '
00239      *                           THERE ARE MORE OLD MASTER RECS
00240                PERFORM A3-COPY-REMAINING-OLD-MASTER
00241                  UNTIL OLD-MASTER-RECORDS-LEFT = 'NO '
00242              ELSE
00243      *                           THERE ARE MORE CARDS, SO
00244                PERFORM A4-ADD-REMAINING-CARDS
00245                  UNTIL CARDS-LEFT = 'NO '.
00246              PERFORM A5-REINITIALIZE-FOR-TAPE-WRITE.
00247              PERFORM A6-LIST-CONTENTS-OF-MASTER
00248                UNTIL NEW-MASTER-RECORDS-LEFT = 'NO '.
00249              PERFORM A7-END-OF-JOB.
00250              STOP RUN.
00251
00252          A1-INITIALIZE.
00253              OPEN    INPUT    APPLICATION-CARDS-FILE
00254                               CREDIT-MASTER-OLD-FILE
00255                      OUTPUT   CREDIT-MASTER-NEW-FILE
00256                               UPDATE-LISTING.
00257              MOVE SPACES TO FIRST-CARD.
00258              MOVE SPACES TO SECOND-CARD.
00259              MOVE SPACES TO ACCT-NUM-MATCH.
00260              MOVE SPACES TO PAIR-VALIDITY.
00261              MOVE ZEROS TO ANNUAL-INCOME-WS.
00262              MOVE ZEROS TO ANNUAL-TAX-WS.
00263              MOVE ZEROS TO MONTHLY-NET-INCOME-WS.
00264              MOVE ZEROS TO MONTHLY-PAYMENTS-WS.
00265              MOVE ZEROS TO DISCR-INCOME-WS.
00266              MOVE ZEROS TO CREDIT-FACTOR.
00267              MOVE ZEROS TO CREDIT-LIMIT-WS.
00268              MOVE ZEROS TO TOTAL-CREDIT-GIVEN-WS.
00269              MOVE 'YES' TO CARDS-LEFT.
00270              MOVE 'YES' TO OLD-MASTER-RECORDS-LEFT.
00271              READ APPLICATION-CARDS-FILE
00272                AT END MOVE 'NO ' TO CARDS-LEFT.
00273              PERFORM B1-GET-A-PAIR-OF-CARDS-INTO-WS.
00274      * FIRST PAIR OF CARDS IN WS: FIRST CARD OF SECOND PAIR IN BUFFER
00275              READ CREDIT-MASTER-OLD-FILE
00276                AT END MOVE 'NO ' TO OLD-MASTER-RECORDS-LEFT.
00277      * FIRST OLD MASTER RECORD IS IN BUFFER
00278              WRITE PRINT-LINE-OUT FROM LOG-HEADER-WSA1
00279                                   AFTER ADVANCING 3 LINES.
00280
```

```
00281        A2-UPDATE-MASTER.
00282    * BEFORE COMPARING THE UPDATE WITH THE MASTER, WE MUST CHECK
00283    * THAT WE HAVE A VALID PAIR OF CARDS — IF YOUR PROGRAM DOES
00284    * NOT MAKE THIS TEST, IT WILL ONLY WORK WITH VALID PAIRS OF
00285    * CARDS
00286        IF   PAIR-VALIDITY = 'BAD '
00287            PERFORM B1-GET-A-PAIR-OF-CARDS-INTO-WS
00288        ELSE IF ACCT-NUM-WS IS GREATER THAN ACCT-NUM-MAS-OLD
00289    *                             ACCT-NUM-WS IS CARD ACCOUNT NUM
00290            MOVE CREDIT-MASTER-OLD-RECORD TO
00291                CREDIT-MASTER-NEW-RECORD
00292            WRITE CREDIT-MASTER-NEW-RECORD
00293            READ CREDIT-MASTER-OLD-FILE
00294                AT END MOVE 'NO ' TO OLD-MASTER-RECORDS-LEFT
00295        ELSE IF ACCT-NUM-WS = ACCT-NUM-MAS-OLD
00296            PERFORM B2-CHANGE-OR-DELETE-MASTER
00297            PERFORM B1-GET-A-PAIR-OF-CARDS-INTO-WS
00298            READ CREDIT-MASTER-OLD-FILE
00299                AT END MOVE 'NO ' TO OLD-MASTER-RECORDS-LEFT
00300        ELSE
00301    *                             ACCT-NUM-WS IS LESS THAN
00302    *                             ACCT-NUM-MAS-OLD
00303            PERFORM B3-ADD-NEW-MASTER
00304            PERFORM B1-GET-A-PAIR-OF-CARDS-INTO-WS.
00305
00306        A3-COPY-REMAINING-OLD-MASTER.
00307            MOVE CREDIT-MASTER-OLD-RECORD TO
00308                CREDIT-MASTER-NEW-RECORD
00309            WRITE CREDIT-MASTER-NEW-RECORD.
00310            READ CREDIT-MASTER-OLD-FILE
00311                AT END MOVE 'NO ' TO OLD-MASTER-RECORDS-LEFT.
00312
00313        A4-ADD-REMAINING-CARDS.
00314            PERFORM B3-ADD-NEW-MASTER.
00315            PERFORM B1-GET-A-PAIR-OF-CARDS-INTO-WS.
00316
00317        A5-REINITIALIZE-FOR-TAPE-WRITE.
00318            CLOSE APPLICATION-CARDS-FILE
00319                CREDIT-MASTER-OLD-FILE
00320                CREDIT-MASTER-NEW-FILE.
00321            OPEN INPUT CREDIT-MASTER-NEW-FILE.
00322            WRITE PRINT-LINE-OUT FROM HEADER-WSA5
00323                AFTER ADVANCING 10 LINES.
00324            MOVE 'YES' TO NEW-MASTER-RECORDS-LEFT.
00325            READ CREDIT-MASTER-NEW-FILE
00326                AT END MOVE 'NO ' TO NEW-MASTER-RECORDS-LEFT.
00327
00328        A6-LIST-CONTENTS-OF-MASTER.
00329            MOVE SPACES TO CREDIT-MASTER-PRINT-LINE.
00330            MOVE CREDIT-MASTER-NEW-RECORD TO CREDIT-MASTER-OUT.
00331            WRITE PRINT-LINE-OUT FROM CREDIT-MASTER-PRINT-LINE
00332                AFTER ADVANCING 2 LINES.
00333            READ CREDIT-MASTER-NEW-FILE
00334                AT END MOVE 'NO ' TO NEW-MASTER-RECORDS-LEFT.
00335
00336        A7-END-OF-JOB.
00337            CLOSE CREDIT-MASTER-NEW-FILE
00338                UPDATE-LISTING.
```

```
00340          B1-GET-A-PAIR-OF-CARDS-INTO-WS.
00341              PERFORM C1-EDIT-FIRST-CARD.
00342              PERFORM C2-MOVE-FIRST-CARD-TO-WS.
00343              READ APPLICATION-CARDS-FILE
00344                AT END MOVE 'NO ' TO CARDS-LEFT.
00345              PERFORM C3-EDIT-SECOND-CARD.
00346              IF   (FIRST-CARD = 'GOOD')
00347                  AND (SECOND-CARD = 'GOOD')
00348                  AND (ACCT-NUM-MATCH = 'GOOD')
00349                      MOVE 'GOOD' TO PAIR-VALIDITY
00350                      MOVE CREDIT-INFO-IN TO CREDIT-INFO-WS
00351              ELSE
00352                  MOVE 'BAD ' TO PAIR-VALIDITY
00353              PERFORM C4-FLUSH-CARDS-TO-ERROR-LINES.
00354              READ APPLICATION-CARDS-FILE
00355                AT END MOVE 'NO ' TO CARDS-LEFT.
00356
00357          B2-CHANGE-OR-DELETE-MASTER.
00358              IF   CHANGE-CODE-WS = 'CH'
00359                  PERFORM C5-MERGE-UPDATE-WITH-OLD-MAST
00360                  MOVE 'RECORD CHANGED' TO UPDATE-MESSAGE-AREA
00361                  PERFORM C6-LOG-ACTION
00362                  WRITE CREDIT-MASTER-NEW-RECORD
00363              ELSE IF   CHANGE-CODE-WS = 'DE'
00364          *                      CHECK IF DELETE VALID
00365                      IF   CREDIT-INFO-WS IS EQUAL TO SPACES
00366                          MOVE 'RECORD DELETED' TO UPDATE-MESSAGE-AREA
00367                          PERFORM C6-LOG-ACTION
00368                      ELSE
00369                          MOVE 'REC NOT DELETED' TO UPDATE-MESSAGE-AREA
00370                          MOVE CREDIT-MASTER-OLD-RECORD TO
00371                              CREDIT-MASTER-NEW-RECORD
00372                          PERFORM C6-LOG-ACTION
00373                          WRITE CREDIT-MASTER-NEW-RECORD
00374              ELSE
00375                  PERFORM C7-INVALID-CHANGE-CODE.
00376
00377
00378          B3-ADD-NEW-MASTER.
00379              PERFORM C8-CALC-DISCRETNRY-INCOME.
00380              PERFORM C9-CALC-CREDIT-LIMIT.
00381              PERFORM C10-ASSEMBLE-NEW-MASTER-RECORD.
00382              MOVE 'RECORD ADDED ' TO UPDATE-MESSAGE-AREA.
00383              PERFORM C6-LOG-ACTION.
00384              WRITE CREDIT-MASTER-NEW-RECORD.
00385
00386          C1-EDIT-FIRST-CARD.  COPY EDT1STCD.
00387 C            MOVE 'GOOD' TO FIRST-CARD.
00388 C            IF NAME-IN IS EQUAL TO SPACES
00389 C                MOVE '*** NAME MISSING ***' TO NAME-IN
00390 C                MOVE 'BAD ' TO FIRST-CARD.
00391 C            IF ADDRESS-IN IS EQUAL TO SPACES
00392 C                MOVE '*** ADDRESS MISSING ****' TO ADDRESS-IN
00393 C                MOVE 'BAD ' TO FIRST-CARD.
00394 C            IF PHONE-IN IS EQUAL TO SPACES
00395 C                MOVE 'NO PHONE **' TO PHONE-IN
00396 C                MOVE 'BAD ' TO FIRST-CARD.
00397
```

```
00398        C2-MOVE-FIRST-CARD-TO-WS.
00399            MOVE NAME-IN TO NAME-WS.
00400            MOVE ADDRESS-IN TO ADDRESS-WS.
00401            MOVE PHONE-IN TO PHONE-WS.
00402            MOVE CHANGE-CODE-IN TO CHANGE-CODE-WS.
00403            MOVE ACCT-NUM-IN1 TO ACCT-NUM-WS.
00404
00405        C3-EDIT-SECOND-CARD.  COPY EDT2NDCD.
00406 C          MOVE 'GOOD' TO SECOND-CARD.
00407 C          MOVE 'GOOD' TO ACCT-NUM-MATCH.
00408 C          IF CARD-TYPE-IN IS NOT EQUAL TO 'C'
00409 C              MOVE 'BAD ' TO SECOND-CARD.
00410 C          IF ACCT-NUM-IN2 IS NOT EQUAL TO ACCT-NUM-WS
00411 C              MOVE 'BAD' TO ACCT-NUM-MATCH.
00412
00413        C4-FLUSH-CARDS-TO-ERROR-LINES.  COPY FLUSHCDS.
00414 C          MOVE FIRST-CARD TO FIRST-CARD-ERR1.
00415 C          MOVE NAME-WS TO NAME-ERR1.
00416 C          MOVE ADDRESS-WS TO ADDRESS-ERR1.
00417 C          MOVE PHONE-WS TO PHONE-ERR1.
00418 C          MOVE ACCT-NUM-WS TO ACCT-NUM-ERR1.
00419 C          MOVE SECOND-CARD TO SECOND-CARD-ERR2.
00420 C          MOVE CREDIT-INFO-WS TO CREDIT-INFO-ERR2.
00421 C          IF ACCT-NUM-MATCH = 'BAD '
00422 C              MOVE 'ACCOUNT NUMBERS DO NOT MATCH'
00423 C                                    TO MESSAGE-ERR-LINE-2
00424 C          ELSE
00425 C              MOVE SPACES TO MESSAGE-ERR-LINE-2.
00426            MOVE SPACES TO PRINT-LINE-OUT.
00427            WRITE PRINT-LINE-OUT FROM CARD-ERROR-LINE1-WS
00428                            AFTER ADVANCING 1 LINES.
00429            MOVE SPACES TO PRINT-LINE-OUT.
00430            WRITE PRINT-LINE-OUT FROM CARD-ERROR-LINE2-WS
00431                            AFTER ADVANCING 1 LINES.
00432
00433        C5-MERGE-UPDATE-WITH-OLD-MAST.
00434            MOVE ACCT-NUM-MAS-OLD TO ACCT-NUM-MAS-NEW.
00435            MOVE NAME-AND-ADDRESS-WS TO NAME-AND-ADDRESS-MAS-NEW.
00436            MOVE AREA-CODE-WS TO AREA-CODE-MAS-NEW.
00437            PERFORM D1-REMOVE-HYPHEN-FROM-TEL-NUM.
00438      * THE SECOND INPUT CARD HAS CREDIT DATA, IF THIS HAS TO BE
00439      * UPDATED THEN THE DISCRETIONARY INCOME CALC HAS TO BE RUN
00440            IF CREDIT-INFO-WS EQUAL TO SPACES
00441                MOVE CREDIT-INFO-MAS-OLD TO CREDIT-INFO-MAS-NEW
00442                MOVE ACCOUNT-INFO-MAS-OLD TO ACCOUNT-INFO-MAS-NEW
00443            ELSE
00444                PERFORM C8-CALC-DISCRETNRY-INCOME
00445                PERFORM C9-CALC-CREDIT-LIMIT
00446                MOVE SEX-WS                       TO SEX-MAS-NEW
00447                MOVE MARITAL-STATUS-WS            TO MARITAL-STATUS-MAS-NEW
00448                MOVE NUMBER-DEPENS-WS             TO NUMBER-DEPENS-MAS-NEW
00449                MOVE INCOME-HUNDREDS-WS           TO INCOME-HUNDREDS-MAS-NEW
00450                MOVE YEARS-EMPLOYED-WS            TO YEARS-EMPLOYED-MAS-NEW
00451                MOVE OWN-OR-RENT-WS               TO OWN-OR-RENT-MAS-NEW
00452                MOVE MORTGAGE-OR-RENTAL-WS        TO MORTGAGE-OR-RENTAL-MAS-NEW
00453                MOVE OTHER-PAYMENTS-WS            TO OTHER-PAYMENTS-MAS-NEW
00454                MOVE DISCR-INCOME-WS TO DISCR-INCOME-MAS-NEW
00455                MOVE CREDIT-LIMIT-WS  TO CREDIT-LIMIT-MAS-NEW.
00456            MOVE CURRENT-BALANCE-OWING-OLD TO CURRENT-BALANCE-OWING-NEW.
00457            MOVE SPARE-CHARACTERS-OLD TO SPARE-CHARACTERS-NEW.
```

```
00458
00459              C6-LOG-ACTION.
00460                  IF CHANGE-CODE-WS = 'CH'
00461          *                                    WRITE OLD TAPE RECORD
00462          *                                    WRITE CARD CONTENTS & MESSAGE
00463          *                                    WRITE NEW TAPE RECORD
00464                      MOVE SPACES TO CREDIT-MASTER-PRINT-LINE
00465                      MOVE CREDIT-MASTER-OLD-RECORD TO CREDIT-MASTER-OUT
00466                      WRITE PRINT-LINE-OUT FROM CREDIT-MASTER-PRINT-LINE
00467                                    AFTER ADVANCING 3 LINES
00468                      MOVE SPACES TO UPDATE-RECORD-PRINT-LINE
00469                      MOVE APPLICATION-DATA-WSB2 TO APPLICATION-DATA-OUT
00470                      MOVE UPDATE-MESSAGE-AREA TO MESSAGE-AREA-OUT
00471                      WRITE PRINT-LINE-OUT FROM UPDATE-RECORD-PRINT-LINE
00472                                    AFTER ADVANCING 1 LINES
00473                      MOVE SPACES TO CREDIT-MASTER-PRINT-LINE
00474                      MOVE CREDIT-MASTER-NEW-RECORD TO CREDIT-MASTER-OUT
00475                      WRITE PRINT-LINE-OUT FROM CREDIT-MASTER-PRINT-LINE
00476                                    AFTER ADVANCING 1 LINES
00477                  ELSE IF CHANGE-CODE-WS = 'DE'
00478          *                                    WRITE OLD TAPE RECORD
00479          *                                    WRITE CARD CONTENTS & MESSAGE
00480                      MOVE SPACES TO CREDIT-MASTER-PRINT-LINE
00481                      MOVE CREDIT-MASTER-OLD-RECORD TO CREDIT-MASTER-OUT
00482                      WRITE PRINT-LINE-OUT FROM CREDIT-MASTER-PRINT-LINE
00483                                    AFTER ADVANCING 3 LINES
00484                      MOVE SPACES TO UPDATE-RECORD-PRINT-LINE
00485                      MOVE APPLICATION-DATA-WSB2 TO APPLICATION-DATA-OUT
00486                      MOVE UPDATE-MESSAGE-AREA TO MESSAGE-AREA-OUT
00487                      WRITE PRINT-LINE-OUT FROM UPDATE-RECORD-PRINT-LINE
00488                                    AFTER ADVANCING 1 LINES
00489                  ELSE IF CHANGE-CODE-WS = ' '
00490          *                                    WRITE CARDS FOR ADDITION
00491          *                                    WRITE NEW TAPE RECORD
00492                      MOVE SPACES TO UPDATE-RECORD-PRINT-LINE
00493                      MOVE APPLICATION-DATA-WSB2 TO APPLICATION-DATA-OUT
00494                      MOVE UPDATE-MESSAGE-AREA TO MESSAGE-AREA-OUT
00495                      WRITE PRINT-LINE-OUT FROM UPDATE-RECORD-PRINT-LINE
00496                                    AFTER ADVANCING 3 LINES
00497                      MOVE SPACES TO CREDIT-MASTER-PRINT-LINE
00498                      MOVE CREDIT-MASTER-NEW-RECORD TO CREDIT-MASTER-OUT
00499                      WRITE PRINT-LINE-OUT FROM CREDIT-MASTER-PRINT-LINE
00500                                    AFTER ADVANCING 1 LINES
00501                  ELSE PERFORM C7-INVALID-CHANGE-CODE.
00502
00503              C7-INVALID-CHANGE-CODE.
00504          * THIS ROUTINE WILL HANDLE CARDS WITH NEITHER CH OR DE IN CC73/74
00505
00506              C8-CALC-DISCRETNRY-INCOME.  COPY DISCINCM.
00507 C               COMPUTE ANNUAL-INCOME-WS  = INCOME-HUNDREDS-WS * 100.
00508 C               COMPUTE ANNUAL-TAX-WS     = ANNUAL-INCOME-WS * TAX-RATE-WS.
00509 C               COMPUTE MONTHLY-NET-INCOME-WS ROUNDED
00510 C                  = (ANNUAL-INCOME-WS − ANNUAL-TAX-WS) / MONTHS-IN-YEAR.
00511 C               COMPUTE MONTHLY-PAYMENTS-WS = MORTGAGE-OR-RENTAL-WS
00512 C                                          + OTHER-PAYMENTS-WS.
00513 C               COMPUTE DISCR-INCOME-WS   = MONTHLY-NET-INCOME-WS
00514 C                                         − MONTHLY-PAYMENTS-WS
00515 C                  ON SIZE ERROR MOVE 999 TO DISCR-INCOME-WS.
00516 C       * DISCRETIONARY INCOMES OVER $999 PER MONTH ARE SET AT $999
00517
```

```
00518           C9-CALC-CREDIT-LIMIT.  COPY CALCREDT.
00519 C    *    MARRIED?              Y Y Y Y N N N N   THIS DECISION TABLE       *
00520 C    *    OWNED?                Y Y N N Y Y N N   SETS OUT COMPANY POLICY    *
00521 C    *    2 OR MORE YEARS?      Y N Y N Y N Y N   FOR DETERMINING CREDIT     *
00522 C    *    ----------------------------------------------------------- LIMIT FROM DISCRETIONARY *
00523 C    *    CREDIT   FACTOR  1               X X   INCOME.  FACTOR1 ETC ARE   *
00524 C    *    LIMIT IS         2        X   X        SET UP IN WS33.            *
00525 C    *    MULTIPLE         3          X                                     *
00526 C    *    OF DISCR         4    X X                                         *
00527 C    *    INCOME.          5  X                                             *
00528 C        IF MARRIED
00529 C            IF OWNED
00530 C                IF YEARS-EMPLOYED-WS NOT LESS THAN 02
00531 C                    MOVE FACTOR5 TO CREDIT-FACTOR
00532 C                ELSE
00533 C                    MOVE FACTOR4 TO CREDIT-FACTOR
00534 C            ELSE
00535 C                IF YEARS-EMPLOYED-WS NOT LESS THAN 02
00536 C                    MOVE FACTOR4 TO CREDIT-FACTOR
00537 C                ELSE
00538 C                    MOVE FACTOR2 TO CREDIT-FACTOR
00539 C        ELSE
00540 C            IF OWNED
00541 C                IF YEARS-EMPLOYED-WS NOT LESS THAN 02
00542 C                    MOVE FACTOR3 TO CREDIT-FACTOR
00543 C                ELSE
00544 C                    MOVE FACTOR2 TO CREDIT-FACTOR
00545 C            ELSE
00546 C                MOVE FACTOR1 TO CREDIT-FACTOR.
00547 C        COMPUTE CREDIT-LIMIT-WS = DISCR-INCOME-WS * CREDIT-FACTOR.
00548 C        IF CREDIT-LIMIT-WS IS GREATER THAN UPPER-LIMIT-WS
00549 C            MOVE UPPER-LIMIT-WS TO CREDIT-LIMIT-WS.
00550 C        ADD CREDIT-LIMIT-WS TO TOTAL-CREDIT-GIVEN-WS.
00551
00552           C10-ASSEMBLE-NEW-MASTER-RECORD.
00553           MOVE ACCT-NUM-WS TO ACCT-NUM-MAS-NEW.
00554           MOVE NAME-AND-ADDRESS-WS TO NAME-AND-ADDRESS-MAS-NEW.
00555           MOVE AREA-CODE-WS TO AREA-CODE-MAS-NEW.
00556           PERFORM D1-REMOVE-HYPHEN-FROM-TEL-NUM.
00557           MOVE SEX-WS                    TO SEX-MAS-NEW
00558           MOVE MARITAL-STATUS-WS         TO MARITAL-STATUS-MAS-NEW
00559           MOVE NUMBER-DEPENS-WS          TO NUMBER-DEPENS-MAS-NEW
00560           MOVE INCOME-HUNDREDS-WS        TO INCOME-HUNDREDS-MAS-NEW
00561           MOVE YEARS-EMPLOYED-WS         TO YEARS-EMPLOYED-MAS-NEW
00562           MOVE OWN-OR-RENT-WS            TO OWN-OR-RENT-MAS-NEW
00563           MOVE MORTGAGE-OR-RENTAL-WS     TO MORTGAGE-OR-RENTAL-MAS-NEW
00564           MOVE OTHER-PAYMENTS-WS         TO OTHER-PAYMENTS-MAS-NEW.
00565           MOVE DISCR-INCOME-WS TO DISCR-INCOME-MAS-NEW.
00566           MOVE CREDIT-LIMIT-WS TO CREDIT-LIMIT-MAS-NEW.
00567           MOVE ZEROS TO CURRENT-BALANCE-OWING-NEW.
00568           MOVE SPACES TO SPARE-CHARACTERS-NEW.
00569
00570           D1-REMOVE-HYPHEN-FROM-TEL-NUM.
00571               MOVE NUMBR-WS TO TEL-NUMBR-WITH-HYPHEN
00572               MOVE EXCHANGE-IN TO EXCHANGE
00573               MOVE FOUR-DIGIT-NUMBR-IN TO FOUR-DIGIT-NUMBR
00574               MOVE TEL-NUMBR-WITHOUT-HYPHEN TO NUMBR-MAS-NEW.
```

7.3 Random access devices

Suppose you had a master file on tape, as maintained by MAINTMFS, with 30,000 records on it, and suppose you wanted to know the credit limit of Morris Median, who is the 21,475th record on the file. You would need to use a program that read through the master file, checking each record until his was found. This could take several minutes, even at computer speeds. If, five minutes later, you wanted the credit limit for Marcia Mean, who had the 20,799th record, you would have to go through the whole process again. In practice, it is usually not economical to search sequentially through a complete tape file for one name at a time, so *inquiries* about data in a sequentially organized file are batched until there are enough to make a run through the file worthwhile. Of course, this means that it can take some time to get the answer to a question about data in a sequential file; for example, if the program is run once a day, it could take 24 hours or more to find out someone's credit limit.

Very frequently, we want to access records in *random* order at a rapid speed as, for example, when a customer of a bank wants to know the balance of his account. Or, when a potential customer calls a supplier to find out whether he can deliver a certain spare part, he doesn't want to wait. In each case, we are making an *inquiry* on the files, and there is no way of predicting which order the inquiries will come in, or when they will come. If the file that holds the relevant data is on tape, you may need to search through the whole of a reel of tape to find the information, which, as we have seen, can take too long; having answered one inquiry, you must rewind the tape and search all the way through again for the next inquiry.

For this reason, *random access storage devices* (sometimes called direct access storage devices, or DASD) were developed, which can locate any desired record in a fraction of a second. The most successful DASD to date is the rotating magnetic disk, shown on the following page in Fig. 7.4.

Each surface of the disk can hold recorded data as a stream of pulses on a series of *tracks*. The *read-write heads* can be moved by a precision mechanism to sit over any one of the tracks as the disk revolves.

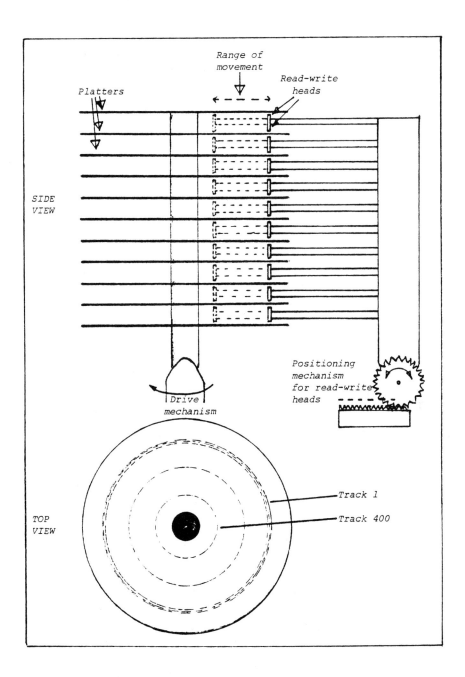

Figure 7.4. Schematic representation of magnetic disk drive.

In any one position of the head movement mechanism, of course, you can read a number of tracks, one for each read-write head. For example, the IBM 3330 disk drive, which is typical of the disks used on a variety of computers, has 11 platters. Each of these can be recorded on both surfaces, except for the very top and bottom surfaces (which might be damaged) and the top surface of the bottom platter (used to position the heads).

Q. How many tracks can be read with a single position of the read-write mechanism?

A. 19 (count them): 11 platters makes 22 sides, less 3 that cannot be used.

The 19 tracks that can be read at one position of the heads are called a *cylinder*. Every position of the heads (the IBM 3330 has 400 possible positions across the face of the platter) reads a different cylinder.

Q. Suppose that the data for Victor Grasper is written on track 79 on the side of the platter read by head 11, and that the heads are currently stationed over track 100. What has to happen before we can retrieve information pertaining to Victor Grasper's credit limit?

A. 1. The read-write heads have to be moved from track 100 to track 79.

2. The disk control program must select head 11 to read.

3. The system has to read track 79 under head 11 as the disk rotates, until it finds Victor Grasper's account number; then it must transfer the data to the input buffer.

The process of moving the heads to the correct position is called a *seek;* the process of reading the track as the disk rotates under the head is called a *search*.

Now, let's consider the mind-boggling calculations. The 3330 model holds 13,000 characters on each track; there are 19 tracks in each cylinder, and 400 cylinders on each disk pack. So, each 3330 drive can hold

13,000 × 19 × 400 or about 100 *million* characters.

That's roughly 1,250,000 fully punched cards, or a tray of punched cards half a mile long! And the 3330 can locate any item in about one-thirtieth of a second! That's what we mean by random access.

7.3.1 Organization of randomly accessed files

You can put sequentially organized files onto disk, just as you put them onto tape; but to randomly access a file, you have to supply enough information to enable the disk control system to work out which track the desired record is on. This is done in two ways, with *indexed* organization or *relative* organization. We shall deal with each in turn in the next two sections.

7.4 Indexed file organization

An indexed file is like a sequential file, except that at the beginning it has another small file, called the index, specifying in which cylinder and track each group of records is to be found. When you issue a READ, calling for a particular record, the operating system directs the read-write head to the index file, where it looks up the cylinder and track; it then goes directly to the track to find the record.

Suppose we had 38,000 customers on our master file, each with a record that is 128 characters long. Since an IBM 3330 can hold 13,000 characters per track, we would get about 100 customer records on each track. Since there are 19 tracks per cylinder, we would need about 20 cylinders to hold the file; that is, 38,000/(19 × 100).

Suppose, further, that the 38,000 account numbers range from 100000 to 999999 (with gaps), and that we want customer number 876543, whose record is actually on track 11 of cylinder 16 of the disk drive. If this were a sequential file, we would have to read through every track on every cylinder, record by record, saying, "Is this account number 876543? If not, read next record."

In an indexed file, the first cylinder has an index to all other cylinders, which in this case would be like this:

Record Key Range	Cylinder
100000 — 145000	1
145001 — 190500	2
190501 — 230499	3
.	.
.	.
.	.
850001 — 895000	16
.	.
.	.

With just one positioning of the read-write head, the disk control program reads this index and compares the range of keys for each cylinder with the so-called nominal key of the record for which we are looking, i.e., 876543. When it gets the match, the control program sends the read-write head to sit over cylinder 16. Now the head is in the correct position, but which of the 19 tracks is the right one to read from?

You guessed it: On the first track of each cylinder is a *track index*, giving the range of record keys to be found on each track, like this:

Cylinder 16 Record Key Range	Track
850001 — 852500	2
852501 — 854500	3
.	.
.	.
875001 — 880000	11
.	.
.	.

The control program then switches on to read-write head 11 and searches the track (serially) until it finds the record for 876543. Thus, with only two seeks of the read-write head (one to the index and one to the cylinder), we have located the correct record from 37,999 others.

As you can appreciate, the programming required to do all of this is somewhat complex; fortunately, the computer manufacturer supplies you with a Disk Control Program, which takes the COBOL commands and works out exactly what to do. You can write commands in your COBOL program to *create* indexed files, *access* a record randomly as described above, *read* the file sequentially, *update* records on the file, *add* new records, and *delete* records. Let's look at each of these actions in turn.

7.4.1 Creating an indexed file

In the FILE-CONTROL paragraph, you need to specify the information that tells the compiler to create an index; the file itself is created as a sequential file of records, and then the control program builds the index.

```
FILE-CONTROL.
    SELECT file-name-in-FD ASSIGN TO        DA-I-CUSTMAST
    ORGANIZATION IS INDEXED
    ACCESS IS SEQUENTIAL
    RECORD KEY IS data-name.                 a typical system-name
```

The RECORD KEY is whatever field that you will use to search the file; in our case, it would be ACCT-NUM.

The system-name, for example DA-I-CUSTMAST above, may be different depending upon the operating system used by your installation. This example uses an IBM Operating System name; earlier we used IBM Disk Qperating System names — the equivalent DOS name might be SYSnnn-DA-2314-I.

In the Data Division, you need to write an FD for the new indexed file, normally specifying LABEL RECORDS ARE STANDARD and containing a BLOCK CONTAINS clause. The input file must be a sequential file, usually card or tape, with the keys arranged in ascending order.

In the Procedure Division, OPEN the new file as OUTPUT. READ from the input file and WRITE to the new indexed file. If, for any reason, the records are out of order or there are two records with the same key (a *duplicate key condition*), the disk system control program will not know what to do. For this reason, the INVALID KEY clause is provided; the format of the WRITE statement becomes

WRITE indexed-record FROM data-name INVALID KEY imperative.

e.g., **WRITE CREATE-INDEX-REC**
       INVALID KEY PERFORM DUPLICATE-OR-SEQUENCE-ERROR.

With this information, you now are required to write a program that creates an indexed file from the customer master file currently held in sequential form on tape. This will be the first step in a project to give the Marketing Manager immediate access to a customer's unpaid balances and to other information. Use ACCT-NUM as the record key, with a block size of ten records. If you find an invalid key, print out the entire tape record with an appropriate message, and go on to the next record. Call this program CREATEMFI.

A model solution is presented on the following pages. You will see that, unlike the previous programs in the book, it has not been compiled. This is because, at the time of writing, this particular form of indexed file, though specified by the 1974 American National Standard (ANS) for COBOL, had not been implemented by any manufacturer. You should check whether your installation has ANS-74 COBOL, or a compiler that conforms to the earlier standard, ANS-68. ANS-68 compilers have some minor differences in handling indexed and relative files, and you should seek advice on what these are. We hope that, by the time you read this, you will have an ANS-74 compiler with which to work.

```
IDENTIFICATION DIVISION.
PROGRAM-ID.  CREATEMFI.

ENVIRONMENT DIVISION.
INPUT-OUTPUT SECTION.
FILE-CONTROL.
        SELECT TAPE-MASTER          ASSIGN TO UT-S-TAPEINPT.
        SELECT DISK-MASTER          ASSIGN TO DA-I-CUSTMAST
                                    ORGANIZATION IS INDEXED
                                    ACCESS IS SEQUENTIAL
                                    RECORD KEY IS ACCT-NUM-MAS.
        SELECT ERROR-LIST           ASSIGN TO UR-S-SYSPRINT.

DATA DIVISION.
FILE-SECTION.

FD  TAPE-MASTER
    LABEL RECORDS ARE STANDARD
    BLOCK CONTAINS 10 RECORDS.
01  TAPE-MASTER-RECORD.
    05   ACCT-NUM-IN                PIC 9(6).
    05   ACCT-INFO-IN               PIC X(102).
    05   FILLER                     PIC X(20).

FD  DISK-MASTER
    LABEL RECORDS ARE STANDARD
    BLOCK CONTAINS 10 RECORDS.
01  INDEXED-MASTER-RECORD.
    05   ACCT-NUM-MAS               PIC 9(6).
    05   ACCT-INFO-OUT              PIC X(102).
    05   FILLER                     PIC X(20).

FD  ERROR-LIST
    LABEL RECORDS ARE OMITTED.
01  PRINT-LINE-OUT                  PIC X(132).

WORKING-STORAGE SECTION.

01  COMMON-WS.
    05   TAPE-RECORDS-LEFT          PIC X(3).

01  ERROR-RECORD-WS.
    05   FILLER                     PIC X(40)
         VALUE 'DUPLICATE OR SEQUENCE ERROR ON ACCT NO   '.
    05   ACCT-NUM-ERR               PIC 9(6).
    05   FILLER                     PIC X(50)
         VALUE 'THIS RECORD IGNORED:  CHECK INPUT AND FILE CONTENTS'.
```

```
PROCEDURE DIVISION.

    PERFORM A1-INITIALIZATION.
    PERFORM A2-LOAD-DISK-FILE
        UNTIL TAPE-RECORDS-LEFT = 'NO '.
    PERFORM A3-END-OF-JOB.
    STOP RUN.

A1-INITIALIZATION.
    OPEN    INPUT    TAPE-MASTER
            OUTPUT   DISK-MASTER
                     ERROR-LIST.
    MOVE 'YES' TO TAPE-RECORDS-LEFT.
    READ TAPE-MASTER
        AT END MOVE 'NO ' TO TAPE-RECORDS-LEFT.
* FIRST TAPE RECORD IN BUFFER

A2-LOAD-DISK-FILE.
    MOVE SPACES TO INDEXED-MASTER-RECORD.
    MOVE ACCT-NUM-IN TO ACCT-NUM-MAS.
    MOVE ACCT-INFO-IN TO ACCT-INFO-OUT.
    WRITE INDEXED-MASTER-RECORD
        INVALID KEY PERFORM B1-DUPLICATE-OR-SEQUENCE-ERROR.
    READ TAPE-MASTER
        AT END MOVE 'NO ' TO TAPE-RECORDS-LEFT.

A3-END-OF-JOB.
    CLOSE   TAPE-MASTER
            DISK-MASTER
            ERROR-LIST.

B1-DUPLICATE-OR-SEQUENCE-ERROR.
    MOVE ACCT-NUM-MAS TO ACCT-NUM-ERR.
    MOVE SPACES TO PRINT-LINE-OUT.
    WRITE PRINT-LINE-OUT FROM ERROR-RECORD-WS.
```

7.4.2 Randomly accessing an indexed file

Now that we have an indexed file on disk, we want to be able to access any record on demand. For example, we might want to be able to get a customer's credit profile by specifying only his account number. To make an *inquiry* on the file like this, we want to feed in an account number, or a series of account numbers, in any order we please, and have the response to each inquiry printed out.

To make random inquiries, specify ACCESS IS RANDOM in the SELECT statement for the file, and move the key value of the record to be retrieved into the field named RECORD KEY, before READing the indexed file. If the record for which you ask cannot be found, an INVALID KEY condition will exist, and you will have to specify what the program should do in this case.

Suppose we want to develop such an inquiry program, called INXINQIR, which will read in cards, in any order, each with a six-digit account number punched in cc 2 − 7, and with an I (for inquiry) in cc 1. The program is to retrieve the corresponding record for each account number from the master file, and simply list the contents of the disk record on the printer. If the record for that account number can't be found, the account number should be printed out with an appropriate message.

The following program will execute this basic inquiry:

```
IDENTIFICATION DIVISION.
PROGRAM-ID.  INXINQIR.

ENVIRONMENT DIVISION.
INPUT-OUTPUT SECTION.
FILE-CONTROL.
        SELECT CARD-FILE        ASSIGN TO UR-S-SYSIN.
        SELECT DISK-MASTER      ASSIGN TO DA-I-CUSTMAST
                                ORGANIZATION IS INDEXED
                                ACCESS IS RANDOM
                                RECORD KEY IS ACCT-NUM-MAS.
        SELECT REPORT-LIST      ASSIGN TO UR-S-SYSPRINT.
DATA DIVISION.
FILE-SECTION.

FD  CARD-FILE
    LABEL RECORDS ARE OMITTED.
01  INQUIRY-CARD.
    05   CARD-TYPE              PIC X.
    05   ACCT-NUM-IN            PIC 9(6).
    05   FILLER                 PIC X(73).
```

```
FD  DISK-MASTER
    LABEL RECORDS ARE STANDARD
    BLOCK CONTAINS 10 RECORDS.
01  INDEXED-MASTER-RECORD.
    05  ACCT-NUM-MAS                        PIC 9(6).
    05  ACCT-INFO-MAS                       PIC X(102).
    05  FILLER                              PIC X(20).

FD  REPORT-LIST
    LABEL RECORDS ARE OMITTED.
01  REPORT-LINE.
    05  PRINT-LINE-OUT                      PIC X(132).

WORKING-STORAGE SECTION.

01  COMMON-WS.
    05  CARDS-LEFT                          PIC X(3).
    05  MASTER-IS-FOUND                     PIC X(3).

01  ERROR-LINE-WS.
    05  FILLER                              PIC X(15)
        VALUE 'ACCOUNT NUMBER '.
    05  ACCT-NUM-ERR                        PIC 9(6).
    05  FILLER                              PIC X(25)
        VALUE 'NOT FOUND IN MASTER FILE '.
    05  FILLER                              PIC X(86).

PROCEDURE DIVISION.

    PERFORM A1-INITIALIZATION.
    PERFORM A2-PROCESS-INQUIRIES
        UNTIL CARDS-LEFT = 'NO '
    PERFORM A3-END-OF-JOB.
    STOP RUN.

A1-INITIALIZATION.
    OPEN    INPUT    CARD-FILE
                     DISK-MASTER
            OUTPUT   REPORT-LIST.
    MOVE 'YES' TO CARDS-LEFT.
    READ CARD-FILE
        AT END MOVE 'NO ' TO CARDS-LEFT.

A2-PROCESS-INQUIRIES.
    MOVE ACCT-NUM-IN TO ACCT-NUM-MAS.
    MOVE 'YES' TO MASTER-IS-FOUND.
    READ DISK-MASTER-RECORD
        INVALID KEY MOVE 'NO ' TO MASTER-IS-FOUND.
    IF MASTER-IS-FOUND = 'YES'
            WRITE PRINT-LINE-OUT FROM INDEXED-MASTER-RECORD
    ELSE
            MOVE ACCT-NUM-MAS TO ACCT-NUM-ERR
            WRITE PRINT-LINE-OUT FROM ERROR-LINE-WS.
    READ CARD-FILE
        AT END MOVE 'NO ' TO CARDS-LEFT.

A3-END-OF-JOB.
    CLOSE CARD-FILE DISK-MASTER REPORT-LIST.
```

When you have compiled a crude skeleton program similar to INXINQIR and have tested it with some account numbers known to be on the file, as well as with some that are not, you will have shown that you successfully can retrieve some records from the master file.

A more complex version of this program might check the first column of the card, and reject the card if it did not have an I in cc 1, printing an appropriate message. How would you modify the logic of INXINQIR to do this?

A still fuller version would present the information retrieved for each account as a profile, as we did in CREDCALC. How would you enhance the program to do this? To what extent could you use the Source Statement Library?

7.4.3 Updating an indexed file, adding and deleting records

Suppose that a customer changes his address or his phone number, or that his credit circumstances change. We will want to alter the fields in his record, just as we did when the master file was on tape. Similarly, we want to be able to create new records for new customers, and delete records when customers close their accounts.

Changing fields is performed with a REWRITE command, adding records with a WRITE (there shouldn't be a duplicate key because this is new), and deleting records with a DELETE command. In all cases, the file is specified with ACCESS IS RANDOM.

There is, of course, no need to create a fresh copy of an indexed file, as we did with the tape. When you modify the file, the disk control program reorganizes the index to keep track of all the records; since the index shows where each record is located, we can add records in any order. This is especially useful when, as in most cases, there are many fewer changes to the file than there are original records. For example, if we update only 150 records on a tape containing 38,000 records, we have to rewrite all 38,000 records again onto a new tape. If we use indexed files, by contrast, we need only change and rewrite the 150 records.

Let us summarize the program considerations in each case:

Updates

OPEN the indexed file as I-O (input and output).

The RECORD KEY field should contain the value of the record to be updated.

READ the indexed file INVALID KEY PERFORM RECORD-NOT-FOUND.

MOVE the new values to the appropriate fields in the record. (Don't change the key field! If you do, you will update the wrong record, or get an invalid key.)

REWRITE the indexed file INVALID KEY PERFORM SERIOUS-ERROR. If the invalid key condition exists, it can be because either the key has been changed between READ and REWRITE, or perhaps the READ was not done in the first place; this would indicate the existence of a bug in your program.

Additions

OPEN the indexed file as I-O.

Make sure that the RECORD KEY field contains the new value.

WRITE the new record INVALID KEY PERFORM RECORD-ALREADY-IN-FILE.

Deletions

OPEN the indexed file as I-O.

MOVE the key of the record to the key field.

DELETE indexed-file-name RECORD INVALID KEY PERFORM RECORD-NOT-FOUND.

Having created our indexed master file, and being able to make inquiries on it, we also want to develop a file maintenance program, so that we can add new customers, change information on existing customers, and delete the records of customers whose accounts have been closed. This program, to be called MAINTMFI, will read pairs of cards laid out as in SAMPLE-4; and changes, additions, and deletions will be submitted using the same card conventions as with MAINTMFS. The only difference will be that where a record is to be added, it will carry the code 'AD' in cc 73-74.

Use these specifications to develop the high-level logic of MAINTMFI. Where the details of a module are not clear, or not vital to the main logic, define the module by name but code only a skeleton version or *stub* as a temporary measure. There are many ways of implementing stubs; the simplest way is to code the paragraph-name and add a comment to remind yourself that the code has yet to be written. The compiler will reject your program if you do not at least define the paragraph!

Another means of implementing a stub is to print a simple debugging message when you enter the module. With just a defined name, there is no way of checking that your stub was performed in the right place, unless you are using READY TRACE. We will discuss other stubs in Part 2, Chapter 14 of this series.

An early version of MAINTMFI is shown on the following pages for comparison.

```
IDENTIFICATION DIVISION.
PROGRAM-ID.  MAINTMFI.
•
INPUT-OUTPUT SECTION.
FILE-CONTROL.
     SELECT CUST-MAST-FILE          ASSIGN TO DA-I-CUSTMAST-R
                                    ORGANIZATION IS INDEXED
                                    ACCESS IS RANDOM
•                                   RECORD KEY IS ACCT-NUM-MAS.
•
PROCEDURE DIVISION.
    PERFORM A1-INITIALIZATION.
    PERFORM A2-UPDATE-INDEXED-FILE
        UNTIL CARDS-LEFT = 'NO '.
    PERFORM A3-END-OF-JOB.
    STOP RUN.

A1-INITIALIZATION.
    OPEN    INPUT     UPDATE-FILE
            I-O       CUST-MAST-FILE
            OUTPUT    UPDATE-LISTING.
    MOVE 'YES' TO CARDS-LEFT.
    PERFORM B1-GET-A-PAIR-OF-CARDS-INTO-WS.
    MOVE ACCT-NUM-WS TO ACCT-NUM-MAS.

A2-UPDATE-INDEXED-FILE
    IF CHANGE-CODE-WS = 'AD'
        PERFORM B2-ASSEMBLE-NEW-MAST
        PERFORM B3-WRITE-CUSTOMER-MAST
        IF INVALID-KEY-FLAG = 'YES'
            PERFORM B4-DUPLICATE-REC-ON-FILE
        ELSE
            PERFORM B5-PRINT-CHANGE
    ELSE IF CHANGE-CODE-WS = 'CH'
        PERFORM B6-READ-CUSTOMER-MAST
        IF INVALID-KEY-FLAG = 'YES'
            PERFORM B7-CUSTOMER-NOT-FOUND
        ELSE
            PERFORM B8-MERGE-CHANGES-WITH-MAST
            PERFORM B9-REWRITE-CUSTOMER-MAST
            IF INVALID-KEY-FLAG = 'YES'
                PERFORM B10-DSK-OR-PRGM-ERR
            ELSE
                PERFORM B5-PRINT-CHANGE
    ELSE IF CHANGE-CODE-WS = 'DE'
        PERFORM B11-DOUBLE-CHECK-DELETE
        PERFORM B12-DELETE-CUSTOMER-MAST
        IF INVALID-KEY-FLAG = 'YES'
            PERFORM B10-DSK-OR-PRGM-ERR
        ELSE
            PERFORM B13-PRINT-DELETION-MSG
    ELSE
        PERFORM B14-INVALID-CHANGE-CODE.
    PERFORM B1-GET-A-PAIR-OF-CARDS-INTO-WS.
```

```
A3-END-OF-JOB.
    CLOSE   UPDATE-FILE
            CUST-MAST-FILE
            UPDATE-LISTING.


B1-GET-A-PAIR-OF-CARDS-INTO-WS.  COPY GETPRCDS.


B2-ASSEMBLE-NEW-MAST.
* THIS ROUTINE WILL BE COPIED FROM THE MAINTMFS PROGRAM

B3-WRITE-CUSTOMER-MAST.
    MOVE 'NO ' TO INVALID-KEY-FLAG.
    WRITE CUSTOMER-MAST-RECORD
        INVALID KEY MOVE 'YES' TO INVALID-KEY-FLAG.


B4-DUPLICATE-REC-ON-FILE.
* THIS ROUTINE WILL BE LEFT AS A STUB FOR EARLY TESTS


B5-PRINT-CHANGE.
* THIS ROUTINE WILL BE ADAPTED FROM THE MAINTMFS PROGRAM

B6-READ-CUSTOMER-MAST.
    MOVE 'NO ' TO INVALID-KEY-FLAG.
    READ CUST-MAST-FILE
        INVALID KEY MOVE 'YES' TO INVALID-KEY-FLAG.


B7-CUSTOMER-NOT-FOUND.
* THIS ROUTINE WILL BE LEFT AS A STUB FOR EARLY TESTS

B8-MERGE-CHANGES-WITH-MAST.
* THIS ROUTINE WILL BE COPIED FROM THE MAINTMFS PROGRAM

B9-REWRITE-CUSTOMER-MAST.
    MOVE 'NO ' TO INVALID-KEY-FLAG.
    REWRITE CUST-MAST-RECORD
        INVALID KEY MOVE 'YES' TO INVALID-KEY-FLAG.


B10-DSK-OR-PRGM-ERR.
* THIS ROUTINE WILL BE LEFT AS A STUB FOR EARLY TESTS

B11-DOUBLE-CHECK-DELETE.
* THIS ROUTINE WILL BE LEFT AS A STUB FOR EARLY TESTS

B12-DELETE-CUSTOMER-MAST.
    MOVE 'NO ' TO INVALID-KEY-FLAG.
    DELETE CUST-MAST-FILE RECORD
        INVALID KEY MOVE 'YES' TO INVALID-KEY-FLAG.


B13-PRINT-DELETION-MSG.
* THIS ROUTINE WILL BE LEFT AS A STUB FOR EARLY TESTS

B14-INVALID-CHANGE-CODE.
* THIS ROUTINE WILL BE LEFT AS A STUB FOR EARLY TESTS
```

7.4.4 Other facilities with indexed files

Should you want to print out a complete listing of a file, you can read an indexed file sequentially by specifying ACCESS IS SEQUENTIAL and writing the READ statement as you would for a tape file. Suppose you want to look at a group of records with keys close together, say, the ten records following account 876543. Of course, you don't want to read through the whole file sequentially to find those records, and you may want to make other random accesses in the same program. With ANS-74 COBOL compilers, you can avoid the first and accomplish the latter by specifying ACCESS IS DYNAMIC, READing the first record you want to see, and then writing

READ file-name NEXT RECORD.

This enables you to mix random access and sequential processing, if your problem demands it.

7.4.5 Disadvantages of indexed files

We said that you can access any record with only two movements of the read-write heads, one to the cylinder index and one to the cylinder. This is true when an indexed file is newly created. However, once you start to add records to a file, the disk control system inserts them in their sequential position in the file, moving other records up to make room. Once a track is full, records may go into a special *overflow area,* which may be on another cylinder or cylinders. When a lot of records have been added to the file, the overflow situation may be such that to find any given record can require four seeks of the read-write head. This can slow processing significantly.

The other type of random access file organization, relative organization, attempts to speed up random access by going directly to the record. This is discussed in the next section.

Of course, if you never require random access, you can create a sequential file on disk to have the same features as a sequential file on tape. The statements used are very similar to those for a sequential tape file, and you should consult the manufacturer's COBOL reference manual for your installation if you need to use a disk sequential file. Bear in mind that holding sequential files on tape is much cheaper than on disk.

7.5 Relative file organization

The idea behind relative file organization is to look up each record by specifying to the disk control system its *relative* position in the file. With relative organization, the disk control system knows the number of records on each track, and the track at which the file begins. So, if we specify that the record we want is 379th in the file, the disk control system can work out which track this record is on, and position the read-write heads to read or write the record. The *relative record number* (RRN), 379 in this case, is a unique number specifying the relative position of the record in the file.

Notice that, once we specify the RRN, the read-write heads can reach the record in only one seek movement, compared with a minimum of two seeks for an indexed file. This makes relative organization inherently faster than indexed organization.

The drawback is that it can be quite difficult to arrange the record keys so that the programmer can specify the RRN. However, in some cases, the nature of the problem makes this a comparatively simple task. For instance, suppose we want to keep a day-to-day record of the volume of business conducted by our company. We also want to retrieve this information, by specifying the Julian date of the day's business volume record that we wish to see. The Julian date is the number of the day in the year: January 31 (a Gregorian date) corresponds to a Julian date of 031. February 27 has a Julian date of 058. We could use the Julian date as the RRN for the file, and write a program that would convert each date, supplied as MMDDYY, to the Julian date before reading the relatively organized disk file.

> Q. Apart from the inconvenience in programming, what are the disadvantages of this approach, assuming no business is done on Saturdays, Sundays, and holidays?

A. A considerable amount of disk space will be wasted, because the disk control system will leave a space for each Julian date, no matter whether there is a record or not.

Situations like this, in which the relative record number can be obtained directly, are rare. Consider the case of our mail-order master file. Suppose we have 500 records, with account numbers from 000001 through 999999. How can we transform each account number into a RRN?

One way is to use a *randomizing* routine: Divide the account number by the prime number that is just less than the total number of records in the file. Use the remainder as the RRN. For example, if you were to divide Victor Grasper's account number, 010101, by 499 (a prime number), the integer result is 20 and the remainder is 121. Victor Grasper thus will become the 121st record in the file. If a customer were assigned the account number 010480, the result would be 21 and the remainder would be 1. This account therefore would be the first record. Since the remainder always will be between 0 and 498, adding 1 to these remainders will make them usable as RRNs.

Q. What is the drawback of this method?

A. You may have two account numbers which randomize to the same remainder. For example, 998121 randomizes to the same RRN as does Victor Grasper's account number. These two account numbers — 010101 and 998121 — are said to be *synonyms*. With only 500 accounts spread across one million possible account numbers, the probability of synonyms is rather low. But what if there were 100,000 accounts?

If relative organization is used, the programmer has to specify what action should be taken in the case of synonyms. For this reason, indexed file organization is much more common than relative file organization; relative files mainly are used in the following cases:

- cases in which speed of response to inquiries or speed of dating is very important, or

- cases in which the keys can be transformed easily to relative record numbers

The COBOL that you write for relative files is very similar to that for indexed files, the main difference being in the SELECT statement; as an example,

```
SELECT DISK-MASTER ASSIGN TO DA-R-RELMAST
    ORGANIZATION IS RELATIVE
    ACCESS IS RANDOM
    RELATIVE KEY IS ACCT-NUM-REMAINDER.
```

Relative organization is dealt with in greater detail in Chapter 12, in Part 2 of this series.

7.6 Controlling printer spacing and paging

Until now, we have controlled spacing on printed output by adding AFTER ADVANCING *n* LINES to each WRITE statement. As you will have noticed, the continuous forms used for printer output usually have perforations every 11 inches (or, at 6 lines per inch, 66 lines). We simply have written over these perforations.

For professionally produced reports, we may want to print headings at the top of each page, or jump to the top of a new page when we get near the bottom of the page being printed. This can be done by specifying the page layout desired in an optional LINAGE clause in the FD for the printer file. The variables that you can specify are shown in the diagram on the next page.

Thus, if you were to write the following in SAMPLE-3:

```
FD   PROFILE-LISTING
     LABEL RECORDS ARE OMITTED
     LINAGE IS 60 LINES
         WITH FOOTING AT 56
         LINES AT TOP 3
         LINES AT BOTTOM 3.
```

each page would start three lines from the top, and the compiler automatically would set up a field called LINAGE-COUNTER, which is set to a value of 1 at the top of each page, and is incremented appropriately by every WRITE statement. Before each WRITE, the program will test to see whether the LINAGE-COUNTER has reached or exceeded the LINAGE value specified in the FD. If it has, the printer will jump to the top of the next page, leaving three lines at the bottom of the previous page.

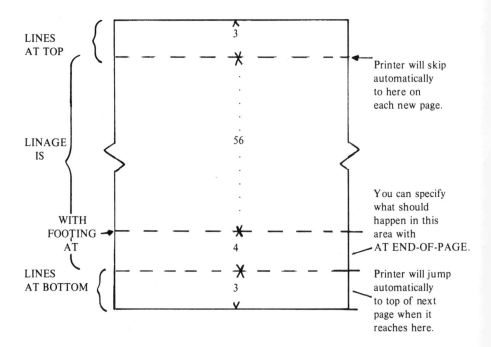

This *automatic page overflow* can be inconvenient when, as in SAMPLE-3, you are printing lines in groups of three, because it might cause a group to split between pages. For this reason, you have an optional AT END-OF-PAGE clause in the WRITE statement. The END-OF-PAGE condition exists when the LINAGE-COUNTER is equal to or greater than the FOOTING value. If you were to modify the WRITE-PROFILE paragraph in SAMPLE-3 like this:

```
WRITE-PROFILE.
    MOVE SPACES TO PRINT-LINE-OUT.
    WRITE PRINT-LINE-OUT FROM LINE-1-WS
        AFTER ADVANCING 4 LINES.
    MOVE SPACES TO PRINT-LINE-OUT.
    WRITE PRINT-LINE-OUT FROM LINE-2-WS
        AFTER ADVANCING 1 LINES.
    MOVE SPACES TO PRINT-LINE-OUT.
    WRITE PRINT-LINE-OUT FROM LINE-3-WS
        AFTER ADVANCING 1 LINE
        AT END-OF-PAGE
            WRITE PRINT-LINE-OUT FROM HEADER-WS
            AFTER ADVANCING PAGE.
```

causing the group of three lines to end at or below the line specified in WITH FOOTING AT, the AFTER ADVANCING PAGE instruction would cause the printer to skip to the top of the next page (as specified in LINES AT TOP) and write a heading. Always check your printing layout to be sure that the footing area is large enough for all the lines that you possibly might want printed in it, so that automatic overflow does not spoil your report.

These very useful facilities only apply to ANS-74 COBOL compilers. Although some ANS-68 compilers have the END-OF-PAGE facility, often it is the programmer's responsibility to keep track of where he is on the page. Once again, you must check the provisions of your COBOL compiler.

7.7 Top-down implementation of a useful accounting system

7.7.1 Functional specifications

Now that we have our customer master file created and maintainable as an indexed file, we are in a position to start doing business. When we get an order for goods from a customer, we send those goods in the mail with an invoice, stating the date of shipment, a serial number, a description of the order, and the amount payable. When the customer receives the goods, he or she will send us a check, money order, or cash in payment.

At the end of each month, we want to send each customer a statement with details of all invoices sent out, payments received, and net amount owing, if any. Naturally, we would not want to send goods to someone if that would mean the amount owed exceeded the particular credit limit. Nor do we want to send out goods to someone who is not on our master file.

The system that you have to design and write will have three main functions:

- to accept orders and payments, and to keep a record of transactions and balances for each account

- to check the credit information on the master file for each person who orders; to reject orders from people who do not have accounts, or who would be exceeding their credit limit; and to produce invoices for good orders

- to produce a statement at intervals for each account that has had a transaction since the last statement

The information we need to store about an order is

- customer's account number

- date that the order was processed

- invoice serial number consisting of three letters for the initials of the account representative plus a three-digit serial number, e.g., CPG903

- ten letters of description of the item, e.g., SNOWMOBILE

- amount of the invoice in dollars and cents up to $9999.99; ignore tax

The information we need to store about a payment is

- customer's account number

- date that payment was received

- serial number of the check or money order

- method of payment (check, money order, cash)

- amount of payment in dollars and cents

Clearly, these two transaction types have a lot in common; perhaps we can use the same card layout for each. In addition, each invoice should contain the following information and should resemble the sample layout:

YOURDON MAIL-ORDER CORPORATION
1133 AVENUE OF THE AMERICAS   NEW YORK, NY 10036 212 730-2670

TO: VICTOR S GRASPER
             990 GAUNTLET AVE
             BURLINGAME CA
                 94010

DATE	INVOICE SERIAL NO	DESCRIPTION	AMOUNT $
MAY 8th 1977	CPG421	SNOWMOBILE	1191.12

PAYMENT IS DUE ON RECEIPT OF GOODS.
PLEASE QUOTE YOUR ACCOUNT NUMBER 010101 ON ALL
PAYMENTS AND CORRESPONDENCE.

Each statement should look like this:

YOURDON MAIL-ORDER CORPORATION
1133 AVENUE OF THE AMERICAS NEW YORK, NY 10036 212 730-2670

TO: VICTOR S. GRASPER
990 GAUNTLET AVE
BURLINGAME CA
94010

STATEMENT OF ACCOUNT AT MAY 31st 1977

BALANCE OWING AT APRIL 30th 1977   293.24

DATE	DESCRIPTION		AMOUNT $	BALANCE $
MAY 8th	INVOICE CPG421	SNOWMOBILE	1191.12	1484.36
MAY 17th	CHECK 423	RECEIVED-THANK-YOU	293.24	1191.12
MAY 29th	INVOICE CPG903	BOOKS	8.88	1200.00

BALANCE OWING AT MAY 31st 1977 $1200.00

YOU ARE REMINDED THAT PAYMENT IS DUE ON RECEIPT OF GOODS.
PLEASE QUOTE YOUR ACCOUNT NUMBER 010101 ON ALL PAYMENTS
AND CORRESPONDENCE.

The systems analyst tells you to allow for up to twenty invoices per account in one month; you can assume that there never will be more than one item per invoice, or more than one invoice per day. There may be up to five, but usually only one, payments per month.

Give some thought to a system that would meet these functional specifications, knowing that you already have the indexed master file and MAINTMFI. Its usefulness will be clear when a customer calls to ask how much he owes, or if management wants to know a specific customer's balance.

7.7.2 Systems design

Let us assume that the transactions will be punched onto cards, with a card format that we will specify later. We need to edit these cards, first to make sure as much as possible that the punching has been done correctly, and to check that the customer account number exists on our master file. Next, orders must be validated to ensure that they will not exceed the credit limit. Then, invoices can be printed.

For reference and for auditing purposes, we want to print a *journal,* or log, of every transaction in the order in which it was received, giving full details of the transaction and the reason for rejection, if any. You are free to design your own layout.

Many commercial systems sort orders and payments into two batches, and edit them with separate programs. We do not want to do this, as it puts an extra clerical load on the people opening the mail; you should design a card input format that can be used for invoices or payments, using a transaction-type code so that the system can tell which is which.

The data flow diagram for daily processing looks thus:

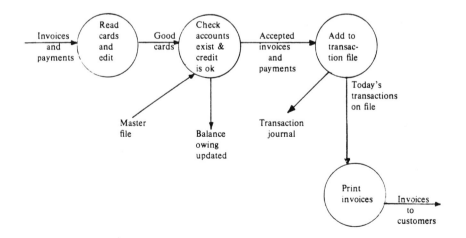

There is no theoretical reason to prevent you from printing the invoice at the same time as you print the transaction journal, except that many computers have only one printer, making it necessary for the operator to go through the printout and separate the invoices. Furthermore, we need to save only the transactions in order to generate end-of-month statements. A structure chart for this system follows:

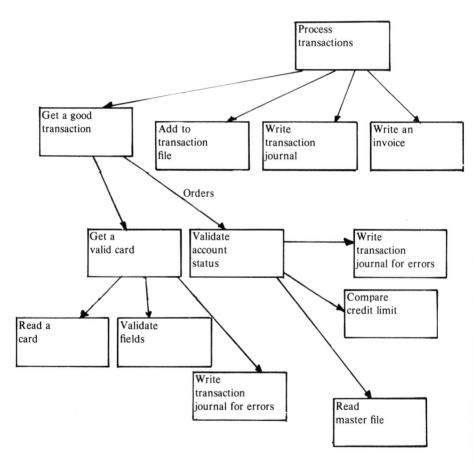

You could implement this structure with two programs: one to build the transaction file, and one to read the transaction file to write the invoices. Or, you could do it all with one program that, like CREATEMF, closes the transaction file and reopens it to write the invoices. This packaging choice largely depends on the size of program that you can run on your computer, and, if the invoices are to be written on special paper, is at the convenience of the operator. The monthly statement-writing program must be kept separate.

7.7.3 File design

The transactions, of course, will come in random order, depending on what arrives in the mail each day. When we produce the statements, we want to do so one account at a time — with the transactions for that statement all together in date order. This involves *sorting* the transactions in some way to get them into order, a facility which we have not yet covered, or loading the transactions to an indexed file in such a way as to be able to retrieve them in the desired way by reading the file sequentially.

This is achieved by making the record key of the transaction file a field which is a combination of account number, transaction date in the form MMDD, and transaction type. Thus, the data for the invoice shown previously could be stored in a record with the key 0101015081 where I is the code for invoice. An invoice the following day would have the key 01010105091 and be retrieved next in a sequential read.

7.8 Building the system with a skeleton and successive versions

Keeping these main design considerations in mind, prepare a detailed design of the file and of the programs as shown in the structure chart above. Writing in pseudocode, the main logic of "Get a good transaction" might be

```
IF the transaction is for an invoice
    Add the invoice amount to the current balance owing
    IF the new current balance would be greater than the credit limit
        Write a message to the transaction journal and reject
    ELSE
        Write the new value of the current balance on the master file
        Write the transaction to the transaction file
ELSE (transaction is a payment)
    Subtract the amount from the current balance on the master file
    Write the transaction to the transaction file
```

If you can work with some colleagues, divide the work among you, with perhaps one being responsible for the editing of cards, one for invoice production, and one for statement production.

Whenever several people and their programs must interface, it is best to code the high levels of each program first, leaving as much as possible as stubs in the way we did with MAINTMFI, and get a *skeleton* or *Version* ∅ of the whole system working as soon as possible. Your system's Version ∅ might

- read in a correctly punched order card and a correctly punched payment card

- do no editing of fields for numeric, alphabetic, or others

- verify that the account exists but will assume that the credit check is OK

- write the transactions to the transaction file

- write an unformatted invoice for the order from the transaction file with, for example, no conversion of dates to the form specified

That is, Version ∅ would contain almost no editing, no transaction journal, and no statement. However, it would prove that your team could load and read the transaction file, as well as read the master file.

Version 1 might write a crude statement, simple transaction journal, and a formatted invoice. Version 2 might reject orders for credit, and edit some fields in the cards, rejecting them if they are not numeric or not alphabetic when they should be. It could require a fully formatted invoice and statement.

This so-called top-down implementation of a system has the advantage that communication between people on a project is simplified, because everyone can work with the same skeleton version of the system on the machine. It also lets you see visible progress much earlier in the project than if you were to code each program completely before putting the system together.

CONCLUSION

If you have understood everything that you have read so far, and if you have completed the program exercises and produced working programs, you are competent to be a junior member of a programming team. You have learned the basics of COBOL, and can use them, with the structured techniques, to solve a wide variety of commercial problems. There are a number of features and facilities in COBOL that you have yet to learn; they will be covered in Part 2 of this series.

If you find that you have to maintain or enhance programs written by other people, you may see use of the GO TO statement, which transfers control to some other part of the program. Unlike the PERFORM statement, the GO TO does not return control to the original point, and, unless used with great care, the GO TO can make the program difficult to follow. If you have trouble working with programs that use it, express the programs as structured flowcharts, and rewrite the code using the structures with which you are familiar.

APPENDICES

Appendix A: Reserved Words

This list of reserved words includes all those specified by the 1974 American National Standard,* plus others (marked with an asterisk, *) that may be found in other compilers, but that are not part of the standard. You should avoid using any of the words on this list as programmer-defined names, even if they are not reserved words for the compiler that you are using. Be sure to check out each compiler that you use to see that it has no other reserved words.

ACCEPT	* BEGINNING	COLUMN
ACCESS	* BINARY	* COM-REG
* ACTUAL	BLANK	COMMA
ADD	BLOCK	COMMUNICATION
* ADDRESS	BOTTOM	COMP
ADVANCING	BY	* COMP-1
AFTER		* COMP-2
ALL		* COMP-3
ALPHABETIC	CALL	* COMP-4
ALSO	CANCEL	COMPUTATIONAL
ALTER	* CARD-PUNCH	* COMPUTATIONAL-1
ALTERNATE	* CARD-READER	* COMPUTATIONAL-2
AND	* CBL	* COMPUTATIONAL-3
* APPLY	CD	* COMPUTATIONAL-4
ARE	CF	COMPUTE
AREA	CH	CONFIGURATION
AREAS	* CHANGED	* CONSOLE
ASCENDING	* CHANNEL	CONTAINS
* ASCII	CHARACTER	CONTROL
ASSIGN	CHARACTERS	CONTROLS
AT	CLOCK-UNITS	COPY
AUTHOR	CLOSE	* CORE-INDEX
	COBOL	CORR
	CODE	CORRESPONDING
* BASIS	CODE-SET	COUNT
BEFORE	COLLATING	* CSP

---

* *American National Standard Programming Language COBOL,* (New York: American National Standards Institute, 1974), pp. I-109-10.

CURRENCY
* CURRENT-DATE
* CYL-INDEX
* CYL-OVERFLOW
* C01
* C02
* C03
* C04
* C05
* C06
* C07
* C08
* C09
* C10
* C11
* C12

DATA
DATE
DATE-COMPILED
DATE-WRITTEN
DAY
DE
* DEBUG
DEBUG-CONTENTS
DEBUG-ITEM
DEBUG-LINE
DEBUG-NAME
DEBUG-SUB-1
DEBUG-SUB-2
DEBUG-SUB-3
DEBUGGING
DECIMAL-POINT
DECLARATIVES
* DEFERRED
DELETE
DELIMITED
DELIMITER
* DENSITY
DEPENDING
* DEPTH
DESCENDING
DESTINATION
DETAIL
DISABLE
* DISP
DISPLAY
* DISPLAY-ST
* DISPLAY-6
* DISPLAY-7
DIVIDE
DIVISION

DOWN
DUPLICATES
DYNAMIC

* EBCDIC
EGI
* EJECT
ELSE
EMI
ENABLE
END
END-OF-PAGE
* ENDING
ENTER
* ENTRY
ENVIRONMENT
EOP
EQUAL
* EQUALS
ERROR
ESI
* EVEN
EVERY
* EXAMINE
EXCEPTION
* EXHIBIT
EXIT
EXTEND
* EXTENDED-SEARCH

FD
FILE
FILE-CONTROL
* FILE-LIMIT
* FILE-LIMITS
FILLER
FINAL
FIRST
FOOTING
FOR
* FORTRAN
* FORTRAN-IV
FROM

GENERATE
GIVING
GO
* GOBACK
GREATER
GROUP

HEADING
HIGH-VALUE
HIGH-VALUES

I-O
I-O-CONTROL
* ID
IDENTIFICATION
IF
IN
INDEX
INDEXED
INDICATE
INITIAL
INITIATE
INPUT
INPUT-OUTPUT
* INSERT
INSPECT
INSTALLATION
INTO
INVALID
IS

JUST
JUSTIFIED

KEY
* KEYS

LABEL
* LABEL-RETURN
LAST
LEADING
* LEAVE
LEFT
LENGTH
LESS
LIMIT
LIMITS
LINAGE
LINAGE-COUNTER
LINE
LINE-COUNTER
* LINE-PRINTER
LINES
LINKAGE
LOCK
LOW-VALUE
LOW-VALUES

* MACRO	PF	RESET
* MAP4	PH	RETURN
* MAP5	PIC	* RETURN-CODE
* MAP6	PICTURE	REVERSED
* MAP7	PLUS	REWIND
* MAP8	POINTER	REWRITE
* MASTER-INDEX	POSITION	RF
MEMORY	* POSITIONING	RH
MERGE	POSITIVE	RIGHT
MESSAGE	* PRINT-CONTROL	ROUNDED
MODE	* PRINT-SWITCH	RUN
MODULES	PRINTING	
* MORE-LABELS	PROCEDURE	
MOVE	PROCEDURES	SAME
MULTIPLE	PROCEED	SD
MULTIPLY	* PROCESSING	SEARCH
	PROGRAM	SECTION
	PROGRAM-ID	SECURITY
* NAMED		* SEEK
NATIVE		SEGMENT
NEGATIVE	QUEUE	SEGMENT-LIMIT
NEXT	QUOTE	SELECT
NO	QUOTES	SEND
* NOMINAL		SENTENCE
NOT		SEPARATE
* NOTE	RANDOM	SEQUENCE
* NSTD-REELS	RD	SEQUENTIAL
NUMBER	READ	* SERVICE
NUMERIC	* READ-AHEAD	SET
	* READY	SIGN
	RECEIVE	SIZE
OBJECT-COMPUTER	RECORD	* SKIP1
OCCURS	* RECORD-OVERFLOW	* SKIP2
* ODD	* RECORDING	* SKIP3
OF	RECORDS	SORT
OFF	REDEFINES	* SORT-CORE-SIZE
OMITTED	REEL	* SORT-FILE-SIZE
ON	REFERENCES	SORT-MERGE
OPEN	RELATIVE	* SORT-MESSAGE
OPTIONAL	RELEASE	* SORT-MODE-SIZE
OR	* RELOAD	* SORT-RETURN
ORGANIZATION	REMAINDER	SOURCE
* OTHERWISE	* REMARKS	SOURCE-COMPUTER
OUTPUT	REMOVAL	SPACE
OVERFLOW	RENAMES	SPACES
	* REORG-CRITERIA	SPECIAL-NAMES
	REPLACING	STANDARD
PAGE	REPORT	STANDARD-1
PAGE-COUNTER	REPORTING	START
* PAPER-TAPE-PUNCH	REPORTS	STATUS
* PAPER-TAPE-READER	* REREAD	STOP
* PARITY	RERUN	STRING
PERFORM	RESERVE	SUB-QUEUE-1

SUB-QUEUE-2
SUB-QUEUE-3
SUBTRACT
SUM
SUPPRESS
* SWITCH
SYMBOLIC
SYNC
SYNCHRONIZED
* SYSIN
* SYSIPT
* SYSLST
* SYSOUT
* SYSPCH
* SYSPUNCH
* S01
* S02

TABLE
* TALLY
TALLYING
TAPE
TERMINAL
TERMINATE
TEXT
THAN
* THEN
THROUGH
THRU
TIME

* TIME-OF-DAY
TIMES
TO
* TODAY
TOP
* TOTALED
* TOTALING
* TRACE
* TRACK
* TRACK-AREA
* TRACK-LIMIT
* TRACKS
TRAILING
* TRANSFORM
TYPE

UNIT
UNSTRING
UNTIL
UP
UPON
* UPSI-0
* UPSI-1
* UPSI-2
* UPSI-3
* UPSI-4
* UPSI-5
* UPSI-6
* UPSI-7
USAGE

USE
* USER-NUMBER
USING

VALUE
VALUES
VARYING

WHEN
WITH
WORDS
WORKING-STORAGE
WRITE
* WRITE-BEHIND
* WRITE-ONLY
* WRITE-VERIFY

ZERO
ZEROES
ZEROS

$+$
$-$
$*$
$/$
$**$
$>$
$<$
$=$

Appendix B:
Lesson Plans and Lecture Notes

The following pages outline suggested lesson plans and lecture notes for 30 three-hour sessions, suitable for a three-week full-time course for industry entrants or for a two-semester college course.

The references are to pages in this book, which serves as the text for such a course.

Session 1

Preparation:

A card with Hollerith code (p. 5) for each student.

Lecture:

Administration, hours, and other details. Assess the class level by asking each student's background in DP, if any.

Introduce function of computers at sufficiently technical level for class' background, stressing that the machine obeys the programmer.

Explain in simple terms COBOL, compiler, and machine language.

Explain the coupon listing problem (p. 2).

Get students to compare list of raw names, addresses, and phone numbers with printed output (pp. 3-4).

Have students count number of columns required for each field. Show a typical card.

Give each student a coded card and explain Hollerith code, row, column, 12-row, 11-row, 9-edge, corner cut, interpreted, digit, letter, special character, ampersand, hyphen, not-sign, apostrophe, quote, and hash-mark.

Explain how card data gets into the computer, and the function of card-reader, hopper, and stacker.

Explain in simple terms the function of the CPU and the printer (pp. 6-7).

How are the holes made in the card? Explain functions of keypunch, including duplication (but not control card).

Exercise:

Demonstrate keypunch, if one is available, and assign each student to punch a transaction card from the list on page 3.

(If the class is too large for the number of keypunches available, demonstrate by punching only one card, and have the others already punched.)

Lecture:

Explain the printer spacing chart (p. 8). Have students compare field lengths on card with printer spacing chart. Refer to spaces as fillers.

Session 2

Preparation:

One source deck of SAMPLE-1 ⎫   for
One compilation listing   ⎬   each
One execution listing   ⎭   student

Lecture:

Review Session 1.

What must the programmer do?

Explain SAMPLE-1 line by line. Stress that the detailed meaning will be made clear later in the course, but that the important thing is to see how everything fits together.

Hand out decks to each student. Have students compare the deck with the visual.

Exercise:

Visit the machine room. Identify pieces of hardware. Compile a deck, then execute the data cards punched during the morning.

Allow each student to do this if time and cost permit.

Lecture:

Hand out compilation listings and execution listings.

Review the process of compilation and execution. Explain that the result of compilation may be stored internally or punched out in an object deck.

Session 3

Preparation:

Execution of SAMPLE-1 without statement 48 (MOVE SPACES TO PRINT-RECORD.).

Lecture:

Review SAMPLE-1 again, comparing compilation deck with compilation listing and with COBOL coding sheets. Answer any questions as simply as possible. Review structure of the course now that the students have seen a program and had an overview.

Explain MOVE using a nonnumeric example, and just treating main storage as a number of storage positions. Have students work out how to swap two fields with MOVEs (p. 15).

Explain the need for initializing to blanks. Use of MOVE SPACES. Hand out execution listing of SAMPLE-1 without print-lines initialized and show the garbage in the print-lines. Get students to explain why garbage stays the same after the first line.

Explain qualified data-names (p. 16).

Explain literals (p. 17).

Explain numeric MOVEs and contrast with nonnumeric (pp. 18-20).

Direct students to do exercise on numeric moves.

Explain ZEROS by comparison with SPACES.

Explain difference between numbers represented by PIC X and by PIC 9.

Review IF statement in SAMPLE-1.

Explain that process of execution is normally sequential, but that the IF allows the computer to choose, and so appear to "think" (pp. 22-23).

Explain structured flowchart and have students answer questions.

Exercise:

Students transform structured flowcharts to code (pp. 23-24).

Session 4

Preparation:

COBOL coding pads. Decks of additional cards for insertion in SAMPLE-1 to make SAMPLE-2. Decks of data cards for SAMPLE-2.

Lecture:

Review the PERFORM statement in SAMPLE-1.

Define a procedure.

Explain a flow of control in a PERFORM statement that is executed only once.

Explain meaning of PERFORM . . . UNTIL . . . .

Show structured flowchart representation (p. 26).

Have students answer questions about PERFORM.

Explain specification for SAMPLE-2 (p. 28).

Exercise:

Students draw a structured flowchart, then explain their solution.

Lecture:

Distribute COBOL coding pads and review Margins A and B, and numbering of statements.

Exercise:

Students code SAMPLE-2 with closed books (allow about one hour).

Let students compare their solution with the listing on p. 31 and with SAMPLE-1.

Hand out decks of additional cards (or have students punch cards needed), and have each student submit his job of SAMPLE-2.

Session 5

Lecture:

Review compilations (and executions of successful compiles) of SAMPLE-2.

Define character set, special characters, alphabetic, numeric, and alphanumeric (p. 34).

Explain elementary item, group item, and level number.

Explain PIC, A, 9, and X.

Define division names, section names, procedure-names, and data-names.

Explain rules for programmer-defined names.

Have students work the exercise on p. 40.

Explain good practice on data-names.

Explain punctuation rules: Define statement and sentence.

Explain good practice on layout.

Explain handwriting conventions (p. 43).

Explain rules and good practice for comments and continuation (pp. 44-45).

Explain that FDs set up I/O areas (buffers), for use by READ and WRITE.

Explain need for W-S.

Explain use of flags.

Explain VALUE statement, and diagram of W-S.

Explain level 88 condition-names.

Have students answer Review Quiz (p. 52).

Session 6

Preparation:

Data cards for SAMPLE-3. Coding supplies.

Lecture:

Explain specifications for SAMPLE-3 (pp. 53-54).

Explain specimen report (p. 55).

Exercise:

Students produce a printer spacing chart and check it against the report.

Lecture:

Discuss program design: Lead students to the proper conclusions that the input is really a 92-character record, which should be set up in W-S for each pair of cards, and that the output is three 132-character lines, which also should be set up in W-S.

Explain DATA RECORDS ARE (p. 58).

Exercise:

Students code Data Division and check it with sample (pp. 59-60).

Lecture:

Develop the program graph.

Show how the structure chart is derived and explain passing of control up and down the chart.

Develop pseudocode from the chart. Have students draw a structured flowchart and check it with sample.

Explain WRITE AFTER ADVANCING.

Get students to code Procedure Division and to compare it with sample.

Arrange for keypunching and submission of solutions. Provide JCL for compilation.

Session 7

Preparation:

Copies of SAMPLE-3 compilation with some interesting diagnostics.

Lecture:

Explain briefly why job control cards are needed and the function of operating system. Specify JCL to compile and to execute on your installation.

Review SAMPLE-3 solution, answering any questions. Explain diagnostic codes (-W, -C, -E, -D) or relevant severity levels if non-IBM (p. 73).

Exercise:

Students locate cause of diagnostics in each other's SAMPLE-3 output.

Lecture:

Explain two forms of ADD (p. 76).

Explain two forms of SUBTRACT.

Explain two forms of MULTIPLY.

Explain two forms of DIVIDE.

Exercise:

Students code instructions to determine discretionary income.

Lecture:

Explain rounding (pp. 79-80).

Explain COMPUTE, stressing the importance of ON SIZE ERROR.

Explain use of signed variables.

Exercise:

Assign Review Quiz (p. 84).

Session 8

Preparation:

Catalog SAMPLE-3 data structures and paragraphs on Source Statement Library (pp. 97-99).

Lecture:

Explain purpose of SSL and its advantages to the programmer.

Explain COPY and COPY REPLACING (pp. 85-88).

Review the steps in developing a program (pp. 88-90).

Explain program checks, with an example of a data exception (pp. 91-92).

Explain READY TRACE and EXHIBIT NAMED, with their respective use to locate a data exception (pp. 92-94).

Explain the specification for SAMPLE-4.

Guide students through the development of the structure chart.

Walk through the modules available on the SSL.

Exercise:

Students code SAMPLE-4 using SSL and COPY.

Session 9

Exercise:

Students complete coding of SAMPLE-4, and review each other's coding sheets in pairs before keypunching, compiling, and testing.

Session 10

Lecture:

Explain five types of logical conditions (pp. 107-14).
- relational: advise not to use > <
- class
- condition-name
- sign
- complex: relate to truth table

Explain the use of nested IFs to structure AND conditions (p. 116).

Have students code a nested IF (p. 119).

Explain the block structure problem and ways of solving it (pp. 120-23).

Explain the null ELSE (pp. 123-24).

Explain the CASE structure (pp. 125-27) and let students code one.

Session 11

Lecture:

Review ways to simplify nested IFs (pp. 127-29).

Describe the conventions for decision tables, including conditions, actions, rules, and explain how to derive the number of rules in an exhaustive table.

Exercise:

Students draw a decision table from an English statement (p. 129).

Lecture:

Explain selective decision tables, the "don't-care" entry, and the ELSE rule (p. 133).

Exercise:

Students produce an exhaustive decision table for credit limit as specified on p. 135, and simplify it as much as possible.

Review decision table, and have students code a nested IF to express the logic (p. 137).

Session 12

Exercise:

Explain the full specification for CREDCALC (p. 138).

Have students design at all levels including pseudocode, and review their designs in pairs.

Lecture:

Discuss a model structure for CREDCALC and walk through pseudocode for each module.

Sessions 13 and 14

Preparation:

Test data deck for CREDCALC.

Exercise:

Students code, compile, and test CREDCALC, using COPY whenever possible.

Session 15

Preparation:

Additional CREDCALC module that is cataloged on COPY-LIB (p. 164).

Lecture:

Explain that cards become inconvenient in high volume.

Define magnetic tape, characters per inch, IRG, blocking, BLOCK CONTAINS, labels, and LABEL RECORDS ARE STANDARD (pp. 158-60).

Explain the difference between sequential and random access, UR, UT, DA, and SELECT statement for tape file on your installation.

Explain the function of OPEN and CLOSE, READ and WRITE for single-volume, single-file tapes (pp. 160-61).

Explain specification for CREATEMF: Have students produce a structure chart and pseudocode (p. 163).

Session 16

Exercise:

Students complete coding of CREATEMF and compare their solution with the model (pp. 165-79).

Visit installation to see tape units and disks demonstrated and tape file loaded.

Session 17

Lecture:

Discuss the considerations in updating the sequential master file with a presorted addition, deletion, and change file and explain specification for MAINTMFS (p. 187).

Develop program graph for students.

Have students draw structure chart and pseudocode.

Walk through solution (pp. 189-99).

Session 18

Lecture:

Explain random access, magnetic disk, track, read-write head, platter, cylinder, seek, search, rotational delay (p. 200).

Exercise:

Students calculate the capacity and average access time from basic data of the disk drives used in installation.

Lecture:

Explain indexed file organization, track, index, and record key (p. 203).

Explain creation of an indexed file, FILE-CONTROL paragraph, ORGANIZATION, ACCESS, and RECORD KEY.

Explain use of INVALID KEY.

Walk through model for CREATEMFI (pp. 207-208).

Explain differences for accessing the new indexed file randomly from other methods and walk through a model (pp. 209-10).

Session 19

Lecture:

Explain updating, addition, and deletion of records on an indexed file using REWRITE and DELETE (p. 211).

Explain specification for MAINTMFI (p. 212). Have students develop structure chart and pseudocode, and review.

Sessions 20 and 21

Preparation:

Master file on disk built by CREATMFI. Updates, addition, and deletion cards for master file.

Exercise:

Students code, review, compile, and test MAINTMFI.

Session 22

Lecture:

Explain disadvantages of indexed files, and how overflow leads to long access times (p. 216).

Explain relative file concept, transforming a key to a relative record number and retrieving with a single access.

Give example of division by prime number and using remainder.

Explain synonyms and how they may be handled.

Explain difference between coding indexed and relative files.

Explain differences between ANS-74 and access methods used in your installation.

Session 23

Lecture:

Explain the printer spacing facilities of ANS-74, the LINAGE clause and its options, the AT END-OF-PAGE option, and other options of the WRITE statement (pp. 219-20).

Explain the printer control features of your COBOL compiler if not ANS-74.

Session 24

Lecture:

Explain specification for credit account system: processing transactions of invoice and payment data against master file to keep a balance owing available on-line against credit limit, and printing statements of account when required (pp. 222-23).

Exercise:

Students work in pairs on the system's design; then review a structure chart with them.

Plan the successive versions for top-down implementation of a system.

Sessions 25 — 30

Exercise:

Have students implement the credit account system top-down to as great a level of detail as time allows.

Appendix C

Answers to Chapter 3 REVIEW QUIZ

1. Which of the characters shown in the specimen card on p. 5 are *not* in the COBOL character set?

    11 characters: &, !, *, ¬, %, _ ,?, :, #, @, "

2. What is wrong with this FD?

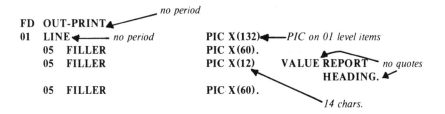

```
                          no period
FD  OUT-PRINT
01    LINE        no period    PIC X(132)    PIC on 01 level items
      05   FILLER              PIC X(60).
      05   FILLER              PIC X(12)     VALUE REPORT   no quotes
                                             HEADING.
      05   FILLER              PIC X(60).
                                                14 chars.
```

3. What is wrong with this FD?

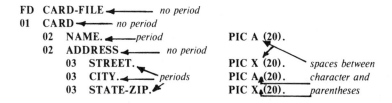

```
FD  CARD-FILE        no period
01    CARD           no period
      02   NAME.      period       PIC A (20).
      02   ADDRESS        no period
           03   STREET.           PIC X (20).   spaces between
           03   CITY.    periods  PIC A (20).   character and
           03   STATE-ZIP.        PIC X (20).   parentheses
```

253

4.   Here are some programmer-defined names. Decide if they are OK as data-names, or as procedure-names, and if not, why not.

Name	Data-Name	Procedure-Name
MASTER-FILE-INVENTORY-CODE	OK	OK
M9999	OK*	OK*
HEADING-	Ends with hyphen	same
-TITLE-	Begins and ends with hyphen	same
111X	OK*	OK*
LINE-COUNTER	OK	OK
ZIP CODE	Spaces in name	same
ZIP CODE	Special character	same
POSITION	OK**	OK*
666	Data name *must* contain at least one alpha character	OK*

5.   What is wrong with this Working-Storage Section?

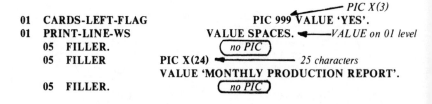

```
01   CARDS-LEFT-FLAG              PIC 999 VALUE 'YES'.
01   PRINT-LINE-WS                VALUE SPACES.
     05   FILLER.
     05   FILLER           PIC X(24)
                           VALUE 'MONTHLY PRODUCTION REPORT'.
     05   FILLER.
```

PIC X(3)
VALUE on 01 level
no PIC
25 characters
no PIC

6.   Write the FD entries to set up meaningful condition-names for a one-column card code called JOB-CODE with the following meanings:

T Trainee   P Programmer
J Junior Programmer A Systems Analyst

---

* Meaningless name
**Ambiguous name, possibly meaningless

```
FD  CARD-FILE.
01  CARD.
    05  JOB-CODE                     PIC X.
        88  TRAINEE                  VALUE 'T'.
        88  JNR-PROG                 VALUE 'J'.
        88  PROGRAMMER               VALUE 'P'.
        88  SYS-ANALYST              VALUE 'A'.
    05  FILLER                       PIC X(79).
```

7. Rewrite the Working-Storage Section specified in Question 5, using correct COBOL, and changing the print-line to read REPORT OF MONTHLY SALES, PRODUCTION AND PROF-ITABILITY, centered in a 132-position print-line.

```
01  CARDS-LEFT-FLAG                  PIC X(3)  VALUE 'YES'.
01  PRINT-LINE-WS.
    05  FILLER                       PIC X(39).
    05  FILLER                       PIC X(53)
        VALUE 'REPORT OF MONTHLY SALES, PRODUCTION
        ' AND PROFITABILITY'.
    05  FILLER                       PIC X(40).
```

Answers to Chapter 4 REVIEW QUIZ

1. Write the code to increase the value of VERMOUTH by the amount stored in GIN, and store the new value in MARTINI.

    ADD GIN VERMOUTH GIVING MARTINI.
    or
    COMPUTE MARTINI = GIN + VERMOUTH.

2. Write the code to increase the value of LOOP-COUNT by 1.

    ADD 1 TO LOOP-COUNT.

3. If field TOTAL contains 480 and field NUMBR contains 24, what is in each field after executing

    DIVIDE NUMBR INTO TOTAL.

    NUMBR: 24
    TOTAL: 20

4. If RESULT is defined as PIC 9V99, what is in RESULT after execution of

    DIVIDE 8 INTO 9 GIVING RESULT ROUNDED.

    RESULT: 1.13

5. If ABSOLUTE-VALUE is defined as PIC 9(3), what is in ABSOLUTE-VALUE after execution of

    SUBTRACT 1000 FROM 2 GIVING ABSOLUTE-VALUE.

    ABSOLUTE-VALUE: 998   The sign will be missing since ABSOLUTE-VALUE was not defined as PIC S9V99.

6.　Use the COMPUTE statement to write the code calculating the interest due on an amount up to $100,000 at a rate of interest which may be set to the nearest one-quarter percent up to twenty percent, over a period to the nearest year, expressing the result to the nearest cent. Include the Data Division entries for your data-names.

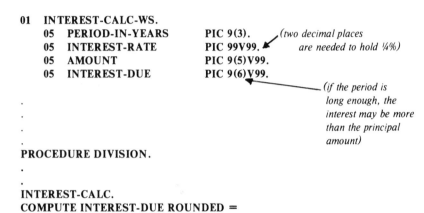

WORKING-STORAGE SECTION.

```
01   INTEREST-CALC-WS.
     05   PERIOD-IN-YEARS      PIC 9(3).          (two decimal places
     05   INTEREST-RATE        PIC 99V99.         are needed to hold ¼%)
     05   AMOUNT               PIC 9(5)V99.
     05   INTEREST-DUE         PIC 9(6)V99.
                                                  (if the period is
     .                                            long enough, the
     .                                            interest may be more
     .                                            than the principal
     .                                            amount)
PROCEDURE DIVISION.

     .

     .

INTEREST-CALC.
COMPUTE INTEREST-DUE ROUNDED =
   (AMOUNT * INTEREST-RATE * PERIOD-IN-YEARS) / 100.
```

Learning to Program in Structured COBOL Part 2

Timothy R. Lister
and
Edward Yourdon

DEDICATION

This book is for the women in our lives —
with special appreciation to our cleaning lady,
who for many months
recognized that the hundreds of tiny scraps of paper
represented a manuscript in progress,
rather than mere trash.

PREFACE

This book is intended for two audiences: the programmer trainee who has successfully completed *Learning to Program in Structured COBOL, Part 1* and the experienced COBOL programmer who is learning the techniques of Structured Programming. Sections of this text address specific instructions and their rules of usage and, therefore, may seem to be of little use to the experienced professional. However, we urge our audience to read the entire text, if for no other reason than to brush up on the 1974 ANS COBOL standard facilities.

We have not tried to produce a palatable reference manual for COBOL; rather, we have tried to present a text which introduces COBOL within the environment of applications development. In attempting to accomplish this goal, we occasionally have slipped into non-ANS COBOL, often into IBM-defined COBOL. This has not been done as an endorsement of any particular vendor, but only to better prepare the student for the business applications world.

8 Programming for Change

8.1 Characteristics of a good COBOL program

What are we trying to accomplish when we write a COBOL program? The most obvious answer is that we are trying to make a computer solve some well-defined problem. That is, our aim is to write a program that works according to its specifications.

That may seem like a trivial statement — *of course* our aim is to write a working program. However, it is a demanding task, and we should not underestimate the difficulty of producing a correct — demonstrably correct — program. Our orders to the computer must be exact. If we make even one error, one error in thousands of statements, the entire program may fail. A program either works, or it doesn't — programmers are rarely congratulated for almost solving a problem. So, let's keep in mind that the first and foremost characteristic of a COBOL program is, it works.

What are some other characteristics of a good COBOL program? Should it be efficient? elegant? devious? You'll find many of your colleagues striving to develop programs with these characteristics — but it's our strong feeling that the second most important characteristic of a COBOL program is its readability. We should be able to read what we write. Sooner or later, we will be asked to add a new feature to our program, or change some aspect of its operation; indeed, sooner or later, someone else will be asked to change our program — and we may not be around to answer any questions about it. In order to make the modification process easy, it is important that we — or the unfortunate maintenance programmer who has been stuck with the job of looking after our program — understand (a) *what* the code is trying to accomplish, (b) *how* the code accomplishes its purpose, and (c) *where* the alterations should go.

Thus, our COBOL program must be understandable to human beings, as well as to the computer that will execute it. Indeed, we must pay a great deal of attention to the human beings who will read our code — for they (and we) have a limited ability to understand complex, obscure, devious logic. All of the COBOL code in this book is written with the intention of being readable, as well as correct.

A third — and also very important — characteristic of all good COBOL programs is their ability to be changed easily. If the specification for the program changes in a minor way, then the changes to the actual code should be simple, localized, and limited in number. Major alterations to a program are time-consuming, costly, and error-prone, and we should be able to avoid them if we design and implement our programs properly.

Changes to computer systems will continue as long as the enterprise that uses the computer system (e.g., the business organization) continues to evolve. We don't want to treat program specifications as a never-changing oil portrait, but as a single frame of a motion picture. We want to organize our programs in such a way that we don't have to rewrite the entire program when the next frame comes into focus.

In summary, we should ask ourselves three important questions before we announce that our program is finished:

1.   Have I solved the problem defined by the specifications?

2.   Would another COBOL programmer easily understand how I have solved the problem?

3.   Can my program be modified easily when the changes come?

Unless the answer is yes to all three questions, we are not finished.

Are there other characteristics of a good COBOL program? Yes, there are at least two: It should be economical to develop, and it should be economical to operate. We find that if a program is designed for easy maintenance and modification, it is usually easy — and, therefore, economical — for the original programmer to develop. That is, the same things that will make it difficult for someone else to understand your program five years from now will make it difficult for you to understand the program while you're in the midst of coding and debugging it. Similarly, we find that attention to understandability and maintainability usually produces a reasonably efficient program, one that does not consume too much memory or too many microseconds of CPU time. It may still be possible to improve the efficiency of such a program, so we will discuss some guidelines for optimizing programs in Chapter 15.

A final comment about maintainability: Your use of the COBOL programming language goes a long way toward making a program easy to understand and easy to modify. Indeed, one of the major reasons why COBOL is the most widely used business-oriented programming language is its relative independence from specific hardware features. The American National Standards Institute (ANSI) sets standards requirements for the COBOL language, and most major computer manufacturers adhere to those standards.[1] Thus, by writing in ANSI COBOL, we should be able to run our programs on a wide range of computers. The same programs should work on Burroughs, IBM, Honeywell, and a host of other machines — a versatility that is not characteristic of several other programming languages. Thus, COBOL's popularity is strong evidence of the computer industry's desire for changeable, maintainable programs.

---

[1]Some COBOL statements are not required by ANSI, but are supplied by individual computer manufacturers as "extensions" to the language. They are probably marked in your COBOL reference manual in some special way; it is common for such nonstandard statements to be shaded in gray. You should ascertain your installation's non-ANSI COBOL statements, and determine whether they are to be used.

8.2 Hierarchies and structure charts

One of the best ways to organize flexible, maintainable systems is in a *hierarchical* fashion. All kinds of systems can be viewed as hierarchies. For example, here is a piece of the hierarchy of the animal kingdom:

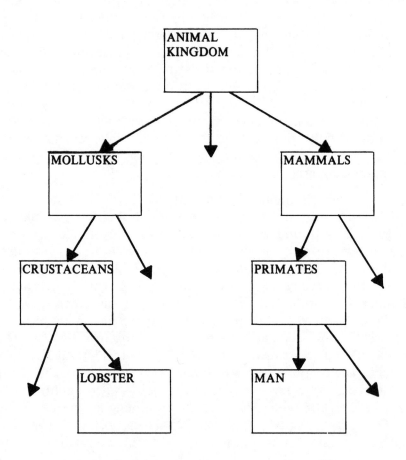

The company that you work for, or the school that you attend, is probably organized in a hierarchical fashion; there's probably a president at the top, and it's likely that you're a great deal closer to the bottom of the hierarchy than to the top.

As you will recall from Part 1 of this series,[2] we design computer programs and systems in a hierarchical fashion, and document those designs in a fashion that highlights the hierarchy. For example, here is a structure chart for a system that will write payroll checks for three types of workers:

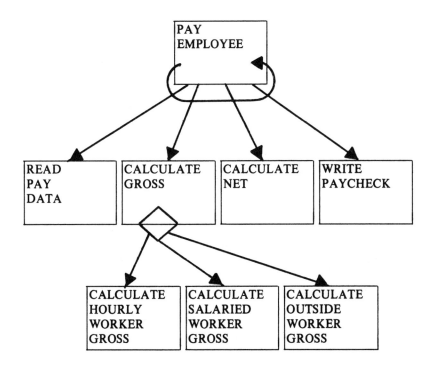

Note that the structure chart shows that there are workers who are paid on an hourly basis, other workers who are salaried, and non-regular workers who are paid on a contract basis.

---

[2]Edward Yourdon, Chris Gane, Trish Sarson, *Learning to Program in Structured COBOL, Part 1* (New York: YOURDON inc., 1976).

The boxes in the diagram on the previous page are known as modules; the arrows, which are also called connections, show the references made from one module to another. There is a one-to-one relationship between the modules in a structure chart, and groups of code in our COBOL program; indeed, every instruction in a COBOL program is a member of one, and only one, module.

The curved arrow wrapping around the connections from PAY EMPLOYEE is our notation for a loop. In this case, the chart clearly shows that PAY EMPLOYEE refers to READ PAY DATA, CAL-CULATE GROSS, CALCULATE NET, and WRITE PAYCHECK in a re-petitive fashion, within a loop. Without this loop, the program would calculate only one employee's paycheck. Although the structure chart does not show the details of the loop, we can as-sume that the top-level module invokes the four second-level modules repeatedly until all of the employee paychecks have been processed.

There is another graphic convention that we should point out. The diamond at the base of CALCULATE GROSS is the sym-bol for a decision. It shows that CALCULATE GROSS contains some instruction, or instructions, to determine whether CALCU-LATE HOURLY WORKER GROSS, or CALCULATE SALARIED WORK-ER GROSS, or CALCULATE OUTSIDE WORKER GROSS should be in-voked. We may assume that for each employee only one of the three modules will be invoked.

Typically, we read a structure chart from the top down. The topmost module is the module that begins and ends the pro-gram. Each module on the second level receives control from PAY EMPLOYEE, carries out its task, and returns control to its in-voker — i.e., to PAY EMPLOYEE. These second-level modules do not return to the first executable statement in PAY EMPLOYEE, but rather to the statement immediately following the instruction that gave them control. All of the modules in the structure chart are assumed to behave in this fashion — if they did not, the structure chart would not represent a true hierarchy in the sense in which we will be using that word.

It is permissible for a module to have more than one in-voker — that is, more than one "boss." For example, the structure chart below shows that CHECK FOR NUMERICS will return control to EDIT ACCOUNT NO or to EDIT ZIP CODE, depending on which of those "bosses" called it.

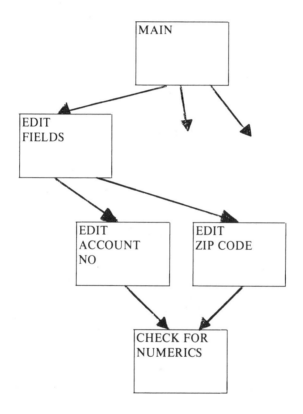

All modules and all connections between modules are shown on a structure chart, but it is not necessary to show *all* of the loops and decisions. Indeed, to show all of the loops and decisions would unnecessarily clutter most structure charts; thus, as a rule of thumb, we usually only show the most important loops and decisions on the structure chart — i.e., those that are important for an understanding of the overall program or system.

8.3 Cohesion and coupling in modular systems

How do we go about designing programs in a hierarchical fashion? Unfortunately, many programmers design in a rather haphazard manner, so they really have no idea of the kind of hierarchy that will evolve. For example, an alternative design for the payroll system we discussed in the previous section might look like this:

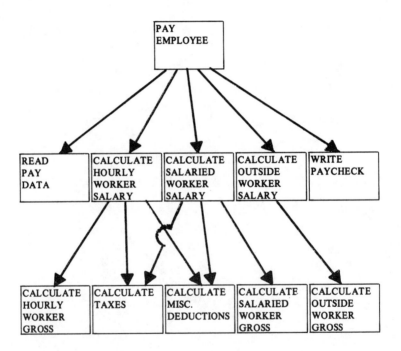

Which design is better — the one above, or the one discussed in Section 8.2? Perhaps our first design was better; after all, it had fewer boxes. Or, perhaps the design shown above is better; after all, it has boxes that individually carry out smaller (and presumably simpler) tasks. Obviously, we need some method of determining which of these hierarchies is "better" — that is, better in the sense discussed in Section 8.1. Which of the designs is more likely to be correct? Which design is easier to understand? Which design will be easier to modify? Which design will be more economical to develop and operate?

One method of evaluating a structure chart is to investigate the relationship between instructions inside a module, as well as the relationship between the modules themselves. In order to understand the entire system, we should be able to focus our attention on one module at a time — without having to worry about its interaction with various other modules in the system. Thus, the fewer interactions between modules on the structure chart, the more likely it is that the design will be easy to understand and easy to modify.

Paradoxically, the easiest way to make certain that the modules in a system are not too highly interrelated is to ensure that the individual instructions inside each module are very highly interrelated. That is, the instructions inside any single module should all be involved in the same task — a *single* task.

This concept of relatedness among instructions inside a module (or, more generally, the strength of association of subordinates to a given module) is known as *cohesion*. The more highly cohesive a module is, the more likely that module is involved in a single, well-defined task — and, as a corollary, the less likely that module will have subtle, unclear connections with other modules in the system.

The best — or strongest — type of cohesion that a module can display is *functional* cohesion: All of the instructions in the module work together to carry out one, and only one, task. For example, CALCULATE HOURLY WORKER GROSS is a functionally cohesive module. It does not calculate gross salary for all types of workers. It does not do anything special with some hourly workers; it does nothing but calculate the gross salary for hourly workers, using the same algorithm each time it is activated.

A module is considered *logically* cohesive when it carries out tasks that seem similar, but are not related in any way pertinent to the problem being solved. For example, we would consider CALCULATE TAXES to be a logically cohesive module, because it does many similar tasks: It calculates federal, state, local, and FICA taxes. Some employees may not have to pay local taxes; others may have already paid their full share of FICA taxes and need no further deduction in that category for the rest of the year.

As a result, we would expect CALCULATE-TAXES to be fairly large and complicated, particularly since it is common for programmers to take advantage of apparently similar logic situations in the processing of federal, state, local, and FICA taxes. The result could well be a module for which a modification to the federal tax logic would cause unexpected bugs in the FICA tax calculations.

In general, we try to avoid logically cohesive modules. While we cannot guarantee that such modules will be difficult to understand or modify, it seems silly to gamble. Virtually no extra work is required (and it is, indeed, often more efficient) to break a logically cohesive module into separate, functionally cohesive modules.

When we are designing a COBOL program, we should not worry too much about the eventual size of the various modules; instead, we should concern ourselves with the function of the modules. If it turns out that a functionally cohesive module is "trivial" (i.e., contains only a few COBOL statements), we may decide to incorporate it internally within the next higher-level superordinate. This decision should be made only after we have finished the design, and have convinced ourselves that the design is satisfactory. The decision to "push" a module into its superordinate is shown on a structure chart in the following way:

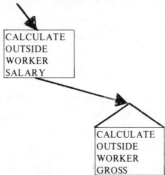

In the illustration, the triangular "hat" on CALCULATE OUTSIDE WORKER GROSS means that it is "lexically included" in the higher-level module that invokes it. When we read the code for this program, we will find the code to calculate an outside worker's gross salary within the module CALCULATE OUTSIDE WORKER SALARY.

Another thing we can look for in a design is so-called black-box behavior. A black box is any construct that can be used without any knowledge of its internal workings. We can make use of a black box if we know what inputs it requires, what outputs it will produce, and what its function is.

A good example of a black box, for most of us, is the common automobile. We know its inputs: gasoline, oil, water, and an occasional kick when it doesn't start. We know its outputs: energy used to spin the rear wheels. And we know its function: to transport a moderate number of people over a moderate distance for a moderate amount of money, within certain safety constraints. Most of us cannot explain the workings of a combustion engine, how the automobile is put together on an assembly line, or even how the cigarette lighter works. Fortunately, most states in the U.S. do not require such knowledge in order to obtain a driver's license!

Following is an example of a black-box module: You are writing a program that issues assignments to secret agents. The boss does not want any one programmer to know everything about the system. You must write the part of the program that matches assignments with free, qualified agents. Once an agent is eligible and meets the requirements, you must check a top-secret subroutine for the final approval. This subroutine is so secret, in fact, that the boss does not want you to know *anything* about how it works. You are given your instructions:

When you are ready to make the final check before assigning an agent, code PERFORM SECRET-OK CHECK. Make sure that you have defined the agent's code number as AGENT-CODE-NO, and the assignment code as MISSION-CODE.

Also, define a four-position alphanumeric switch called SECRET-OK. After PERFORMing this subroutine, the SECRET-OK indicator will be set to "OKAY" if the agent is cleared, or "NYET" if the agent cannot be assigned to this mission.

Your structure chart might look as follows:

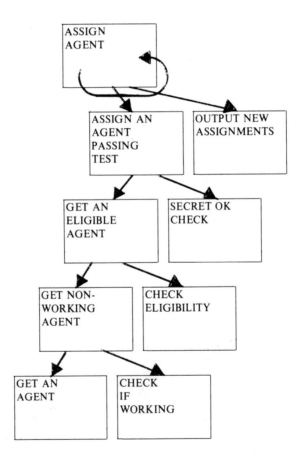

ASSIGN AN AGENT PASSING TEST, the module which invokes the secret subroutine, knows that the subroutine checks eligibility, but does not know how. It does not even know whether SECRET-OK CHECK is one module, or only the topmost of many modules. The important thing to remember is, it doesn't *need* to know.

When we use black-box modules, each module knows only of the existence of those modules that it invokes. This is of great benefit to programmers. For example, what if the rules for SECRET-OK CHECK need to be changed? Someone can change that module without affecting the other modules.

We do not have to work for a spy ring to realize that black-box modules make future modifications easier. By using black boxes wherever we can, we limit the impact of many changes.

Another way of evaluating a structure chart is to examine the nature and strength of the interactions between one module and another. We use the term *coupling* to describe the strength of connections between one module and another. As you would expect, our goal is to develop systems with loosely coupled modules, so that a modification of one module will have a minimum chance of affecting some other module. For example, the SECRET-OK CHECK module is loosely coupled to the other modules in the system, because it needs only a small amount of information — AGENT-CODE-NO, MISSION-CODE, and SECRET-OK — to do its work.

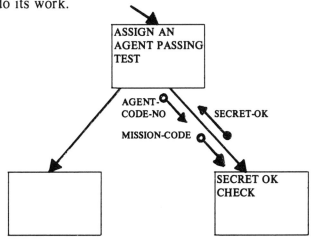

One method of evaluating the coupling between modules is to check the number of data items they must share. The fewer the items of data shared between modules, the more loosely coupled the design. If we pass many switches, indicators, and data items between modules, it becomes more likely that a modification to one module will affect some other module.

Coupling often can be reduced by rearranging the existing hierarchy of modules. As an example, consider the following extension to the spy design described above. Our spy ring uses its computer to write out "The Secret Code Word for the Day" to its agents. Because the word is top-secret, the keypunch operators punch only one letter per card. No single keypunch operator punches more than one letter; therefore, only the boss, who collates the cards, knows the entire word. The boss inserts dummy input before and after the code word, so that the computer operators will have little chance of determining the code word when they read the cards into the program. The word begins immediately after a card with a zero in column 1, and ends with a card containing a zero in column 1. In the example below, the code word is SNEAKY.

Below are two designs, labeled "Version 1" and "Version 2." From our description of the problem, you should be able to determine the interfaces between the modules — i.e., the data and control information that must pass between the various modules. When you do this, you should be able to decide which is better.

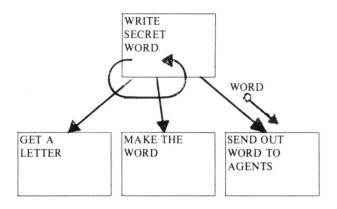

Version 1

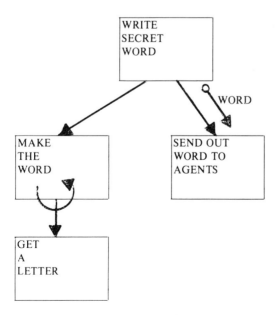

Version 2

The modules in Version 2 are less strongly coupled; therefore, we would judge that to be the better design. By contrast,
note that in Version 1, MAKE THE WORD must return a flag to
WRITE SECRET WORD to indicate whether it has finished making a
word. Note that Version 2 does not require any flags.

In most cases, strong coupling between modules is an indication of low cohesion; conversely, a system with highly cohesive
modules usually exhibits very low intermodular coupling. As an
example, consider the following structure chart with a logically
cohesive module FORMAT ALL ERRORS. (By the way, can you tell
why it is a logically cohesive module?)

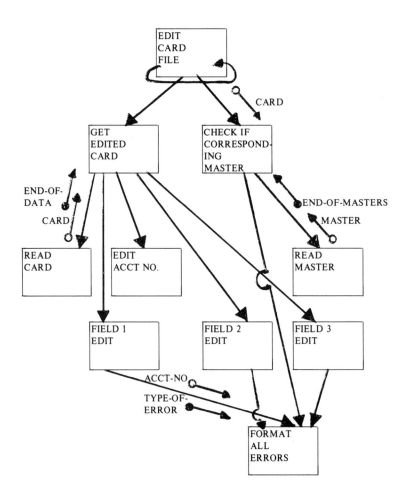

The program shown above edits cards that have an account number and three fields of information on them. The cards will be used by another program to update certain fields of a master file once they have been accepted by this editing program. Notice that the logically cohesive module requires a flag to determine *which* error has occurred. Now compare that structure chart with the following one:

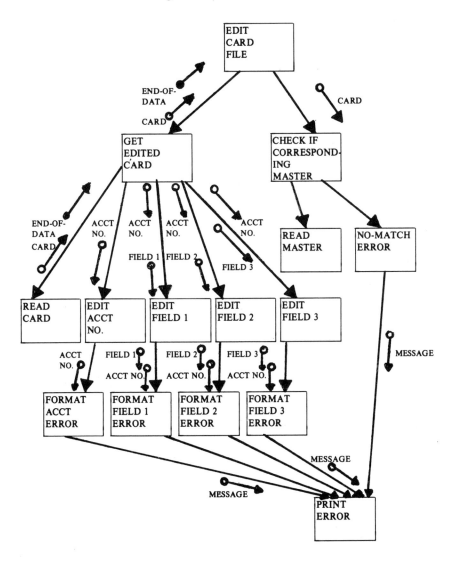

In this second design, the functionally cohesive error modules require no flag at all. If, during the actual coding of these modules, we discover that they are too small (i.e., only a few COBOL statements), then we can always "push them up" into their superordinate.

8.4 COBOL modules and connections

Thus far, we have concentrated on program design without much regard for COBOL. This has been intentional. Our concepts of good design practice are independent of any specific programming language. That is, we should strive for highly cohesive, loosely coupled, black-box modules regardless of the programming language we use — and it *is* possible to develop such modules, regardless of whether we code in FORTRAN, COBOL, or PL/I.

Nevertheless, our interest in this book obviously is in the development of COBOL modules; so let's turn our attention to the design of good programs and good modules in COBOL.

We'll begin with a careful definition of a module. In formal terms, a program module is usually defined as a contiguous group of statements having a single name by which it can be invoked as a unit.[3] In COBOL, this means that a module — i.e., one of the rectangular boxes drawn in a structure chart — can be either a paragraph, a SECTION, or an entire COBOL program.

We have not yet looked at an example of a SECTION in the PROCEDURE DIVISION; the code that follows illustrates this portion of a module. As you will see in the example, the SECTION is one method of grouping statements under a single name. A SECTION consists of zero or more paragraphs, each paragraph having its own COBOL statements. The SECTION must be given a name, immediately followed by the key word SECTION and a

---

[3]For a precise definition of module, see *Structured Design* by Edward Yourdon and Larry L. Constantine (New York: YOURDON inc., 1975).

period. A SECTION ends when another SECTION begins, or when the PROCEDURE DIVISION ends.

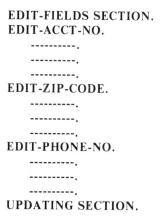

EDIT-FIELDS SECTION.
EDIT-ACCT-NO.
    ----------.
    ----------.
    ----------.
EDIT-ZIP-CODE.
    ----------.
    ----------.
    ----------.
EDIT-PHONE-NO.
    ----------.
    ----------.
    ----------.
UPDATING SECTION.

The PERFORM statement is used to transfer control from one module to another, regardless of whether the module consists of a paragraph or a SECTION. Thus, we might find ourselves connecting paragraphs by coding:

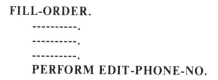

FILL-ORDER.
    ----------.
    ----------.
    ----------.
    PERFORM EDIT-PHONE-NO.

Equivalently, we might connect sections this way:

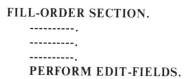

FILL-ORDER SECTION.
    ----------.
    ----------.
    ----------.
    PERFORM EDIT-FIELDS.

We prefer to use paragraphs as the building block for modules. Our primary reason for this preference is that the use of paragraphs ensures that there will be only one way of entering the module (via the paragraph-name), and only one way of leaving the module (by returning to the module which PERFORMed the paragraph). Thus, we find that COBOL programs built from paragraphs tend to have the black-box behavior that we discussed in Section 8.3.

We are less able to guarantee this black-box behavior when we use SECTIONs as the basic building block of a COBOL program. To illustrate the problem, recall the example of the EDIT-FIELDS SECTION code above. It is possible that some other module in the program may contain the statement

PERFORM EDIT-ZIP-CODE.

Although this is perfectly legal, it is poor COBOL practice. Why? Because the module which contains this PERFORM statement obviously knows that the EDIT-FIELDS SECTION module has a side-door entrance named EDIT-ZIP-CODE. The black-box quality of EDIT-FIELDS is now seriously impaired. In general, a SECTION may have many such possible entry points (the SECTION name, plus all of the paragraph-names within it); it is therefore more difficult to maintain as a black box.

You may find that your programming group uses SECTIONs instead of paragraphs; indeed, there are some situations in which SECTIONs are highly desirable (e.g., to simulate a CASE structure), or absolutely necessary (e.g., in conjunction with the SORT verb, discussed in Chapter 13). From our discussion, you can see that the best approach is one of consistency: To form modules, you should either use SECTIONs consistently, or you should use paragraphs consistently. And, if you do use SECTIONs, be sure to avoid any temptation to PERFORM individual paragraphs within a SECTION.

Unfortunately, there is some confusion when we use paragraphs as the basic form of a module. Because of some quirks in the COBOL language, not every paragraph is a "meaningful" module. For example, consider the following program which copies card images onto magnetic tape:

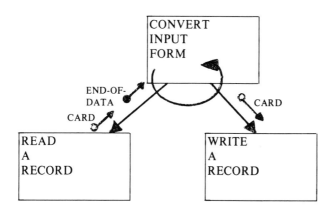

The structure chart is fairly straightforward; we can see that there are three modules. Now, let's look at the code:

```
PROCEDURE DIVISION.
A1-CONVERT-INPUT-FORM.
    OPEN RECD-IN INPUT
        RECD-OUT OUTPUT.
    MOVE 'NO' TO RECD-EOF.
    PERFORM B1-READ-A-RECORD.
    PERFORM PROCESS-LOOP
        UNTIL RECD-EOF = 'YES'.
    CLOSE RECD-IN
        RECD-OUT.
    STOP RUN.
PROCESS-LOOP.
    MOVE INPUT-RECORD TO OUTPUT-RECORD.
    PERFORM B2-WRITE-A-RECORD.
    PERFORM B1-READ-A-RECORD.
B1-READ-A-RECORD.
    READ RECD-IN
        AT END
            MOVE 'YES' TO RECD-EOF.
B2-WRITE-A-RECORD.
    WRITE OUTPUT-RECORD.
```

Note that PROCESS-LOOP exists because we need a paragraph-name for the PERFORM-UNTIL statement — that is, PROCESS-LOOP contains all those statements which may be executed iteratively. It did not appear in the structure chart because it never occurred to the designer to identify it as a distinct module; PROCESS-LOOP is only the body of a loop, and is really only a fragment of a "meaningful" module.

So what should we do about all of this? Most COBOL programmers prefer to think of a module like PROCESS-LOOP as an "artificial" module. They do not show it on their structure chart, but they do ensure that, in the program listing, PROCESS-LOOP is placed near the module containing the PERFORM-UNTIL which invokes PROCESS-LOOP. Other COBOL programmers feel that there should be a strict one-to-one correspondence between the paragraphs in their program and the rectangular boxes in their structure chart. Such programmers would deal with the situation by drawing the structure chart as follows:

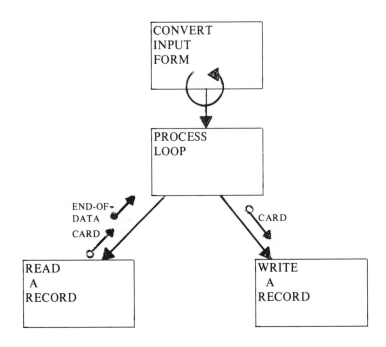

Once again, our primary concern is that you do things in a consistent fashion; most COBOL programmers will be able to understand either approach, as long as consistency is maintained.

Q.   In the example above, how many times will PROCESS-LOOP be PERFORMed?

A.   Once for each record in the RECD-IN file. The loop exits when RECD-EOF = 'YES', and 'YES' is moved to that flag when the RECD-IN file is AT END. Don't forget that the imperative clause following AT END is executed the *first* time there are no more records. If we try to READ after we have executed the AT END clause, the program will almost certainly abort (or it will begin to behave in an undefined fashion).

Q.   Is the previous answer true under all possible conditions?

A.   Yes, it is. If the file has no records, then the PROCESS-LOOP will never be executed. This is because the PERFORM-UNTIL statement tests its termination clause *before* executing the specified paragraph.

8.5 Program-to-program linkage

In the previous section, we mentioned some of the advantages and disadvantages of paragraphs and SECTIONs. There is an additional disadvantage of both paragraphs and SECTIONs that we should mention: By definition, any paragraph and any SECTION may access any data elements defined in the DATA DIVISION, regardless of whether the module has any legitimate reason for accessing the data.

For example, one module may require a field of data, properly defined in the DATA DIVISION, to hold an intermediate value when carrying out its calculations. No other module needs to know that this field even exists, yet every module in the program has the ability to refer to this field or even alter it. As you can imagine, this has serious consequences for maintenance and debugging.

Think, for example, of a large COBOL program (by large, we mean any program larger than 10,000 COBOL statements — many programs in industry today are more than 100,000 statements long!), which you have to modify. If you need to alter the length of a field, then you must find every reference to that field in the entire program; this is crucial, for you must ensure that the unchanged code (code in modules other than the ones you explicitly intended to modify) still will work correctly when the data field is changed. If your compiler does not produce a cross-reference listing of all data elements, this job will be tedious and error-prone — you may easily miss an obscure reference to your data element.

Q.   How is it possible that some code in other parts of a program may stop working correctly if the length of a field is changed?

A.   It is possible because the code may have made assumptions about the size of a number that the field contained. If the code assumes that the field never contains a number larger than 99 (decimal), peculiar things then would happen if the field were changed to a PIC 9(3).

The point of all this is very simple: If we partition code in the PROCEDURE DIVISION into black-box modules, then we should also try to partition data in the DATA DIVISION so that modules can access only that data which they require in order to carry out their function. How can we do this?

The most straightforward way, in COBOL, is to make each module a separately compiled program, rather than a paragraph or a SECTION. It is not necessary for a COBOL program to be invoked directly by the operating system on our computer; indeed, it is relatively easy to write programs that are invoked by other COBOL programs!

Remember the SECRET OK CHECK module that some other programmer wrote? Well, it turns out that the boss has decided to make that subroutine a separate program — and he wants you to fix your code to accommodate this change. (In case you have forgotten, you wrote the rest of the modules shown on the structure chart.) The name for the new program is SECRETOK.

Somewhere in ASSIGN AN AGENT PASSING TEST, you might find the statement

PERFORM SECRET-OK-CHECK.

If you changed that statement to

PERFORM SECRETOK.

the COBOL compiler would flag it. Why? Because it is illegal to PERFORM an entire COBOL program. If you compiled the program with the PERFORM statement shown above, the compiler would certainly produce an error message — for the simple reason that it could not find a paragraph named SECRETOK in your program.

So how does it work? We need a new statement that will allow one COBOL program to pass control to another. That statement is known as the CALL statement, discussed below.

8.6 The CALL statement

To connect one COBOL program to another, you must use the CALL statement. For example, in our spy system, we would simply change the PERFORM statement to read

CALL SECRETOK.

The CALL statement functions just like the PERFORM statement, except that it is used to connect two programs: the one containing the CALL, and the one named in the CALL statement.

Q.   If you saw the program SECRETOK, where do you think that name would be defined?

A.   In the PROGRAM-ID. You would find the statement

PROGRAM-ID. SECRETOK.

As you may remember, the SECRET OK CHECK module (when it was in the form of a paragraph) required the agent code and the mission code as its input; it returned the authorization status flag as its output. SECRETOK, the COBOL program, still needs the input codes, and must still produce the flag as its output. Somehow, we must be able to pass the necessary information between two programs. (Remember, each program has its own FILE SECTION and WORKING-STORAGE SECTION.) With the COBOL mechanisms that we have discussed up to this point, it is not possible to refer to fields defined outside the boundaries of a program.

In order to pass information across program boundaries, the CALLing program must explicitly state to what data the receiving program may refer. This is done with the USING option of the CALL statement. Since we must pass the two fields and the flag, the CALL statement will look like this:

```
CALL SECRETOK
    USING    MISSION-CODE
             AGENT-CODE-NO
             SECRET-OKAY.
```

The rules of the CALL-USING statement are: Every data-name in the USING clause must be defined with an 01- or 77-level-number in the CALLing program. The data-names may be defined in the FILE SECTION or the WORKING-STORAGE SECTION.

Incidentally, although the CALL acts somewhat like the PER-FORM statement, it does not have precisely the same syntax. For example, it is illegal to write

CALL SUB-PGM
USING AFIELD
UNTIL X = Y.

Unfortunately, the CALL statement may have only the USING option; however, the USING option is not necessary if the CALLing program does not need to pass any information to the CALLed program.

    Q.   How would you accomplish the kind of logic that was attempted with the illegal CALL statement shown above? That is, how can you call a subprogram iteratively?

    A.   The following code is the most common approach used by COBOL programmers:

PERFORM SUB-PGM-LOOP UNTIL X = Y.
    ----------.
    ----------.
    ----------.
SUB-PGM-LOOP.
    CALL SUB-PGM
        USING AFIELD.

8.7 The LINKAGE SECTION

Now that we've introduced the CALL statement, let's look at the new version of SECRETOK. If we were to look at its listing, we would immediately notice a new SECTION — something called the LINKAGE SECTION. The LINKAGE SECTION is the receiving end of the data passed in the CALL statement, and it is coded immediately after the WORKING-STORAGE SECTION. The LINKAGE SECTION for SECRETOK appears on the following page.

```
LINKAGE SECTION.
01  CODE-FOR-MISSION        PIC 9(5).
01  AGENT-ID-CODE           PIC 9(4).
01  CLEARANCE-FLAG          PIC X(3).
PROCEDURE DIVISION
     USING     CODE-FOR-MISSION
               AGENT-ID-CODE
               CLEARANCE-FLAG.
```

It may appear to you that there is a mistake here. After all, the CALLing statement was

```
CALL SECRETOK
     USING     MISSION-CODE
               AGENT-CODE-NO
               SECRET-OKAY.
```

All of this is perfectly legal. The data-names in the LINKAGE SECTION of the CALLed program need not be the same as the data-names in the CALLing program; indeed, if the two programs were written by different people at different times, it is unlikely that they would be identical. However, the data-names in the CALLed program and the CALLing program must describe data that are of the same length (and preferably of the same type) because the CALLed program will actually access the data in the CALLing program's DATA DIVISION. It is also important that the two programs agree on the order (or sequence) of the data elements. The order of the data elements is established by the US-ING clause in the PROCEDURE DIVISION statement of the CALLed program. Thus, we have the following correspondence in the SECRETOK situation:

	1st	2nd	3rd
CALL SECRETOK			
USING	MISSION-CODE	AGENT-CODE-NO	SECRET-OKAY.
PROCEDURE DIVISION			
USING	CODE-FOR-MISSION	AGENT-ID-CODE	CLEARANCE-FLAG.

Every field passed in a CALL must be defined in the LINK-AGE SECTION as an 01-level or 77-level entry. However, you are free to subdivide the fields in any way you find convenient — just as you would with data elements defined in the FILE SECTION or the WORKING-STORAGE SECTION. Thus, we might find that SECRETOK's LINKAGE SECTION would look like this:

```
LINKAGE SECTION.
01   CODE-FOR-MISSION.
     05   AREA-CODE                       PIC 9(2).
     05   DANGER-LEVEL                     PIC 9.
     05   SECRECY-LEVEL                    PIC 9(2).
01   AGENT-ID-CODE.
     05   AGENT-NUM                        PIC 9(2).
     05   AGENT-SECURITY-CLEARANCE         PIC 9.
     05   AGENT-PROFICIENCY-RATING         PIC 9.
01   CLEARANCE-FLAG                        PIC X(3).
PROCEDURE DIVISION
          USING      CODE-FOR-MISSION
                     AGENT-ID-CODE
                     CLEARANCE FLAG.
```

When the CALL statement is executed, control is passed to the SECRETOK program. Execution begins with the first statement in the PROCEDURE DIVISION of SECRETOK, as you would expect. SECRETOK carries out its prescribed task of deciding whether the specified agent qualifies for the assignment, and then returns to the program that CALLed it.

How does SECRETOK know where to return, and how does it actually accomplish this return? Unlike paragraphs and SEC-TIONs (which exit when the end of the PROCEDURE DIVISION is reached, or when another paragraph or SECTION is encountered), and unlike programs invoked directly by the operating system (which exit to the operating system when a STOP RUN statement is encountered), a CALLed subprogram must explicitly exit by executing an EXIT PROGRAM statement. This statement has a simple syntax: It must be the only statement in a sentence; that sentence must be the only one in the paragraph. Thus, SECRET-OK probably would contain a paragraph like this:

```
SECRETOK-EXIT.
     EXIT PROGRAM.
```

Here is a graphic representation of the communication between CALLing and CALLed COBOL programs:

```
CALLING PROGRAM.                  SECRETOK PROGRAM.


----------.                       PROGRAM-ID. SECRETOK.
----------.                       LINKAGE SECTION.
----------.                       01    CODE-FOR-MISSION  PIC 9(5).
----------.                       01    AGENT-CODE        PIC 9(4).
----------.                       01    CLEARANCE-FLAG    PIC X(3).
CALL SECRETOK                     PROCEDURE DIVISION
   USING                             USING
      MISSION-CODE                      CODE-FOR-MISSION
      AGENT-NO                          AGENT-CODE
      SECRET-OKAY.                      CLEARANCE-FLAG.
IF SECRET-OKAY = 'YES'                ----------.
----------                           ----------.
----------                           ----------.
ELSE                                 ----------.
----------                           ----------.
----------.                       EXIT-SECRETOK.
----------.                           EXIT PROGRAM.
```

8.8 Using CALL to build systems

In developing large systems, veteran COBOL programmers use CALLed programs as their basic building block. This approach enables them to modify and recompile one program without necessarily having to modify or recompile any other programs in the system. In addition, the use of the LINKAGE SECTION forces the designer to define, explicitly, the interfaces between the modules. By contrast, designers who use paragraphs or SECTIONs as their basic building block often find that they have ignored the intermodular interfaces.

To illustrate the use of CALLed modules in a COBOL system, let's consider the design of an editing system for an airline charter business having the unlikely name of Wing-and-a-Prayer Charter Tours. It happens that business has increased so much at W&P that the company is beginning to computerize its current manual charter air tour system, which is known as CATS.

Our task is to design a program that will edit the incoming client transactions. These transactions eventually will be used to update the charter tour master file so that clients can be booked on their choice of tours.

The input to the program is shown in Table 8.1 on the following page. Each client has one record, occupying an 80-position card. There will be two outputs from the program: an Edited Client File (ready for further processing), and a listing of the errors that were found. Each input record either will generate an output record on the Edited Client File, or will generate a message on the error listing. The format of the Edited Client File is identical to that of the card input file. The general format of the error listing is shown in Table 8.2. The precise format of the error messages is up to you; just be sure that they are appropriate.

The input cards have already been organized in ascending order by Tour Number; within every tour, clients are batched together by group. A group is identified by client records with the same Client Number. The Number in Group field should contain the same number as there are clients with identical Client Numbers. If there is disagreement, an error should be noted.

As you can see in Table 8.1, the editing criteria are fairly straightforward. However, a few of the edits merit special explanation. The Airport Choice code is the three-letter international airport code; it should be a three-character alphabetic field. For example, LAX is the official designation for the Los Angeles International Airport. Unfortunately, W&P only operates from a few airports; here is a list of the acceptable airports:

JFK	John F. Kennedy Airport, New York
ORD	O'Hare Airport, Chicago
LAX	Los Angeles International Airport
SFO	San Francisco International Airport
DFW	Dallas/Fort Worth Airport
IAD	Dulles Airport, Washington, D.C.

Any airport code other than the ones listed above should be treated as an error.

Table 8.1. Format of input cards.

FIELD NAME	LENGTH	EDITING CRITERIA	POSITIONS
Tour Number	4 positions	numeric	pos 1-4
Client Number	4 positions	numeric	pos 5-8
Number in Group	1 position	numeric	pos 9
1st Airport Choice	3 positions	alpha	pos 10-12
1st Airline Choice	2 positions	alpha	pos 13-14
1st Flight Number	3 positions	numeric	pos 15-17
1st Seating Choice	1 position	numeric	pos 18
*2nd Airport Choice	3 positions	alpha or blank	pos 19-21
*2nd Airline Choice	2 positions	alpha or blank	pos 22-23
*2nd Flight Number	3 positions	numeric or blank	pos 24-26
*2nd Seating Choice	1 position	numeric or blank	pos 27
Client Name	15 positions	must be present	pos 28-42
Street Address	16 positions	must be present	pos 43-58
City	15 positions	must be present	pos 59-73
State	2 positions	alpha	pos 74-75
Zip Code	5 positions	numeric	pos 76-80

*For second-choice information to be valid, all fields must pass the specific edit or all must be blank.

Table 8.2. Layout of error listing.

ERRORS FOUND ON ◄——————— center
CLIENT CARDS   header

	TOUR NO.	CLIENT NO.	NAME	MESSAGE	FIELD	sub-head aligned with columns
should	1234	7777	Joe Smith	Bad Zip	12A45	
fit 60	2246	8111	Selma Smith	Illegal Airport	LAG	
detail	3468	9001	Max Fly	No State		
lines						
per page						

Airline Choice is the two-letter code for the airlines. W&P buys blocks of seats on regularly scheduled airlines for its charter tours. Depending on the airport, it uses certain carriers:

AIRPORT	CARRIERS			
JFK	TW	PA	BA	AF
ORD	PA	AM		
LAX	PA	QF	JA	
SFO	JA	PA	TW	
DFW	PA			
IAD	BW	AF	PA	AL

The airline abbreviations have the following meanings:

CODE	AIRLINE
TW	Trans World Airlines
PA	Pan American
BA	British Airways
AF	Air France
AM	Aeronaves de Mexico
JA	Japan Airlines
BW	British West Indies Airlines
AL	Alitalia Airlines
QF	Qantas Airways

Our program should permit only tours flying on authorized airlines (listed above) from authorized airports.

At the present time, W&P only requires a numeric editing test for the Flight Number field; at some later time, they may wish the test to be more sophisticated. The Seating Choice field should be either a 1 (for first class), or a 2 (for coach); any other code is an error.

If all of the individual Client Records pass the edits, then check to ensure that they all have the identical first-choice and second-choice airport/airline/flight/seating information. If they are truly a group, they must be traveling together!

If a group of records passes this final test, then each of the records in the group should be written to the Edited Client File. We are to write only those records which pass every edit, including the group edits.

Once you are certain that you understand the problem, develop a structure chart for your solution. Be sure that you show all of the data and control information that must be passed between the modules. Don't worry about the size of the modules now — your primary concern is to design modules of high cohesion and loose coupling. Take your time; nobody produces a good structure chart quickly for a problem of this size.

When you have finished your structure chart, look at the suggested solution in the Appendix. If yours differs dramatically, spend some time comparing the two. If you have any questions, this is a good time to talk to your instructor.

8.9 Structured program design methodologies

How did you arrive at the solution for the Wing-and-a-Prayer system in the previous section? Chances are, you used intuition to develop your solution — and you should be neither surprised nor disappointed if you had to scrap several poor designs before arriving at a good one. Nor should you be terribly disappointed if your design looks somewhat different from the one in this book.

Our solution for the W&P system — and most other systems discussed in this book — was developed with a methodology known as *transform analysis,* or *transform-centered design.* Transform-centered design is a "cookbook" approach that usually produces good designs (good from the point of view of cohesion and coupling) for common data processing applications. We shall provide only a brief summary of the design strategy here; for a more comprehensive discussion, consult Yourdon and Constantine's *Structured Design.* [4]

---

[4]Edward Yourdon and Larry L. Constantine, *Structured Design* (New York: YOURDON inc., 1975).

The first step in transform-centered design is to represent the problem in a nonprocedural form known as a program graph or bubble chart. You may recall seeing program graphs in the brief discussion of program design in Section 3.10 of Part 1 of this series. For the W&P system, the program graph can be drawn as follows:

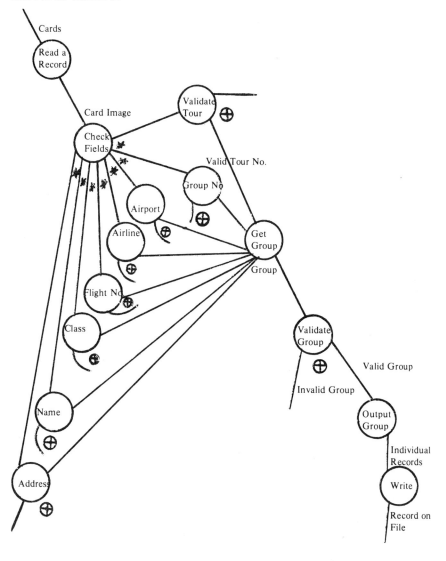

The second step is often described as "looking for the point of highest abstraction." We follow the flow of data along the program graph to see where the input ends — that is, the point where the data can no longer be regarded as input. In the case of the W&P system, card images are obviously input — indeed, the difference between a card image and a card is hardly more than semantic. The next recognizable piece of data in the program graph is the tour data associated with a "valid individual"; certainly, this type of data can still be regarded as input to the system.

The next type of data is a group of individuals; this is a more aggregate, and therefore more logical, form of data. Note, for example, that it is no longer evident at this stage whether the data has anything to do with such physical forms of data as a card image.

Finally, we see a valid group as the next form of data in the program graph. At this point, we know that each individual's tour has been checked, and that the individuals have been checked against one another for consistency. If we go one step further in the program graph, we find that we are dealing with an edited file record, which clearly represents an output from the W&P system. So, we determine that the most logical, or most highly processed, input to the W&P system is a valid group.

The third step of the transform-centered design strategy is to work our way backward from the output end(s) of the program graph, looking for the first point at which we have something resembling output. This, too, could be regarded as a point of highest abstraction — i.e., a form of data that is definitely an output from the system, but which has not yet been put into proper form for physical outputting.

In the case of the W&P system, we first notice a form of data that consists of a record to be written on an Edited Customer File. While this is definitely an output from the system, it is not necessarily the most logical output. Indeed, if we go inward (toward the middle of the program graph) one step further, we next find a valid group — a *collection* of records to be written. Recall that this was also the data element that we regarded as the most logical form of input — so there is no point tracing inward any further on the program graph for logical forms of output.

What does all this mean? Simply that the W&P system, at the highest level, appears to be a simple input-output program: It obtains valid groups of customers, then writes them to the Edited Customer File. Everything else in the program is a *detail* having to do with input or output. If we mark on the program graph where the input ends and the output begins, we would have something like this:

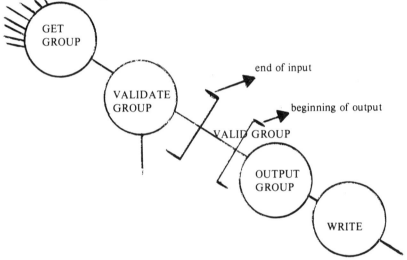

We must emphasize that the W&P system is unusually simple in that it has no calculations, or central transforms. Most of the COBOL programs that you develop will have a number of bubbles in the program graph *between* the point where input ends and the point where output begins.

After we have gotten this far, we can begin to build a structure chart. The purpose of finding the most logical inputs and the most logical outputs is to determine where the top-level module in the W&P system will be attached to other modules in the hierarchy. To see how this works, imagine the program graph as a collection of cardboard disks with pieces of string connecting them. Taking a pair of scissors, we snip the string at the end of the input, and again at the beginning of the output. Now we introduce a cardboard rectangle, which is named EDIT-CLIENT-TRANSACTIONS. It, too, has strings dangling from it.

Taking strings from the rectangle, we tie one to the snipped end of the input and another to the beginning of the output. If we lift the whole mess by the rectangle, we'll get something that looks like this:

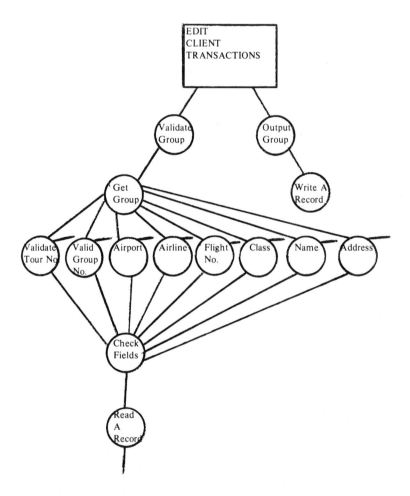

If we convert each bubble to a rectangular box, we can see that we have a rough approximation of a structure chart. Obviously, we need to further partition the modules into one or more levels of highly cohesive subordinate modules. And we must examine our structure chart for possible coupling problems, although they should be minimal if the program graph was drawn properly. Regardless of whether we implement the modules with CALLed subprograms of PERFORMed paragraphs (or SECTIONs), it is important that we give careful attention to the interfaces between the modules.

9 More Powerful Facilities

9.1 Traditional flowcharts

There's a good chance that your organization uses flowcharts as its documentation for each program. Flowcharts emphasize the procedural aspects of the program; they show every action and every decision, connected in the time-order in which they occur. For example, the flowchart on the following page shows a program that will read three cards and store them in three areas. If an end-of-file condition is noted, or if a blank card is found, the program finishes by setting the end-of-file indicator or blank-card indicator; if it finds three non-blank cards, it finishes without setting any indicator.

One alternative to the traditional flowchart is the so-called structured flowchart. Most people refer to it as a Nassi-Shneiderman diagram, named for Isaac Nassi and Ben Shneiderman, who first described the technique.[1] Compare the traditional flowchart on the next page with the Nassi-Shneiderman diagram of procedural logic that follows it. Both represent the same program that we saw before in flowchart form.

There is yet another alternative to the flowchart: *pseudocode*, also called structured English, program design language, or computer Esperanto. Its purpose is to give the programmer a good balance between the precision of programming languages like COBOL and the informality of English.

---

[1] I. Nassi and B. Shneiderman, "Flowchart Techniques for Structured Programming," *ACM SIGPLAN Notices*, Vol. 8, No. 8 (August 1973), pp. 12-26.

ACTION ──────▶ MOVE SPACES
TO   AREA-1
        AREA-2
        AREA-3

MOVE 'NO' TO
EOF-CARD

MOVE 'NO' TO
CARD-BLANK

MOVE 0 TO
RECD-COUNT

LINE CONNECTOR ──▶ ◯
(no instruction)

MOVE
'YES' TO   AT END   READ
EOF-CARD   CARD   INPUT OR
                                        OUTPUT FUNCTION

ADD 1 TO
RECD-COUNT

Y   CARD =   N
       SPACES

                    Y   RECD-   N
                           COUNT = 1

MOVE   Y   RECD-   N
'YES' TO   COUNT = 2
CARD-BLANK   MOVE CARD
               TO AREA-1
                                  MOVE CARD   MOVE CARD
                                  TO AREA-2   TO AREA-3

                    COUNT > 3   N

                          Y

                          ◯

Traditional flowchart.

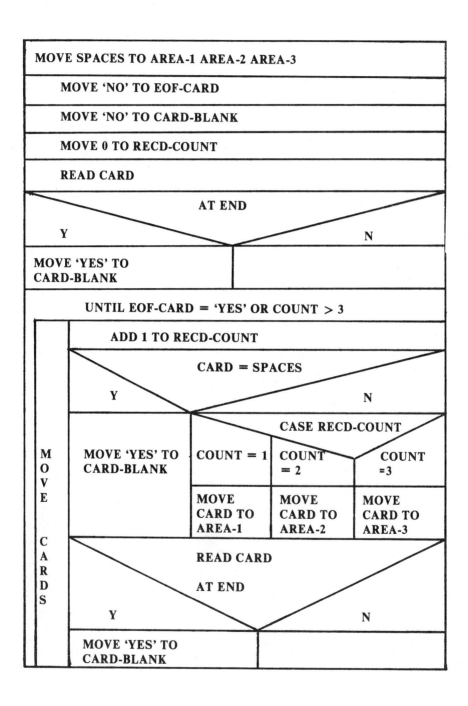

Nassi-Shneiderman diagram.

A pseudocode version of our simple card-reading program might look as follows:

```
MOVE SPACES TO AREA-1 AREA-2 AREA-3
MOVE 'NO' TO EOF-CARD
MOVE 'NO' TO CARD-BLANK
MOVE 0 TO RECD-COUNT
READ CARD
  AT END MOVE 'YES' TO EOF-CARD
UNTIL EOF-CARD = 'YES' OR RECD-COUNT > 3
    ADD 1 TO RECD-COUNT
    IF CARD = SPACES
       MOVE 'YES' TO CARD-BLANK
    ELSE IF RECD-COUNT = 1
       MOVE CARD TO AREA-1
    ELSE IF RECD-COUNT = 2
       MOVE CARD TO AREA-2
    ELSE
       MOVE CARD TO AREA-3.
```

Which form of procedural documentation should we use? The only proper answer is, use whatever works for you. Throughout the 1950's and 1960's, most EDP organizations used flowcharts; however, most programmers today agree that flowcharts have some major drawbacks. The first problem has to do with the correspondence between the flowchart and the COBOL code. You'll find that a strict interpretation of the flowchart almost inevitably leads to coding with GO TO statements, which we try to avoid.

A more significant problem has to do with maintenance. If we change the COBOL coding, what are the chances that the flowchart will be modified appropriately? Most EDP organizations have found that it is almost impossible to guarantee that the flowcharts and the COBOL coding will remain consistent after several years of maintenance. Indeed, it is very common to find that a programmer will not draw the flowchart for his program until *after* he has finished debugging the program! This means that he will have a flowchart of what he thinks his program is doing, which may or may not be the same as what his program really is doing.

This emphasizes an important point about detailed documentation for our programs. When a program is modified, what happens if the COBOL coding and the documentation disagree? Obviously, we are forced to believe the code, since that is what the computer executes. Thus, if there is any chance that the documentation will *not* be updated when the code is updated, the documentation is worthless. There are three ways of interpreting this observation:

1. Maintaining the current documentation for a program is as important as maintaining the code itself.

2. The form of documentation should be something that a programmer will find *easy* to maintain. If the documentation is difficult or awkward to update, there is more chance that it will be ignored. This would suggest that pseudocode is the best form of documentation, since it is the easiest for the programmer to generate. The problem with both Nassi-Shneiderman diagrams and flowcharts is that they require the programmer to become involved with "artwork"; chances are that it will be done sloppily if a maintenance effort has to be done in the middle of the night.

3. In a real-world environment, there is a good chance that *no* detailed documentation will be kept up-to-date. We feel — based on our own experience — that the most reliable form of documentation is a standard structure chart (which does not change very much during maintenance), combined with neat, formatted, COBOL source code.

9.2 Details of the PERFORM statement

In addition to the MOVE statement and the arithmetic statements, the statement we will use most often is the PERFORM. Therefore, it is imperative that we thoroughly understand its capabilities.

Thus far, we have used the simple PERFORM as a connector of two modules:

PERFORM EDIT-ACCT-NUM.

However, there is another version of the PERFORM which can be used as a connector. It is the PERFORM-THRU, illustrated by the following statement:

PERFORM EDIT-ACCT-NUM THRU EDIT-ZIP-CODE.

This version of the PERFORM statement will pass control to the EDIT-ACCT-NUM paragraph; execution will then continue through *all* of the paragraphs following EDIT-ACCT-NUM until EDIT-ZIP-CODE is reached. EDIT-ZIP-CODE will be executed, too — and, at its conclusion, control will return to the statement immediately following the PERFORM THRU.

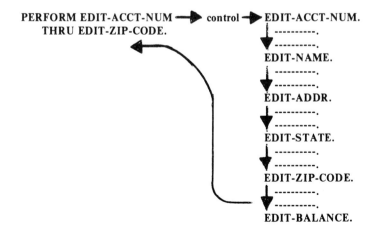

Although the PERFORM-THRU is legal in COBOL, we prefer to use the simple version of the PERFORM. Adapting the example shown above, we would write:

```
PERFORM EDIT-ACCT-NUM.
PERFORM EDIT-NAME.
PERFORM EDIT-ADDR.
PERFORM EDIT-STATE.
PERFORM EDIT-ZIP-CODE.
```

Why do we prefer the simple version of the PERFORM? It allows us to insert extra paragraphs among the existing EDIT paragraphs without affecting the nature of the control logic. With the PERFORM-THRU, the EDIT paragraphs are strongly coupled together; they *must* remain physically adjacent, and no new code may be inserted without affecting what happens when the PERFORM-THRU is executed. We've learned, after many long nights of debugging, that it's dangerous to depend upon the fact that control "falls" from one paragraph to the next.

Some programmers use the PERFORM-THRU as the standard connection between COBOL paragraphs. In such cases, the custom is to follow each paragraph with an EXIT paragraph. Thus, we might see code like this:

```
PERFORM EDIT-ACCT-NUM THRU EDIT-ACCT-EXIT.
---------------.
EDIT-ACCT-NUM.
     ----------.
     ----------.
     ----------.
EDIT-ACCT-EXIT.
     EXIT.
```

The EXIT statement must appear as the only statement in a paragraph; its sole purpose is to mark the *end* of a procedure — in this case, the account-number-edit procedure. Programmers often use this form of PERFORM-THRU in order to facilitate the use of GO TO statements *within* the procedure; e.g., to provide for an early exit from the module by passing control to the EXIT paragraph. As an example, consider the following fragment of code:

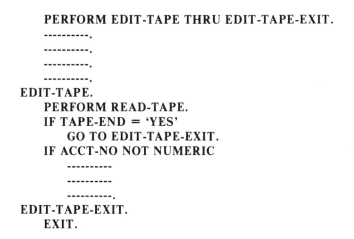

```
PERFORM EDIT-TAPE THRU EDIT-TAPE-EXIT.
----------.
----------.
----------.
----------.
EDIT-TAPE.
    PERFORM READ-TAPE.
    IF TAPE-END = 'YES'
        GO TO EDIT-TAPE-EXIT.
    IF ACCT-NO NOT NUMERIC
        ----------
        ----------
        ----------.
EDIT-TAPE-EXIT.
    EXIT.
```

The same logic could be coded without the GO TO statement as follows:

```
PERFORM EDIT-TAPE.
----------.
----------.
----------.
----------.
EDIT-TAPE.
    PERFORM READ-TAPE.
    IF TAPE-END = 'NO' AND
        ACCT-NO NOT NUMERIC
        ----------
        ----------
        ----------.
EDIT-TAPE-EXIT.
    EXIT.
```

Note that with this arrangement of code, the final EXIT paragraph really isn't necessary. Indeed, this is generally true. If we organize our logic properly, the GO TO statement is superfluous.

Although we prefer the simple PERFORM as a connector between modules, you should follow whatever standards have been determined by your programming organization. The important thing, as always, is to be consistent.

9.3 The PERFORM-UNTIL statement

The PERFORM statement is used in yet another way: to form a *loop*. This is done with the PERFORM-UNTIL construct. An example of such a construct is

```
PERFORM PROCESS-RECDS
    UNTIL END-OF-RECDS = 'YES'.
```

The important thing about the PERFORM-UNTIL statement is that the UNTIL clause is tested *before* the specified paragraph is invoked. Thus, if END-OF-RECDS had been set to 'YES' *before* the PERFORM-UNTIL statement was invoked, PROCESS-RECDS would be invoked *zero* times. For most normal applications, we would expect PROCESS-RECDS to be invoked at least once, and we would expect that the code within PROCESS-RECDS would eventually set END-OF-RECDS to 'YES'. But it is important to remember that the PERFORM-UNTIL statement may execute the specified paragraph zero times, since it tests the terminating condition before it carries out the PERFORM.

Obviously, you must plan your logic so as to take this into account. In the example above, the programmer might ensure that PROCESS-RECDS is executed at least once by explicitly initializing the value of END-OF-RECDS. Thus, we might see

```
MOVE 'NO' TO END-OF-RECDS.
PERFORM PROCESS-RECDS
    UNTIL END-OF-RECDS = 'YES'.
```

It is permissible to specify *compound* conditions in the UN-TIL clause of a PERFORM-UNTIL. For example, we might write

```
PERFORM PROCESS-RECDS
    UNTIL END-OF-RECDS = 'YES'
        OR BAD-RECD = 'YES'.
```

If you do use compound conditions, it is considered good style to enclose any pairs of conditions in parentheses. Thus, we might see code like this:

```
PERFORM PROCESS-RECDS
    UNTIL BAD-MSTR = 'YES'
        OR (END-TRANS = 'YES' AND END-MSTR = 'YES').
```

If we write the code this way, anyone reading it will understand exactly what conditions will cause the loop to terminate.

Note that the PERFORM-UNTIL statements we have seen will continue looping — i.e., continue invoking a named paragraph — until some *logical condition* occurs. We don't know when we write the code whether the loop will be executed six, one hundred, or one million times. Since there often are programming situations in which we *want* to specify the *number* of times the loop will execute, COBOL provides a TIMES option on the PER-FORM statement. Thus, we can write

```
PERFORM EDIT-FIELDS
    6 TIMES.
```

or

```
PERFORM EDIT-FIELDS
    NUMBER-OF-FIELDS TIMES.
```

If we use the second version of the TIMES option, we must be certain that the "iteration variable" — in this case, NUMBER-OF-

FIELDS — is defined as a *numeric integer.* If its value is negative or zero, then the specified paragraph, EDIT-FIELDS, will not be executed at all.

There is another restriction of which you should be aware: It is illegal to change the value of the iteration variable during the execution of the PERFORM-UNTIL statement. In the example above, we may not change the value of NUMBER-OF-FIELDS from the first time we invoke EDIT-FIELDS until after we have finished executing the entire PERFORM-UNTIL statement. After the PERFORM-UNTIL has finished executing, the value of the iteration variable will be the same as when we first began executing it; the looping process will not affect the field in any way.

In practice, we seldom use the TIMES option on the PER-FORM statement. In most situations, the programmer is unable to specify the number of iterations of a loop with a constant, or even with a simple variable. It is more common to introduce one variable to indicate which iteration is currently being performed, and another variable to indicate how many iterations should be carried out for this particular execution of the PER-FORM loop. We often see COBOL coding of the following sort:

```
MOVE ZERO TO FIELD-NUMBER.
PERFORM EDIT-FIELDS
    UNTIL FIELD-NUMBER = MAX-NUMBER-OF-FIELDS.
```

Note that we accomplished this loop — which is definitely of an iterative nature — with the familiar PERFORM-UNTIL construct that we discussed earlier.

We should point out that there often is more than one reason for terminating a loop. One terminating condition, for example, might be based on an iteration count, while another terminating condition might be based on a logical condition. As a result, we often see COBOL coding such as is shown on the following page:

```
MOVE ZERO TO FIELD-NUMBER.
PERFORM EDIT-FIELDS
      UNTIL FIELD-NUMBER = MAX-NUMBER-OF-FIELDS
      OR EDITING-ERROR = 'YES'.
```

Regardless of the type of PERFORM loop you code, there is one important rule to keep in mind: You *must* state the conditions of looping correctly. Common mistakes in this area are:

1. The programmer instinctively assumes that his PERFORM loop will be executed at least once — and fails to construct his logic so that the loop will "do nothing gracefully"[2] when the UNTIL clause is satisfied the first time it is tested.

2. The loop does not execute correctly on the first iteration — e.g., the programmer forgets to initialize subscripts or other variables properly for the first iteration of the loop.

3. The programmer fails to prepare correctly for the next iteration of the loop. Typically, the next iteration will require that the next transaction be read, or that a subscript be incremented.

4. The programmer fails to terminate the loop correctly. It is common for a loop to iterate one time too many, or one time too few; it is in this area that you must be particularly careful to remember that the UNTIL clause is tested *before* the specified paragraph is PERFORMed. On rare occasions, a programmer constructs an infinite loop — a loop that never terminates — but such a bug is so obvious that it is quickly remedied

---

[2]B.W. Kernighan and P.J. Plauger, *The Elements of Programming Style* (New York: McGraw-Hill, 1974), p. 88.

Consider the following fragment of code, which reads through a sequentially ordered transaction file until it finds a transaction with an account number matching the account number of a master record:

```
PERFORM READ-TRANS
    UNTIL TRANS-ACCT = MSTR-ACCT.
```

But what if there is a transaction with no corresponding master record? If the transaction file is in ascending sequence by account number, we could code

```
PERFORM READ-TRANS
    UNTIL TRANS-ACCOUNT NOT < MSTR-ACCT.
IF TRANS-ACCT > MSTR-ACCT
    PERFORM NO-MATCH-TRANS
ELSE
    PERFORM MATCH-PROCESSING.
```

What must we be able to assert immediately before the PER-FORM? That we indeed have a master account number available for comparison! We need to ask ourselves if the master file could be at end of file when we execute the loop.

Before we code a loop, we must be able to convince our-selves that we have the necessary elements for proper control of the loop. The conditions for terminating the loop must be stated so that no matter what happens during the iterations of the loop, we will eventually exit. We must also ensure that the code fol-lowing the PERFORM-UNTIL loop will be able to execute properly regardless of the reason for terminating the loop. Remember: Anything that *can* happen *will* happen, sooner or later — and it invariably will be the least convenient thing that happens. So, plan your loops with great care.

9.4 CASE structures with GO TO DEPENDING ON

It is common for a field — i.e., a variable — to have more than two possible values. In such situations, different actions that are dependent on those values usually must be taken. This is accomplished with a construct known as a CASE. We saw a structured flowchart of a CASE construct in Section 9.1, a portion of which is extracted as follows:

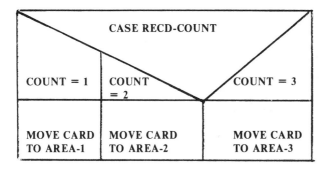

We could code this using IF-ELSE statements:

```
IF RECD-COUNT = 1
    MOVE CARD TO AREA-1
ELSE IF RECD-COUNT = 2
    MOVE CARD TO AREA-2
ELSE
    MOVE CARD TO AREA-3.
```

Note that we don't indent this code as we would with a nested IF statement. Why? Because the actions are mutually exclusive. In the code above, for instance, we move a card to only one area each time the code is activated. Since the actions are mutually exclusive, we arrange the indentation to emphasize that the actions occur at the same logical level. It is important to recognize that this indentation means nothing to the COBOL compiler, the operating system, or the computer hardware; it is done solely for the benefit of the human reader trying to understand what the author of the code intended.

There is another way to implement the CASE construct in COBOL, using the GO TO DEPENDING ON statement:

```
MOVE-CARD-TO-AREA.
    GO TO      RECD-AREA-1
               RECD-AREA-2
               RECD-AREA-3
               DEPENDING ON RECD-COUNT.
RECD-AREA-1.
    MOVE CARD TO AREA-1.
    GO TO AREA-EXIT.
RECD-AREA-2.
    MOVE CARD TO AREA-2.
    GO TO AREA-EXIT.
RECD-AREA-3.
    MOVE CARD TO AREA-3.
    GO TO AREA-EXIT.
AREA-EXIT.
    EXIT.
```

This piece of code could be executed using the statement

```
PERFORM MOVE-CARD-TO-AREA THRU AREA-EXIT.
```

Here, we have used a PERFORM-THRU to make it obvious to the reader of our program that the scope of the CASE construct is everything from the paragraph-name, MOVE-CARD-TO-AREA, to the final AREA-EXIT paragraph.

The rules of the GO TO DEPENDING ON statement are very restrictive. The field which is the object of the DEPENDING ON clause — RECD-COUNT in the example above — must contain a positive *numerical* value. Control is then transferred to the first, second, third, . . . or nth paragraph, depending on the numerical value of the field.

If the field contains a value that is "out of range," the GO TO DEPENDING ON is effectively ignored, and control is passed to the first statement *after* the GO TO DEPENDING ON. Looking back at our example, RECD-COUNT must contain the numerical value of 1, 2, or 3 in order for the code to behave in a meaningful way. If RECD-COUNT is zero, or 6, or 'YES', or *anything* but 1, 2, or 3, control will pass to the first statement after the GO TO DEPEND-ING ON — i.e., to paragraph RECD-AREA-1.

This can be a dangerous procedure: If there were a bug somewhere else in the program which caused RECD-COUNT to be set to some illegal value, the program could continue behaving as if everything were all right, and it might take quite a while to determine that RECD-COUNT was out of range.

Consequently, it is considered good programming style to introduce an error paragraph immediately following the GO TO DEPENDING ON statement — unless the object of the DEPENDING ON clause always can be guaranteed to be in range when the GO TO DEPENDING ON is encountered.

Q.   Does the following illustrate legal use of the GO TO DEPENDING ON statement?

```
REGION-CHECK.
    GO TO   EAST-REG
            EAST-REG
            CENTRAL-REG
            ROCKY-REG
            WEST-REG
            DEPENDING ON REGION-CODE.
ERROR-REG.
    ----------.
    ----------.
    GO TO REG-EXIT.
EAST-REG.
    ----------.
    ----------.
    GO TO REG-EXIT.
CENTRAL-REG.
    ----------.
    ----------.
    GO TO REG-EXIT.
ROCKY-REG.
    ----------.
    ----------.
    GO TO REG-EXIT.
WEST-REG.
    ----------.
    ----------.
    GO TO REG-EXIT.
REG-EXIT.
    EXIT.
```

A.   Yes, it is perfectly legal. Note that two values of REGION-CODE result in control being passed to the same paragraph.

Q.   What is the legal range of REGION-CODE in the example above?

A.   1 through 5, inclusive.

Q.   What would happen if there were no GO TO statements at the end of each paragraph, *and* the value of REGION-CODE were 1?

A.   Control would fall through all four paragraphs; that is, through EAST-REG, CENTRAL-REG, ROCKY-REG, and WEST-REG.

Q.   What would happen if the significant values of REGION-CODE were 1, 14, 60, and 94?

A.   We would have to list 94 paragraphs in the GO TO DEPENDING ON statement, all but four of which would cause control to be transferred to an error paragraph.

Q.   What would be a more straightforward way of coding the CASE construct if the values of REGION-CODE were 1, 14, 60, and 94?

A.   Using the IF-ELSE construct, we could build the following CASE mechanism:

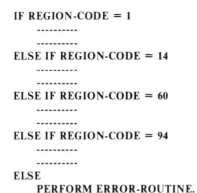

```
IF REGION-CODE = 1
    ----------
    ----------
ELSE IF REGION-CODE = 14
    ----------
    ----------
ELSE IF REGION-CODE = 60
    ----------
    ----------
ELSE IF REGION-CODE = 94
    ----------
    ----------
ELSE
    PERFORM ERROR-ROUTINE.
```

(In the above example, the final ELSE clause is used to catch all situations in which REGION-CODE is not equal to 1, 14, 60, or 94.)

Unless circumstances *naturally* argue in favor of the GO TO DEPENDING ON construct, it is better style to use the IF-ELSE-IF construct for a CASE. We strongly recommend that you avoid converting a non-numeric field to a numeric value in order to take advantage of the GO TO DEPENDING ON. In most cases, the conversion is a waste of time — yours and the computer's. Similarly, we suggest that you avoid assigning clever, artificial numerical codes to variables, if your only reason for doing so is to take advantage of the GO TO DEPENDING ON. In such cases, the user of the program ends up having to remember the meaning of some arbitrary set of numerical codes, rather than having the convenience of mnemonic alphanumeric names for his data.

9.5 Literals, and why you shouldn't use them

Thus far, we have been using literals in many of our coding examples. It is time to recognize that literals usually are *not* the best way to represent a constant in a COBOL program. To illustrate our point, consider the following example:

```
MULTIPLY NUMBER-OF-GIZMOS TIMES 2.19
    GIVING TOTAL-GIZMO-PRICE.
```

By looking at this code, we deduce that the price of a single Gizmo is $2.19. However, it is highly likely that the price of a

Gizmo will change at some point in the near future. What will happen if we raise the price of a Gizmo to $2.99? We will have to hunt through the entire program looking for instances of the literal 2.19, and change each one to 2.99. As you might expect, several things can go wrong:

1.   We might overlook an instance of the literal 2.19 — and the boss will not be pleased when we underbill the client!

2.   While changing a literal from 2.19 to 2.99, we may have to repunch an entire COBOL statement — increasing the possibility that errors and bugs will be introduced into the program.

3.   We may inadvertently change a literal of 2.19 that had nothing to do with the price of Gizmos. It might turn out, for example, that the price of a Widget is also $2.19.

Far better programming style would be to define a field with the value of the current price of a Gizmo; we could then reference that field from any part of our program. For example, we might write

```
77  PRICE-PER-GIZMO          PIC 9V99   VALUE 2.19.
    ----------.
    ----------.
    ----------.
    MULTIPLY NUMBER-OF-GIZMOS
       TIMES PRICE-PER-GIZMO
       GIVING TOTAL-GIZMO-PRICE.
```

Now if the price changes, all we have to do is change the VALUE clause of the data definition. No instructions in the PROCEDURE DIVISION will have to be changed. With our Gizmo example, we would merely change the PIC definition as follows:

```
77  PRICE-PER-GIZMO          PIC 9V99   VALUE 2.99.
```

What we are saying, then, is that any change that is likely to occur should be accommodated by changing just one line of source program text, as we have done in the example above. Literal values are often used repeatedly in a program, and, as we pointed out earlier, they can be hard to spot when making modifications — *especially* when one is under a lot of pressure to fix a bug at 3:00 a.m. So, watch out for literals — and avoid them whenever you can.

9.6 The ALTER statement

In Chapter 8 we observed that the GO TO statement should be avoided if we wish to write *understandable* programs. Unfortunately, there is a statement that is even *worse* than the GO TO: the ALTER statement. It normally is used in conjunction with the GO TO statement to dynamically modify the paragraph-name to which the GO TO transfers control. Here is an example of an ALTER statement:

```
PROCEDURE DIVISION
     USING      CARD-AREA
                CARD-EOF.
OPEN-BYPASS.
   GO TO OPEN-FILE.
OPEN-FILE.
   OPEN INPUT CARD-FILE.
   ALTER OPEN-BYPASS TO PROCEED TO READ-FILE.
READ-FILE.
   READ CARD-FILE INTO CARD-AREA
      AT END
         MOVE END-CARDS TO CARD-EOF
         CLOSE CARD-FILE.
EXIT-READ.
   EXIT PROGRAM.
```

As you can see, this program either OPENs and READs from a file of cards, or simply READs from the file, or READs and CLOSEs the file. The first time the program is CALLed, the file is OPENed, *and* the GO TO statement in OPEN-BYPASS is modified so that subsequent CALLs will skip around the OPEN-FILE paragraph and proceed directly to READ-FILE.

The GO TO statement, which serves as the object of the ALTER, must be in a paragraph by itself — the ALTER statement references the paragraph-name in which the GO TO resides. The GO TO cannot have a DEPENDING ON clause. Any number of ALTER statements may modify a single GO TO, as long as the ALTERs and the GO TO are in the same PROCEDURE DIVISION.

What's so horrible about the ALTER? It is nearly impossible to debug programs containing ALTER statements, because it makes a lie out of the program listing! Imagine, for example, that something has gone wrong with one of your programs. While debugging, you come across a statement that says

GO TO OPEN-FILE.

Naturally, you would innocently turn to paragraph OPEN-FILE and continue reading the code. But that is not what the GO TO "said" at *execution* time. Four pages after the GO TO statement, there is an ALTER lurking among some other statements . . . and it modified the GO TO statement to make control proceed to FORMAT-RECORD, which lies 15 pages away from OPEN-FILE. How long will it take you to discover that you are following the wrong trail?

The ALTER statement can cause so many debugging problems that many EDP organizations have banned its use completely. Chances are good that your programming group won't allow its use.[3] Even if your company allows its use, we strongly recommend that you avoid it. And even if you think you can handle an ALTER without getting personally confused, it eventually may cause problems for someone else — e.g., for the maintenance programmer who has to work with your programs several years after you've finished them. Indeed, if you discover an ALTER statement in an old program that you are maintaining, it is usually a good idea to remove it — *if* you can do so easily.

---

[3]Indeed, chances also are good that the American National Standards Institute (ANSI) soon will drop the ALTER statement from the official ANS definition of COBOL.

9.7 MOVE, ADD, and SUBTRACT CORRESPONDING

In all previous programming examples, we have given a unique name to every field of data — regardless of whether it was defined in the FILE SECTION, the WORKING-STORAGE SECTION, or the LINKAGE SECTION. Technically, we don't *have* to do it this way — and there are often good reasons for using the same field names in multiple structures of data. Consider the following example:

```
01   TAPE-IN.
       05   NAME           PIC     X(20).
       05   STREET-ADDR    PIC     X(30).
       05   CITY           PIC     X(15).
       05   STATE          PIC     X(2).
       05   ZIP-CODE       PIC     9(5).
    -----------.
    -----------.
    -----------.
01   PRINT-LINE.
       05   FILLER         PIC     X(2).
       05   NAME           PIC     X(20).
       05   FILLER         PIC     X(10).
       05   STREET-ADDR    PIC     X(30)
       05   FILLER         PIC     X(10).
       05   CITY           PIC     X(15).
       05   FILLER         PIC     X(10).
       05   STATE          PIC     X(2).
       05   FILLER         PIC     X(10).
       05   ZIP-CODE       PIC     9(5).
       05   FILLER         PIC     X(18).
    -----------.
    -----------.
    -----------.
MOVE NAME IN TAPE-IN
     TO NAME IN PRINT-LINE.
    -----------.
    -----------.
    -----------.
```

Different fields defined with the same name are called *qualified data-names*. In order to refer to a nonunique data-name, we must give not only the data-name but also the group name of the group item to which it belongs. The group name *must* be unique; however, the group name does not have to be the immediately superior level to the data-name that is being qualified. The following code illustrates this point:

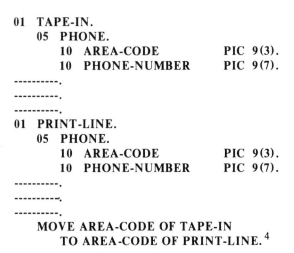

```
01  TAPE-IN.
    05  PHONE.
        10  AREA-CODE          PIC 9(3).
        10  PHONE-NUMBER       PIC 9(7).
    ----------.
    ----------.
    ----------.
01  PRINT-LINE.
    05  PHONE.
        10  AREA-CODE          PIC 9(3).
        10  PHONE-NUMBER       PIC 9(7).
    ----------.
    ----------.
    ----------.
        MOVE AREA-CODE OF TAPE-IN
            TO AREA-CODE OF PRINT-LINE. [4]
```

When working with qualified data-names, we can move them one at a time:

```
        MOVE NAME OF TAPE-IN
            TO NAME OF PRINT-LINE.
        MOVE STREET-ADDR OF TAPE-IN
            TO STREET-ADDR OF PRINT-LINE.
        MOVE CITY OF TAPE-IN
            TO CITY OF PRINT-LINE.
    ----------.
    ----------.
    ----------.
```

[4]In COBOL, we can use either the key word OF or the key word IN when describing a qualified data reference.

Or, we can move them all at once:

MOVE CORRESPONDING TAPE-IN TO PRINT-LINE.

The MOVE CORRESPONDING statement will MOVE every elementary data field — a field defined with type and length, e.g.,
X(6) — to another field with the same data-name, providing that
the qualification of the fields is identical to, but *not* including, the
group names stated in the MOVE CORRESPONDING. Fields meeting this criterion will not be moved if they contain a RENAMES,
REDEFINES, or OCCURS clause. Don't worry about this at the
moment — we'll examine those clauses in the next two chapters.

Besides moving fields, we can also ADD CORRESPONDING or
SUBTRACT CORRESPONDING. The rules are the same whether we
MOVE, ADD, or SUBTRACT with the CORRESPONDING clause.
Here's an example of ADD CORRESPONDING:

```
05  CUSTOMER-BALANCE.
    10  DUE-LAST-MONTH       PIC     9(5)V99.
    10  DUE-THIS-MONTH       PIC     9(5)V99.
    10  PAID-LAST-MONTH      PIC     9(5)V99.
 ----------.
 ----------.
 ----------.
05  TOTAL-MONTHLY-BALANCE.
    10  DUE-LAST-MONTH       PIC     9(6)V99.
    10  PAID-LAST-MONTH      PIC     9(6)V99.
    10  DUE-THIS-MONTH       PIC     9(6)V99.
 ----------.
 ----------.
 ----------.
ADD CORRESPONDING CUSTOMER-BALANCE
    TO TOTAL-MONTHLY-BALANCE.
 ----------.
 ----------.
 ----------.
```

Notice that the elementary items are not in the same order
in the two group items shown above. That's perfectly acceptable.
Also, note that the receiving fields are larger than the sending
fields. That's all right, too, since the ADD CORRESPONDING
statement will behave as if we had written the following code:

```
ADD DUE-LAST-MONTH OF CUSTOMER-BALANCE
    TO DUE-LAST-MONTH OF TOTAL-MONTHLY-BALANCE.
ADD PAID-LAST-MONTH OF CUSTOMER-BALANCE
    TO PAID-LAST-MONTH OF TOTAL-MONTHLY-BALANCE.
ADD DUE-THIS-MONTH OF CUSTOMER-BALANCE
    TO DUE-THIS-MONTH OF TOTAL-MONTHLY-BALANCE.
----------.
----------.
----------.
```

The MOVE, ADD, and SUBTRACT CORRESPONDING statements look pretty handy, don't they? *Wrong!* One of the most frequently changed parts of a program is the format of input records and output records. When such record definitions change, it is very easy to foul up the requirements for the CORRESPONDING clause. In the long run, it is better to use the straightforward MOVE, ADD, and SUBTRACT statements. They explicitly state what is happening, and, therefore, are significantly easier to follow.

9.8 The COMPUTE statement

Occasionally, you'll find that the simple ADD, SUBTRACT, MULTIPLY, and DIVIDE statements are not sufficient to easily express a computation. For example, we could write

```
MULTIPLY SIDE BY SIDE
    GIVING SQUARE-FEET.
```

but it would be more convenient to use the *exponentiation* (raising a number to a power) operator "**" and the COMPUTE statement to do the same thing:

```
COMPUTE SQUARE-FEET = SIDE ** 2.
```

The COMPUTE statement should be used whenever a computation is sufficiently complicated that it would be excessively verbose to express with ADDs, MULTIPLYs, and so forth. Similarly, the COMPUTE statement should be used whenever a well-known formula is to be invoked or exponentiation is required. Incidentally, we can even use the COMPUTE statement to determine *roots* of a number:

COMPUTE SIDE = SQUARE-FEET ** 0.5.

We now have seen the complete set of arithmetic operators: i.e., +, −, *, /, and **. However, there is one topic that remains to be discussed: the *precedence* of these arithmetic operators. For example, how would the COBOL compiler interpret the following statement?

COMPUTE A = +9/4 * E + F ** 3 − C.

The first operation is to make the 9 a "+9". This is called unary arithmetic — simply making "plus" numbers positive, and "minus" numbers negative. The next operation performed is exponentiation: F is to be raised to the third power. The next lower "precedence" is division and multiplication, both of which have the same level of "binding." [Remember the commutative law of arithmetic? A*(B/C) is the same as (A*B)/C.]

Since multiplication and division are at the same level, the compiler works from left to right on the COBOL statement that it is analyzing. Thus, the expression 9/4 is resolved, and the result is then multiplied by E. Next come addition and subtraction, which operate at the same level of precedence. Consequently, addition and subtraction are carried out in a left-to-right fashion; so, the expression (+9/4)*E is added to the expression F**3, and C is then subtracted.

To generalize from this example, we can see that the order — or precedence — of arithmetic operations is as follows:

first	unary arithmetic operators
second	exponentiation
third	multiplication, division (performed left to right)
fourth	addition, subtraction (performed left to right)

An important, additional point should be made: Even though the COBOL compiler *knows* the order in which computations should be carried out, you should act as if it doesn't. Why? Because our biggest problem is writing programs that can be understood by people. Imagine your dilemma if you were a maintenance programmer desperately trying to find a bug at 3:00 a.m., and you narrowed the bug down to the general vicinity of the following statement:

COMPUTE A = +9/4 * E + F ** 3 − C.

Naturally, you would begin to wonder (a) if your memory of the precedence of exponentiation, multiplication, and addition were correct, (b) if there were a bug in the COBOL compiler, and (c) whether the original programmer really knew the order in which the computations were to be carried out. How much better it would have been had the original programmer simply written

COMPUTE A = ((+9/4) * E) + (F ** 3) − C.

In addition to the strong argument of readability, there is another practical reason for using parentheses liberally in a COM-PUTE statement: Doing so allows us to change the order of computation so that the compiler will work from the innermost parentheses outward. For example, parentheses are *extremely* desirable — and absolutely necessary — in a COBOL statement such as the following:

COMPUTE BALANCE-DUE =
  (TOTAL-DUE − LAST-PAYMENT) / MONTHS-REMAINING. [5]

---

[5]Note that the presence of a "space" character changes the meaning of the "-" character from a "hyphen" to a "minus."

If we are carrying out a complex computation, it is better programming style to break the COMPUTE down into a series of smaller COMPUTEs, introducing *meaningful* data-names to hold intermediate results. For example, suppose we were required to calculate the minimum payment for a credit card holder. Let's assume that the minimum payment is defined as 10 percent of the outstanding balance, where outstanding balance is defined as last month's balance minus last month's payment, plus 1 percent interest on that outstanding amount, plus any new charges. We could write the following code:

```
COMPUTE THIS-MONTH-BALANCE =
    (((LAST-MONTH-BALANCE − PAYMENT) * INTEREST)
    + NEW-CHARGES) / NUMBER-OF-PAYMENTS.
```

but it would be far more understandable if we wrote

```
COMPUTE OUTSTANDING-BALANCE =
    (LAST-MONTH-BALANCE − PAYMENT) * INTEREST.
COMPUTE TOTAL-DUE =
    OUTSTANDING-BALANCE + NEW-CHARGES.
COMPUTE THIS-MONTH-BALANCE =
    TOTAL-DUE / NUMBER-OF-PAYMENTS.
```

As always, readability is the most important consideration. The COMPUTE statement can either aid or hinder the understandability of your program, depending on how it is used.

9.9 The INSPECT/EXAMINE statement

This book is based on the version of COBOL defined by the American National Standards Institute in 1974 — otherwise known as 1974 ANS COBOL. The American National Standards Institute previously defined a standard version of COBOL in 1968. Today, many COBOL compilers still adhere to the 1968 standards, rather than the 1974 standards.

One of the major differences between the 1968 and 1974 versions of COBOL is the elimination of the EXAMINE statement (from 1968 ANS COBOL) and the addition of the more flexible INSPECT statement. If your COBOL compiler is based on the 1968 standards, you will have to use the EXAMINE statement because the INSPECT statement will not be recognized. Both instructions are useful for counting and/or replacing characters in a string of data.

To illustrate the use of the INSPECT/EXAMINE statements, suppose we want to write a program to read cards that describe the amount of money owed to us by our clients. Let's assume that the card has a five-position field for the amount of money. However, the keypunch operators have been told that they do not have to keypunch leading zeroes if the amount occupies four or fewer positions. Thus, we might have a card that looks like the following:

> bb295

(Note that we have used the character "**b**" to represent the "blank" character.) Before we can do any arithmetic with this number, we must make it purely numeric. The following statements will do the trick:

> **EXAMINE CLIENT-BALANCE**
> **REPLACING LEADING SPACES BY ZEROS.**

> or

> **INSPECT CLIENT-BALANCE**
> **REPLACING LEADING SPACES BY ZEROES.**

(Note that COBOL accepts both ZEROS and ZEROES as the plural for ZERO. For the sake of consistency, pick one spelling and stick with it.) The result of this operation can be summarized with the following example:

BEFORE	AFTER
bb295	00295

Not only can we replace LEADING characters, but we also can use the EXAMINE statement to replace ALL, FIRST, and UNTIL FIRST. Here's an example:

FIELD-A BEFORE	COBOL STATEMENT	FIELD-A AFTER
bb2b7b	EXAMINE FIELD-A REPLACING ALL SPACES BY ZEROES.	002070
bb2b7b	EXAMINE FIELD-A REPLACING UNTIL FIRST '7' BY '3'.	33337b

The INSPECT can do whatever the EXAMINE can do, plus much more. Not only can we replace characters before the first occurrence of a specified character, but also after the specified character. For example:

FIELD-A BEFORE	COBOL STATEMENT	FIELD-A AFTER
bb2b7b	INSPECT FIELD-A REPLACING CHARACTERS BY ZEROES AFTER INITIAL '2'.	bb2000
bbbb1111	INSPECT FIELD-A REPLACING CHARACTERS BY ZEROES BEFORE INITIAL '1'.	00001111
ESEZINP	INSPECT FIELD-A REPLACING ALL 'E' BY 'A', 'S' BY 'M', 'P' BY 'G'.	AMAZING

In addition to using INSPECT and EXAMINE to replace characters, you can also count characters. There is a special field called TALLY, defined by and known to the COBOL compiler. This field is the repository of the count when you use either the INSPECT or the EXAMINE statement. You don't have to define TALLY in your DATA DIVISION; it is defined automatically as a 9(5) item, as shown on the following page:

BEFORE	COBOL STATEMENT	AFTER	TALLY
002107	**EXAMINE FIELD-A TALLYING ALL ZEROES.**	002107	3
002107	**INSPECT FIELD-A TALLYING ALL '1'.**	002107	1

After either of these instructions, you may reference TALLY as you would any other field. For example:

IF TALLY GREATER THAN ZERO ...

or

ADD TALLY TO ZERO-COUNT.

You can even count and replace characters simultaneously, as the following example illustrates:

BEFORE	COBOL STATEMENT	AFTER	TALLY
bbb322	**EXAMINE FIELD-A TALLYING LEADING SPACES REPLACING BY ZEROES.**	000322	3

or

0064.22	**INSPECT FIELD-A TALLYING ZERO-COUNT FOR LEADING ZEROES REPLACING ALL '.' BY ZERO.**	0064022	ZERO-COUNT=2

Notice that the INSPECT in the example above included the clause TALLYING ZERO-COUNT. When counting with the INSPECT statement, we can have the TALLY count placed in any field we wish, provided we define the field as a numeric elementary item.

Thus, we might define ZERO-COUNT as follows:

77 ZERO-COUNT   PIC 9(2).

Unfortunately, this particular feature is not available with the EX-AMINE statement.

Both the EXAMINE and the INSPECT statements are very powerful and have a myriad of options. Whether you use the 1968 EXAMINE statement, or the 1974 INSPECT statement, you should take a look at all of the possibilities in your COBOL manual. One or two common uses of INSPECT/EXAMINE should probably be made part of your standard repertory of programming tools.

Following are a few problems for you to try. For each coding example, describe the effect on the test-field and on TALLY. The answers can be found in the Appendix.

BEFORE	COBOL STATEMENT	AFTER	TALLY

b1274

      EXAMINE TEST-FIELD
      TALLYING UNTIL FIRST '4'
      REPLACING BY SPACE.

BANANA

      EXAMINE TEST-FIELD
      REPLACING ALL 'A' BY 'E'.

b$1346

      INSPECT TEST-FIELD
      TALLYING NUMB-COUNT
      FOR CHARACTERS AFTER INITIAL '$'
      REPLACING FIRST '$' BY SPACE.

ELEMENT

      INSPECT TEST-FIELD
      REPLACING ALL 'LE' BY 'DA',
      FIRST 'E' BY 'Q'.

9.10 The STRING/UNSTRING statement

We have seen how we can use the MOVE CORRESPONDING statement to copy elementary items of one group into their counterparts in another group. The STRING statement is, in a sense, the opposite of MOVE CORRESPONDING. That is, the STRING statement can be thought of as a move *not* corresponding. The STRING statement can accept fields from diverse sources and order them, one after another, into an elementary alphanumeric data item. This sounds as if it is just another way of disguising a series of simple MOVEs, but the STRING statement has some features which go well beyond that.

Suppose, for example, that we had to write a CALLable program which would format a "detail" line for subsequent printing. Our program will receive a client-record, a balance-due field, and a flag representing the client's billing status. It eventually will call a subordinate module, PRINTCL,[6] passing it a formatted print-line to be written. The piece of the structure chart that we are working on looks like this:

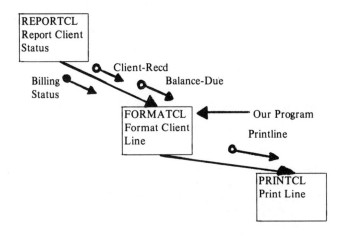

---

[6]Unfortunately, most implementations of COBOL allow a maximum of eight alphanumeric characters for a program name. Thus, CALLed programs often have non-mnemonic names.

When this program is CALLed once, the print-line passed to PRINTCL should contain this information:

MR. S. SPADE 44221 21 W. 43 ST. NY NY 10036 2140.83 (0 — STATUS *) 60 DAYS IN ARREARS, SEND LETTER

We might imagine that the "0" status means that the client's bill is 60 days in arrears, and that he should be sent a letter.

```
IDENTIFICATION DIVISION.
PROGRAM-ID. FORMATCL.

ENVIRONMENT DIVISION.

DATA DIVISION.

WORKING-STORAGE SECTION.

01    BEST-MSG              PIC X(11)        VALUE 'A1-STATUS *'.
01    OKAY-MSG              PIC X(10)        VALUE 'C-STATUS *'.
01    BAD-MSG               PIC X(10)        VALUE '0-STATUS *'.
01    END-OF-STATUS         PIC X            VALUE '*'.
01    STATUS-MSG            PIC X(11).
01    1ST-WARNING           PIC X(26)
                            VALUE 'NOTIFY 30 DAYS IN ARREARS-'.
01    2ND-WARNING           PIC X(32)
                            VALUE '60 DAYS IN ARREARS, SEND LETTER-'.
01    ATTORNEY-MSG          PIC X(31)
                            VALUE '90 DAYS LATE, NOTIFY ATTORNEYS-'.
01    END-OF-ACTION         PIC X            VALUE '-'.
01    ACTION-TO-TAKE        PIC X(32).
01    PRINTLINE             PIC X(132).
01    NORMAL-INDENT         PIC 9(3)         VALUE 5.
01    BLANK-3               PIC X(3)         VALUE SPACES.
01    BLANK-5               PIC X(5)         VALUE SPACES.

LINKAGE SECTION.
01    CLIENT-RECORD.
      05    CLIENT-NAME      PIC X(20).
      05    CLIENT-NUMBER    PIC 9(5).
      05    CLIENT-ADDR      PIC X(30).
      05    CLIENT-ZIP       PIC 9(5).
      05    CLIENT-STATUS    PIC 9.
            88    EXCELLENT-STATUS              VALUE 1.
            88    OKAY-STATUS                   VALUE 2.
            88    POOR-STATUS                   VALUE 3.

01    BALANCE-DUE           PIC 9(4)V99.

01    BILLING-STATUS        PIC 9(2).
      88    30-DAYS-LATE                        VALUE 30.
```

```
          88    60-DAYS-LATE                 VALUE 60.
          88    90-DAYS-LATE                 VALUE 90.
     EJECT


* FORMATCL IS A PROGRAM CALLED BY REPORTST WHICH FORMATS A
* PRINTLINE DEPENDING ON THE BILLING STATUS INDICATOR.
* IT PASSES THE PRINTLINE ONTO 'PRINTCL' TO HANDLE WRITING


PROCEDURE DIVISION
     USING                        CLIENT-RECORD
                                  BALANCE-DUE
                                  BILLING-STATUS.


CHECK-STATUS.
     IF EXCELLENT-STATUS
          MOVE BEST-MSG TO STATUS-MSG
     ELSE IF OKAY-STATUS
          MOVE OKAY-MSG TO STATUS-MSG
     ELSE IF POOR-STATUS
          MOVE BAD-MSG TO STATUS MSG.

     IF 30-DAYS-LATE
          MOVE 1ST-WARNING TO ACTION-TO-TAKE
     ELSE IF 60-DAYS-LATE
          MOVE 2ND-WARNING TO ACTION-TO-TAKE
     ELSE
          MOVE ATTORNEY-MSG TO ACTION-TO-TAKE.
     MOVE SPACES TO PRINTLINE.
          STRING
          CLIENT-NAME DELIMITED BY SIZE

          CLIENT-NUMBER DELIMITED BY SIZE
          BLANK-3 DELIMITED BY SIZE
          CLIENT-ADDR DELIMITED BY SIZE

          CLIENT-ZIP DELIMITED BY SIZE
          BLANK-5 DELIMITED BY SIZE
          BALANCE-DUE DELIMITED BY SIZE

          STATUS-MSG DELIMITED BY END-OF-STATUS
          ACTION-TO-TAKE DELIMITED BY END-OF-ACTION
     INTO PRINTLINE
          WITH POINTER NORMAL-INDENT.

     CALL 'PRINTCL' USING PRINTLINE.

EXIT-FORMATCL.
     EXIT PROGRAM.
```

The STRING statement works left to right on the receiving field. For example, the INTO PRINTLINE WITH POINTER clause directs the ordering of fields — and it indicates that we should begin with the fifth position of the line. If we had omitted this clause, then "stringing" would begin in the first position of the line. The size of the field acting as a pointer must be large enough to hold the length of the receiving field *plus one*. The length of PRINTLINE is 132, so (length of PRINTLINE) + 1 is 133 — thus, the pointer is defined as a three-position field. Each field is listed in the order in which it is to be placed on the line.

The DELIMITED BY SIZE clause means that the entire field should be moved. If we wish, we can move just a part of a field. For example, STATUS-MSG is DELIMITED BY END-OF-STATUS, which has a value of '*'. This tells the STRING statement to move only that part of the field which is to the left of the *first* occurrence of an asterisk.

As you can see, STRING is most useful when packing a series of items into a linear sequence. It helps us to avoid writing many MOVEs and, more important, to avoid writing complex record layouts for output lines. All of the complexity is kept in one place: in the STRING statement itself.

The UNSTRING statement takes an elementary alphanumeric data item as its input, and moves data from that alphanumeric data item to separate fields. The fields can be defined as numeric, alphanumeric, or alphabetic data items. The UNSTRING statement is used most often in reformatting raw input so that each field may be edited.

To illustrate the UNSTRING statement, suppose we want to write a CALLed program that will build a charge card record for billing a commercial airline flight. The input to the program is a card in the following format: charge number/from airport/to airport/flight number/number of seats/coach or first class/departure date/. For example, both of the following two cards are valid:

00427689757100AX/JFK/LAX/10/7/C/012177/
38180056290006DC/LAG/LGN/351/3/F/022777/

The card that follows is invalid because it has too few fields:

00476972237686AX/SFO/ATL/222/3/C/

The output returned to the CALLing program follows:

00427689757100AX 012177 JFK LAX 10b 1bbC 3818005629000bDC 022277 LAG LGN 351 3bbF

We are not supposed to edit the field — all we have to do is re-format the input field into the kind of output shown above. If any field is missing, or if there are extra fields, we should print the entire card, and an error message — which will be accomplished by CALLing a program known as ERROROUT, which expects the entire card and an appropriate message.

```
IDENTIFICATION DIVISION
PROGRAM-ID. BUILDREC.

ENVIRONMENT DIVISION.

DATA DIVISION.
WORKING-STORAGE SECTION.

01   CARD-AREA            PIC X(80).
01   END-OF-CARDS         PIC X(3)   VALUE SPACES.
01   NUMBER-OF-FIELDS     PIC 9.
01   TOO-MANY-FIELDS      PIC X(3).
01   MARKER               PIC X      VALUE '/'.
01   PROPER-NUMBER        PIC 9      VALUE 7.
01   TOO-MANY-MSG         PIC X(24)  VALUE 'REJECTED TOO MANY FIELDS'.
01   TOO-FEW-MSG          PIC X(24)  VALUE 'REJECTED TOO FEW FIELDS '.

LINKAGE SECTION.

01   CHARGE-RECORD.
     05   CHARGE-CODE      PIC X(16).
     05   DEPART-DATE      PIC X(6).
     05   FROM-AIRPORT     PIC X(3).
     05   TO-AIRPORT       PIC X(3).
     05   FLIGHT-NUMBER    PIC X(3).
     05   NUMBER-OF-SEATS  PIC X(3).
     05   FIRST-OR-COACH   PIC X.
01   EOF-RECORDS          PIC X(3).
* THIS PROGRAM, CALLED BY EDITREC, FORMATS A CARD ACCORDING TO THE
* LAYOUT OF CHARGE-RECORD. IF FIELDS ARE MISSING OR THERE IS EXTRA
* DATA, THE CARD IS REJECTED AND 'ERROROUT' IS CALLED.  IT GETS A CARD
* BY CALLING 'GETCARD'.

PROCEDURE DIVISION
        USING     CHARGE-RECORD
                  EOF-RECORDS.
REFORMAT.
        MOVE ZEROES TO NUMBER-OF-FIELDS.
        CALL 'GETCARD'
           USING CARD-AREA
                 END-OF-CARDS.

        PERFORM REFORMAT-LOOP
           UNTIL END-OF-CARDS = 'YES'
              OR NUMBER-OF-FIELDS = PROPER-NUMBER.
        IF END-OF-CARDS = 'YES'
           MOVE 'YES' TO EOF-RECORDS.
REFORMAT-EXIT.
        EXIT PROGRAM.
```

```
REFORMAT-LOOP.
    MOVE 'NO' TO TOO-MANY-FIELDS.
    MOVE ZEROES TO NUMBER-OF-FIELDS.

    UNSTRING
    CARD-AREA DELIMITED BY MARKER
        INTO CHARGE-CODE
            FROM-AIRPORT
            TO-AIRPORT
            FLIGHT-NUMBER
            NUMBER-OF-SEATS
            FIRST-OR-COACH
            DEPART-DATE
        TALLYING IN NUMBER-OF-FIELDS
        ON OVERFLOW MOVE 'YES' TO TOO-MANY-FIELDS.

    IF TOO-MANY-FIELDS = 'YES'
        CALL 'ERROROUT'
            USING    CARD-AREA
                     TOO-MANY-MSG
        CALL 'GETCARD'
            USING    CARD-AREA
                     END-OF-CARDS
    ELSE IF NUMBER-OF-FIELDS LESS THAN PROPER-NUMBER
        CALL 'ERROROUT'
            USING    CARD-AREA
                     TOO-FEW-MSG
        CALL 'GETCARD'
            USING    CARD-AREA
                     END-OF-CARDS.
```

Note that the UNSTRING statement in the code above strips off the fields delimited by a '/'. It also keeps count of the number of fields it has moved in NUMBER-OF-FIELDS. If there should be more fields on the card and the receiving fields have all been used, the UNSTRING statement will carry out the actions specified by the ON OVERFLOW clause. Similarly, the ON OVERFLOW clause is normally used with the STRING statement for occasions when the receiving field may be too small to hold all the fields.

We have shown a relatively simple example of the UN-STRING statement. The UNSTRING, like the STRING, can have a WITH POINTER clause, and can count the number of positions moved into any receiving field. These facilities will enable you to perform many useful operations, but you may wish to refer to your COBOL language manual for other uses of this sophisticated instruction.

9.11 The ACCEPT/DISPLAY statement

The DISPLAY statement normally is used to output a small message — usually to the computer operator. For example, one might write the following statement:

**DISPLAY 'INVALID MASTER FOUND, ACCOUNT-' MSTR-ACCOUNT
UPON CONSOLE.**

The coding above causes the literal and a master record account number to be DISPLAYed. Literals are DISPLAYed by enclosing them in single quotes; the contents of various fields can be DISPLAYed by listing the field-name in the DISPLAY statement. The UPON CONSOLE clause will send the message to the computer operator's console terminal (which almost always is located in the computer room, right next to the tapes, disks, printers, and CPU). Messages can also be DISPLAYed upon any other device that is normally used to receive output data; to do this, merely write UPON "device-name" instead of UPON CONSOLE. Device-name must be specified in the SPECIAL-NAMES paragraph of the ENVIRONMENT DIVISION.

The 1974 ANS COBOL standards permit you to obtain the date, day, and time of day by using the ACCEPT statement. For example, one might write

ACCEPT TODAY-DATE FROM DATE.

DATE is an internally defined field — like TALLY; you need not worry about defining it in your DATA DIVISION. In effect, it is a 9(6) item, in the format YYMMDD. Thus, July 4, 1976 would be represented as 760704.

The ACCEPT statement also can be used to input small amounts of data — typically, from the operator's console terminal, or some other on-line typewriter. We might write the following code:

```
MOVE SPACES TO REPORT-ANSWER.
DISPLAY 'SUMMARY REPORT TO BE PRINTED?
   - REPLY Y OR N'.
PERFORM GET-ANSWER
   UNTIL REPORT-ANSWER = 'Y'
      OR REPORT-ANSWER = 'N'.
----------.
----------.
----------.
```

GET-ANSWER.
```
ACCEPT REPORT-ANSWER FROM CONSOLE.
IF REPORT-ANSWER NOT EQUAL 'Y'
   AND REPORT-ANSWER NOT EQUAL TO 'N'
   DISPLAY 'SUMMARY REPORT TO BE PRINTED?
      - REPLY Y OR N'.
```

Because their use is extremely implementation-dependent, ACCEPT and DISPLAY should be used sparingly, if at all. It is best to hide them in CALLed modules, so that only the module need change when a program is moved from one environment to another. Indeed, some EDP organizations have banned the use of ACCEPT and DISPLAY in order to ensure the portability of COBOL programs from one computer environment to another.

9.12 The STOP RUN statement

The STOP RUN statement will cause a program to return to the operating system. Only the topmost module in a hierarchy of modules should have a STOP RUN statement; ideally, it should be the physically last statement of the top-level module. All other modules (i.e., CALLed subprograms) should have an EXIT PROGRAM statement to cause them to return to the CALLing program. This is an important point: If a low-level module (which has been CALLed by a module, which was CALLed by some other module, which was CALLed by some other module, and so forth) should execute a STOP RUN statement, then the entire hierarchy of modules will exit to the operating system. Since we want all modules to have a single entry point and a single exit, we would expect to have only one STOP RUN or EXIT PROGRAM statement per program.

10 Internal Coding and the DATA DIVISION

10.1 Representing numbers with ones and zeroes

If someone asked you, "What was the largest number of home runs hit in one season by a major league baseball player?" how would you respond? Assuming that you knew, you would answer, "61." Without even thinking about it, we naturally express numerical quantities as base ten numbers. Thus, 61 is convenient shorthand for 6 tens and 1 one. If, instead, we assumed that 61 were a base seven number (written as 61_7), then 61 would be equivalent to 6 sevens and 1 one — or 43_{10}.

When dealing with computers, the basic unit of information is the bit, which is a binary, or base two, digit. When representing binary numbers, only 1's and 0's are valid digits. The following example illustrates this:

$$
\begin{aligned}
101101_2 \quad = \quad & 1 \times 2^5 & = & \quad 32 \\
+\ & 0 \times 2^4 & = & \quad 0 \\
+\ & 1 \times 2^3 & = & \quad 8 \\
+\ & 1 \times 2^2 & = & \quad 4 \\
+\ & 0 \times 2^1 & = & \quad 0 \\
+\ & 1 \times 2^0 & = & \quad 1 \\
\hline
& & & \quad 45_{10}
\end{aligned}
$$

When dealing with long strings of bits (they grow in length more rapidly than decimal numbers), it is easier to represent them as hexadecimal, or base 16, numbers. Since 16 is equal to 2^4, each hexadecimal digit summarizes four bits of information: A number expressed by 12 binary digits could be expressed in three hexadecimal digits. When writing hexadecimal numbers, 0 through 9 have the same value as 0 through 9 in the base ten system; the letters A through F are used to signify values of ten through 15. For example:

$$3D = (3 \times 16) + (13 \times 1) = 61_{10}$$

A four-position binary field has 16 possible values, from 0000 (0_{16}), to 1111 (F_{16}). To convert any binary number to its hexadecimal equivalent, work from right to left, grouping four bits at a time. For example:

In most computers, the next unit of information after the bit is the byte. The number of bits within a byte varies from vendor to vendor. Most machines are designed eight bits to the byte, but some have six- or nine-bit bytes. Assuming that you have an eight-bit per byte machine, what is the largest number — in base 16 — that a byte can contain?

$$1111\ 1111_2 = FF_{16} = 255_{10}$$

The byte is the basic unit of internal storage for holding data. When we define data — e.g., an elementary item in WORKING-STORAGE — the size of the internal storage needed to hold that item is computed in terms of bytes.

10.2 Representing characters: USAGE DISPLAY, COMP, COMP-3

There are several forms we can use to represent byte-oriented information. The simplest form is *numeric character,* in which one byte contains one character. Numeric character format is known as DISPLAY in COBOL. It is the only way we can store non-numeric data — e.g., alphabetic strings such as ABC, or alphanumeric strings such as A97B. Indeed, we have been using the DISPLAY form exclusively in this book; it is the default form when defining data. Thus,

```
01 CUSTOMER-STATE   PIC XX.
01 CUSTOMER-STATE   PIC XX
      USAGE DISPLAY.
```

define CUSTOMER-STATE in exactly the same way; both define a two-character field to hold a two-letter state code.

With the DISPLAY format, each number, letter, or special character (e.g., "$", ".", ",", or "+") is assigned a unique eight-bit binary value, that is, a unique byte value. The most popular system for representing the character codes is known as EBCDIC — an acronym for Extended Binary Coded Decimal Interchange Code. The other popular coding scheme is known as ASCII, which is an acronym for American Standard Code for Information Interchange. We will use EBCDIC code, shown in Table 10.1 on the following page.

Note that we show the characters in ascending order of binary value. This is called the *collating sequence;* it determines the result when we compare one field with another — i.e., the binary value of 3 is less than the binary value of 4.

To illustrate the use of DISPLAY, suppose we define the following field:

```
01 PRESIDENT          PIC X(6)   VALUE 'CARTER'.
```

The six-position field, with the value CARTER, would be expressed as the following hexadecimal quantity:

Table 10.1. Letters and Numbers in EBCDIC.

Binary Value	Hexadecimal Value	Character
1100 0001	C1	A
1100 0010	C2	B
1100 0011	C3	C
1100 0100	C4	D
1100 0101	C5	E
1100 0110	C6	F
1100 0111	C7	G
1100 1000	C8	H
1100 1001	C9	I
1101 0010	D1	J
1101 0011	D2	K
1101 0011	D3	L
1101 0100	D4	M
1101 0101	D5	N
1101 0110	D6	O
1101 0111	D7	P
1101 1000	D8	Q
1101 1010	D9	R
1110 0010	E2	S
1110 0011	E3	T
1110 0100	E4	U
1110 0101	E5	V
1110 0110	E6	W
1110 0111	E7	X
1110 1000	E8	Y
1110 1001	E9	Z
1111 0000	F0	0
1111 0001	F1	1
1111 0010	F2	2
1111 0011	F3	3
1111 0100	F4	4
1111 0101	F5	5
1111 0110	F6	6
1111 0111	F7	7
1111 1000	F8	8
1111 1001	F9	9

When we define any numeric field with the DISPLAY format, it is important to remember that the sign is carried somewhere within the confines of the number, not as a separate character. Notice in Table 10.1 that the digits 0 through 9 are represented as hexadecimal F0 through F9. The four bits comprising the F are called *zone bits,* while the four bits which describe the integer are called *numeric bits* (thus the *numeric* format we mentioned earlier). Different vendors hold the sign of numeric fields in different locations, but all vendors include the sign within the number itself. In the IBM 360/370 series, when a number is defined as a positive quantity, the zone bits of the low-order digit will be a hexadecimal C instead of an F; if the number is negative, the low-order zone bits will be a D. For example, the COBOL statement

01   DEDUCTION   PIC   S9(4)   VALUE   +1500.

would cause DEDUCTION to be stored internally in the following format:

F1	F5	F0	C0

In the programs and the examples we have seen thus far, we did arithmetic — ADD, SUBTRACT, MULTIPLY, DIVIDE, and COMPUTE — with numeric fields in DISPLAY form. When we do arithmetic with DISPLAY fields, the fields are usually converted to another format before the calculations actually take place. For IBM COBOL, arithmetic always is done on fields in *packed decimal* format. IBM COBOL's name for packed decimal is COMP-3, which is an abbreviation for COMPUTATIONAL-3.[1] In the COMP-3 format, the zone bits are dropped — so that two numeric digits can be held in one eight-bit byte. In order to preserve the sign of the number, the low-order sign byte of the DISPLAY form has its zone and numeric bits reversed when converting to the COMP-3 format.

---

[1] COMP-3 is actually a vendor name. Packed decimal is not defined in the ANSI COBOL standards.

For example, the data item DEDUCTION introduced above could be represented in either of the following two forms:

DEDUCTION as DISPLAY   DEDUCTION as COMP-3

F₁F₅F₀C0   01500C

We have packed four bytes of DISPLAY data into three bytes of COMP-3 data. Obviously, the saving in memory is greater if we are dealing with longer numbers — it can be as much as 50 percent. Note also that a high-order zero was added to the COMP-3 form of DEDUCTION; this is done automatically by COBOL, since (on almost all computers) each data item must begin and end on a byte boundary.

It is simple to define COMP-3 fields in the WORKING-STORAGE SECTION of our program. For example:

01 P1 PIC S9V9999   VALUE +3.1426   USAGE COMP-3.

or

01 P1 PIC S9V9999   VALUE +3.1426   COMP-3.

In this example, we still define the field in terms of the number of positions needed to express it as a decimal quantity. That is, the PIC clause must indicate that P1 is a numeric item that requires five decimal digits and a decimal point. When defining the data, we do not worry about the number of bytes that will be used to hold the number internally in the computer.

With IBM COBOL, use the COMP-3 format on all fields that are defined by the programmer, and intended for use in arithmetic statements. By defining fields in this fashion, we avoid the time-consuming conversion from DISPLAY to COMP-3, which otherwise would take place every time the DISPLAY field was referenced in an arithmetic statement.

There is a third format for holding numeric data. It is known as COMP, and is used to represent data in a binary form. The COMP format requires that the field be either two bytes (i.e., a half-word on computers such as the IBM System/370), or four bytes (a full word on the IBM System/360). Of the 16 bits that are available in a two-byte quantity, 15 are used to represent the number, and one is used to indicate the sign. Thus, such numbers must be in the range $\pm 32767_{10}$. Normally, we use COMP numbers in COBOL to do arithmetic when using non-IBM COBOL compilers, and to describe subscripts and indexes for all compilers. Subscripts and indexes are discussed in Chapter 11.

10.3 Alignment of fields: SYNC, JUSTIFIED

When we work with binary (COMP) fields, we must ensure that they are always aligned on an internal computer boundary. Every byte of internal storage has a unique *address* — that is, a number that describes a specific position in the internal storage area (or memory) of the computer. Most computers that run COBOL programs have millions of such bytes of internal storage.

With IBM COBOL, every half-word (i.e., a two-byte quantity) must begin on a *half-word boundary;* that is, the left-most byte of the pair must have an address that is divisible by two. Similarly, full-word binary fields must be aligned in such a way that the left-most byte has an address divisible by four. We should point out that all this is necessary because of hardware requirements. Almost all modern computers are particular about the alignment of data.

As a COBOL programmer, you do not have to be concerned about the alignment of data if you are defining a binary (COMP) field. If it should turn out that the binary field does not have an even-numbered address, the COBOL compiler will arrange things so that (a) the binary field is moved to a properly aligned area of memory, (b) the specified arithmetic operation is carried out, and (c) the results are moved back to the original storage area allocated for the binary field. All of this is transparent — that is, COBOL makes it look as if the arithmetic operation has taken place directly on the mis-aligned field.

As you might imagine, this moving of binary fields back and forth can be rather time-consuming; in some cases, it can slow your program significantly. We can avoid all of this internal work, however, by adding the clause SYNC to the data definition. SYNC tells the COBOL compiler to leave space, if necessary, between one data field and another — to ensure that each data field begins on the proper boundary. SYNC is an abbreviation for SYNCHRONIZED; either word is acceptable to COBOL. An example of a data item defined with SYNC follows:

05 TABLE-SUB   PIC S99   USAGE IS COMP SYNC   VALUE IS +01.

SYNC ensures that the original definition of TABLE-SUB is properly aligned. Wherever you define a binary field, it is best to include the SYNC clause.

SYNC is used to properly justify a field within *internal* storage; it should not be confused with the JUSTIFIED clause in a data definition. JUSTIFIED is used when moving alphanumeric fields. Why do we need the JUSTIFIED clause? To deal with situations in which we do not want to accept COBOL's normal tendency to left-justify alphanumeric fields. Normally, if a sending alphanumeric field is larger than the receiving field, the extra positions on the right are truncated. For example:

FIELD A	moved to	FIELD B
BETSY ROSS		BETSY RO

Similarly, if the sending field is shorter than the receiving field, the receiving field is left-aligned and blank-filled on the right. To illustrate:

FIELD A	moved to	FIELD B
BETSY ROSS		BETSY ROSS**bbb**

When we add the JUSTIFIED clause — which can be abbreviated as JUST — to the data definition of the receiving field, the
alphanumeric field is right-aligned; and if the receiving field is
too short, the extra left-most positions are truncated:

FIELD A	moved to	FIELD B
BETSY ROSS		TSY ROSS

If, on the other hand, the receiving field is longer than the sending field, the field is right-aligned and blank-filled on the left.
For example:

FIELD A	moved to	FIELD B
BETSY ROSS		**bbb**BETSY ROSS

To define a field as JUSTIFIED, we simply code

```
05  FIELD-B    PIC X(13)  JUST.
```

Remember: The JUSTIFIED clause may be used for elementary
alphanumeric items only.

10.4 Negative numbers and the SIGN clause

We have seen that when defining signed numeric fields, it
is as easy to define negative numbers as it is to define positive
numbers. For example, we can code

```
01 DISCOUNT              PIC S9V99   COMP-3  VALUE -2.55.
```

From our discussion in Section 10.2, we know that DISCOUNT
would have the following format in internal storage:

255D

In many accounting applications, data is entered with a separate "+" or "−" to represent either a credit or a debit. For example, suppose we are required to write a program to update a sequential master account file, using transaction cards which contain an account number and a numeric quantity with a trailing "+" or "−" representing a credit or debit. Once the matching account is found, we are to adjust the field named ACCOUNT-BALANCE. We could define the card format as follows:

```
01 TRANSACTION-CARD.
   05  ACCOUNT-NUMBER        PIC  9(5).
   05  CARD-AMOUNT           PIC  9(3)V99.
   05  CREDIT-DEBIT          PIC  X.
   05  FILLER                PIC  X(69).
```

We could then write the following code:

```
IF CREDIT-DEBIT = CREDIT-MARK
    ADD CARD-AMOUNT TO ACCOUNT-BALANCE
ELSE IF CREDIT-DEBIT = DEBIT-MARK
    SUBTRACT CARD-AMOUNT FROM ACCOUNT-BALANCE
ELSE
    PERFORM ERROR-ROUTINE.
```

With this example, CREDIT-MARK is defined as a "+", and DEBIT-MARK is defined as a "−". A positive ACCOUNT-BALANCE would mean a credit, and a negative ACCOUNT-BALANCE would indicate an amount owed by the customer.

There is nothing wrong with the code above — but COBOL allows it to be written much more compactly. We can define the field known as CREDIT-DEBIT as nothing more than the sign for CARD-AMOUNT. This would be done as follows:

```
01 TRANSACTION-CARD.
   05  ACCOUNT-NUMBER      PIC  9(5).
   05  CARD-AMOUNT         PIC  S9(3)V99
        SIGN IS TRAILING SEPARATE CHARACTER.
   05  FILLER              PIC  X(69).
```

We could then write the following code:

```
ADD CARD-AMOUNT TO ACCOUNT-BALANCE.
*IF CARD-AMOUNT IS NEGATIVE, IT IS A DEBIT.
*IF CARD-AMOUNT IS POSITIVE, IT IS A CREDIT.
```

With the SIGN IS TRAILING SEPARATE CHARACTER clause, COBOL counts the "S" in the definition of CARD-AMOUNT as a position. Exactly *where* the S is placed is unimportant — the SIGN clause states that the S is the last character. Without the SIGN IS TRAILING SEPARATE CHARACTER clause, CARD-AMOUNT would be considered to be a five-position field with the sign contained *within* the right-most digit. When the clause is present in your data definition, COBOL considers the field to be a six-position numeric field with the sign *alone* in the right-most position. The SIGN IS . . . clause is permitted only for numeric items with a DISPLAY format. The sign must be either a plus or a minus. If we wanted the sign to immediately *precede* the numeric field, we could have used SIGN IS LEADING SEPARATE CHARACTER.

When we input data from cards, the sign of an amount field can be overpunched on the right-most digit. For example, if a number is to represent a credit, no overpunch is made; thus, an amount of 15075 would simply be keypunched as 15075. However, if the amount is a debit — i.e., a negative quantity — the last digit is overpunched: First, the numeric digit is punched, and then the "−" character is punched over it. Thus, to represent −15075, we would keypunch 1507 5̲.

How on earth can our COBOL program unravel all of this? It all works because of the EBCDIC coding scheme for numbers and letters. When you punch a "−" character on a standard keypunch, it causes a hole to be placed in the 11-row of the card. Punching a numeric digit, on the other hand, causes a single hole to be punched in any of the 0 through 9 rows. Thus, punching a 5, and then overpunching a "−", causes a hole to be punched in the 5-row of the card, and then another hole to be punched in the 11-row.

This particular combination of punches is equivalent to the alphabetic character N in the EBCDIC coding scheme (you might want to try all of this on your keypunch just to convince yourself). If you look at the EBCDIC table presented in Section 10.2, you'll find that the character N is represented *internally* by the binary sequence 11010101, or the hexadecimal value D5. Which leads us to the point of all this: A hexadecimal D5 can be interpreted as a −5 when that byte is described as S9 in a PICTURE clause. And since the sign of a DISPLAY numeric field is in the zone bits of the low-order digit, 15075 equals -150.75 when the field is described as S9(3)V99.

In situations where we want to explicitly indicate that a number is positive, we can overpunch − but not with a " + ", as you might have thought. Because of the coding scheme on the cards, the appropriate character for overpunching a " + " number is the ampersand character, "&".

On many computers, we can overpunch either the right-most digit, *or* the left-most digit. If we overpunch the right-most digit, we use SIGN IS TRAILING SEPARATE CHARACTER, and if we overpunch the left-most digit, we use SIGN IS LEADING SEPARATE CHARACTER. Check the details of your COBOL compiler as well as the standards in your programming group, before you begin using the overpunch facility.

10.5 Editing fields with PIC

When we are asked to write a program that will print some numbers for a report, we are usually expected to print the numbers in their most readable form. For example, a field named NUMBER-OF-CARDS, defined as 9(6), might produce a number like 000024 or 384601 when moved directly to a printline. However, the program user might prefer seeing just 24; and for large numbers, he might prefer something like 384,601.

How can we ensure that numbers are printed in their most readable form? Well, we could use INSPECT or EXAMINE to replace leading zeroes with spaces. And we could use TALLY to count the number of digits being printed; if the TALLY is greater than three, we could insert a comma by moving the number, one part at a time, to the print-line. However, there is an easier way of doing it. We could simply write the statement

MOVE NUMBER-OF-CARDS TO CARD-TOTAL-ON-LINE.

This is not a feat of prestidigitation, but just an example of editing a field by using the COBOL editing features. The receiving field — the field that receives the number when the MOVE is done — is CARD-TOTAL-ON-LINE. It is defined as follows:

```
01  PRINT-LINE.
    05  CARD-TOTAL-ON-LINE    PIC ZZZ,ZZZ.
```

The letter Z is a position in the receiving field that automatically causes a leading zero in that position to be converted to a blank. The comma in the PIC clause tells COBOL to insert a comma if a non-blank character precedes it. Here are some more examples of editing specifications in the PIC clause:

PIC & VALUE OF SENDING FIELD		PIC OF RECEIVING FIELD	RESULT
9(5)	01000	ZZ,ZZZ	1,000
9(5)	00227	ZZ,ZZZ	227
9(5)	00000	ZZ,ZZZ	
9(5)	37624	ZZ,ZZZ	37,624

Notice the third example: The result column is blank. Chances are that if you read a report, and saw a line that read NUMBER OF NEW CUSTOMERS ADDED-, you might think that the computer program had an error in it. In a case like this, it would be better to print NUMBER OF NEW CUSTOMERS ADDED - 0.

We can accomplish this by changing the PIC clause of the receiving field to ZZ,ZZ9. The 9 indicates to COBOL that it should print this digit and all subsequent digits, if any — even if the digit is a leading zero. Here are some examples of the Z specification combined with the 9 specification:

PIC & VALUE OF SENDING FIELD		PIC OF RECEIVING FIELD	RESULT
9(5)	12345	Z9,999	12,345
9(5)	00024	Z9,999	0,024
9(5)	00006	ZZ,999	006

We can use a decimal point in the PIC clause in much the same way that we have been using the comma. However, the decimal point does have one special effect: It causes the decimal point of the sending field to be lined up with the decimal point of the receiving field's editing PIC. (By the way, only one decimal point is allowed in each field.) As an example, suppose we have to edit the following field:

05   AVERAGE-ACREAGE-PER-SALE   PIC 9V99.

Now suppose that the receiving field is defined as

05   AVERAGE-ACREAGE-PRINT   PIC 99.999.

Now, if we simply execute the statement

**MOVE AVERAGE-ACREAGE-PER-SALE TO
AVERAGE-ACREAGE-PRINT.**

the fields will be aligned properly. For example, if the sending field had contained the value 4.36, then the result, after moving, would be 04.360. On the other hand, if the editing PIC in the receiving field had been ZZ.99, the result would have been 4.36.

Here are some more examples:

PIC & VALUE OF SENDING FIELD	PIC OF RECEIVING FIELD	RESULT
9(5)V99 01244.68	ZZ,ZZ9.99	1,244.68
9(5)V99 00000.03	ZZ,ZZ9.99	0.03
9(5)V99 00000.03	ZZ,ZZZ.99	.03

Note that the third example resulted in a receiving field of .03 because, unlike the comma, the decimal point in a PIC editing clause terminates any further zero suppression. One last point about commas and decimal points as editing characters: It is illegal for either a decimal point or a comma to be the *last* character in an editing PIC, or for a Z to follow a 9 or a decimal point.

Thus far, we have been illustrating the editing of *unsigned* numeric fields. Now suppose that we are required to show — perhaps on an output report — whether a numeric field is positive or negative. There are several easy ways to do this. Let's take the straightforward case first. If a field is negative, we wish to print a leading "−"; if it is positive, we wish to print the number only. To do this, we use the character "−" in the editing PIC of the receiving field. Remember that the sign is carried in the zone bits of the low-order byte for a DISPLAY format numeric field. In the examples below, we will show the sign of a number above the low-order digit.

PIC & VALUE OF SENDING FIELD	PIC OF RECEIVING FIELD	RESULT
S9(4) 012$\bar{3}$	-9999	-0123
S9(4) 123$\dot{4}$	-9999	1234
S9(4) 246$\bar{8}$	9999-	2468-
S9(4) 357$\dot{9}$	9999-	3579
S9(4) 000$\bar{0}$	-9999	0000

Notice that 0000, whether positive or negative, will have a result with no sign. We can suppress leading zeroes and place a minus sign immediately before the first non-zero digit by using the

"—" in the same way we used the Z editing character. The examples below illustrate this.

PIC & VALUE OF SENDING FIELD		PIC OF RECEIVING FIELD	RESULT
S9(4)	0076̄	----9	-76
S9(4)	0076̟⁺	----9	76
S9(4)	6666̄	-----	-6666
S9(4)	0000̟⁺	----	

When we use zero suppression with the "—" character, we must construct the receiving field with an extra position. If the sending field, for example, has a length of three, then the receiving field must be at least four positions — to accommodate the possible three numeric positions as well as the minus sign.

Now let's imagine that we want to indicate positive numbers by preceding such numbers with a "+" character; at the same time, we want to continue editing negative numbers with a "—" character. All of this can be done with the "+" character in the editing PIC. We can also use the "+" to suppress leading zeroes. Just like the "—", the resulting "+" character can be made to either precede or trail the number. Try to determine the result of each MOVE operation in the exercises below. The answers can be found in the Appendix.

PIC & VALUE OF SENDING FIELD		PIC OF RECEIVING FIELD	RESULT
S9(3)V9	024.6̟⁺	+++9.9	
S9(3)V9	006.7̄	+++9.9	
S9(4)	2468̟⁺	++,++9	
S9(4)	0022̟⁺	++,++9	
S9(3)	001̄	+ZZ9	
S9(3)	006̄	+ZZ9	
S9(4)	0016̟⁺	ZZZ9-	
S9(2)V99	22.06̄	ZZ.999-	
S9(2)V99	00.01̄	ZZ.99+	

There will be many programming situations in which we know that the numeric quantities represent dollars and cents. Regardless of whether our program produces paychecks, sales reports, or expenditure reports, it usually is desirable to show amounts of money in their most readable form. COBOL supplies an editing PIC with some characters specifically dealing with monetary amounts; as you might expect, the editing character that we use is the dollar sign. We can use "$" to specify either a fixed-position dollar sign, or a floating-position dollar sign. Here are some examples of both:

PIC & VALUE OF SENDING FIELD		PIC OF RECEIVING FIELD	RESULT
9(4)	0022	$ZZZ9	$ 22
9(4)	0022	$$$$9	$22
9(6)	012448	$$$$,$$9	$12,448

When we are dealing with both dollars and cents, we can use the decimal point as well as the "$" in our editing PIC. Once again, this can be done in either a fixed-position format or in a floating-position format. Here are some examples:

PIC & VALUE OF SENDING FIELD		PIC OF RECEIVING FIELD	RESULT
9(3)V99	009.79	$ZZ9.99	$ 9.79
9(3)V99	000.39	$ZZZ.99	$ .39
9(5)V99	06224.71	$$$,$$9.99	$6,224.71
9(5)V99	00016.23	$$$,$$9.99	$16.23

If we have to contend with both negative and positive dollar amounts — e.g., if we are dealing with both credits and debits — then we can use the "+" and "−" editing characters to our advantage. For instance, look at the following editing examples:

PIC & VALUE OF SENDING FIELD		PIC OF RECEIVING FIELD	RESULT
S9(3)V99	022.6$\bar{7}$	$$$9.99-	$22.67-
S9(3)V99	106.0$\bar{2}$	$$$9.99+	$106.02+
S9(3)V99	321.9$\bar{6}$	$$$9.99+	$321.96-
S9(3)V99	016.3$\bar{2}$	$$$9.99-	$16.32

There is another convenient way of dealing with positive and negative dollar amounts. We can print the characters CR (for credit) or DB (for debit) as the right-most characters of the result. It works like this: If a field is negative, then either CR or DB will be printed to the right of the number — depending on which one we specify in the editing PIC. If the field is positive or unsigned, then two spaces will be printed to the right of the number if we have used *either* CR or DB in the editing PIC. Depending on the nature of the application, the person reading our output will have to know whether a negative amount represents a debit or a credit. Here are some examples:

PIC & VALUE OF SENDING FIELD		PIC OF RECEIVING FIELD	RESULT
S99V99	21.4$\bar{3}$	$$9.99CR	$21.43CR
S99V99	00.4$\bar{3}$	$$9.99CR	$0.43
S99V99	62.1$\bar{9}$	$$9.99DB	$62.19DB
99V99	06.77	$$9.99DB	$6.77

Unfortunately, the editing PIC does not give us the facility to print CR for positive numbers and DB for negative numbers — or vice versa. It prints two spaces for positive (or unsigned) numbers, leaving you to determine whether negative numbers should be printed as a CR or a DB. If you do want to print CR next to positive numbers, and DB next to negative numbers, you'll have to do some extra programming of your own.

We have seen that the editing character Z is useful for suppressing leading zeroes and replacing them with blanks. There are some applications in which it may be convenient to re-place leading zeroes by asterisks as follows:

PIC & VALUE OF SENDING FIELD	PIC OF RECEIVING FIELD	RESULT
9(3)V99 004.46	$**9.99	$**4.46

This facility is particularly useful when printing dollar amounts on checks or other financial documents. By filling the area to the left of the high-order digit with asterisks, we make it more difficult for someone to alter the check.

So far, our discussion about editing PIC characters has been confined to numeric fields. Most of the real-world editing prob-lems that you'll face will involve the formatting of numeric quantities on output reports. However, there are also a number of other editing characters that we can use to edit alphanumeric and numeric fields. We can easily instruct COBOL to insert zeroes, blanks, or slashes ("/") in such fields. For example:

PIC & VALUE OF SENDING FIELD	PIC OF RECEIVING FIELD	RESULT
S9(3) 01$\overset{+}{2}$	$$9.00	$12.00
S9(4) 1446	Z,ZZ9,000	1,446,000
X(6) XYZ446	XXXBBXXX	XYZ 446
9(10) 2127302670	999/999/9999	212/730/2670
9(9) 085423174	999B99B9999	085 42 3174

As you can see from these examples, simple insertions are useful for formatting Social Security numbers, telephone numbers, and various other fields that are to be stored in a compressed format but printed in a "humanized" format.

We have seen many editing features in this section. Don't be concerned about memorizing them. Whenever you need to print numeric or alphanumeric information in a formatted manner, just consult your COBOL manual to see if one of the PIC editing characters will do the job for you automatically. Certain common editing applications — such as zero suppression — eventually will become so familiar that you won't have to look them up every time you use them.

Before we consider other topics, there are a few final rules about editing — rules that pertain to all of the editing characters we have seen in this section:

1. Once a field has been edited, the edited (receiving) field is considered to be alphanumeric — regardless of whether the sending field was numeric or alphanumeric. After the field has been edited, it can be MOVEd, but *no arithmetic operation can be done with it.*

2. The PIC string for editing may not exceed 30 characters in length, and the receiving field must be long enough to hold the largest possible value of the sending field.

3. Only elementary items may be edited using the editing PIC characters.

10.6 Figurative constants

COBOL has certain reserved words that identify specific constant values. These reserved words are known as *figurative constants*. We already have used two of the most popular figurative constants: SPACES and ZEROES. When comparing a field with either of these constants, the COBOL compiler automatically adjusts the constant to be the same length as that of the other field, so that the comparison will test the entire field. When SPACES or ZEROES are used without reference to a specific field — e.g., in the STRING or UNSTRING statements — the length of the figurative constant is assumed to be one.

The figurative constants HIGH-VALUES and LOW-VALUES are used most often in comparing numeric quantities; as a pair, they are used for testing end-of-file conditions on sequentially ordered files. As you would expect, they are the largest possible number and the smallest possible number that can be represented on the computer. Depending on the specific COBOL compiler, HIGH-VALUES may be represented by a field of all 9's, or it may be represented by a field with hexadecimal FF in every byte. Similarly, LOW-VALUES may be represented by all zeroes, or by hexadecimal 00 in every byte.

Before you use HIGH-VALUES or LOW-VALUES in a programming application, check your COBOL manual to see how they actually are represented internally. This may help you to avoid some subtle, but very unpleasant, bugs in your program. If you find, for example, that HIGH-VALUES is represented internally by a field of all 9's, it may be dangerous to use the field in certain kinds of comparisons. For example, you may be reading records from a master file whose records are in ascending order by customer account number. To determine whether you have reached the end of the file, you might be tempted to code as shown on the following page, but this might cause serious trouble. There could well be a *legitimate* account number whose value is 9999. Indeed, many organizations use an account number (or an employee number, or a part number, or any other kind of number) of all 9's to indicate a special account.

```
      PERFORM READ-MASTER.
      PERFORM PROCESS-MASTER-LOOP
          UNTIL ACCOUNT-NUMBER EQUALS HIGH-VALUES.
      STOP RUN.
      ----------.
      ----------.
      ----------.
  READ-MASTER.
      READ MASTER-FILE
          AT END
              MOVE HIGH-VALUES TO ACCOUNT-NUMBER.
```

Another problem with some compilers is that HIGH- and LOW-VALUES are non-numeric values, that is, X′FF′ and X′00′, respectively; and may cause compiler diagnostics if they are compared to numeric fields.

A less commonly used figurative constant is QUOTES, having the value of a literal *single* quote, or "'". The QUOTES constant is useful for enclosing a field in quotes on a print-line. Since most such applications require the printing of a *double* quote, we would have to move QUOTES to *two* one-position fields immediately preceding the field we wish to print, and to *two* one-position fields immediately following it.

As we observed earlier, COBOL allows us to spell the figurative constants in a variety of ways. Any of the following spellings is legal:

SPACE	ZERO	HIGH-VALUE	LOW-VALUE	QUOTE
SPACES	ZEROS	HIGH-VALUES	LOW-VALUES	QUOTES
	ZEROES			

10.7 The RENAMES clause

When defining data, we may need to refer to the same field in several different ways. See, for example, the definition of an employee record on the following page.

```
01  EMPLOYEE-REC.
    05  EMPLOYEE-NUM.
        10  EMPLOYEE-PREFIX        PIC 9(4).
        10  EMPLOYEE-JOB-CODE      PIC 9(2).
    05  EMPLOYEE-NAME              PIC X(30).
    05  DATE-HIRED.
        10  YEAR-HIRED             PIC 9(2).
        10  MONTH-HIRED            PIC 9(2).
        10  DAY-HIRED              PIC 9(2).
    05  FILLER                     PIC X(38).
66  JOB-NAME-FIRST-YEAR
    RENAMES EMPLOYEE-JOB-CODE THRU YEAR-HIRED.
```

With this definition, we can refer to each field defined in the record, and we can separately refer to JOB-NAME-FIRST-YEAR, which includes EMPLOYEE-JOB-CODE, EMPLOYEE-NAME, and YEAR-HIRED. When we use the level-66 RENAMES clause, the RENAMES must *immediately* follow the record that holds the renamed data. It is perfectly legal to use several level-66's to rename the same record, and the data they rename may overlap. For example, we could add another level-66 to the employee record we coded above:

```
66  EMPLOYEE-NUM-AND-NAME
    RENAMES EMPLOYEE-NUM THRU EMPLOYEE-NAME.
```

A RENAMES clause can begin and/or end with a group name. If it does, the span of renamed data begins with the first elementary item of the first group item, and ends with the last elementary item in the last group name.

Although the RENAMES clause can be very handy in some applications, in practice it is seldom used. Indeed, some programming organizations do not permit the use of RENAMES. Such organizations argue that the use of RENAMES could cause problems if the record definition changes. For example, if a new field is inserted in the middle of a record, it may affect the span of a RENAMES.

10.8 The REDEFINES clause

In COBOL applications, it is very common to read a file that contains different kinds of records. For example, we may be reading a card file that contains an information card and an account card for each customer. To handle a case like this, we would probably code two 01-level record descriptions, with the FD for the card file. Within the FD statement, we would expect to see the clause

      DATA RECORDS ARE CUSTOMER-INFO
          ACCOUNT-INFO.

What have we done? First, we have defined the records in the card file as CUSTOMER-INFO; then, we have *redefined* the same area in storage, and told COBOL that the specified area will contain records known as ACCOUNT-INFO. The redefinition of the record area is accomplished by listing all the 01-level records in the DATA RECORDS ARE . . . clause.

While this approach is appropriate for the redefinition of entire records, it is not sufficient when we want to redefine a portion of a record, or certain WORKING-STORAGE fields. To accomplish this, we use the REDEFINES clause, as demonstrated by the following example:

```
05  CURRENCY-CODE              PIC X.
    88  U-S-A                   VALUE 'U'.
    88  JAPAN                   VALUE 'J'.
    88  FRANCE                  VALUE 'F'.
05  DOLLARS-CENTS              PIC 9(4)V99.
05  YEN REDEFINES DOLLARS-CENTS PIC 9(6).
05  FRANCS-CENTIMES REDEFINES
        DOLLARS-CENTS          PIC 9(4)V99.
```

The storage area is shown on the next page:

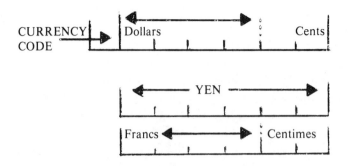

We could now code:

```
IF U-S-A
    MOVE DOLLARS-CENTS TO AMT-DUE
ELSE IF JAPAN
    MULTIPLY YEN BY JAPAN-RATE GIVING AMT-DUE
ELSE IF FRANCE
    MULTIPLY FRANCS-CENTIMES BY FRANCE-RATE
        GIVING AMT-DUE
ELSE
    PERFORM ERROR-ROUTINE.
```

We can use REDEFINES to redefine either a group item or an elementary item. However, in all cases, the level given to the description of the redefinition must be the same as that of the original definition; also, the REDEFINES statement must immediately follow the field being redefined. Redefinition concludes when a level-number equal to or less than the redefinition level is encountered. To illustrate this, here's an example of an illegal REDEFINES:

```
05  A.
    10  B           PIC X(2).
    10  C           PIC X(4).
05  Q REDEFINES B   PIC 9(2).
```

This is illegal because the REDEFINES statement is at an 05-level, and it is attempting to redefine a field of data that was defined as a 10-level. To do it correctly, we would code as follows:

```
05  A.
    10  B                   PIC X(2).
    10  Q REDEFINES B       PIC 9(2).
    10  C                   PIC X(4).
```

Here's an example of a legal redefinition of a data item:

```
05  A.
    10  B                   PIC X(2).
    10  C                   PIC X(4).
05  Q REDEFINES A.
    10  R                   PIC X.
    10  S.
        15  T               PIC 9(2).
        15  U               PIC X(3).
05  Z.
----------.
----------.
----------.
```

Note that a redefinition of data does not have to involve the same data type as the original definition. For example, the original definition of A above was alphanumeric (as indicated by the definition of the elementary items B and C); but T is defined as numeric. This is perfectly legal.

10.9 Example

To illustrate many of the concepts discussed in this chapter, let's imagine that we have to write a program named FORMATDL. Its job will be to format detail lines for a billing report associated with tour sales of the Wing & Prayer organization, discussed in Chapter 8.

Our program will be CALLed by BILLREPT, and will be given a client record to format. When FORMATDL has properly formatted the line, it should CALL a subordinate module PRINTDL, passing a detail line as its only parameter. Thus, we are dealing with a structure chart that looks like the one on the following page.

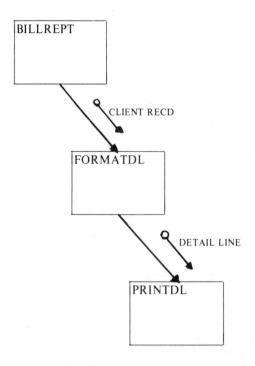

When FORMATDL is called, it is given a fixed length record, CLIENT-RECD, which is 80 positions long, and has the following format:

FIELD	TYPE	POSITIONS
Client Number	Numeric	1-6 (6)
Independent/Agent	Alpha (I or A)	7 (1)
Tour Number	Numeric	8-13 (6)
Client Name	Alphanumeric	14-43 (30)
Number in Group	Numeric	44-45 (2)
Cost for One	Signed Numeric ($$$$¢¢)	46-51 (6)
Deposit	Signed Numeric ($$$$¢¢)	52-59 (8)
Departure Date	Numeric (YYMMDD)	60-65 (6)
Filler	—	66-80 (15)

The output print-line is 132 positions long. It is to be formatted in slightly different ways, depending on whether the client is an independent or a travel agent:

POSITIONS	FIELD	FORMAT
1-5	Filler	Spaces
6-13	Tour Number	99/999/9
14-18	Filler	Spaces
19-25	Client Number	9/99999 (if independent)
26	Filler	Space (if independent)
19-26	Client Number	99/999/9 (if agent)
27-31	Filler	Spaces
32-61	Client Name	30 Alphanumeric positions
62-66	Filler	Spaces
67-68	Number in Group	99 — suppress leading zeroes
69-73	Filler	Spaces
74-84	Total Cost	$999,999.99 — float $, suppress leading zeroes
85-89	Filler	Spaces
90-100	Deposit	$999,999.99 — float $, suppress leading zeroes
101-105	Filler	Spaces
106-119	Balance Due	$999,999.99CR — float $, suppress leading zeroes
120-124	Filler	Spaces
125-132	Departure Date	MM/DD/YY

The Total Cost field is computed as the Cost for One multiplied by the Number in Group. Similarly, the Balance Due field is computed as Total Cost minus Deposit. If the Deposit is larger than the Total Cost, then CR should appear following the Balance Due.

When the output line is properly formatted, we should CALL PRINTDL, and pass the line as a parameter.

Take some time to study these specifications, and then try writing the program. Do *not* look at the sample program in the Appendix until you've made an attempt of your own.

11 Using Tables

11.1 Introduction

In this chapter, we discuss one of the most important concepts in programming: tables. Programmers often talk about tables, arrays, subscripts, pointers, and indexes when they discuss their programming applications; indeed, you will sometimes hear programmers discuss an approach to programming known as *table-driven programs.*

The first objective of this chapter is to make you aware of the usefulness and importance of this table-oriented approach to programming. Then, we will discuss the method of defining tables in the COBOL DATA DIVISION as well as the methods of accessing tables in the PROCEDURE DIVISION.

Surprisingly, many veteran COBOL programmers are not familiar (or comfortable) with the concept of tables. In our opinion, skill at table-handling is one of the things that distinguishes a good COBOL programmer from an average one. So, we urge you to read this chapter carefully and practice the examples — it will pay off!

11.2 Defining related data items

Let's imagine that we want to write a program that totals our company's sales on a product-by-product basis. The company sells 25 different products, each with its own unique product code. A clever systems analyst has assigned unique codes of 01 through 25 to the products.

Obviously, we need 25 accumulators to hold the daily sales totals for each product. We could define the accumulators in WORKING-STORAGE as follows:

```
01  PRODUCT-TOTALS.
    05  ACCUM01        PIC S9(5).
    05  ACCUM02        PIC S9(5).
    05  ACCUM03        PIC S9(5).
    ----------.
    ----------.
    ----------.
    05  ACCUM25        PIC S9(5).
```

Let's assume that the details of each sale of a specific product are keypunched on a card, defined in WORKING-STORAGE as follows:

```
01  SALE.
    05  PRODUCT-CODE PIC 99.
    05  NUMBER-SOLD  PIC 9(3).
```

In order to accumulate the sales of each product properly, we could write the following code in the PROCEDURE DIVISION:

```
IF PRODUCT-CODE = '01'
    ADD NUMBER-SOLD TO ACCUM01
ELSE IF PRODUCT-CODE = '02'
    ADD NUMBER-SOLD TO ACCUM02
ELSE IF . . .
    ----------.
    ----------.
    ----------.
ELSE IF PRODUCT-CODE = '25'
    ADD NUMBER-SOLD TO ACCUM25.
```

Although this approach will solve the problem, it is time-consuming, error-prone, and boring. And what if the company has 2,500 products instead of just 25?

Fortunately, COBOL enables us to handle problems of this type much more easily. Instead of defining each of the 25 accumulators separately, we can write

```
01  PRODUCT-TOTALS.
    05  ACCUM      PIC S9(5)    OCCURS 25 TIMES.
```

By using the OCCURS clause, space is reserved for 25 S9(5) fields, just as if we had defined each one individually. In this fashion, we have created a table of accumulators — a table whose entries all are named ACCUM. However, we no longer have a unique name for each of the 25 fields — for example, there is no longer an ACCUM17 to which we can refer.

Obviously, we must have some way to add the NUMBER-SOLD into the proper accumulator. How can we do this? By using the PRODUCT-CODE field as the key to the proper accumulator for the addition of NUMBER-SOLD. The definitions of PRODUCT-CODE and NUMBER-SOLD remain the same:

```
01  SALE.
    05   PRODUCT-CODE      PIC 99.
    05   NUMBER-SOLD       PIC 9(3).
```

Since PRODUCT-CODE is the key to the proper accumulator, it can be used as a subscript, or "pointer," for ACCUM; that is, it acts as a pointer to the particular occurrence of ACCUM that is to be used. We make use of this concept by writing the following statement in the PROCEDURE DIVISION:

ADD NUMBER-SOLD TO ACCUM (PRODUCT-CODE).

When we use a field as a pointer to a specific item of data within an OCCURS clause, the pointer field is known as a subscript; PRODUCT-CODE is a subscript in the example above.

When a field is used as a subscript, it must be enclosed in parentheses. Most COBOL compilers are very finicky about one other formatting aspect of subscripts: There must be *at least* one space between the table name (the field defined within an OCCURS clause) and the opening parenthesis of the subscript. Thus,

ADD NUMBER-SOLD TO ACCUM(PRODUCT-CODE).

is *not* correct COBOL syntax for all compilers, while

ADD NUMBER-SOLD TO ACCUM   (PRODUCT-CODE).

is correct on all compilers.

One other point: Any field may be used as a subscript (in addition to being used for other computational purposes) as long as it is defined as one of the numeric types of data.

It should be evident from this simple example that subscripting — and the use of tables — allows us to code many applications much more simply. Keep in mind that the alternative to subscripting would be to write out a long sequence of code in the form

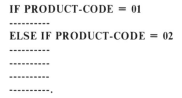

```
IF PRODUCT-CODE = 01
----------
ELSE IF PRODUCT-CODE = 02
----------
----------
----------
----------.
```

Q. Is there any other way to organize the code for the example discussed above?

A. Yes. We could use a GO TO DEPENDING ON statement and write the following code:

```
GO TO P1, P2, . . . , P25
DEPENDING ON PRODUCT-CODE.
```

Q. What are the advantages and disadvantages of the three approaches we have seen for implementing the sales-totals application?

A. The nature of the programming application will usually determine which of the three approaches is most appropriate. If, for example, we had only three product codes in the example above, and if we could be sure that the company would not require new product codes in the future, it probably would be simpler to use the IF . . . ELSE IF . . . coding approach. After all, it doesn't require setting up a table with an OCCURS clause.

The GO TO DEPENDING ON approach has the advantage

(with most implementations of COBOL) of being reasonably efficient. Within the computer hardware, control is transferred to the appropriate paragraph with machine instructions very similar to the subscripting approach that we have already seen in COBOL. However, the GO TO DEPENDING ON approach does have the disadvantage of requiring 25 separate paragraph-names (in the sales-totals example). Thus, while it is fairly efficient in terms of execution speed, this approach usually will be relatively inefficient in terms of memory requirements. The GO TO DEPENDING ON approach is most practical when different types of processing must be carried out for each value of the subscript.

Assuming that there are more than three or four distinct values of the subscript variable and that the processing to be carried out for each distinct variable is virtually the same (e.g., adding NUMBER-SOLD to the appropriate accumulator), the subscript approach is easier to code, more efficient in terms of execution speed and memory requirements, and generally much easier to change.

11.3 Defining tables

As we saw in the example in Section 11.2, identical data items often can be defined with the OCCURS clause. In most instances, this data must be defined internally, in the WORKING-STORAGE SECTION of the program. When data are defined by the programmer in this way, the group of items is called a table.

Let's look at another example to illustrate the use of tables. At the end of Chapter 8, you were asked to design a program to edit incoming transactions for the charter airline booking system. One of the modules in our solution shown in the Appendix is called CHECKAIR. This module's function is to check to see if Airport Choice is valid. CHECKAIR is given a three-position Airport Code and a three-position "valid-invalid" switch. The module's purpose is to set the switch appropriately. While there are many ways of coding CHECKAIR, one easy way is to use a table of valid Airport Codes. We might write the following:

```
IDENTIFICATION DIVISION.
PROGRAM-ID. CHECKAIR.
ENVIRONMENT DIVISION.
DATA DIVISION.
WORKING-STORAGE SECTION.
01   AIRPORT-ABBREVIATIONS.
     05   ENTRY-1.
          10   FILLER              PIC X(3)        VALUE 'JFK'.
          10   FILLER              PIC X(15)       VALUE 'NEW YORK'.
     05   ENTRY-2.
          10   FILLER              PIC X(3)        VALUE 'LAX'.
          10   FILLER              PIC X(15)       VALUE 'LOS ANGELES'.
     05   ENTRY-3.
          10   FILLER              PIC X(3)        VALUE 'SFO'.
          10   FILLER              PIC X(15)       VALUE 'SAN FRANCISCO'.
     05   ENTRY-4.
          10   FILLER              PIC X(3)        VALUE 'ORD'.
          10   FILLER              PIC X(15)       VALUE 'CHICAGO'.
     05   ENTRY-5.
          10   FILLER              PIC X(3)        VALUE 'DFW'.
          10   FILLER              PIC X(15)       VALUE 'DALLAS-FT WORTH'.
     05   ENTRY-6.
          10   FILLER              PIC X(3)        VALUE 'IAD'.
          10   FILLER              PIC X(15)       VALUE 'WASHINGTON DC'.
01   AIRPORT-TABLE REDEFINES AIRPORT-ABBREVIATIONS.
     05   FILLER
               OCCURS 6 TIMES.
          10   AIRPORT             PIC X(3).
          10   AIR-CITY            PIC X(15).
01   THIS-AIRPORT                  PIC S9(8)       COMP SYNC.
01   NUMBER-OF-AIRPORTS            PIC S9(3)       COMP-3   VALUE 6.
LINKAGE SECTION.
01   AIRPORT-CODE                  PIC X(3).
01   FOUND-AIR-SW                  PIC X(3).
01   CITY                          PIC X(15).
PROCEDURE DIVISION
     USING         AIRPORT-CODE
                   FOUND-AIR-SW
                   CITY.
LOOKUP-AIR.
     MOVE SPACES TO CITY.
     MOVE 'NO' TO FOUND-AIR-SW.
     MOVE 1 TO THIS-AIRPORT.
     PERFORM CHECK-AIR
          UNTIL FOUND-AIR-SW = 'YES'
               OR THIS-AIRPORT IS GREATER THAN
                    NUMBER-OF-AIRPORTS.
EXIT-CHECKAIR.
     EXIT PROGRAM.
CHECK-AIR.
     IF AIRPORT-CODE = AIRPORT (THIS-AIRPORT)
          MOVE 'YES' TO FOUND-AIR-SW
          MOVE AIR-CITY (THIS-AIRPORT) TO CITY
     ELSE
          ADD 1 TO THIS-AIRPORT.
```

Note that it is perfectly legal, and often very useful, to define a table with more than one field in each entry. Each field within the table can be pointed to by a single subscript.

11.4 Indexes and the SET statement

There is an interesting difference between the subscripting example in Section 11.2 and the airport example in Section 11.3. In Section 11.2, a variable called PRODUCT-CODE was already available for use as a subscript; that is, PRODUCT-CODE would have been a part of the program regardless of whether we had used a table. On the other hand, a field had to be defined for use as a subscript for the table of airports; THIS-AIRPORT had nothing to do with the definition of the problem.

When there is no field that will act naturally as a subscript, it often is preferable to define a field as an *index* instead of as a subscript. The following code redefines the airport table using the INDEXED BY clause:

```
01  AIRPORT-TABLE
        OCCURS 6 TIMES
        INDEXED BY AIRPORT-IND.
    05  AIRPORT-CODE        PIC X(3).
    05  AIRPORT-CITY        PIC X(15).
```

When a field is named with the INDEXED BY clause, we don't have to define it elsewhere. The COBOL compiler internally gives it a PIC clause. One great advantage of indexes is that they are declared within the definition of the table. This usually makes table-related code much easier to follow.

There is a special set of instructions for adjusting the values of an index. Just as with subscripts, it is the programmer's responsibility to initialize and adjust index values. Arithmetic and MOVE statements may not be used with indexes; instead, all indexes are SET, as shown by the following examples:

1.   SET AIRPORT-IND TO 1 (to point the index at the first entry in the table)

2.   SET AIRPORT-IND TO AIR-CODE (the value of the field AIR-CODE is adjusted to the value of AIRPORT-IND)

3.   SET AIRPORT-IND UP BY 1 (add 1 to the existing value of AIRPORT-IND)

4.   SET AIRPORT-IND DOWN BY AIR-CODE (subtract the value of AIR-CODE from the value of AIRPORT-IND)

Examples 1 and 2 are functionally equivalent to the MOVE statement. Example 3 is the equivalent of an ADD statement. Example 4 is the index equivalent of a SUBTRACT statement. If you inadvertently attempt to carry out a MOVE statement or arithmetic on an index, the COBOL compiler will issue an error message when it compiles your program.

For practice, recode the last version of CHECKAIR (the one that returns a full city name) using indexes instead of subscripts.

11.5 Sequential searches

For most of the remainder of this chapter, we will be talking about the *searching* techniques of COBOL. Searching means nothing more than looking through items in a table to find a specific item. The most common method of searching is known as a sequential, or linear, search. By sequential, we mean that our program proceeds one entry at a time, starting with the first entry in the table, until the desired entry is found. The searches in our airport examples in the previous sections were sequential in nature.

Let's take a look at another example: Assume that we are given a shuffled deck of cards, and are asked to find the eight of clubs in the deck. Using a sequential search, we would start at the top of the deck — i.e., the first entry — and proceed, card by card, until we find the eight of clubs. We may find our card at the top of the deck, but, if we're unlucky, it may be the last card that we draw. On average, given absolutely random shuffling of the deck, we would expect to find the eight of clubs in 26 examinations.

In a COBOL program, the sequential search is accomplished by initializing a subscript or index to the value one — thereby pointing to the first entry in the table. A PERFORM UNTIL loop is then implemented, with the loop terminated when the search is complete, or when the end of the table is reached. As seen in the airport examples, the paragraph that is invoked by the PERFORM UNTIL must increment the pointer by using an ADD or a SET.

The following pseudocode summarizes this:

```
initialize subscript or index to first entry
WHILE the desired entry has not been found
        and there are more entries in the table
   check if this is the desired entry
   IF it is not the desired entry
        increment subscript or index by 1
```

COBOL offers a variation of the PERFORM UNTIL, which will accomplish the initialization of the subscript, the incrementing of the subscript, and the termination of the loop in a single statement. With the addition of the VARYING, FROM, and BY clauses to the PERFORM UNTIL, we accomplish all of the work necessary to step sequentially through a table. Following is an example:

```
                                        ( SUBSCRIPT )
PERFORM TABLE-LOOKUP VARYING   {              }
                                        ( INDEX     )
   FROM 1 BY 1
        UNTIL ENTRY (SUB) = desired entry
           OR SUB GREATER THAN number of entries
```

The FROM clause takes care of initialization, allowing the programmer to initialize a subscript or index to any desired value — even the value of another field. In most cases, however, initializing the subscript or index to point to the first entry in the table will be sufficient; the BY clause will handle the increment-ing of the pointer-field. In the example above, the pointer-field is set to the value one the first time the loop is executed; it is then incremented by one for each successive iteration. The VARYING clause names the field that will be initialized by the FROM clause and incremented by the value stated in the BY clause. The UNTIL statement acts exactly as it does in a simple PERFORM-UNTIL. (Remember that if the UNTIL clause is true immediately after initializing the subscript or index, the loop will not be executed at all.)

To obtain some practice in the use of tables and the PER-FORM VARYING statement, try the following: Write a CALLed program that will calculate the amount due on book orders. Eight different books are available to customers, with the cost per book depending on the number of books ordered. Each book has its own code — 01 through 08. Here is a list of the book prices:

Book code	Unit price 1-5 books	Unit price 6-11 books	Unit price 12 or more books
01	9.95	8.95	7.00
02	16.50	14.00	12.00
03	34.49	32.49	28.00
04	7.75	7.25	6.75
05	12.50	11.50	10.50
06	3.50	3.50	3.50
07	19.95	18.50	17.00
08	4.00	3.50	2.95

Give the program a two-position, numeric BOOK-CODE field; in addition, use a two-position, numeric field identifying the number of books ordered, and a six-position — S9(4)V99 — numeric field called AMT-DUE. Your program should calculate the amount due for the order placed, and return the information to the CALLing program in the AMT-DUE field. If the BOOK-CODE field is not 01 through 08, your program should return zeroes in AMT-DUE. Assume that the information in BOOK-CODE will al-ways be numeric, even though it possibly may be out of range.

The solution can be found in the Appendix.

11.6 The SEARCH and SEARCH ALL statements

Instead of using the PERFORM-VARYING-FROM-BY-UNTIL to carry out a table search, you can take advantage of two built-in COBOL statements: SEARCH and SEARCH ALL.

The SEARCH statement is used to carry out *sequential* table searches of the type we saw in Section 11.5 — i.e., a search that proceeds, one entry at a time, through the entire table. The SEARCH statement automatically picks up the index from the name of the table being searched. This means that there must be an INDEXED BY clause with the table definition if we are to use the SEARCH statement. An example of the SEARCH statement follows:

```
* THIS CODE IS BASED ON THE SOLUTION OF
* THE BOOK-CODE PROBLEM AT THE BACK OF THE BOOK

CALC-AMT-DUE.
   SEARCH BOOK-ENTRY
      VARYING THIS-BOOK
      AT END
         MOVE ZEROES TO AMT-DUE
      WHEN BOOK-CODE-TB (THIS-BOOK) = BOOK-CODE-LK
         MOVE 'YES' TO BOOK-FOUND.

   IF BOOK-FOUND NOT EQUAL TO 'YES'

* THE CODE TO FIND THE AMOUNT DUE WOULD BE HERE, NOW
* THAT WE KNOW THE UNIT PRICE OF THE BOOK.
```

Note that the AT END clause will be activated when the end of the table has been reached and no true conditions were found with the WHEN clause. After the AT END clause is invoked, control passes to the first statement following the period in the SEARCH statement.

You can have as many WHEN clauses as you wish in a single SEARCH statement. However, keep in mind that there is an implied OR condition connecting each of the WHEN clauses.

There are times when a sequential search is not the best way of locating an entry in a table; in such cases, we can use the COBOL SEARCH ALL statement to carry out a *binary* search. Instead of starting at the first entry of a table and searching one by one, we begin in the *middle* of the table, and proceed by cutting the table successively in half, then in half again. In order to carry out such a search, the table must be arranged in ascending or descending order on the field that we are using as a search key.

Using our book-code table, we will test to see if the book code in the middle of the table matches the order — i.e., the fourth entry in the table. If so, the search is finished; if not, we can eliminate either the "top" half of the table or the "bottom" half. For example, if the comparison indicates that BOOK-CODE is greater than the fourth entry in the table, we can disregard the first, second, and third entries. Now only 05, 06, 07, and 08 are possible matches. Once again, COBOL tries the entry in the middle.

Since the strategy is based on dividing by two and then comparing, it is called binary. By continuing to narrow the number of possible entries, the SEARCH ALL can discover the match (or the fact that there are *no* matches) in far fewer tries than generally is possible with the sequential search.

For example, let's assume that we have a table with 64 entries. With a sequential search, we can expect an average of 32 comparisons in order to get a match, while a binary search will make six comparisons at most.

The larger the table, the more likely it is that the binary comparison will be preferable to a sequential search. For example, if our table is 32,768 entries long, then a sequential search will require (on average) 16,384 comparisons, while a binary search will require only 15. Remember that the binary search is preferable only if

1.   The table is ordered in a sequence.

2.   Any one entry is as likely to be the matching
entry as is any other entry.

The SEARCH ALL statement could be used as follows:

```
* THIS CODE IS ALSO BASED ON THE BOOK-CODE SOLUTION
 .
 .
01 BOOK-TABLE REDEFINES BOOK-VALUES.
   05  BOOK-ENTRY
          OCCURS 8 TIMES
          ASCENDING KEY IS BOOK-CODE-TB
          INDEXED BY THIS-BOOK.
  .
  .
  .
CALC-AMT-DUE.
   SEARCH ALL BOOK-ENTRY
      AT END
          MOVE ZEROES TO AMT-DUE
      WHEN BOOK-CODE-TB (THIS-BOOK) = BOOK-CODE-LK
          MOVE 'YES' TO BOOK-FOUND.

   IF BOOK-FOUND NOT EQUAL TO 'YES'

* THE CODE TO CALCULATE THE AMOUNT-DUE WOULD BE
* HERE, NOW THAT WE KNOW THE UNIT PRICE OF THE BOOK
```

Notice that when we REDEFINE the table, we add the clause
ASCENDING KEY IS BOOK-CODE-TB. The SEARCH ALL requires
this clause as a source of information about the *order* of the table
layout. Where it is appropriate, we can also use the clause DES-
CENDING KEY IS. . . . However, whether we arrange the table
layout in ascending or descending order, the key must be a
numeric data type.

11.7 Multidimensional tables

Sometimes, it is useful to have a *multidimensional* table —
that is, a table of tables. For example, a two-dimensional table is
organized like a simple table — but each entry within the table
is, in itself, a table. To properly manipulate such a table, we

need two subscripts, or two indexes. One index points to the entries of the outer table; visualize this pointer as operating vertically. The other index points at the specific entries within the outer entry; think of this pointer as moving horizontally.

To illustrate this concept, let's return to the airport problem. Now, instead of confirming that the airport is one that our charter business uses, we must also confirm that the airline is valid for that specific airport. The specifications remain the same as before, except that a new two-dimensional alpha field is now passed; this field is the AIRLINE-CODE. We use up to four different airlines from any given airport. We will arrange a two-dimensional table of airports and their airlines; to manipulate the table, we will need an index to point at the airports, and another index to point at the airlines. The table looks like this:

		Index to slide along airlines			
	JFK	PA	TW	BA	AF
Index	ORD	PA	AF	TW	
to	LAX	QA	PA		
slide	SFO	PA	AJ	TW	
along	DFW	AM	PA		
airports	IAD	AF	TW	PA	BA

PA	=	Pan American
TW	=	Trans World Airlines
BA	=	British Airways
AF	=	Air France
QA	=	Qantas Airways
AJ	=	Air Japan
AM	=	Aeronaves de Mexico

Now look at our sample code for the expanded airline example:

```
WORKING-STORAGE SECTION.
01   AIR-VALUES.
     05   FILLER                      PIC X(3)  VALUE 'JFK'.
     05   FILLER                      PIC X(8)  VALUE 'PATWBAAF'.
     05   FILLER                      PIC X(3)  VALUE 'ORD'.
     05   FILLER                      PIC X(8)  VALUE 'PAAFTW   '.
     05   FILLER                      PIC X(3)  VALUE 'LAX'.
     05   FILLER                      PIC X(8)  VALUE 'QAPA     '.
     05   FILLER                      PIC X(3)  VALUE 'SFO'.
     05   FILLER                      PIC X(8)  VALUE 'PAAJTW   '.
     05   FILLER                      PIC X(3)  VALUE 'DFW'.
     05   FILLER                      PIC X(8)  VALUE 'AMPA     '.
     05   FILLER                      PIC X(3)  VALUE 'IAD'.
     05   FILLER                      PIC X(8)  VALUE 'AFTWPABA '.
01   AIR-TABLE REDEFINES AIR-VALUES.
     05   AIRPORT-ENTRY
                    OCCURS 6 TIMES
                    INDEXED BY THIS-PORT.
          10   AIRPORT-TB       PIC X(3).
          10   LINE-ENTRY.
               15   AIRLINE-TB  PIC X(2)
                    OCCURS 4 TIMES
                    INDEXED BY THIS-LINE.
01   LINES-PER-PORT             PIC S9    VALUE 4.
01   NOT-YES-NOT-NO             PIC X(3)  VALUE 'XXX'.
01   NOT-FOUND                  PIC X(3)  VALUE 'NO '.
01   FOUND                      PIC X(3)  VALUE 'YES'.

LINKAGE SECTION.
01   AIRPORT-LK                 PIC X(3).
01   AIRLINE-LK                 PIC X(2).
01   FOUND-SW-LK                PIC X(3).


PROCEDURE DIVISION
     USING          AIRPORT-LK
                    AIRLINE-LK
                    FOUND-SW-LK.
CHECK-CARRIERS.
     MOVE NOT-YES-NOT-NO TO FOUND-SW-LK.
     SET THIS-PORT TO 1.
     SEARCH AIRPORT-ENTRY
          VARYING THIS-PORT
          AT END
               MOVE NOT-FOUND TO FOUND-SW-LK
          WHEN AIRPORT-LK = AIRPORT-TB (THIS-PORT)
               PERFORM FIND-LINE
                    VARYING THIS-LINE
                    FROM 1 BY 1
                    UNTIL AIRLINE-TB (THIS-LINE) OF LINE-ENTRY (THIS-PORT) = AIRLINE-LK
                              OR THIS-LINE GREATER THAN LINES-PER-PORT
          IF THIS-LINE GREATER THAN LINES-PER-PORT
               MOVE NOT-FOUND TO FOUND-SW-LK
          ELSE
               MOVE FOUND TO FOUND-SW-LK.
CHECK-EXIT.
     EXIT PROGRAM.
FIND-LINE.
     EXIT.
* A DUMMY PARAGRAPH FOR AIRLINE LOOKUP.
```

The reason we use a PERFORM-VARYING-FROM-BY-UNTIL to check the airlines is that COBOL will not permit us to subscript or index the name of the field we SEARCH. That is, we may *not* code SEARCH LINE-ENTRY (THIS-PORT) . . .

11.8 Variable length tables

Sometimes, tables have a variable number of entries; that is, the number of entries varies from one execution of the program to another. We can easily define such tables with the COBOL OCCURS X TO Y DEPENDING ON clause. For example, here is a module that selects records having account numbers corresponding to an entry in a passed table. A table containing the number of entries is also passed to the CALLed program:

```
IDENTIFICATION DIVISION.
PROGRAM-ID. SELECTRD.

ENVIRONMENT DIVISION.
INPUT-OUTPUT SECTION.
FILE CONTROL.
    SELECT SELECT-RECDS
        ASSIGN TO SYS005-UT-2400-S.

DATA DIVISION.
FILE SECTION.
FD   SELECT-RECDS
     LABEL RECORDS ARE OMITTED.
     DATA RECORD IS PICKED-RECD.
01   PICKED-RECD                    PIC X(100).

WORKING-STORAGE SECTION.

LINKAGE SECTION.
01   NUMBER-ENTRIES                 PIC S9(2).
01   RECD-IN.
     05    ACCT-NO-RECD             PIC 9(5).
     05    FILLER                   PIC X(95).
01   ACCT-NO-TABLE.
     05    ACCT-NO-TB
           OCCURS 1 TO 99 TIMES
           DEPENDING ON NUMBER-ENTRIES
           ASCENDING KEY IS ACCT-ENTRY
           INDEXED BY THIS-ENTRY.
           10    ACCT-ENTRY         PIC 9(5).

PROCEDURE DIVISION
     USING        NUMBER-ENTRIES
                  RECD-IN
                  ACCT-NO-TABLE.
SELECT-RECD.
     OPEN INPUT SELECT-RECDS.
     SEARCH ALL ACCT-NO-TB
          WHEN ACCT-ENTRY (THIS-ENTRY) = ACCT-NO-RECD
              WRITE PICKED-RECD FROM RECD-IN.
     CLOSE SELECT-RECDS.
SELECT-RECD-EXIT.
     EXIT PROGRAM.
```

Note that the PROCEDURE DIVISION code remains the same for fixed length and variable length tables, since the OCCURS DEPENDING ON clause lets us hide the variations from the code.

11.9 Precautions with tables

Before concluding this chapter, we must caution you on the use of tables. COBOL's table-building and table-handling facilities are *very* powerful, and you will soon discover they are so useful that they are nearly indispensable for most non-trivial applications. Unfortunately, tables have a Jekyll-and-Hyde characteristic to them — they are a likely spot for bugs in your code.

Perhaps the most common problem is the so-called boundary problem. COBOL assumes that if we reference the 4,265th entry in a table that was defined in the DATA DIVISION as only ten entries long, we must know what we are doing; it therefore allows us to proceed. The normal result is that our program aborts, and we are left wondering what went wrong.

The obvious moral: Whenever you finish coding a program that makes use of a table, inspect the code for possible boundary errors. Ask yourself if it is possible for your program to set the index or subscript to a value one greater or one less than the number of entries in the table? If so, what will happen? Similarly, ask yourself what happens if the program does *not* find a match in a table lookup? If you assume that such a situation will never occur, you are leaving yourself open for problems.

Your code should always include an "if table exhausted" clause along with the "if match found" clause. The following pseudocode is the basic form for every table lookup:

```
PERFORM table-lookup
    VARYING index
        FROM first-entry BY one-entry
        UNTIL entry (index) = element
            OR no-more-entries.
IF entry (index) = element
    THEN found-match
ELSE
    THEN no-match-in-entire-table.
```

or

SEARCH table-entries VARYING index
    AT END
        there-was-no-match
    WHEN
        there-is-a-match.
IF there-was-a-match

ELSE no-match

    ----------.

or

SEARCH ALL table-entries
    AT END
        there-was-no-match
    WHEN
        there-was-a-match.
IF there-was-a-match

ELSE

    ----------.

12 Advanced Input-Output Techniques

12.1 IDENTIFICATION DIVISION options

In this chapter, we discuss how a COBOL program interfaces with the operating system, and how this makes your work as a programmer much easier. We also discuss several COBOL options which simplify input-output (or I/O for short) no matter how a file is organized. The chapter concludes with remarks about two special COBOL features: teleprocessing (or data communications) and the report writer facility.

Before beginning the I/O discussion, let's take a look at the various options available when using the IDENTIFICATION DIVISION. All of our programs include the PROGRAM-ID paragraph because it *must* appear in every program. The AUTHOR paragraph, plus several other IDENTIFICATION DIVISION paragraphs, are optional; however, your data processing organization may have standards requiring you to include them in your program.

Aside from the PROGRAM-ID paragraph, COBOL treats other IDENTIFICATION DIVISION paragraphs as comments in the program. You, therefore, may want to check their accuracy very carefully, since COBOL won't. An example of a typical IDENTIFICATION DIVISION follows:

```
IDENTIFICATION DIVISION.
PROGRAM-ID. COMPTAX.
AUTHOR. MY NAME.
INSTALLATION. CORP-HEADQRTRS.
DATE-WRITTEN. 10-17-77.
DATE-COMPILED.
SECURITY. PAYROLL CLEARANCE NECESSARY.
```

The DATE-COMPILED clause is left blank when you write your program, because the COBOL compiler automatically will insert the current date each time the program is compiled. This is a very useful feature, since it may help you to determine whether you are reading the current version of a program or an obsolete version. Occasionally, a programmer will forget to replace an obsolete version of a program source listing with the most recent one — and, as a result, often spends frustrating hours debugging the wrong version of the program. This error may be caught if the DATE-COMPILED entry is suspiciously old. Most data processing organizations demand that DATE-COMPILED be included for just that reason.

12.2 ENVIRONMENT DIVISION options

The CONFIGURATION SECTION provides a place to designate the type of computer on which your program is to be compiled and executed. For example, we could code

```
ENVIRONMENT DIVISION.
CONFIGURATION SECTION.
SOURCE-COMPUTER. IBM-370.
OBJECT-COMPUTER. IBM-370.
```

The SOURCE-COMPUTER clause indicates which computer will be used to compile your program, while OBJECT-COMPUTER specifies the computer on which the program will be executed.

As with the IDENTIFICATION DIVISION, these clauses in the ENVIRONMENT DIVISION are optional and may be treated as comments by your particular COBOL compiler. Consequently, the ENVIRONMENT DIVISION options often are overlooked by programmers since they neither define nor operate upon data. However, these options contain information for which many a programmer is thankful when he is responsible for changing the code in an alien program — that is, a program coded by someone who is no longer around to explain what the program does. So, follow your organization's COBOL standards for the IDENTIFICATION DIVISION and for the ENVIRONMENT DIVISION.

12.3 Options of the OPEN and CLOSE statements

The variations of both the OPEN and CLOSE statements depend largely on the physical file-storage medium. For example, the possibilities for handling a magnetic tape (on which records usually can be accessed only in a sequential fashion) are vastly different from the options for manipulating a disk (on which records can be accessed sequentially, randomly, or directly). In Section 12.5, we'll learn more about accessing records from a disk file, but, first, let's look at the various ways of OPEN-ing a file that resides on magnetic tape.

A standard OPEN statement for a magnetic tape file positions the tape so that the first record on the tape is accessed when the first READ statement in the program is executed. Subsequent READ statements will access the second, third, fourth, and following records in an obvious fashion. For many common EDP applications, this approach is sufficient: Each record in a file has to be printed in a report, or processed to produce paychecks, or examined to see whether processing is necessary.

Sometimes, though, our processing is not so straightforward — and, for unusual applications, COBOL provides an OPEN REVERSED statement. As the name implies, it positions the tape so that the first READ statement in the program selects the *last* record in the file, with subsequent READs producing the immediately previous record.

Why would anyone want to read a tape backwards? As an example, suppose we had a tape file containing customer information, with each record having a unique five-digit customer number. It happens that all government agencies with which we do business have account numbers beginning with 99 — e.g., 99001, 99002, and so forth. Let's also imagine that the file is sequenced in ascending order by customer number, and that we have several thousand customers on the file. Now, suppose that we wish to create a listing of all the government agencies, without any particular regard for the actual sequence of customer numbers. We could OPEN the file in the normal fashion and read through all of the customer records until we finally found one with a customer number starting with 99. Or, if it is important that our program execute relatively quickly, we could OPEN the file in a REVERSED fashion, and begin printing the government agencies immediately.

Here's how we code the REVERSED option:

OPEN INPUT CUST-FILE REVERSED.

In this case, the end-of-file condition is handled in the same way as for normal READ operations, except that the AT END clause is activated when a READ is attempted *after* READing the physically first record on the file.

Just as there are various options on opening a file, so are there options for closing the file. A simple CLOSE statement will cause a magnetic tape file to be rewound. (This usually occurs for the convenience of the computer operator, who will remove the tape file from the magnetic tape drive.) However, the CLOSE statement also has the advantage of physically positioning the file so that another program can efficiently OPEN the same file (i.e., the OPEN statement will find that the file has already been positioned at the first record) and begin reading it.

It is possible — and sometimes desirable — to CLOSE WITH NO REWIND. As you would expect, this statement closes the file, and leaves the tape exactly where it was at the time of the CLOSE. Normally, this is used in situations in which one program will CLOSE a file WITH NO REWIND and a subsequent program will OPEN the file REVERSED. To code such a CLOSE statement, we could write:

CLOSE CUST-FILE WITH NO REWIND.

There is an important option that can be used to CLOSE any type of file: the WITH LOCK option. When a file is CLOSEd WITH LOCK, no matter how the program runs, that file cannot be OPENed again during the execution of the program that issued the CLOSE. This prevents the file from being reopened and overwritten if a bug exists in your program.

12.4 Buffering and blocking

So far, we have talked about records without saying very much about the actual manner in which they are stored on a tape or disk, or the actual manner in which the computer reads the records from the I/O device and provides them to your program. These physical details, which we've left for late in the book, often can have an important effect on the efficiency of your program. The two major concepts to be discussed in this section are *blocking* and *buffering*.

Records are stored on tape or disk in blocks. In the case of disks, the blocks are usually of a fixed maximum size — some disks have 512-character blocks, while others have 3,844-character blocks. With magnetic tapes, however, the blocks can be as long or as short as the situation requires — although it is customary for all blocks on the same tape to be the same length.

On a magnetic tape, a block is really just a contiguous group of records; the blocks are separated by interrecord gaps, which are the lengths of blank tape that signal the computer when one block has ended and another is about to begin. Since the interrecord gaps take up space on the tape (typically, 3/4 inch), it is more economical to use blocks that are relatively large compared to the interrecord gaps.

If, for example, we stored only about 200 characters of data in each block, we probably would find that about 50 percent of the available space on the tape was being used up by interrecord gaps (the precise figures depend on such things as the *recording density* used to record data on the tape, and other physical characteristics that may vary from one hardware manufacturer's tape drive to another's).

We have implied that when a READ statement is executed, a record magically is read from the tape or disk file and is brought into an area of memory (typically called a *buffer*), where it is made available to the program. While that explanation was sufficient before, we now should point out that it only *appears* to work that way. Actually, a number of records are grouped into one block. Each block is considered a *physical record* by the operating system, while each record referenced with a READ statement is called a *logical record.* Operating systems work with physical records; programs work with logical records.

The number of logical records in a block (or physical record) is stated in the BLOCK CONTAINS *n* RECORDS clause of a file's FD. Alternatively, the number may be part of the information contained in the Job Control Language (JCL) provided with your program in order to tell the operating system how to run your program.

When a file is OPENed, two areas — or buffers — are set up to receive records from a file. Each buffer is large enough to hold one physical record. Then, as part of the OPEN statement, the first two physical records are read into the buffers. When a READ statement is executed, the first logical record contained within the first physical record is made available to the program.

As subsequent READing is done, the first physical record is exhausted — and the next READ automatically will receive the first logical record in the second buffer. This switch of buffers also triggers the actual reading of the next physical record into the first buffer, overlaying the records previously used by the program. To the programmer, the records appear to be coming into memory one after the other from the input-output device; in fact, the input is accomplished asynchronously with the READ commands.

With sequential files, WRITE statements work in exactly the same way. Every time a WRITE is executed, a logical record is appended to the current physical record in a buffer. When a physical record has been composed from the appropriate number of logical records, the operating system begins writing the physical record, and simultaneously switches to the other buffer for assembly of the next physical record.

What if we were READing or WRITEing records in blocks of 20, but our file had only 15 logical records? Let's examine these two cases separately. If we were READing, the last block (or physical record) would contain only 15 logical records. Therefore, when we attempted to READ the sixteenth record (which doesn't exist), our program would get an end-of-file indication. Thus, we don't need to organize our file in such a way as to guarantee that the number of logical records is an exact multiple of the number of physical records — the last physical record can be short, without affecting our programming.

If we were WRITEing, the last physical record would not be complete — it, too, would contain only 15 logical records, and the last block automatically would be written to the I/O device when the CLOSE statement for the file was executed.

In almost all programs, two buffers are sufficient to accomplish efficient overlapping of input-output and actual processing — that is, a program will work on the logical records in one buffer while the operating system is doing the physical input-output in another buffer.

In special situations requiring more than two buffers, the RESERVE *n* ALTERNATE AREAS clause can be used with the SELECT statement, with *n* specifying the number of buffers needed *in addition to* the one buffer which a program must have if it is to accomplish any input-output.

By specifying RESERVE NO ALTERNATE AREAS, you can ensure that only one buffer will be set up for your file. While this will save a certain amount of memory (how much memory depends on the size of your physical records), it generally will slow your program — simply because your program will be forced to wait while the next physical record is read into or written out of the buffer. Similarly, reserving more than one alternate buffer will increase the amount of memory your program consumes, but it may speed up your program.

It is likely that your data processing organization has guidelines for blocking factors — specifying, for example, how many logical records should be contained in a physical record — and for buffering. Before you decide to increase or decrease the number of buffers or the block size, you should consult those guidelines.

12.5 Indexed input-output

Thus far in this chapter, we have been concerned with sequential access of records. Although this is the most common method used in business data processing applications, it does have its limitations: In order to look at one specific record, it is necessary to READ each preceding record, even though those records are of no interest to us. This process can be quite time-consuming — especially since files used in today's computer systems frequently contain more than a million records.

Direct access into a file for a specific record can be accomplished by using *indexed* organization.[1] This is specified in the SELECT statement with the ORGANIZATION IS INDEXED clause. (A small but important reminder: You cannot arbitrarily change the organization of a file. When the file is created, it is given a certain organization that remains constant for the file's lifetime.) Along with the ORGANIZATION clause, a RECORD KEY IS clause must be specified to indicate which field will act as a pointer to a specific record in the file.

For example, let's suppose that we want to access directly a client on the charter tour customer file. Assuming that each client has a unique customer number, we could write RECORD KEY IS CLIENT-NUMBER. This indexed file organization would allow us to access any customer by CLIENT-NUMBER. Or, if we state in the SELECT statement that ACCESS MODE IS SEQUENTIAL, we could retrieve clients in the order in which the file is organized, from the first record to the last record (i.e., just as if it were a magnetic tape file).

---

[1] For more information on indexed file organization, see *Learning to Program in Structured COBOL, Part 1*, Section 7.4.

COBOL also provides an alternate path into a file when using indexed I/O. By using the ALTERNATE RECORD KEY IS clause in the SELECT statement, a specific record in the charter tour system could be accessed by, say, the customer phone number.

In addition to allowing a second direct path into a file, the ALTERNATE RECORD KEY is very useful for accessing groups of records whose key fields have the same value. Unlike the key stated in the RECORD KEY IS clause (often known as the prime key), the ALTERNATE RECORD KEY may be a field that does not have a unique value in each record.

In the charter tour system, for example, there might be multiple records with the same tour number; this could be coded as ALTERNATE RECORD KEY IS TOUR-NUMBER WITH DUPLICATES. This permits us to access directly the first record with a specific tour number, then all of the rest of the records with the identical tour number. If a request is made for all clients booked on tour 16872, we need not read through *all* of the client records testing each one for the requested tour.

The entire SELECT statement for the client file might be something like this:

```
SELECT CUST-FILE
    ASSIGN TO UT-I-SYS001
    ORGANIZATION IS INDEXED
    ACCESS MODE IS DYNAMIC
*THIS ALLOWS BOTH INDEXED AND SEQUENTIAL ACCESS
    RECORD KEY IS CLIENT-NUMBER
    ALTERNATE RECORD KEY IS TOUR-NUMBER WITH DUPLICATES.
```

Additional verbs besides READ and WRITE have the ability to access records directly. For example, we can code

```
DELETE CUST-FILE RECORD
    INVALID KEY
        DISPLAY 'RECORD ' CLIENT-NUMBER ' NOT THERE'
        UPON CONSOLE.
```

This deletes the record corresponding to the key at the time of the DELETE statement. If there is no corresponding record, and the access mode is not sequential, then the INVALID KEY clause will be activated.

Or, we can write

READ CUST-FILE NEXT RECORD.

When we have specified a dynamic access mode in our SELECT statement, the NEXT RECORD clause permits retrieval of the *next* record asynchronously with the record currently being processed. That is, input is done in a buffered fashion as if READing were being done sequentially.

We can also code

REWRITE CUST-RECD.

This will cause the specified record to be written back onto the disk in its original place. This particular technique is called updating in place.

Finally, we can code

$$\text{START CUST}-\text{FILE KEY} \begin{Bmatrix} \text{IS EQUAL TO} \\ \text{IS GREATER THAN} \\ \text{IS NOT LESS THAN} \end{Bmatrix} \text{field}-\text{name}$$

This will position the file so that the pointer locates the first record that satisfies the condition.

12.6 Relative input-output

Relative I/O is another organization which permits either sequential or direct access. As with indexed I/O, it is necessary to have a key to access a relative file. However, the similarity ends there. An indexed file requires that each record have a unique value for its key field, while a relative file does not depend on any field value.

Instead, the relative file works with a key based on relative position of a record in the file. If the RELATIVE KEY field is equal to 50, the record in the fiftieth slot is returned, regardless of whether record slots 01 through 49 contain any records. This permits direct access for files that do not have a natural key field within every record. We would code this as follows:

```
SELECT CUST-FILE
    ASSIGN TO UT-R-SYS001
    ORGANIZATION IS RELATIVE
                    [SEQUENTIAL
    ACCESS MODE IS  [RANDOM     ]  , RELATIVE KEY IS R-POINTER
                    [DYNAMIC    ]
```

As shown in the code above, there are three possible access modes: SEQUENTIAL, which allows access of one record after another from the first to the last; RANDOM, which permits access only by RELATIVE KEY; and DYNAMIC, which permits RANDOM and SEQUENTIAL access.

We can use the same verbs for accessing relative files that we use for accessing indexed files: READ, WRITE, DELETE, REWRITE, and START.

12.7 File status

There is another aspect of the physical world that we need to discuss: the possibility of errors and unusual, unanticipated situations when doing I/O. It is possible (although not common) that our COBOL program will be unsuccessful in its attempt to OPEN, CLOSE, READ, START, WRITE, or REWRITE. Unless we specify a suitable action, our program will abort if an error is detected on any of these I/O operations. In many cases, this is unnecessary: Processing often can continue (with, perhaps, the erroneous record being deleted or ignored) once the error is detected, noted on an error report, and circumvented. This is particularly true of programs that may run for hours while processing hundreds of thousands of I/O operations. It is impractical and inefficient to let one I/O error abort the entire job.

To check the success or failure of an I/O operation, COBOL offers the FILE STATUS IS clause in the SELECT statement. For example, we could code

FILE STATUS IS CUST-INDICATOR.

CUST-INDICATOR must be a two-position alphanumeric field defined by the programmer; consequently, it can have a name chosen by the programmer. Each of the two positions contains useful information concerning the status of the file, which we typically will want to examine *after* an I/O operation has been executed. It is convenient to refer to the left-most position of CUST-INDICATOR as key 1, and the right-most position as key 2.

For *sequentially organized* files, key 1 will have the following values and meanings:

'0'	-	successful I/O operation
'1'	-	end of file reached
'3'	-	permanent error
'9'	-	defined by the computer vendor

Key 2 contains the following information:

'0'	-	no further information
'4'	-	when key 1 = '3', an attempt was made to use more space than was allocated by the operating system

When key 1 = '9', key 2 contains values that have been defined by the computer vendor.

For *relative organization,* key 1 has the following values:

'0'	-	successful I/O operation
'1'	-	end of file reached
'2'	-	invalid key
'3'	-	permanent error
'9'	-	defined by the computer vendor

If key 1 = '9', key 2 will be defined by the computer vendor. However, if key 1 = '2', key 2 provides more information about the nature of the invalid key error. In this case, the possible values for key 2 are:

'0'	-	no further information
'2'	-	an attempt was made to write a record that would have created a duplicate key
'3'	-	no record found
'4'	-	an attempt was made to write beyond the defined boundaries of the file

If *indexed organization* is used, the values of key 1 can be '0', '1', '2', '3', or '9'; the meaning of these values is exactly the same as for relative file organization. However, the details regarding key 2 vary slightly.

If key 1 = '0' and key 2 = '0', then the I/O operation was successful, and the operating system has no further information to provide. However, if key 1 = '0' and key 2 = '2', then *either* a duplicate key has just been written (or rewritten) for the alternate key value, *or* if a READ has just been executed, then the record just read and the *next* record have duplicate keys.

If key 1 = '2', an invalid key situation has occurred. In this case, key 2 will be coded as follows:

'1'	-	a sequence error has occurred when the indexed file was being accessed sequentially (records must be in ascending order by record key)
'2'	-	an attempt was made to write or rewrite a record that would have caused a duplicate key to be created
'3'	-	no record on the file has the specified key
'4'	-	ran out of space

Use of the keys enables you to continue running your program even though an I/O operation has failed. However, testing key values after each I/O operation can be tedious as well as awkward. Fortunately, the task is simplified considerably by the USE statement, detailed in Section 12.8 below.

12.8 The USE statement and DECLARATIVES section

We now know that COBOL makes it possible to determine whether an I/O error has occurred. In most programs, we can specify the type of error-checking that is to be carried out in the DECLARATIVES. DECLARATIVES must immediately follow the PROCEDURE DIVISION statement and must end with the sentence END DECLARATIVES. For example, we might code

PROCEDURE DIVISION.
DECLARATIVES.
section-name SECTION.
USE statement.
.
.
.
END DECLARATIVES.

Within the DECLARATIVES section the USE statement defines the particular conditions under which the error-handling routines should be executed.

The most common form of USE statement is

USE AFTER STANDARD ERROR PROCEDURE ON CUST-FILE.

Instructions for handling *any* I/O error for the CUST-FILE follow this statement; together, these statements comprise an entire *section* of code within the DECLARATIVES part of the program.

Since you may have several files, you may need several USE statements, each with its own section of error-handling code. It is also possible to have USE statements for input, output, or I/O, rather than for specific files, although this is less common.

Control automatically will pass to the DECLARATIVES when an error is encountered; control will return to the statement following the I/O statement when the END DECLARATIVES is encountered (or, in most cases, when the appropriate USE statement or statements have been executed). That is, the program operates just as if you had written the following code, using the DECLARATIVES:

```
READ CUST-FILE
    IF ANY ERROR FOUND
        PERFORM DECLARATIVES.
```

instead of writing

```
READ CUST-FILE.
```

If, for some reason, you want to have the DECLARATIVES handle end-of-file conditions, all you need do is omit the AT END clause on READ statements. Control automatically will pass to DECLARATIVES when end of file is found. If a program contains both DECLARATIVES and AT END, the AT END clause takes precedence over DECLARATIVES.

12.9 Introduction to Report Writer and Data Communications

There are two special features of COBOL that rarely are used because of their complex qualities: the Report Writer feature and the Data Communications feature. The Report Writer allows the programmer to code the report layout in the DATA DIVISION in such a way that COBOL automatically will accomplish most of the work of writing the reports without any coding in the PROCEDURE DIVISION.

Within the DATA DIVISION, the *Record Description* (RD) is defined in much the same way that an FD is defined. The Report Writer can handle page counting, accumulating of totals, detail line formatting, heading and footing titles, and much more. (We will make no attempt in this book to teach you the intricacies of the Report Writer — that would take a book in itself![2] If your organization uses this feature, refer to your COBOL manual for a thorough description.)

COBOL uses the Data Communications feature to deal with the special situations of teleprocessing. There are many problems that may arise when messages (input transactions) enter a system from remote terminals. The Data Communications feature, along with a message control system, provides COBOL with the ability to handle this situation. The feature is complex and seldom used, since teleprocessing systems rarely are written in COBOL.

12.10 Benefits of an operating system

Many of the topics discussed in this chapter will affect you only indirectly, since the operating system will allocate buffers as well as read from and write to the files.

Operating systems are resident (always in the computer) programs, built specifically to make the job of writing and executing application programs easier. They operate like black boxes, since the COBOL programmer need not know how the operating system actually handles details — all he needs to know is that the input or output is actually accomplished when a READ or WRITE is executed.

---

[2]Relatively few versions of COBOL actually have implemented the Report Writer, and *very* few organizations use it. Hence, our decision not to elaborate on this aspect of COBOL.

When a COBOL program is to be run, special instructions can be given to the program via the operating system's Job Control Language. The JCL usually supplies information to the operating system about what files will be needed by the program, what files will be created, how much space on a storage medium a new file will require, which files should be saved at the completion of the program's execution, which files should be deleted, and how much memory the program will require.

All of this information is used by the operating system to help schedule the job, and to help manage the resources of the entire computer system as efficiently as possible (because, generally, several programs are executing on the computer at the same time). The operating system will not load the program into memory if there are not enough storage devices available to READ and WRITE all of the files. This scheduling — completely hidden from the programmer — helps make the computer operate in a more cost-effective way. It also allows the application programmer to concentrate on solving the business problem rather than playing with the hardware.

There are many different types of operating systems, but they all have the same basic purpose: to let the programmer worry about solving the problem, while leaving the operating system free to handle the details of making good use of the particular computer hardware.

13 Sorting and Merging

13.1 Introduction

Sorting and *merging* are two related procedures that are used frequently by COBOL programmers. Sorting involves the automatic ordering of records under a programmer's direction; merging involves the interleaving of several files into one ordered sequence of records.

Sorting and merging can be accomplished with a single key field, or multiple key fields. For example, the customer records for the charter tour system could be sorted into ascending sequence on CLIENT-NUMBER; or it might be useful to sort these records into ascending sequence on TOUR-NUMBER, and within each tour, into ascending order on CLIENT-NUMBER. Both of these sorts can be accomplished with a single SORT statement.

13.2 The SORT statement

Let's begin by looking at a small, simple program which accomplishes a SORT, shown in the code on the following page.

The program sorts the customer file into ascending TOUR-NUMBER order — and, within that, ascending CLIENT-NUMBER order. In case you think the program is wrong because it lacks OPENs and CLOSEs, don't worry — the SORT automatically OPENs and CLOSEs the files.

The key fields are listed in order from major to minor; we can request ascending or descending sequencing to be done for each. The program uses numeric fields for keys, but the sort can be used with non-numeric keys as well. Sorting into ascending sequence with an alpha field key would produce a file in alphabetic order by key field. As is evident from the code, the USING clause on the SORT statement names the unsorted input file, and the GIVING clause names the sorted file that will be the output.

```
IDENTIFICATION DIVISION.
PROGRAM-ID. SIMPLSRT.

ENVIRONMENT DIVISION.

INPUT-OUTPUT SECTION.
FILE-CONTROL.
    SELECT CUST-FILE-IN ASSIGN TO UT-S-MSTTAPE.
    SELECT CUST-SORT ASSIGN TO DA-S-WORKROOM.
    SELECT CUST-FILE-OUT ASSIGN TO UT-S-NEWTAPE.

DATA DIVISION.
FD  CUST-FILE-IN
    LABEL RECORDS ARE STANDARD
    RECORD CONTAINS 120 CHARACTERS
    BLOCK CONTAINS 0 RECORDS
    DATA RECORD IS OLD-CUST.
01  OLD-CUST            PIC X(120).
SD  CUST-SORT
    RECORD CONTAINS 120 CHARACTERS
    DATA RECORD IS SORT-CUST.
01  SORT-CUST.
    05  TOUR-NUMBER     PIC 9(5).
    05  CLIENT-NUMBER   PIC 9(5).
    05  FILLER          PIC X(110).
FD  CUST-FILE-OUT
    LABEL RECORDS ARE STANDARD
    RECORD CONTAINS 120 CHARACTERS
    BLOCK CONTAINS 0 RECORDS
    DATA RECORD IS NEW-CUST.
01  NEW-CUST           PIC X(120).

PROCEDURE DIVISION.
SORT-CUSTOMERS.
    SORT CUST-SORT
        ON ASCENDING KEY TOUR-NUMBER
        ON ASCENDING KEY CLIENT-NUMBER
        USING CUST-FILE-IN
        GIVING CUST-FILE-OUT.
    STOP RUN.
```

13.3 The SORT description (SD)

In the coding example in Section 13.2, we named an *inter-mediate* file, CUST-SORT, to be used as a work space during the process of ordering the records. A file is considered to be intermediate when it is created *within* the program (i.e., it did not exist before the program began running, in contrast to a *permanent* file), and when it is of no further use at the conclusion of the program's execution.

The COBOL SORT requires work space in order to shuffle the records into the requested sequence. Note that CUST-SORT is assigned a disk with its own SELECT statement. This work file is described by what appears to be a normal file description — except that instead of calling it an FD, we call it a SORT description. The SD and the corresponding record layout describe each record's appearance as it goes into the SORT. The key fields for the sorting sequence must be defined in a record description attached to an SD.

13.4 INPUT and OUTPUT PROCEDUREs

The example shown in Section 13.2 does nothing more than sort the file. However, COBOL permits the programmer to reference and manipulate both the input to the SORT, and the output from it — and, in many cases, the COBOL programmer needs that facility.

If we wish to reference information on a file *before* it is sorted, we use an INPUT PROCEDURE; the INPUT PROCEDURE is declared as part of the SORT statement. Similarly, if we wish to work with sorted records (that is, records that are produced, one at a time, by the sorting mechanism), we declare an OUTPUT PROCEDURE in the SORT statement.

As an example, on the following pages we see a program that selects customers who are flying from a specified airport on a specific date, sorts them by tour and client number, and then prints a listing of these customers:

```
IDENTIFICATION DIVISION.
PROGRAM-ID. FANCYSRT.


ENVIRONMENT DIVISION.

INPUT-OUTPUT SECTION.
FILE-CONTROL.
    SELECT CUST-FILE-IN ASSIGN TO UT-S-MSTTAPE.
    SELECT CUST-SORT ASSIGN TO DA-S-WORKROOM.
    SELECT CONTROL-REC ASSIGN TO UR-S-SYSIN.
    SELECT CUST-LIST ASSIGN TO UR-S-SYSPRINT.


DATA DIVISION.

FILE SECTION.
FD  CUST-FILE-IN
    LABEL RECORDS ARE OMITTED
    RECORD CONTAINS 80 CHARACTERS
    BLOCK CONTAINS 0 RECORDS
    DATA RECORD IS OLD-CUST.
01  OLD-CUST.
    05   FILLER              PIC X(45).
    05   AIR-SELECTED        PIC A(3).
    05   FILLER              PIC X(27).
    05   DEPART-DATE         PIC 9(5).


*
* DEPARTURE DATE IS IN DDDYY FORMAT.
*


SD  CUST-SORT
    RECORD CONTAINS 80 CHARACTERS
    DATA RECORD IS SORTING-CUST.
01  SORTING-CUST.
    05   TOUR-NUMBER         PIC 9(5).
    05   CLIENT-NUMBER       PIC 9(5).
    05   CLIENT-NAME         PIC X(20).
    05   CLIENT-ADDR         PIC X(15).
    05   FILLER              PIC X(3).
    05   BALANCE-DUE         PIC 9(4)V99.
    05   FILLER              PIC X(26).

FD  CUST-LIST
    LABEL RECORDS ARE OMITTED
    RECORD CONTAINS 132 CHARACTERS
    DATA RECORD IS CUSTOMER-LIST.
```

```
01  CUSTOMER-LIST            PIC X(132).
WORKING-STORAGE SECTION.
01  EOF-SORT                 PIC X(3)    VALUE 'NO '.
01  EOF-CUST                 PIC X(3)    VALUE 'NO '.
01  PRINT-LINE.
    05   FILLER              PIC X(2).
    05   TR-NUM              PIC 9(5).
    05   FILLER              PIC X(5).
    05   CL-NUM              PIC 9(5).
    05   FILLER              PIC X(10).
    05   CL-NAME             PIC X(20).
    05   FILLER              PIC X(3).
    05   CL-ADDR             PIC X(15).
    05   FILLER              PIC X(5).
    05   BAL-DUE             PIC $$$$9.99-.
    05   FILLER              PIC X(54).
01  SELECTED-REC.
    05   TOUR-NUMB           PIC 9(5).
    05   CLIENT-NUMB         PIC 9(5).
    05   CLIENT-NAM          PIC X(20).
    05   CLIENT-ADD          PIC X(15).
    05   FILLER              PIC X(3).
    05   BALANCE-DUE         PIC S9(4)V99.
    05   FILLER              PIC X(26).

FD CONTROL-REC
    LABEL RECORDS ARE OMITTED
    RECORD CONTAINS 80 CHARACTERS
    DATA RECORD IS CONTROL-CARD.
01  CONTROL-CARD.
    05   CONTROL-AIR         PIC A(3).
    05   FILLER              PIC X(6).
    05   CONTROL-DATE        PIC 9(5).
    05   FILLER              PIC X(66).

PROCEDURE DIVISION.

SORT-SELECTED.
    SORT CUST-SORT
        ASCENDING KEY TOUR-NUMBER
        ASCENDING KEY CLIENT-NUMBER
        INPUT PROCEDURE SELECT-CUSTOMERS.
        OUTPUT PROCEDURE CREATE-LIST.
END-SORT.
    EXIT PROGRAM.

SELECT-CUSTOMERS SECTION.
GET-CUSTOMERS.
    OPEN INPUT CUST-FILE-IN
        INPUT CONTROL-CARD.
    PERFORM READ-CONTROL.
    PERFORM READ-CUST.
```

```
        PERFORM SELECT-LOOP
            UNTIL EOF-CUST = 'YES'.
        CLOSE CUST-FILE-IN.
        GO TO SELECT-CUSTOMERS-EXIT.
    SELECT-LOOP.
        IF CONTROL-AIR = AIR-SELECTED
            AND CONTROL-DATE = DEPART-DATE
                MOVE OLD-CUST TO SORTING-CUST
                RELEASE SORTING-CUST.
        PERFORM READ-CUST.
    READ-CUST.
        READ CUST-FILE-IN
            AT END
                MOVE 'YES' TO EOF-CUST.
    READ-CONTROL.
        READ CONTROL-CARD
            AT END
                DISPLAY 'NO CONTROL CARD - RUN STOPPED.'
                STOP RUN.

 * NOTE: IF EOF, THERE WAS NO CONTROL CARD AT ALL, SO
 * JOB IS ABORTED

    SELECT-CUSTOMERS-EXIT.
        EXIT.

    CREATE-LIST SECTION.
    FORMAT-LINES.
        OPEN OUTPUT CUST-LIST.
        PERFORM GET-FROM-SORT.
        PERFORM FORMAT-LOOP UNTIL EOF-SORT = 'YES'.
        CLOSE CUST-LIST.
        GO TO CREATE-LIST-EXIT.
    FORMAT-LOOP.
        MOVE SPACES TO PRINT-LINE.
        MOVE TOUR-NUMBER TO TR-NUM.
        MOVE CLIENT-NUMBER TO CL-NUM.
        MOVE CLIENT-NAME TO CL-NAME.
        MOVE CLIENT-ADDR TO CL-ADDR.
        MOVE BALANCE-DUE TO BAL-DUE.
        PERFORM WRITE-LINE.
        PERFORM GET-FROM-SORT.
    GET-FROM-SORT.
        RETURN CUST-SORT RECORD INTO SELECTED-REC
            AT END MOVE 'YES' TO EOF-SORT.
    WRITE-LINE.
        WRITE CUSTOMER-LIST FROM PRINT-LINE.
    CREATE-LIST-EXIT.
        EXIT.
```

This program looks different from our previous examples, primarily because the rules of the COBOL SORT dictate a special arrangement for the INPUT and OUTPUT PROCEDURES.

COBOL treats this program as three separate and distinct phases of processing, all of which are controlled by the SORT statement. The first phase, the INPUT PROCEDURE, is given control immediately from the SORT. It OPENs and READs records, and as each record is ready to be sorted, it is "released" to the sorting mechanism with the RELEASE statement. When the INPUT PROCEDURE is finished, it EXITs (usually when an end of file has been detected on the input file); then the second phase — the actual sort — begins.

When the sort is finished, control is passed to the third phase — the OUTPUT PROCEDURE. The OUTPUT PROCEDURE obtains records, one at a time, in a sorted sequence, by executing a RETURN statement. The RETURN statement can be considered a "READ next record from sorted file" statement. When the OUTPUT PROCEDURE is finished, it EXITs, and control is passed to the statement immediately following the SORT statement.

The rules involved with the COBOL SORT may require the programmer to write GO TO statements, as demonstrated in the example above. The rules for INPUT and OUTPUT PROCEDURES are as follows:

1.   The INPUT PROCEDURE must consist of one or more contiguous COBOL SECTIONS. Similarly, the OUTPUT PROCEDURE must be comprised of adjacent SECTIONS.

2.   The INPUT PROCEDURE may not invoke or reference a paragraph or section outside the INPUT PROCEDURE itself. Similarly, the OUTPUT PROCEDURE may not invoke any paragraphs or sections outside of itself.

3.   No piece of code outside the INPUT PROCEDURE
or OUTPUT PROCEDURE may refer to a paragraph
inside those procedures.

Because the programmer is forced to use adjacent sections for
each SORT procedure, it may be necessary to use a GO TO statement to pass control to the EXIT paragraph in the procedure.
Normally, we would frown on the use of GO TO statements, but
in this case they are unavoidable.

13.5 The MERGE statement

The COBOL MERGE statement combines two or more
identically sequenced files into one ordered file, as specified by
key fields. Its rules are very similar to the SORT. A typical
MERGE statement follows:

```
MERGE MERGE-MONTHS-FILE
    ON ASCENDING KEY TOUR-NUMBER
    ON ASCENDING KEY CLIENT-NUMBER
    USING     JAN-CUST-FILE
              FEB-CUST-FILE
              MAR-CUST-FILE
              APR-CUST-FILE
              MAY-CUST-FILE
              JUN-CUST-FILE
    GIVING FIRST-HALF-YEAR-FILE.
```

The MERGE-MONTHS file must be defined with an SD, just
like a sort file. The rest of the MERGE rules are the same as the
SORT rules, *except* that only an OUTPUT PROCEDURE is allowed.

14 Testing and Debugging

14.1 Introduction to testing

No matter how carefully you write your code, no matter how sure you are that your code is perfect, you still must actually *test* it on a computer. Without testing, the chances of a bug — even in the simplest code — are very high; and the cost of fixing the bugs (known as debugging) and rerunning the job can be very expensive. It is so easy to inadvertently put a bug in code that even the smallest modification to an existing program deserves to be tested on the computer.

If we are to test our program, we need a collection of *test inputs*. These test inputs will produce some outputs — outputs that we should be able to predict before we begin the testing. It is useless to look at test output without knowing whether the output is the correct response to a particular test input; indeed, in such a situation we usually spend most of our time trying to convince ourselves that the test output looks reasonable.

Our test inputs also must exercise *all* of the modules in a program in order to give us confidence that the test is any measure of the program's correctness. For example, if we were testing a program that edits records and produces valid records and an error report, it would be foolish to use only error-free records or only illegal records as test data. Obviously, we need combinations of both to form a worthy set of test data.

14.2 Walkthroughs

In many situations, a program will abort and stop executing when the first bug is encountered. An attempt to divide by zero, an illegal subscript, or any of a number of other bugs may cause the program to be interrupted by the operating system. In such cases, the programmer usually is forced to find the bug that caused the abnormal termination (or "abend," as it is called on some systems), fix it, and then run the test again.

Unfortunately, another bug may be lurking only a few statements further in the code. Naturally, this causes another abend, another effort to find the bug, another recompilation of the program to fix the bug, and yet another test run. This start-and-stop method of testing — in which only one bug is found in each test run — can be long and arduous, as well as expensive. This is particularly true in data processing organizations in which the programmer has to wait for a day or more to have his program compiled, or his test run executed.

In order to avoid this cumbersome process, many organizations use *code walkthroughs* to eliminate as many bugs as possible *before* the first test run. The code walkthrough consists of a review of the program by other COBOL programmers in an attempt to find bugs before the machine does. After the program has been written, and perhaps after it has been compiled (depending on computer turnaround time), the author of the program distributes copies of the code (i.e., program listings or coding sheets) and program specifications to three or four other programmers, giving them a reasonable period of time to review the code privately. The private review process typically takes only an hour, but it usually is advisable to allow two days to ensure that each of the reviewers will be able to squeeze in an hour of reviewing time among his or her other programming duties.

After each programmer has had a chance to review the code, a meeting — or walkthrough — is held to discuss publicly any bugs that might be present *as well as* any deviations from installation standards, major inefficiencies, or any other aspect of the program which the reviewers feel would make it difficult to maintain or modify. Once the author of the program is shown a bug, discussion of that bug usually stops — it is the responsibility of the author to fix the mistake and conduct another walk-through to convince the reviewers that the bug has indeed been eliminated.

If this seems time-consuming, rest assured that, compara-tively, it's not. Time spent reviewing the code in this fashion generally is *much* less than the amount of time the author of the program would require to find a bug using the start-and-stop method of testing. In addition, the walkthrough process usually finds bugs that the author never would have found in his own testing efforts — bugs that usually cause *very* expensive testing, debugging, and rerunning of the program after it has been put into production. Thus, it is important to realize that *all* code needs to be submitted to this walkthrough process; experience has shown us that just as many bugs lurk in simple modules as in complex ones.

Successful walkthroughs are generally very short — usually 30 minutes long, and rarely as long as 60 minutes. Of necessity, this means that a walkthrough normally is used to review a rela-tively small piece of code — typically, 50-100 statements. Many programmers make the mistake of attempting to review too much code, or of prolonging the walkthrough for two or three hours. In both cases, the walkthroughs become superficial, and some bugs are not found. If a large program is being written, a module-by-module review will produce far better results than will one meeting in which bugs are hunted in a 50-page program.

The walkthrough approach also can be very helpful when developing test data. Reviewers must ask themselves the follow-ing questions: Given a certain specification, is this test data a rigorous test of the code? If the program produces the correct results with this test data, can we assume that the program actu-ally does what it is supposed to do?

Chances are good that as you have been learning to write COBOL programs, you and your fellow students have spent many hours wondering why a program abended, or why it pro-duced such mysterious output. Walkthroughs are merely a slightly more formalized version of those brainstorming sessions — except that they take place *before* the program abends!

14.3 Top-down testing

Testing of a COBOL program can be made easier if the code is tested piece by piece, rather than all at once after the entire program has been written. This approach is known as *incremental testing* because it involves coding and testing one module at a time until the entire program is tested. Written in pseudocode, the strategy could be expressed as

> **Code a module**
> **Test that module**
> **WHILE there are more modules in the program**
>   **Code a module**
>   **Test that module with those already tested**

Top-down testing is an incremental testing approach that works down from the topmost module to the lowest modules in the hierarchy. The rule of top-down testing is that the main module is always written first, and every subsequent module that is coded is immediately subordinate to one that already has been coded and tested.

The structure chart on the following page illustrates top-down testing. The program reads in records labeled X and Z, and outputs records labeled XY′ and XY″. Using top-down testing, the first module to be coded and tested would be MAIN MODULE. The structure chart shows that MAIN MODULE invokes modules 1, 2, 3, and 4; thus, if we are going to test MAIN MODULE, we must simulate the work of these modules by using *stubs,* or "dummy" modules. A stub is a quick-and-dirty module that does either no processing, or only a minimal amount of processing to simulate the behavior of the *real* module.

Our structure chart indicates that module 4 receives record XY as its input. A stub for module 4 might be a single COBOL paragraph that DISPLAYs the XY record each time it receives control. The information DISPLAYed would be used to verify that

MAIN MODULE is passing control to module 4 at the proper time, and that it is passing the proper values in XY.

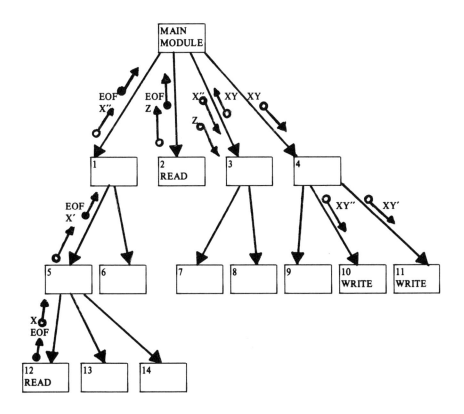

A stub for module 1 is more difficult to code. Somehow, the programmer must simulate a module that returns an X″ record to MAIN MODULE, as well as eventually returning an end-of-file indicator. One possible approach would be to build a table of sample values for X″. The stub for module 1 then could retrieve entries from the table and return them to MAIN MODULE. When the table is exhausted, the stub would return an end-of-file indicator.

Module 3 also could work with a table to return XY records. Or, it could return a constant value of XY, by moving the same value into XY each time it is invoked without regard to the values in X″ and Z. If the programmer decided to return a constant value each time, it would be a good idea to DISPLAY the values of X″ and Z every time the stub is invoked.

Once MAIN MODULE is working, the programmer has a choice of coding and testing modules 1, 2, 3 or 4. The choice generally depends on the programmer's overall implementation strategy for the program. For example, if module 4 is coded, then we could code module 11 immediately afterwards, thereby having our program write out XY′ records long before the program is completely finished.

Alternatively, if module 11 prints out a report, it might be very useful for the user to see an example of the report format. Thus, we might want to start by coding and testing MAIN MODULE, then module 4, and then module 11. If module 11 writes out a file made up of XY′ records, and if some other program in our data processing organization reads those records, then it would be useful to get module 11 working as soon as possible so that we could confirm that the two programs can "talk" to each other.

On the other hand, it may be useful to write module 2 after testing MAIN MODULE. This would mean that we could use a real file of Z records in all subsequent testing. This might be followed by coding modules 1, 5, and 12 in order to be able to use a file of real X records.

The implementation strategy generally will be up to you and the other people involved in the analysis, design, and implementation of your system. The strategy often depends on consideration of whether a primitive version of a system would be useful to the user as a demonstration tool, a training tool, or even as a limited production version of the program. The key to top-down testing is its *incremental* nature: The programmer tests and debugs one piece at a time, rather than writing an entire program and then trying to get all of the modules to work at once.

In the back of the book, there is a structure chart of the program that edits customer records for booking onto flights. The following page shows a strategy for coding and testing the modules of that program in a top-down fashion:

VERSION DESCRIPTION	MODULES WORKING	STUBS
1 This version will write out valid groups exactly as will the finished product; erroneous groups are displayed simply. All editing is simulated.	EDIT-CLIENT TRANSACTIONS GET NEXT VALID GROUP PUT VALID GROUP WRITE A RECORD	GET GROUP CORRECT NUMBER IN GROUP SAME AIRPORTS FORMAT ERROR LIST
2 This version will read in client records, which are assumed to pass all local edits, build clients into groups, check for correct number in a group, check that all members have the same choices for airports, display errors, and write individuals in valid groups.	GET GROUP (CHANGE IN GROUP) CORRECT NUMBER IN GROUP SAME AIRPORTS	FORMAT ERROR LIST GET EDITED CLIENT
3 This version does every-thing that the final ver-sion will do except edit-ing on individual flight information, and on name and address information. It now prints the error listing.	FORMAT ERROR LIST FORMAT HEADER PRINT ERROR LIST	CHECK AIR TRANSPORT INFORMATION CHECK CLIENT INFORMATION
4 This is the production version of the system.	ALL MODULES	

14.4 Common bugs

In this section we will discuss some of the common, garden-variety bugs that creep into almost everyone's programs from time to time. Obviously, the number of possible COBOL mistakes is infinite, so we will confine our discussion to some very common types of errors.

One of the most common bugs is the *data exception:* A program will abort if any field is *defined* in the DATA DIVISION as one type of data, and then *used* in such a way as to cause incompatible types of data to be stored in that field. For example, what would happen if you attempted to add to an accumulator a field containing 'SMITH'. The program would abort with a data exception because arithmetic only can be done with numeric fields.

In many cases, data exceptions occur because the programmer misdefines a record — that is, he accidentally defines one of the fields with an improper length, thereby throwing off the rest of the fields. For example, suppose we have a record which *should* be defined as

```
01  CUSTOMER-RECD.
    05  CUSTOMER-NUMBER     PIC  9(6).
    05  CUSTOMER-NAME       PIC  X(20).
    05  AMT-DUE             PIC  9(4)V99.
```

but, because of a bug, ends up being coded as

```
01  CUSTOMER-RECD.
    05  CUSTOMER-NUMBER     PIC  9(5).
    05  CUSTOMER-NAME       PIC  X(20).
    05  AMT-DUE             PIC  9(4)V99.
```

By misdefining the record, the programmer has caused the following three things to happen:

1. The field CUSTOMER-NAME will include the low-order digit of CUSTOMER-NUMBER. This means that CUSTOMER-NAME probably will contain *alphanumeric* data, which will cause trouble if the program expected it to be purely *alphabetic*.

2. The AMT-DUE field will include the low-order position of the CUSTOMER-NAME field. This means that AMT-DUE probably will end up being alphanumeric instead of pure numeric.

3. The last position of AMT-DUE read in from the file will be dropped, since the *actual* definition of the record is one position less than the amount of data read in.

Under these conditions, it is very likely that the program will abend with a data exception. Indeed, if it doesn't abend, it's pretty obvious that the programmer hasn't implemented very thorough testing! It's very likely, for example, that the program will try to carry out some arithmetic operation on the AMT-DUE field; a data exception will immediately occur, since AMT-DUE generally will contain something like 'R10649'.

There is yet another common cause of data exceptions: failure to initialize WORKING-STORAGE fields that are used as counters or in arithmetic operations. For example, consider the following statement:

ADD 1 TO RECORDS-READ.

This statement could easily cause an abend if the programmer has failed to initialize RECORDS-READ to a numeric value. This happens because COBOL does *not* initialize fields automatically.[1] Instead, the COBOL compiler merely reserves enough space to

---

[1] Actually, fields are initialized to zeroes on some computers — but this is a vendor-dependent feature of which you should definitely *not* take advantage!

hold the field; this means that when your program begins executing, that area of memory usually will contain whatever "garbage" was left behind by the *last* program that occupied that area of memory.

Another common type of COBOL bug, known as "off-by-one errors," can cause different types of abends depending on the specifics of the situation. However, the abends usually are caused by *loops*. For example, when storing entries in a 30-entry table, the programmer may accidentally store 31 entries — thereby overlaying whatever data reside immediately following the thirtieth entry.

Probably the most typical type of off-by-one error is that of iterating through a loop one time too few. To illustrate this, suppose we wanted to count the number of customers we have in each state; let's assume that we've decided to do this with a table lookup using the two-letter state abbreviation. We could cause an off-by-one error by coding

```
PERFORM STATE-COUNTING
    VARYING THIS-STATE FROM 1 BY 1
    UNTIL TABLE-CODE (THIS-STATE) = POSTAL-CODE
        OR THIS-STATE = NUMBER-OF-STATES.
IF THIS-STATE = NUMBER-OF-STATES
    ADD 1 TO FOREIGN-CUSTOMER-COUNTER
ELSE
    ADD 1 TO STATE-COUNTER (THIS-STATE).
```

Presumably, the table with which we are working is NUMBER-OF-STATES entries long. That is, if there are fifty states, we assume that the table has fifty entries, and we assume that NUMBER-OF-STATES has the value of 50. In this case, it turns out that we *never* will match against the last entry in the table (which will be Wyoming, if the table is ordered alphabetically). This is because indexes and subscripts are initialized and incremented *before* the UNTIL clause is tested, and the UNTIL clause is tested *before* the paragraph or section is invoked.

To make this program work the way we want it to, we should have coded

PERFORM STATE-COUNTING
    VARYING THIS-STATE FROM 1 BY 1
      UNTIL TABLE-CODE (THIS-STATE) = POSTAL-CODE
        OR THIS-STATE GREATER THAN NUMBER-OF-STATES.

Whenever you write code for a loop, check the conditions of the loop to ensure that:

1.   The loop will execute correctly the *first* time it is invoked.

2.   The loop is capable of executing *zero* times if that is appropriate — i.e., make sure that your loop can "do nothing gracefully."

3.   The loop "will prepare" for the next iteration. In cases where your program is reading input from a sequential file, for example, it is customary to get ready for the next iteration by reading in the next record as the last executable statement at the bottom of the loop.

4.   The loop will terminate correctly in *all* possible cases. It is a good idea to work out by hand the details of the *last* iteration of the loop. Check the values of the subscript or index upon conclusion.

Yet another common type of bug is the *limit error*. To illustrate this, let's imagine that you have been asked to write a program that will print one grand-total amount-due figure by summing the outstanding balances of all of the customers of your company. Each customer has a record on a master file, and the amount-due field is a six-position field in the form $$$$¢¢. How large should we make the accumulator that will hold the grand total in our program?

The answer is, *we don't know!* It depends on how many customers there are in the file. When defining counters and accumulators, we need to know the volume our program will be expected to handle. If, for example, we are told that the master file contains ten customer records, we can calculate the minimum size for the accumulator by multiplying the largest possible value in any one occurrence by the number of occurrences. In our example with grand totals, we would compute

$$9999.99 \times 10 = 99999.90$$

Thus, our accumulator *could* be defined as

01   **TOTAL-AMT**   **PIC S9(5)V99   COMP-3.**

When defining accumulators, it is far better to assume that every occurrence of a data item that will be added into the accumulator will have its *largest* possible value, rather than an estimated *average* value.

What if the master file in our example has an eleventh customer added to it? Then, it is possible that the grand total could be as large as

$$9999.99 \times 11 = 109999.89$$

Now the accumulator defined as S9(5)V99 may not be large enough to hold the grand total. Consequently, we may encounter a SIZE ERROR when the program is executed; that is, the program will abend with a message telling us that we tried to store a value too large for the field. This means that the accumulator will have to be redefined (perhaps as an S9(7)V99 field); the program will have to be recompiled, and the job will have to be rerun.

Obviously, another factor that we should take into account when defining accumulators is the likelihood that the user will expand the number of items to be summed. If it is possible for such an expansion to take place, it is sensible to build in some surplus capacity in the accumulators — after all, it generally only requires one or two more positions of memory.

Remembering that IBM COBOL arithmetic is done on packed decimal numbers (COMP-3), we can compute a reasonable size for accumulators and counters with the formula

(largest possible value of field) ×
(number of fields, rounded up to next order of magnitude) =
(number which must fit in planned accumulator)

If the formula indicates that the accumulator should have an even number of positions, add an extra high-order position — since COBOL will do it anyway for COMP-3 fields.

Here is an example. Suppose we have to accumulate a total of 65 two-position numeric fields. We would compute

$$99 \times 100 = 9900$$

(Note that we rounded 65 up to the next higher order of magnitude.) Since the smallest field that could hold 9900 would be four positions in length, we add one more position, and define our accumulator as follows:

01   ACCUMULATOR   PIC S9(5)   COMP-3.

14.5 Debugging strategies and techniques

By the time you have gotten to this section, debugging probably will have become a familiar task to you. For most programmers, it is a painful and exasperating task, which consumes hours of checking page after page of code . . . only to discover that the bug was a simple coding blunder. For many programmers, debugging is the blackest of the black magic of programming — yet, it does not have to be such a tortuous task.

The most helpful technique in debugging is to *localize* the bug to a small area of the program. One way of accomplishing this is to remember to *never* attempt to test all of the modules in a COBOL program in one fell swoop. By designing modules that are small and well-defined, and by testing the program in a top-down incremental fashion, you should be able to tell which piece of your program contains the bug that has just caused the entire program to abend.

For example, suppose we have designed a 50-module program. If we compile all 50 modules at once, develop test data for the entire program, run the test, and discover a data exception, we probably will be faced with a rather difficult debugging task. The bug might be in any one of the 50 modules. However, if we run several small tests, each one involving the substitution of a new module for its stub, it is reasonable to expect that a data exception will be located much more quickly.

Once you have localized a bug, you should spend about half an hour looking for it. In general, it is more efficient to look at the source code and the actual program output than to look at octal or hexadecimal memory dumps of the program. If you have not found the bug after 30 minutes, it most certainly is time to call for help.

Find one or two other programmers and, with the listing in front of you, describe the problem to your colleagues. Describe why you think the bug is in the area of code that you are examining, and then walk through the code, line by line, explaining how it works. There is an excellent chance that you will discover the bug yourself — your friends won't even have to open their mouths! In other situations, your friends will point out an obvious bug that escaped your attention — after all, since you were the one who put the bug in the program, it is not surprising that you would continue to think that the logic of your program is correct!

Only as a last resort should you make extensive use of the dump, or trace, facilities that most computer systems have. These packages generally produce vast amounts of paper in which only a tiny amount of useful information is found. It is not surprising to see a programmer produce 200 pages of memory dump printout, only to find that one position of memory was initialized incorrectly. If you *must* use dumps, use them sparingly. Typically, the following types of dumps will be more than sufficient to find even the most elusive bugs:

1. A trace that shows the order in which paragraphs, sections, or subprograms were called. This can usually be invoked as part of a debugging option found in many COBOL systems; if not, you can do it yourself by having each module DISPLAY a message as the first executable statement. Merely by watching the sequence in which modules are called (and by comparing that with the structure chart that you have developed for the program), you can find many of your bugs.

2. A trace that shows the input parameters passed to each module and the output parameters returned from each module. This is most practical when your modules consist of CALLable subprograms; what you want to do is dump the fields defined in the LINKAGE SECTION upon entering each CALLed program, and just prior to exiting. As you can imagine, this produces voluminous output; however, it may be useful in locating a subtle bug that involves the clobbering of certain fields of data.

3. A trace that shows all of the references to and/or all of the modifications to a specified field of data. This approach is usually practical only if you have a debugging package that allows you automatically to invoke the tracing of a field. It would generally be very impractical for you to insert your own debugging code to DISPLAY a message every time a field is refer-

enced (and it may not solve the problem — it may turn out that your field of data is being clobbered because of an off-by-one error that you can't even see). Again, this approach can produce voluminous output and should be avoided if possible. More important, try to avoid a shotgun approach of tracing *all* variables in your program — it will produce more output than you would believe possible!

15 Efficiency and Optimization

15.1 Introduction

From time to time we've mentioned that one programming approach is "more efficient" than another approach. But we've generally said very little about efficiency — and you may have gotten the impression that we aren't particularly concerned about the subject.

To the contrary, we are and *should* be concerned about efficiency. Indeed, efficiency is *so* important that we've saved it for last — *after* we've discussed such basic issues as data representations, table-handling, and input-output operations. Now that you're familiar with all of these COBOL techniques, we can talk about ways of making your program more efficient.

But before we begin, we should ask ourselves some simple questions: What does "efficiency" mean? Does it mean a program that consumes very little CPU time? Does it mean a program that requires very little memory? Or does it imply one that makes very few disk accesses?

It's easy to become overly concerned with one or two narrow views of efficiency. In the final analysis, an efficient program is one that minimizes *total* costs, whether measured in dollars, francs, or rubles, over its entire productive lifetime. Total costs include the cost to develop the program, the cost to run it in a production environment (including the cost of reruns), and the cost of maintaining and modifying the program. Our main topic of discussion in this chapter is that of minimizing the cost of *running* the program.

The cost of running a program is becoming a smaller and smaller fraction of the total budget. There's no mystery behind this — it's simply that the price of computer hardware has dropped sharply during the past twenty years (and is expected to continue dropping for the foreseeable future), while the cost of the *people* who design, code, operate, and maintain the programs has increased (and is expected to continue increasing).

In the mid-1970's, for example, most large data processing organizations found that they spent roughly 50 percent of their budgets on hardware, and the other 50 percent on people-related costs. By the mid-1980's, those same organizations expect to spend only 20 percent on hardware, and 80 percent on people-related costs. Thus, the emphasis is shifting much more to minimizing *people* costs, rather than minimizing *hardware* costs. As a result, it often turns out to be more efficient to computerize a manual system even when the computer hardware is idle 98 percent of the time.

There is one aspect of the trade-off between people costs and hardware costs that needs to be discussed more fully. Except for some relatively trivial techniques for improving the hardware efficiency of a program, we usually find that attempts to make a program *very* efficient also make it considerably harder to develop, understand, debug, and maintain.[1] Thus, as we attempt to *decrease* hardware costs, we often find that we have *increased* people costs.

So, what should we conclude from all of this? *While you are writing the program, don't worry about efficiency.* After the program is operational, you can worry about optimizing it. After all, it's much easier to make a correct program efficient than it is to make an efficient program correct.

---

[1]Try this for yourself and see: Find a friend who has an efficient program of which he is particularly proud. Draw your own conclusions about the ease with which the program can be understood.

A second conclusion: If you must optimize your program, do it in an organized, methodical way. Many programmers waste hours of computer time while they try to make a ten-microsecond procedure run in nine microseconds.

In the next section, we'll discuss a strategy for optimizing programs. Then, we can discuss the actual mechanics of making a program more efficient.

15.2 Strategy for optimization

Many programmers approach program optimization in a disorganized, helter-skelter fashion. This section details a systematic, step-by-step procedure that you should follow when optimizing your program.

First, make sure that your program works! A relatively inefficient program that produces correct output is generally tolerable, at least for the few days that it might take you to optimize the program. An efficient program that produces incorrect output is of little use to anyone.

Second, find out whether anyone cares about the possible inefficiency in your program. It's not unusual for a programmer to feel guilty about wasting three milliseconds of CPU time in a program that requires a *total* of only three seconds, and that executes only once a month in production! If your program runs daily, taking 26 hours of computer time, *then* start worrying!

Third, find out which part of your program is the most inefficient. This is particularly important, since it almost always will turn out that any inefficiencies are localized in a small part of your program. A number of studies have shown that 50 percent of the CPU time of a program typically is consumed by 5 percent of the code. In one real-time system involving roughly 300,000 instructions, approximately 1.5 percent of the code consumes 75 percent of the CPU time!

Unfortunately, most programmers are notoriously poor at *guessing* where the inefficiencies, or "hot spots," are concentrated. Too often, the programmer assumes that the module that was most difficult for him to code also will turn out to be the most inefficient. For all but the most trivial programs, we need some precise way of *measuring* CPU time, memory, disk accesses, and other resource requirements of a program. We will discuss this in more detail in Section 15.3 below.

Fourth, try to estimate how much of an improvement you can make in each module of your program, and roughly how long it will take to make that improvement. Even though you generally will want to optimize the module that is least efficient, a more useful guideline to follow is: *Optimize the module that will produce the largest gain in efficiency for the least cost.* If your program is still too inefficient, then optimize the module that will produce the next largest net improvement in efficiency for the least amount of work, and so forth.

Fifth, make use of any available optimizing compilers and optimizing packages to get cheap improvements in efficiency. These packages generally are hardware-dependent and vendor-dependent, so we will not discuss them here. However, you should check to see if such facilities are available in your organization. It is common for optimizing compilers to produce improvements of 10-20 percent in the efficiency of a program. However, the packages themselves consume considerable memory and CPU time, so they should be used only *after* your program has been debugged.

Sixth, once you have decided which module should be optimized, try to find a better *algorithm* for the module before you resort to clever coding tricks of the sort discussed in Section 15.4. For example, you may find that you have organized your file in a *sequential* fashion, even though you access only 100 records out of a file of 100,000 records. By making the file a *direct* file and accessing only those records required, you may be able to save hours of computer time.

Finally, if you *do* decide to recode a module to make it more efficient, insert copious comments indicating what you've done and why; otherwise, your program may be unintelligible.

15.3 Measuring the inefficiency in your program

As we have pointed out, most programmers are notoriously poor at guessing *where* their program consumes the bulk of its resources. Some organized method of *performance measurement* is usually necessary to avoid making the optimization process an entirely hit-or-miss affair.

Listed below are three basic approaches for measuring performance:

1. Use counters to count the number of times "interesting" events have occurred — for example, count the number of file accesses made, the number of times a table was searched for a particular entry, and, most important, *the number of times selected portions of code have been executed.*

2. Use the computer's real-time clock to measure the elapsed time between one portion of code and another.

3. Use a vendor-supplied package to capture the statistics automatically.

The first method is often satisfactory for taking crude measurements of the behavior of a program. For example, you might decide to count the number of times each paragraph in your program is executed. If there are, say, 100 paragraphs in the program, then you would define a 100-entry table in your DATA DIVISION, with each entry initialized to zero. Then you would add one statement to the beginning of each paragraph. For example:

```
EDIT-CUSTOMER-RECORD.
*
* NOTE: THIS IS THE 17TH PARAGRAPH IN THE PROGRAM
*
    ADD 1 TO PARAGRAPH-COUNTER (17).
    .
    .
    .
```

Just prior to terminating the program, you would print the contents of the table.

While this approach is satisfactory for some simple applications, it has some obvious drawbacks. The primary limitation is that it doesn't tell us how much memory or CPU time is consumed by each paragraph. A somewhat less serious (although often *extremely* annoying) problem is that it requires a lot of tedious work to insert the measurement code, and to eventually remove it. This problem can be alleviated to some extent if you have a *pre-compiler* available. If not, we recommend that you introduce the code and then use a simple flag (whose value can be changed by recompiling the program) to determine whether the statistics actually should be printed.

There is one final disadvantage of the counter approach: The measurement code itself consumes some memory, CPU time, and I/O operations. Thus, it will slow your program and add some extra memory requirements.

The second approach — reading the real-time clock — is more precise, but it involves facilities that are not part of the standard COBOL language. Depending on the type of computer system you use, you may find that you can use the Job Control Language to request the operating system to measure the CPU time of an individual program. This may be a suitable approach if you have separately compiled CALLable subprograms. Alternatively, you may have to CALL an assembly language subroutine, which in turn will call the operating system to read the real-time clock. Inquire about how this operation is accomplished in your installation.

Assuming that you are able to gain access to the real-time clock, you may decide to measure the CPU time consumed by a COBOL section or paragraph, or possibly by even a single COBOL statement. In most cases, you'll want to keep track of the total number of times a unit of code is invoked, as well as the *total* CPU time consumed. From this, you can compute (manually or in a program) the average amount of CPU time required for each unit of code.

This technique for performance measurement has two disadvantages in common with the previous approach: You must modify your code in order to gather the statistics; and you do consume some additional overhead with the performance measurement logic. Even worse, the overhead is *included* with the measurements of your program — that is, if your statistics indicate that your program consumed 100 seconds of CPU time, you can expect that two to three seconds were involved in just *capturing* the statistics. Fortunately, the overhead tends to be relatively small, so you should be able to ignore it.

There is one other practical way to gather performance statistics about your program: Use a vendor-supplied package, if one is available in your EDP organization. Although it is beyond the scope of this book to describe how the variety of available hardware and software monitors work, you should be aware that they exist. Almost all such packages have the advantages that (a) they require little or no modification of your source program, and (b) they add little or no measurable overhead to the CPU time, memory, or other resource requirements of your program.

So, if you have access to a performance measurement package, it's probably the best way to obtain accurate, detailed information about your program. Otherwise, you should use the real-time clock to get accurate measurements of the execution speed of your program, and you should use strategically placed counters to obtain other useful information.

15.4 Programming techniques for efficiency

For every model of computer hardware, operating system, and programming language, there is a list of special tricks that can be used to save a microsecond of CPU time, a byte of memory, or a block of disk storage. While these tricks may be very important from time to time in your efforts to optimize your program, we will make no attempt to describe them in this book. Even if we could capture the thousands of programming tricks on various computers, they would be outdated by the time you read this book.

What we *can* do is discuss five of the most *common* programming techniques that can be used with virtually any version of COBOL to save memory and CPU time. These techniques are detailed in the following subsections.

15.4.1 Avoid Unnecessary Internal Data Conversions

One of the most common causes of inefficiency in a COBOL program is the unnecessary conversion of data from one format to another. As we have pointed out, COBOL expects data fields to be in certain formats in order to carry out certain operations. If the data are *not* in the required format, COBOL automatically will cause the data to be converted *when the program executes.* This conversion process involves some assembly language instructions that add extra memory requirements to the program, as well as slow it down.

For example, COBOL expects to carry out arithmetic operations (ADD, SUBTRACT, and so forth) on packed decimal fields — i.e., fields that have been defined as COMP or COMP-3. Thus, if you have defined a numeric field as

01   **BALANCE-DUE**   PIC 9(5)V99.

you can expect that a certain amount of inefficiency will result from any arithmetic operations on the field. COBOL will have to convert BALANCE-DUE from the DISPLAY format shown above to a packed decimal format for arithmetic operations, and then convert the result from a packed decimal format back into DISPLAY format.

It also is more efficient to define a numeric field as *signed* if your program is going to store data in the field; otherwise, COBOL will carry out specified computations on the field and then compute the *absolute magnitude* of the result to ensure that it is a positive number.

On most computers, it is also more efficient to specify an *odd* number of digits for a signed numeric field. This is because most computers require that a numeric field occupy an *even* number of positions in memory, and that the sign itself occupy one position. If you specify an *even* number of digits for your field, the COBOL compiler will generate instructions which will cause your program, *when it runs,* to (a) move the field to a temporary field that is defined with an odd number of digits, (b) carry out the arithmetic operations on the temporary field, and (c) move the results back into your field.

Another common internal data conversion involves *subscripts.* Since a subscript is used to compute the hardware address of an entry in a table, and since hardware memory locations have *binary* addresses, it follows that subscripts must be defined as a *binary* field.

15.4.2 Organize Searches Efficiently

As we stated in Chapter 11, COBOL provides two statements — SEARCH and SEARCH ALL — to look for entries in a table. With the SEARCH statement, an average of N/2 inspections is required to locate an entry in the table; with the SEARCH ALL statement, an average of log_2N inspections is required. Thus, for a table with more than four entries, the binary search will generally require fewer inspections.

However, the binary search requires more overhead than the sequential search. Prior to each inspection of the table, the SEARCH ALL statement requires a computation to determine *which* table entry should be inspected next; with the SEARCH statement, COBOL merely has to increment a subscript by 1 to determine which entry should be inspected next. Because of this additional overhead, we usually find that it is not worth the bother of using a SEARCH ALL statement unless your table is 50-100 entries long (remember that the SEARCH ALL statement requires the table to be ordered, whereas SEARCH does not).

If you are using the SEARCH statement, and if the entries in your table do not change during execution of the program, there may be another opportunity to improve the efficiency of the SEARCH. Remember, an average of N/2 inspections will be required if *each* table entry has an equal probability of being selected. But in many real-world applications, that is not a reasonable assumption: You may find that 90 percent of all SEARCH statements are looking for one or two specific table entries.

Therefore, you should order the entries in the table so that the most popular entries appear first, and the least popular entries appear last. With this approach, you may find that the SEARCH statement requires only a couple of inspections instead of N/2 inspections.

With larger tables (e.g., tables that are several thousand entries long), you may need more sophisticated searching techniques than are available with the SEARCH and SEARCH ALL statements.[2] One commonly used technique is called a *hash-code,* or "randomizing," search. Its basic objective is to determine a *probable* table entry where the desired item will be found; when it works properly, the hash-code search will retrieve entries in an average of about 1.5 inspections of the table.

To illustrate the hash-code search, let's imagine that we have to maintain a table of the Social Security numbers of some 1,000 people in our organization. We could use a sequential search, but that would be unreasonably slow; even a binary search would require an average of ten inspections of the table before retrieving the desired Social Security number. The hash-code approach would involve (a) using a table of 1,000 entries to store the 1,000 Social Security numbers, (b) using an algorithm to determine where each employee record should be stored in the table, and (c) using the same algorithm to retrieve items from the table.

---

[2]For the numerous variations on the SEARCH mechanism, see Donald Knuth, *The Art of Computer Programming — Volume 3: Searching and Sorting* (Reading, Mass.: Addison-Wesley, 1973).

One simple algorithm for this example would be to divide an employee's Social Security number by the length of the table, and use the *remainder* as a subscript. Thus, an employee with Social Security number 130-34-9025 would be stored in table entry 025, while someone with Social Security number 093-44-7732 would be stored in table entry 732.

But what do we do with someone whose Social Security number is 130-34-5025? Such a situation is called a *collision,* or *overflow.* One reasonable approach would be to try putting Social Security number 130-34-5025 into table entry 026, since table entry 025 is already occupied by Social Security number 130-34-9025. Of course, we run the risk that table entry 026 is occupied, too — in which case, we could then examine entry 027. In other words, we use an algorithm to compute a probable *first* entry to examine; a sequential search (which may have to wrap around the end of the table) is used thereafter. If the distribution of employee numbers is reasonably random, our hash-code search will be very efficient; if it turns out that *all* employees have a Social Security number ending in 025, the search will degenerate into a pure sequential search (in which case, we should choose another algorithm!).

15.4.3 Organize *IF-ELSE-IF* Constructs *Efficiently*

Consider the following sequence of code:

```
IF MARITAL-STATUS = 'DIVORCED'
    PERFORM DIVORCED-ROUTINE
ELSE IF MARITAL-STATUS = 'SEPARATED'
    PERFORM SEPARATED-ROUTINE
ELSE IF MARITAL-STATUS = 'SINGLE'
    PERFORM SINGLE-ROUTINE
ELSE IF MARITAL-STATUS = 'MARRIED'
    PERFORM MARRIED-ROUTINE
ELSE
    PERFORM BAD-MARITAL-STATUS.
```

What if it turns out that 80 percent of the cases we deal with involve a marital status of married, and only 5 percent of the cases we deal with are divorced or separated? Obviously, our program wastes some time before discovering the most likely cases. To make our program more efficient, we should reorganize the sequence of tests so that the most likely conditions will be discovered first.

Of course, the programmer may have had no idea when he wrote this program which case would be most likely — and, as we pointed out in Section 15.1, he should not worry about it then. *After* the program is working, appropriate performance measurement techniques can determine whether this sequence of tests constitutes a serious inefficiency in the program, and which marital status is the most common.

15.4.4 Arrange Blocking and Buffering for Efficiency

As we discussed in Chapter 12, you can specify with the RESERVE *n* ALTERNATE AREAS whether each of your files will have one buffer, two buffers, or *n* buffers. Your program generally will require *more* memory and *less* CPU time if you specify a large number of buffers; conversely, it will require *less* memory and *more* CPU time if you specify only one buffer.

In most cases, a point of diminishing returns is reached after your program is given three or four buffers. If it takes your program significantly longer to process one record than it takes the operating system to bring the next record into memory, then it is pointless to have more than two buffers — the operating system will always be able to overlap its input operation with your program's computing. Similarly, if it takes *much* longer for the operating system to bring the next record into memory than it takes your program to process the record, then it won't help to have 200 buffers. Your program still will get ahead of the operating system, and be forced to wait while the next record is brought into memory. However, it may turn out that your program processes five to ten records very quickly and then spends a considerably longer period of time processing the next record (this is common in sequential file processing, where many records can be examined quickly and then written to the output file, while a relatively small number of records require lengthy processing). In such a case, additional buffers can make the program run much faster.

Similarly, *blocking factors* can be adjusted to make a program more efficient. By making the blocking factor small, we have small physical records and thereby conserve memory. On the other hand, we make *less* efficient use of the storage space on the I/O device, and we incur more physical I/O operations, which will make our program run more slowly. Conversely, a large blocking factor will require more memory (since each physical block read by the operating system will contain more logical records), but will make better use of the physical I/O device and generally will allow our program to run faster.

15.4.5 Change CALL Statements to PERFORM Statements

In some cases, you may find that your program operates inefficiently because of the overhead of the CALL statement and its associated passing of data through the LINKAGE SECTION. This usually will be localized to one or two CALLable subprograms that are invoked frequently. If a module is invoked only a few times, the inefficiency of the CALL statement can usually be disregarded.

There is a disadvantage to replacing CALLs with PERFORMs: Doing so means that all of the modules will share the same DATA DIVISION, thereby increasing the chance that a bug in module A will cause some of module B's data to be mysteriously destroyed. So, it's best to avoid this type of optimization if you possibly can — if you *must* do it, change only those modules that are invoked a substantial number of times.

On occasion, you may even find that the PERFORM statement slows your program more than you can afford. Or, on a virtual memory system, you may find that the module that executes the PERFORM statement is on a different page than the module being PERFORMed. In such cases, it may make sense to code the PERFORMed module *in-line* in the module which invokes it. If the PERFORMed module was invoked from two or three superordinates, use the COPY statement to place an exact copy of the module in-line. Naturally, two or three copies of a module will add memory requirements to your program. However, it generally will make the program run faster, and it may eliminate some nasty thrashing in a virtual memory environment.

AFTERWORD

The purpose of this book has been to make you a productive COBOL programmer, not an expert on every aspect of the language. To become an expert, you would have to memorize the COBOL reference manual, and no one expects that. An excellent programmer knows where to find answers, but does not have to know *all* the answers. As with the programmers before you, your training has just begun, and it will continue until you retire from the profession. The problems we solve are constantly evolving, and the tools we use are changing with them.

We hope that this book has given you a good start, but now we encourage you to continue your education. A COBOL reference manual is a necessary text, and other programmers' code is an endless source of practical information on style and technique. We also recommend that you become a regular reader of at least one of the data processing periodicals. They are heralds of the future, and forums for the problems of the present.

We welcome you to programming. Work, learn, and enjoy!

APPENDIX

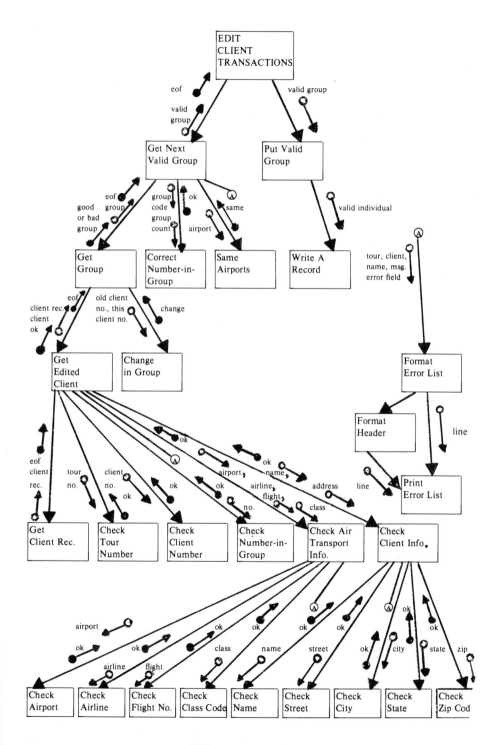

W&P sample flowchart.

1. TALLY = 4, FIELD = **bbbb**4

2. TALLY = UNCHANGED, FIELD = BENENE

3. NUMB-COUNT = 4, FIELD = **bb**1346

4. TALLY = UNCHANGED, FIELD = QDAMENT

1)   +24.6

2)   −6.7

3)   +2,468

4)   +22

5)   + 1

6)   − 6

7)   16+

8)   22.060−

9)   .01−

A note about Problems 5 and 6: With only one occurrence of the "+" in the editing PIC, the "+" is interpreted as fixed in position, regardless of whether leading zeroes are suppressed by Z characters.

```
IDENTIFICATION DIVISION.
PROGRAM-ID. FORMATDL.
ENVIRONMENT DIVISION.
DATA DIVISION.
WORKING-STORAGE SECTION.
*
*
01 PRINT-LINE.
    05 FILLER                    PIC X(5).
    05 PR-TOUR-NUM               PIC 99-999/9.
    05 FILLER                    PIC X(5).
    05 PR-AGT-CLIENT             PIC 99-999-9.
    05 IND-CLIENT REDEFINES PR-AGT-CLIENT.
        10  PR-IND-CLIENT        PIC 9-99999.
        10  FILLER               PIC X.
    05 FILLER                    PIC X(5).
    05 PR-CLIENT-NAME            PIC X(30).
    05 FILLER                    PIC X(5).
    05 PR-NUMBER-GROUP           PIC Z9.
    05 FILLER                    PIC X(5).
    05 PR-TOTAL-COST             PIC $$$$,$$9.99.
    05 FILLER                    PIC X(5).
    05 PR-DEPOSIT                PIC $$$$,$$9.99
    05 FILLER                    PIC X(5).
    05 PR-BAL-DUE                PIC $$$$,$$9.99CR.
    05 FILLER                    PIC X(5).
    05 PR-DEPART-DATE            PIC 99/99/99.
    05 FILLER                    PIC X.
*
01 WS-TOTAL-COST                 PIC S9(6)V99.
01 WS-BAL-DUE                    PIC S9(6)V99.
01 WS-DEPART-DATE.
    05 WS-MONTH-DAY              PIC 9(4).
    05 WS-YEAR                   PIC 99.
*
*
*
LINKAGE SECTION.
*
01 CLIENT-RECD.
    05 CLIENT-NUMBER             PIC 9(6).
    05 IND-OR-AGT                PIC A.
        88  INDEPEND             VALUE 'I'.
        88  AGENCY               VALUE 'A'.
    05 TOUR-NUMBER               PIC 9(6).
    05 CLIENT-NAME               PIC X(30).
```

```
    05  NUM-IN-GROUP              PIC 99.
    05  COST-FOR-ONE             PIC S9(4)V99.
    05  DEPOSIT                  PIC S9(6)V99.
    05  DATE-DEPART.
        10  DEPART-YEAR          PIC 99.
        10  DEPART-MONTH-DAY     PIC 9(4).
    05  FILLER                   PIC X(15).
*
*
 PROCEDURE DIVISION
    USING CLIENT-RECD.
*****
* FORMATDL FORMATS A DETAIL-LINE, NAMED PRINT-LINE
* AND THEN CALLS PRINTDL TO PRINT IT.  FORMATDL
* IS CALLED BY BILL REPT.
*****
 FORMAT-RECD.
    MULTIPLY COST-FOR-ONE BY NUM-IN-GROUP
        GIVING WS-TOTAL-COST.
    SUBTRACT DEPOSIT FROM WS-TOTAL-COST
        GIVING WS-BAL-DUE.
    MOVE DEPART-MONTH-DAY TO WS-MONTH-DAY.
    MOVE DEPART-YEAR TO WS-YEAR.
*
*

    MOVE SPACES TO PRINT-LINE.
    MOVE TOUR-NUMBER TO PR-TOUR-NUM.
    IF INDEPEND
        MOVE CLIENT-NUMBER TO PR-IND-CLIENT
    ELSE
        MOVE CLIENT-NUMBER TO PR-AGT-CLIENT.
    MOVE CLIENT-NAME TO PR-CLIENT-NAME.
    MOVE NUM-IN-GROUP TO PR-NUMBER-GROUP.
    MOVE WS-TOTAL-COST TO PR-TOTAL-COST.
    MOVE DEPOSIT TO PR-DEPOSIT.
    MOVE WS-BAL-DUE TO PR-BAL-DUE.
    MOVE WS-DEPART-DATE TO PR-DEPART-DATE.
*
*

    CALL 'PRINTDL' USING PRINT-LINE.
*
*
 EXIT-FORMATDL.
    EXIT PROGRAM.
```

```
WORKING-STORAGE SECTION.
01 BOOK-VALUES.
    05  FILLER                    PIC 9(2)        VALUE 01.
    05  FILLER                    PIC S9(2)V99    VALUE +09.95.
    05  FILLER                    PIC S9(2)V99    VALUE +08.95.
    05  FILLER                    PIC S9(2)V99    VALUE +07.00
    05  FILLER                    PIC 9(2)        VALUE 02.
    05  FILLER                    PIC S9(2)V99    VALUE +16.50.
    05  FILLER                    PIC S9(2)V99    VALUE +14.00.
    05  FILLER                    PIC S9(2)V99    VALUE +12.00.
    05  FILLER                    PIC 9(2)        VALUE 03.
    05  FILLER                    PIC S9(2)V99    VALUE +34.49.
    05  FILLER                    PIC S9(2)V99    VALUE +32.49.
    05  FILLER                    PIC S9(2)V99    VALUE +28.00.
    05  FILLER                    PIC 9(2)        VALUE 04.
    05  FILLER                    PIC S9(2)V99    VALUE +07.75.
    05  FILLER                    PIC S9(2)V99    VALUE +07.25.
    05  FILLER                    PIC S9(2)V99    VALUE +06.25.
    05  FILLER                    PIC 9(2)        VALUE 05.
    05  FILLER                    PIC S9(2)V99    VALUE +12.50.
    05  FILLER                    PIC S9(2)V99    VALUE +11.50.
    05  FILLER                    PIC S9(2)V99    VALUE +10.50.
    05  FILLER                    PIC 9(2)        VALUE 06.
    05  FILLER                    PIC S9(2)V99    VALUE +03.50.
    05  FILLER                    PIC S9(2)V99    VALUE +03.50.
    05  FILLER                    PIC S9(2)V99    VALUE +03.50.
    05  FILLER                    PIC 9(2)        VALUE 07.
    05  FILLER                    PIC S9(2)V99    VALUE +19.95.
    05  FILLER                    PIC S9(2)V99    VALUE +18.50.
    05  FILLER                    PIC S9(2)V99    VALUE +17.00.
    05  FILLER                    PIC 9(2)        VALUE 08.
    05  FILLER                    PIC S9(2)V99    VALUE +04.00.
    05  FILLER                    PIC S9(2)V99    VALUE +03.50.
    05  FILLER                    PIC S9(2)V99    VALUE +02.95.

01 BOOK-TABLE REDEFINES BOOK-VALUES.
    05  BOOK-ENTRY OCCURS 8 TIMES INDEXED BY THIS-BOOK.
        10  BOOK-CODE-TB          PIC 9(2).
        10  MAX-PRICE             PIC S9(2)V99.
        10  SMALL-DISC-PRICE      PIC S9(2)V99.
        10  BIG-DISC-PRICE        PIC S9(2)V99.
```

```
01  MIN-FOR-SMALL-DISC        PIC 9(2)        VALUE 06.
01  MIN-FOR-BIG-DISC          PIC 9(2)        VALUE 12.
01  NUMBER-OF-BOOKS           PIC 9           VALUE 8.

LINKAGE SECTION.
01  BOOK-CODE-LK              PIC 9(2).
01  NUMBER-ORDERED            PIC 9(2).
01  AMT-DUE                   PIC S9(4)V99.

PROCEDURE DIVISION
     USING                    BOOK-CODE-LK
                              NUMBER-ORDERED
                              AMT-DUE.

CALC-AMT-DUE.
    PERFORM MATCH-CODES
        VARYING THIS-BOOK FROM 1 BY 1
        UNTIL BOOK-CODE-TB (THIS-BOOK) = BOOK-CODE-LK
           OR THIS-BOOK GREATER THAN NUMBER-OF-BOOKS.

    IF THIS-BOOK GREATER THAN NUMBER-OF-BOOKS
        MOVE ZEROES TO AMT-DUE
    ELSE IF NUMBER-ORDERED LESS THAN MIN-FOR-SMALL-DISC
        MULTIPLY NUMBER-ORDERED BY MAX-PRICE (THIS-BOOK)
            GIVING AMT-DUE
    ELSE IF NUMBER-ORDERED LESS THAN MIN-FOR-BIG-DISC
        MULTIPLY NUMBER-ORDERED BY SMALL-DISC-PRICE (THIS-BOOK)
            GIVING AMT-DUE
    ELSE
        MULTIPLY NUMBER-ORDERED BY BIG-DISC-PRICE (THIS-BOOK)
            GIVING AMT-DUE.
EXIT-AMT-CALC.
    EXIT PROGRAM.

MATCH-CODES.
    EXIT.
*
* THIS PARAGRAPH IS A DUMMY BECAUSE THE PERFORM-VARYING HANDLES
* THE ENTIRE TABLE LOOKUP.
*
```

GLOSSARY

abend

an acronym for "abnormal end"; used on many IBM computers to describe a situation that causes a computer program to terminate its execution abnormally.

ANSI

an abbreviation for American National Standards Institute, the organization which (among other things) establishes the standard definition of the COBOL language.

asynchronous execution

a way of organizing two or more processes (in the context of this book, the operating system and a COBOL program) so that each can execute independently of the other, except for occasional references made by one process to the other to check on completion of an event, or to check on progress, or otherwise to *synchronize* its activities with those of the other process.

binary search	a strategy of searching through tables that, after each inspection of the table, reduces the number of remaining entries to be searched by half. Also known as a *logarithmic search,* since the average number of inspections to find a specified entry in the table is $\log_2 N$, where N is the length of the table.
binding	a synonym for *cohesion.*
black box	a common description of a system whose inputs, outputs, and function are known, but whose inner workings are unknown and irrelevant.
blocking	the process of combining several *logical records* into one *physical record.*
blocking factor	an integer which describes the number of *logical records* that have been placed in one *physical record.*
bubble chart	a synonym for *program graph.*
buffer	an area of memory into which the operating system reads records from an input-output device,

or from which the operating system writes records onto an input-output device.

buffering

the process of providing more than one buffer in a program, so that the operating system can *asynchronously* read records into or write records from one buffer while the COBOL program uses the data in another buffer.

central transforms

those *bubbles* in a *program graph* that are involved in computing, or transforming the inputs to the program into the outputs of the program.

cohesion

a measure of the relatedness of elements (e.g., instructions or subordinate modules) of a COBOL module.

collision

a phenomenon that occurs when a *hash-code search* computes the same probable table entry for two unique data elements.

coupling

a measure of the interconnections between COBOL modules.

data exception

an informal, but common term to describe an *abend* caused by a program's attempt to manipulate data that is in a form other than that defined in the PIC clause.

debugging

the process of identifying the location, cause, and cure for a bug, once the existence of the bug has been made known.

direct access

a method of organizing files, so that the program can access a desired record directly without having to read and discard all of the records which precede the desired record. Usually contrasted with *sequential access*.

EBCDIC

an acronym for Extended Binary Coded Decimal Interchange Code. One of several conventions for representing the set of printable characters as binary codes.

functional cohesion

the strongest form of *cohesion*. A module with functional cohesion contains elements (for example, instructions or subordinate modules) which are necessary and

sufficient to carry out
one single, well-defined
task.

hash-code search

a searching algorithm in
which the desired table
entry is used to compute
a probable index in the
table. The algorithm
used to compute the
probable address is used
both to store entries in
the table and to retrieve
entries from the table.

in-line code

a synonym for *lexically
included code.*

incremental testing

a testing strategy in
which one untested (and
potentially bug-ridden)
module is added to a set
of previously tested
modules. The process is
repeated until all
modules have been test-
ed.

interrecord gap

an area between two *phy-
sical records* on an input-
output device (typically,
magnetic tape or disk).
Used by the computer
hardware to detect the
end of one record and
the beginning of another
record.

intermediate file

a file produced as output
by one program, and

	used as input in another program, but which is not saved for any other purpose after the programs have finished executing.
JCL	an abbreviation for *Job Control Language.*
Job Control Language	an informal term used to describe the instructions by which a programmer tells the operating system how the program should be executed — e.g., how much memory the program requires, what priority it should have, what names have been given to the physical files, and so forth.
lexically included code	COBOL statements that have been identified on a structure chart as distinct, cohesive module(s), but which are coded within the body of the next higher-level superordinate module(s).
logical cohesion	one of the weaker levels of *cohesion.* A logically cohesive module contains processing elements (for example, statements or subordinate modules) that perform a variety of similar tasks, but do not

perform one single, well-defined task.

logical record

a data record as seen by the computer program-mer, and as defined in the COBOL program. Usually contrasted with *physical record.*

memory dump

a debugging strategy in which the contents of all or part of the computer's memory is printed, often in almost unreadable form.

merging

the process of combining the records in two or more files, to produce a single file whose records are ordered.

multidimensional table

a table with two or more distinct subscripts.

packed decimal

a form of data represen-tation that permits two decimal digits to be stored in one byte of computer memory.

physical record

a record of data, as stored on an input-output device. A physi-cal record contains one or more *logical records.*

program graph

a diagram that shows the flow of data elements through a program, and

	the transformations of data from one form to another form.
pseudocode	a means of describing procedural logic by using imperative English statements, IF-THEN-ELSE constructs, and DO-WHILE constructs. Also known as structured English, or program design language.
recording density	a measure of the amount of data that can be stored on one unit (e.g., a block or a track) of a physical input/output device.
sequential access	a method of accessing records from a file in which the Nth record may be obtained only by first reading the first N-1 records of the file. Usually contrasted with *direct access*.
sorting	the process of rearranging the records of a file so that they appear in sequential order.
structure chart	a form of program documentation that shows the modules of a COBOL program, and the connections between modules.

stub

a module that provides a primitive simulation of a subordinate module during the testing of a superordinate module. Normally used as part of a process of *top-down testing*.

subordinate module

a module that is CALLed or PERFORMed by some other module, that is, one that is hierarchically lower than some other module.

superordinate module

a module that CALLs or PERFORMs some other module, i.e., one that is hierarchically higher than some other module.

top-down testing

a testing strategy in which higher-level modules are tested first (usually by supplying *stubs* for the subordinate modules), and lower-level modules are tested last. Usually associated with *incremental testing*.

transform analysis

a design strategy that derives a *structure chart* for a program by analyzing the *program graph* for the problem.

transform-centered design

a synonym for *transform analysis*.

INDEX